TM

Guild Press of Indiana, Inc.

Indianapolis, Indiana

Cathedral :

Seventy-five Years

"She's Still

Dear Old Cathedral"

By

Bill Shover, '46
For the years 1917–1975

And

James Obergfell, '92H
For the years 1976–1993

Guild Craft of Indiana
A Division of Guild Press of Indiana, Inc.
6000 Sunset Lane
Indianapolis, IN 46208

Guild Press of Indiana, Inc.
6000 Sunset Lane
Indianapolis, IN 46208

Printed in the United States of America

Library of Congress
Catalog Card Number
93- 080515

ISBN 1-878208-35-7 Hardcover
ISBN 1-878208-36-3 Softcover

CONTENTS

Author's Preface

Every school is more than just a school. It is a place where memories began, of fuzzy, out-of-focus mind pictures of people and events of a time which more than any other indelibly formed our characters. Indeed, the years of youth, the years of adolescence, frame the personality, color our beliefs and prejudices and create the persons we will become for all the future.

So it is with any school, but especially Cathedral High School. The Old Girl evolved from birth on the second story of a grade school building at Thirteenth and Pennsylvania streets, to a 1927 showplace campus at 1416 North Meridian Street, to a sylvan campus of buildings nestled on thirty-nine bucolic acres.

From the oiled-floor and faulty-furnace scents to the aromas of nature, Cathedral has experienced seventy-five full seasons, mild and harsh winters, as well as welcome springs, and served as the crucible for the maturation to adulthood of her sons and daughters.

As a relatively small Catholic school, she has weathered depressions, prejudice, wars, civil unrest and the evolution of society. She has seen Indianapolis change from urban to suburban, from quiet to dramatic.

She has survived the Ku Klux Klan, a world conflict, a police action in Korea, the tragedy of Vietnam, social unrest and world terrorism. She has wept as the lives of eighty of her sons were ended by war. Her patriotism is unsurpassed through gifts of education and dedication to God and country.

For those of us who shared and survived the Cathedral experience, affection will always mark the recollection. But Cathedral is not a flag we salute; it is the place that has molded young men and women, where we formed as the song says, "water-colored memories of the way we were."

We are a proud collection, tending to flaunt the achievement of days in school and the accomplishments of Cathedral's graduates. Perhaps no other school—at least not one of such relatively small enrollment—has seen more graduates shape the formation of Indianapolis than has Cathedral.

This history of Cathedral chronicles the living history of a school that has evolved more change than any other in Indianapolis. Its persistence and achievement is a tribute to an exceptional faculty, especially the Brothers of Holy Cross, who nurtured Cathedral for fifty-four years, and eventually to equally dedicated and competent lay teachers.

As religious vocations were eroded by societal change, Cathedral adapted. But the foundation established in 1918 never changed. The story of Cathedral is, indeed, a chronicle of evolution of Indianapolis and of society itself.

It is the story of a school whose halls have heard the echoes of George M. Cohan, the sounds of the Roaring Twenties, "Begin the Beguine," the memories of FDR and "Ike," the sadness of war and shouts of victory; the hatred of one individual or group towards another, the tragedies of JFK, RFK, and MLK, the emergence of blacks and other races, the challenge to and doubt of patriotism, the great menace to mankind from chemical abuse, the survival of rock and roll, the Beatles, the cacophony of acid and heavy metal and the tragedy of AIDS.

We were, and are, a spectrum of society. From its early years, Cathedral was the only school in Indianapolis melding the Italians of Holy Rosary, the Irish of St. Patrick's, the blacks of Holy Angels and St. Rita's, the Slovenians of Holy Trinity, the Germans of St. Catherine's and a dozen other nationalities and adherents of faiths other than Catholic: rich and poor, sons and finally daughters.

More than any other institution of life a school reflects life itself. And truly it is that the Cathedral lady basks in what is really a reflected glory—that of those whose lives were educated and inspired and who went on to achieve.

This review of seven-and-one-half decades of Cathedral living is testimony to those men and women who taught the lessons of education and of life itself as they launched thousands of lives.

As youth, many of us believed we survived the Cathedral experience. Perhaps we resisted the discipline and academic demands. It is only now, perhaps, that we realize how much Cathedral made us better than we otherwise might have been.

—Bill Shover, '46

DEDICATIONS

TO JOSEPH CHARTRAND—"JOE BISH"—The Founder

If ever a person put his imprint on an institution it was Joseph Chartrand. More than any other man, he created the school to fulfill his dream of building a school where boys could sanctify God and achieve scholastic success and whose love for each other and spirit of unity would surpass that of all other schools.

Not only did he envision, he worked. He found the teachers at Notre Dame. He squeezed a high school into a grade school building. He designed an institution which would make a powerful statement, negotiated the property sale and then told his parishes he needed $1,053, 296.76. And, within weeks in 1924, he assembled their pledges and oversaw construction.

But beyond that, Bishop Chartrand was the soul of Cathedral. He walked the halls almost daily and taught religion there every Friday. He knew the boys by name and provided inspiration and resources when needed.

His "Cathedral boys" as he endearingly called them, believed he was a saint. Yet his presence, though awesome, was personal, kind and sincere.

From his birth in 1870 in St. Louis to his death in the Cathedral Rectory December 8, 1933, "Joe Bish," as he was affectionately called, was a man of God, of the people and a constant friend to his Cathedral boys.

TO THE BROTHERS

"Who are these guys?"

Butch Cassidy asked that question of the "Sundance Kid" and Cathedral boys pondered a similar one: who are these men in black?

For fifty-four years the Brothers of Holy Cross taught rambunctious teen-aged Cathedral boys and, at the same time, organized and ran a school with financial support from the Archdiocese.

But who were these men in cassocks and Roman collars who brought terror, taught knowledge and engendered respect?

As students we knew little about them and feared—but needed—the discipline they demanded and, when necessary, rendered. They had funny-sounding names we didn't have to memorize because we could get by with just addressing them as "Brother."

From our grade school education most of us came to know Sisters and priests but who are Brothers? As fourteen-year-olds we were too distracted to care, except we knew there was to be respect and, yes, admiration.

But what did they do after school? How did they live in those sequestered quarters behind that mysterious door at the rear of the school library?

For the most part they were dedicated to learning and teaching. Many were scholars who constantly replenished their knowledge and had to understand the limitations and distractions of boys growing into youthful manhood.

At an early stage of religious life a Brother makes a decision to teach and to be taught. Each school year the community at Notre Dame assigned up to thirty men to Cathedral.

The ratio of Brothers to student population was, generally, about one to thirty. They lived in rooms ten feet by thirteen feet and spent many of their out-of-class hours grading papers and preparing curricula. They coached, directed extracurricular activities, and did secretarial work and other overlooked tasks which helped keep the school afloat.

We can mind-picture a clutch of men in black hats, black suits, white shirts and black ties sitting together at games cheering their students on. It is a picture older graduates remember. As years passed, of course, less formal attire might be worn by the Brothers when away from the campus.

While we paid no tuition to attend Cathedral until 1934, the Brothers received the smallest of stipends. And even after years of fifty dollars per student tuition (family discounts were available), the Brothers' salaries remained modest. Brother Eugene played organ for three masses a day at the Cathedral—at one dollar per mass. Cathedral was the only Brothers' school to survive without financial aid from the community at Notre Dame. In fact, Cathedral was often able to meet the "proveni tax" on each Brother to support the operation.

Each summer the Brothers continued educating themselves and were allowed two weeks' vacation. The life was confining and regimented and the demands of classroom excellence were constant. Brothers, if invited, were allowed to visit the homes of students for dinner.

After they made the decision to leave Cathedral in 1972, there was anger and disappointment. The Brothers felt they were no longer welcome in Indianapolis with the opening of four Archdiocese-supported high schools and the immediate acceptance of Brebeuf, a Jesuit preparatory high school, which had opened in 1963.

Cathedral sons felt abandoned and many for the first time realized the great contribution of the Congregation of Holy Cross (C.S.C.). The departure was not saluted with the accolades it deserved. The Brothers left as they came fifty-four years earlier: without fanfare or tribute.

Sal Punterelli '45 had his own farewell tribute. Just before the Brothers' departure from the school, the Punterelli family and Bob and Meg Robisch invited the sixteen Brothers of the Cathedral faculty for an evening of Italian food, wine, singing and nostalgia. It was a quiet farewell after five-plus decades of devoted teaching and nurturing boys to manhood.

This book is dedicated to the commitment to life that the Brothers taught to more than five thousand young men who during school years never really understood, but later appreciated them for lessons learned inside and outside the classroom.

TO JOSEPH STANLEY DIENHART

The life of Joe Dienhart, he himself once said, began to develop when he came to Cathedral as basketball coach for the 1928-'29 season. Brother Edgar's team the previous season had compiled a 22-6 record. Dienhart's first team also was 22-6.

As football coach, Dienhart succeeded Joe Sexton '22 who left a 16-7-2 football record. Sexton left to concentrate on a full-time law practice. A native of Lafayette, Dienhart was a three-sport letterman at Jefferson High School. Dienhart entered Notre Dame and played on the "Four Horsemen" Irish varsity football team. He excelled at basketball and was elected Notre Dame team captain, but left the University to accept a position with the United States Shipping Board in Washington, D.C.

After leaving government service, Joe came to Indianapolis and got his degree at Butler University, where he played football for the Bulldogs. Dienhart was Cathedral's first full-time lay teacher and coach. His football teams became state powerhouses, with a record of 41-29-6 against the best competition. The 1931 team was recognized as the unofficial State Champion and the 1934 team won the Central Indiana Championship.

Had Cathedral been a recognized City Championship contender, the Irish would have claimed City titles in 1930, 1931, 1934 and 1935. Dienhart coached Indiana State Catholic Basketball champions in 1929, 1932 and 1933, and the National Catholic championship squad in 1933. His 129-69 won-lost basketball record is second to Tom O'Brien's in victories.

Beyond athletic success, Joe Dienhart formed the bridge to manhood for young men. "He was," said John Ford '32, "more than a coach. Joe Dienhart was a friend, a strong disciplinarian and an understanding mentor." Joe left Cathedral in 1938 to coach football at St. Joseph's College in Rensselaer, Indiana, where he developed a strong football program.

He went on to Purdue University to become assistant football coach and later assistant athletic director. After retirement from Purdue, Dienhart was elected mayor of West Lafayette, Indiana. During ten years of challenging change at Cathedral Joe was the public image of the emerging school. Even though he lacked facilities and equipment, Joe was a successful coach whose personal integrity caused Cathedral to be accepted as a formidable opponent. He was a sportsman, inspiring his players to realize their best as members of a team. He is saluted by dedication of this book, the third "Joe," to be so saluted. Ironically, none of the trio, Joe Chartrand, Joe Dezelan or Joe Dienhart attended the high school they represented in such a dedicated way.

TO JOE DEZELAN: "MR. CATHEDRAL"

Since arriving as a "one-year, no contract" coach in 1944, "Papa Joe"—more than any other person—has been "Mr. Cathedral."

Raised on the City's west side, Joe could not afford the streetcar fare to Cathedral from Haughville, so he settled on George Washington High School, where he was a stellar football star for legendary Coach Henry Bogue.

After graduation from Washington in 1933, Joe went on to captain Butler for another legend, Coach Tony Hinkle. Dezelan didn't graduate from Butler but was offered the Cathedral position forty-nine years ago on the condition that he would continue studies for a degree.

"Here I was, a CYO coach, following two Notre Dame athlete-coaches [Joe Harmon and Milt Piepul] and John Janzaruk from Indiana," Joe recalled. Actually, Joe almost didn't coach his first game, the opener against Shelbyville, because he thought his players questioned his credentials. Prior to the game, Joe put it to the team directly and they committed to his coaching.

The 1944 Irish won their first seven games and lost to Washington, 0-6, for the City Championship. Bob Welch was a guard on that team.

The rest, as they say, is history. Dezelan went on to win a mythical state championship in 1952, and ten City titles ('45, '50, '51, '52, '54, '59, '60, '61, '63 and '68)—more than any other coach.

His 182-60-8 record ranks high among that of all Hoosier coaches. He also coached many athletes who went on to coaching careers themselves, including Mike McGinley at Cathedral, Bob Springer at Washington and Dick Dullaghan at Ben Davis.

Dezelan also was Cathedral's head basketball coach in 1944–45 (won 8 of 19 games).

But beyond athletics and games won, there is Joe Dezelan the man. "No one ever gave more of himself to Cathedral than Joe Dezelan," Bob Welch said in tribute to his coach and friend of forty-eight years.

Joe was named Cathedral's first honorary graduate by the Class of 1963. In 1990 his wife, Yolanda "Londe" Dezelan was the school's first honorary female graduate.

The character of an institution is the sum of its faculty and alumni and friends. Joe Dezelan is the epitome of all as "Mr. Cathedral."

TO: ROBERT VINCENT WELCH
(1927-1992)

Bob Welch was a man of passionate loyalty and intense commitment. He came to Cathedral in 1941 as a freshman from St. Joan of Arc parish.

"I first met Bobby when we were freshmen, a Westside kid and a Northsider," Bob Collins '45 recalled. "For more than fifty years we were tighter than a pair of mail order shoes. We played football and Cathedral had a new varsity coach each season—Joe Harmon, Milt Piepul, John Janzaruk and Joe Dezelan," Collins reflected, "In truth, there is a Cathedral because there was Bob Welch."

The survival and emergence of Cathedral is a tribute to the devotion of the man who perished with his friend Frank McKinney, Jr. '57 and two others in a tragic airplane crash September 11, 1992.

Bob Welch was told this book would be dedicated to his service more than a year before his passing. Collins wrote:

Bobby was a tough businessman. He was gruff and to the point. But that was business; it wasn't Bobby. He was soft as a marshmallow. He was a sucker for good causes. His plate usually was full of volunteer work.

He could move from board room to bar room easier than any man I've ever known. At leisure, he was relaxed and congenial. He had friends in all the strata of Indianapolis life. He walked with the movers and shakers because he was one of them. He served on many boards.

But Bobby was most content when he was with his Gaelic friends. He was, as they say, as Irish as Paddy's pig. He preferred his Irish buddies. We were an ebullient, sometimes raucous group. He helped us sample the grape; like many Irishmen, he had a taste for it. But mostly he sat and laughed. And his laughter should have been quarantined; it was contagious.

Along with Bishop Chartrand, the Brothers of the Holy Cross, Coaches Dienhart and Dezelan, Bob Welch is remembered here. He is the only Cathedral graduate of seven decades to be so honored.

When he played football for Cathedral he often heard the cheer:

He's a man,

Who's a man,

He's a fightin' Cathedral man!

That was Robert Vincent Welch '45.

ACKNOWLEDGMENTS

This work is a product of accurate memories, cherished souvenirs and treasured scrapbooks.

Special thanks go to the special readers: Larry "Bo Connor '43, former managing editor of *The Indianapolis Star*, who reviewed the beginning pages through 1928 and the years 1939–1949.

Frank Widner '35, former news editor of *The Indianapolis Star*, who reviewed the years 1929–1938.

Bob Early '54, editor of *Arizona Highways* magazine, who reviewed the years 1950–1958.

Dan Carpenter '66, former *The Indianapolis Star* columnist and now their copy editor, who reviewed the years 1959–1968.

Chris Zinser Lavelle, Ladywood '70, feature editor of *The Phoenix Gazette*, who reviewed the years 1969 through 1979.

These professionals corrected, challenged and humbled the author; for which he is appreciative.

Special thanks go to other critics and contributors:

Cathedral President Julian Peebles.

Coach Joe Dezelan.

Cathedral teacher Nancy Niblack Baxter, who edited and published this book through Guild Press of Indiana, Inc.

All the students who interviewed former teachers and students.

Cathy McHugh Hess, assistant librarian, *The Indianapolis Star* and *The Indianapolis News*.

And to all the contributing writers, to those who submitted tapes, letters and information.

A special "thanks" to Linda Dillard, my executive secretary, who typed hundreds of pages of this book and who may know more about Cathedral than any other person who did not attend the school.

And thanks especially to my co-author, Cathedral teacher Jim Obergfell, who so capably researched and wrote the history of the years 1976–1993, and aided me in the entire project, start to finish.

Finally and most importantly, to Murny, my wife, who gave me the time to research and write *Cathedral: Seventy-Five Years*.

OUR CATHEDRAL

There is nothing ethnic about Cathedral. She's more like a huge family in which all groups are members.

More Irishmen were exposed (some carried in kicking and screaming) to education at Cathedral than, perhaps all of the people who live in that lovely green island. It was at Cathedral that we threw away the wheelbarrows and picked up the books.

People with names like McHugh, Connor, McLinn, Doyle, Sylvester, and Collins think of Cathedral as an Irish school. Not true.

Cathedral is a school for all people and all seasons; a place where a young person with a curious mind and a reasonable attention span can obtain a superior education.

In my day, when we lived in log cabins and studied by candlelight, Cathedral was an outstanding high school. It still is top of the line.

Of course, Cathedral has girls. Even though my granddaughter was a 1993 graduate, I have trouble writing about Cathedral persons. So, if I lapse into, "guys," I hope the ladies will forgive me.

In my days at Cathedral, girls were strange, untouchable creatures who attended St. Agnes Academy across the street. We stood outside every morning and watched them, making what for the time were ribald comments.

Many years later I discovered that they had the same curiosity about us.

I attended Cathedral through the end of the depression and into World War II. It was another time, another world.

Tuition was twenty-five dollars per semester (eons below the bandit prices Julian Peebles now is charging). Still, many families had trouble making the stipend.

But they came up with the money, a sacrifice offered up to the altar of education. And it paid dividends. Some of the most famous and influential men in the history of Indianapolis are Cathedral graduates. They have left fingerprints on almost every progressive movement.

In my time—the early forties—young men arrived from all over the city, filled with braggadocio—and fear. About the only thing we had in common was pimples. We were from Haughville and Irish Hill (where a gent named William R. Shover once lived) and Holy Rosary and St. Francis and Little Flower and St. Phillip's and St. Joan of Arc, where the only guys with extra coin resided.

The school was a melting pot. Name a language and somebody could speak it. This, of course, does not include the Irish, who still are battling English to a draw. The Brothers of Holy Cross took us and, using books, lectures, knuckles, paddles and yard sticks, turned us into students. Boy, those guys were tough. They would not tolerate students working below their ability. And I was the classic underachiever. I spent so much time in the assistant principal's office a Roman collar grew out of my neck.

But, subtly, they also were nurturing a bonding. We didn't know the meaning of the word, but we felt what was happening. Soon, we were one. We were Cathedral men.

Friendships were formed that lasted a lifetime. For example, I am into the sixty-seventh year of what many would call a zany life, but if I were to name my ten best friends, more than half would be my old Cathedral buddies. I could relate anecdotes until you were comatose. But Bill Shover and Jim Obergfell already have most of them in this wonderful book.

For those who love Cathedral, she always has been a movable feast. Cathedral memories are honed and polished like precious stones. And Bill and Jim, with the help of many others, have put together a book of precious stones that belongs on the shelf of every Cathedral graduate.

The book is dedicated to my late and dear friend Bob Welch. Of course, all Bobby did was save the school when it was about to become a memory. Bobby wouldn't have enjoyed this book, he would have wallowed in it. He was the greatest of all Cathedral men.

To all Cathedral persons (see, I remembered) I say "God Bless."

And allow me to finish with the traditional Irish Toast:

May the road rise to meet you.
May the wind be always at your back.
May the sun shine always on your face.
May the rain fall soft upon your fields.
And until we meet again,
May God hold you in the palm of His hand.

(And may you be gone for an hour before the devil finds out you're dead.)

Bob Collins, '45
February 26, 1993

(Bob Collins is the former daily columnist and Sports Editor of *The Indianapolis Star*.)

*We try to recall these years and get as an answer the
echo of our own voices laden with treasured recollections.*

Donald Flanagan '32
Valedictory Address

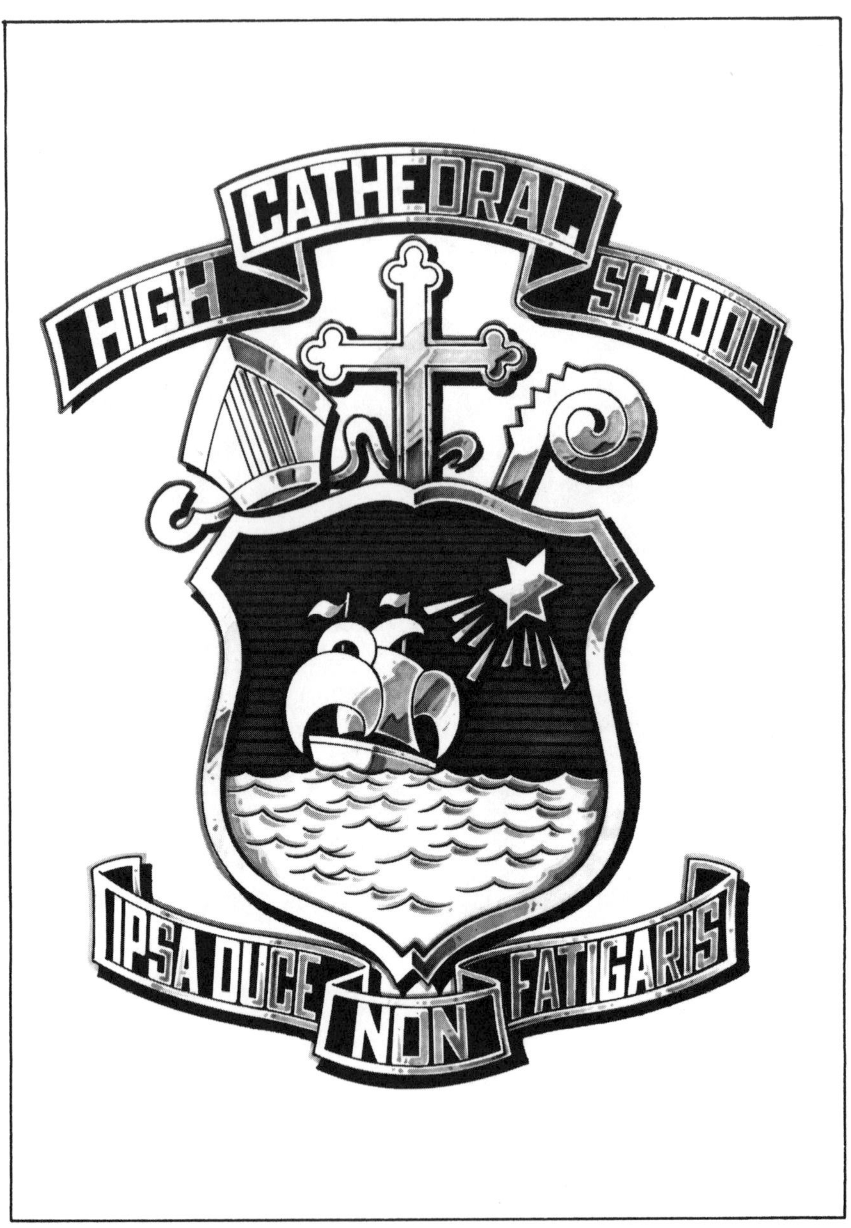

From the shield of Bishop Chartrand
Cathedral adopted its motto in its first year.

Ipsa duce non Fatigaris

"With her leading, you will not tire."

CATHEDRAL, ITS PROLOGUE . . .

Father Joseph Chartrand had a dream that there would be a boys' Catholic high school in a city that had three Catholic girls' academies—St. John's, St. Agnes' and St. Mary's.

Fr. Chartrand had served as principal of Cathedral Grade School after starting the parish in 1892.

He carefully measured space requirements in the red brick building that still stands at 13th and Pennsylvania streets, now the Damien Center for victims of AIDS.

There were more than three hundred grade school children enrolled, but Fr. Chartrand was sure the second floor of the building—approximately 9,500 square feet—could provide classroom space until a larger, better-equipped school building could be erected. He dreamed a dream and, by sheer persistence, he created his high school for boys.

It was a rainy Monday evening on September 17, 1917, when a few dozen fellow visionaries met in the grade school building to assess their desire and commitment. Chartrand, ever the eloquent evangelist, challenged: "There will be a school for boys and each of you has a mission to accomplish." There was nothing but a dream. Fr. Chartrand nine months later would become Bishop Chartrand.

An appeal for subscriptions followed.

Money was tight in a city that was buying Liberty Bonds in a patriotic fervor that swept the nation along to the strains of "Over There."

The money was found. The next task was to attract teachers. Chartrand had heard that at South Bend, the Congregation of Holy Cross had teaching brothers who were new in their work of establishing boys' high schools. Chartrand contacted Rev. Fr. Andrew Morrissey, Provincial of the Congregation of Holy Cross at Notre Dame, Indiana.

The University of Notre Dame was then in its seventy-fifth year, a struggling institution still relatively unknown. Only four years earlier Albert G. Feeney had played center on the football team that electrified the collegiate world. Notre Dame had been invited to West Point to play the Cadets in football. The boys from South Bend, Illinois—as Eastern newspapers had said it, misplacing the school geographically—shocked Army, 35–13. Gus Dorias' passes to Knute Rockne began not only the emergence of Notre Dame football but of offensive football itself.

Feeney and Rockne, friends through their lives, were to be prominent in early Cathedral history.

Fr. Morrissey accepted Chartrand's invitation and assigned Brothers Anthony, Austin, Bernard and Walter as the first faculty. Brother Bernard Gervais served as principal until 1922. Another member of his natural family, Brother Benedict, would later serve as Cathedral principal from 1942–47.

All of this activity was part of the Silver Jubilee of Bishop Chartrand's ordination after the founding of Cathedral parish. Catholics throughout the city responded to the wish of the beloved Chartrand and three hundred and sixty one days after the drive began—Friday the 13th of September, 1918—the wooden and glass doors of the old grade school opened to ninety boys, freshmen and sophomores. Cathedral became the first non-tuition parochial high school in Indiana.

For the most part the sophomore students had come from Shortridge, Manual and Tech, the city's only public high schools.

Three years later, in 1921, eleven young men graduated, and, surprisingly, nine of them matriculated to college. Seven went to Notre Dame, a pattern that continues today.

The early religious training at the new school would inspire young men to the vocations, one of the reasons the Brothers were involved. A second goal of the Holy Cross was to influence Cathedral graduates to matriculate to the University of Notre Dame.

The school's ties with and to Notre Dame are unbroken. Speaking to the first graduating class in 1921, Father John Cavanaugh, C.S.C. said "Your school, like ours, will form a rich heritage of tradition and your sons will go on as ambassadors to improve life in the spirit of Christ." Fr. Cavanaugh later became president of Notre Dame.

Chartrand shared the credit for the establishment of the institution. "The community was lacking and in want of a boys high school. I was only the instigator," he demurred.

For fifteen years Chartrand lived his dream every day.

But the first morning was crisp, springlike, with a temperature of fifty-one degrees. Friday, September 13, 1918, Cathedral High School opened the doors on the first of nearly eighteen thousand school days.

The headline in *The Indianapolis Star* that morning bannered
> *Yanks Cut 5 Miles Into Hun Lines*
> *and Capture 8,000 in First Drive*

The next day *The Star* banner read
> *Americans Capture 13,300 Prisoners in Wiping*
> *Out Pocket at St. Mihiel*

Other events happening that day:
- Labor Leader Eugene V. Debs was convicted of violating the Espionage Act
- Suspension of football loomed as the government put a ban on schedules
- the War Department asked colleges not to arrange programs for 1919
- World Series receipts for 1918 Championship brought $1,108.45 to each victorious Boston Red Sox player (including Babe Ruth)
- National League Champion Chicago Cub regulars received $574 each.

The war in France was going well for the Allies. Sixteen months after the United States had entered the conflict, American men and machines were helping to overcome the Central Powers.

The politically divided German people and the German High Command weren't in sync.

The city of Indianapolis was prospering from industries that fed our war machine. The Indianapolis Motor Speedway had opened in 1909 as a testing track for the new automotive phenomena. Indianapolis was at the beginning of a burgeoning spurt of growth: growth that on the one hand promised a bright economic future as the Great War wound down, and on the other hand had an ominous edge of overwrought patriotism which would soon evolve into the bigoted emotionalism which would bring the Ku Klux Klan to Indiana.

Monument Circle in 1918 looked something like it does today; the Soldiers and Sailors' Monument, built sixteen years earlier, stood as a sincere patriotic testimony to the dedication of Hoosiers in two wars, the Civil War and the Spanish-American conflict. It was, however, dirty already from the coal-smoke haze which hung over the industrial heart of Indianapolis. Miss Liberty needed a bath, the Indianapolis papers reported.

Christ Church Cathedral on the northeast corner was then a venerable and heralded Episcopal parish center; the Columbia Club was eighteen years old. It was a modest structure standing on the east side of the Circle and had not as yet been transformed into the splendid Gothic temple of the twenties; and the Circle Theatre, later to be the revered site of Cathedral graduations, was two years young.

Rumors of an armistice were rampant, but the most deadly attack on the civilian population had been the influenza epidemic which was still ravaging the country. Hundreds of thousands of American lives had been taken by the "Spanish Flu" so far and Indianapolis citizens were still battling the "germ" or recovering from the brain fever and rheumatic problems that followed in the flu's wake.

Though there were clouds on the horizon, Cathedral bravely opened its doors with a few brothers for teachers, a little nest egg from hopeful parishioners to pay the first bills and a group of young men from all over the city determined to meet and get a "Catholic education."

"I rode a bike to school," Stanley Boyle '21, recalled, "and wore a mask over my face. Everybody wore masks. It looked like Halloween but it was necessary."

The three existing public high schools, Shortridge, Manual, and Tech, closed for a month to avoid the contagion of "the grippe," but Cathedral continued its classes.

"We were disappointed," Boyle recalls "but that was to be an indication of the kind of school Cathedral would become."

On that cloudy Friday the 13th of September morning Brother Bernard Gervais stood on the front steps of Cathedral Grade School.

"He personally greeted each student and the parents and showed us to the stairs inside the building that led to the second floor," Stanley Boyle recalled. "Frankly, I wasn't too impressed walking into a grade school. After all, I was thirteen, almost fourteen."

Boyle and the other teen-agers who joined him were an apprehensive lot whose parents—at the suggestion of parish priests who had been urged by Bishop Chartrand—had signed them up as the first classes, seventy-eight freshmen and twelve sophomores.

The dress code mandated ties and jackets and most wore dark clothing and knickers. Many sported tams—the area was suffering a cold spell that would soon intensify the influenza epidemic.

Parents were sending their boys to the school partly because they felt they should go, but mostly because of opportunity. Cathedral was the city's first Catholic high school for boys.

The mission statement promulgated by the Brothers of the Congregation of Holy Cross states that Cathedral's general purpose is explicitly "to train young men to become, under the inspiration of divine grace and the orderly pursuit of intellectual and moral truth, true Christian gentlemen." That purpose has changed only to include, since 1976, young women.

Mark Mooney '22 recalls that "Bishop Chartrand greeted each new student and, as I recall, was at the school nearly every day." The number, ninety boys enrolled on that first day, surpassed expectations, and Brother Walter was later assigned to help the three Brothers already assigned.

Only months before, final arrangements to open the school had been completed with the Very Reverend Andrew Morrissey, Order Provincial at Notre Dame. A residence for the Brothers was purchased south of the school on Pennsylvania Street.

Both parents and students coming up those steps the first day noticed that the early three classrooms were comfortable but cramped. Within three years as enrollment swelled, they had to be expanded for accreditation. Latin, English, algebra, geometry, ancient and modern history, science, civics and religion was the structured pre-college fare.

The first year, in 1918, application was made for a state commission of recognition for Cathedral, but the request was denied because high school classes were held in a building jointly used by a grade school. (In 1922 the State Board of Education finally granted the commission when Cathedral classes were being held in a temporary facility on 14th Street between Illinois and Meridian Streets.)

From its birth the school attracted students from fifteen parishes—all parts of town. The largest group came from the

Northside. Students' family financial statuses were as varied as their intellectual talents. Most came to Cathedral because they were quick to see the advantages of an all-male Catholic high school, a characteristic of school spirit that was to continue through the years.

Some also selected Cathedral because of the opportunity for more personal attention than they would receive at a larger school. Still others were lured by the facility's accessible, central location. Typical was Fred Schoettle, who entered Cathedral in 1920 after having spent two years at St. Meinrad Minor Seminary and two years at another local high school. He entered the school because Bishop Chartrand thought that he would benefit much more from attending Cathedral for an additional two years than by entering college or seeking employment.

There was one common point among all Cathedral students: their deep affection for Bishop Chartrand. Though he was not officially on the faculty, His Excellency taught religion every Friday afternoon. It was often said that he would ask who had received Holy Communion the previous Sunday. If a student had not, the Bishop would ask, "When are you going to join the Roman Catholic Church?"

Curriculum under the brothers was basic and demanding, instruction formal. Chemistry and physics were not originally featured, but were soon added to challenge budding scientists. A new laboratory was installed in the basement of the school building. A fire at the factory manufacturing the apparatus delayed the opening of the labs, however.

Cathedral's social services contribution tradition began in 1920 with the first Bengal Mission to aid Holy Cross Brothers serving the poor of India.

Almost from the school's opening, athletics became a vital focus of Cathedral life. In 1918 the faculty organized an intramural basketball league—"the Insects"—that was to launch varsity sports the following year. Games were played in the Marion Club gymnasium and one team was called "Irish."

The first fighting Irish football squads by necessity played clubs and community centers. These games made up in spontan-eity and rough fun for what they lacked in regularity. The first official contest was a loss; but Cathedral's underclassmen won the rest of the games in 9–1 season against local community center teams. Playing against club and school teams, the original football squad won nine of ten games

1919–1921

On September 9, 1919, the second year of Cathedral's life began with near-double enrollment. Brother Gregory joined the faculty and French, Spanish, U.S. History and trigonometry were added to the curriculum.

Basketball was to be Cathedral's first sport in competition against a high school team. The coach for all seasons was Brother Gregory. Games were played at the then-downtown Shortridge High School gymnasium or at Knights of Columbus Hall when available. The first real school opponent, "Indiana Deaf and Dumb," defeated Cathedral, 31–14. *The Megaphone* noted that the loss was "scarcely encouraging," but later that season the lads trounced IDD soundly.

Another tradition was added that 1919 fall: varsity football. Brother Gregory coached the all-underclass team. Practices began in October and automobile drivers behind the wheels of all-black Ford "Tin Lizzies" pulled aside as they watched Cathedral boys running to practice at Senate Avenue and Fall Creek Boulevard. One puzzled driver was overheard to say, "Did these young men change clothes after school today?"

Though not impressive in attire, the first team did win all three scheduled games (one was a forfeit victory) and thus started a winning football tradition.

As *The Megaphone*, analyzing the 1919 season, commented:

> *The heavy Northwestern A.C.'s were played at North-western Park and trounced, 12–0. The Miami Juniors were carded for the next contest but failed to show up and the game was forfeited to us, 2–0. A return game was played on Thanksgiving Day and Cathedral again defeated Northwestern A.C. by a 12–6 score. The aerial work of [Tom] Ruckelshaus and [Mark] Mooney and the consistent line plunging of [George] Sadlier were the features of the game.*

Ruckelshaus was killed as a pilot flying "The Hump" over Burma in World War II. He was the uncle of William Ruckelshaus who attended Cathedral and served in the cabinets of Presidents Nixon and Reagan. Class President in 1922, Mooney attended Notre Dame and never returned to live in Indianapolis. He retired from General Electric and lives in Tampa, Florida. Sadlier, the team's captain, was Chairman of the Board of First Federal Savings & Loan Association and a noted horseman.

Student theatre began; a sixteen-piece orchestra of violins, banjos, brass, a drum and piano began performing.

And so, Cathedral High School entered its third season, as the nation entered the decade of the "Roaring Twenties."

Newspapers bannered the drama of one of America's great court cases in 1920, the infamous Sacco-Vanzetti murder trial. The Great War was a tragic memory and the League of Nations was formed to outlaw war. The inept New York Yankees, who had never won a pennant, saw promise in a left-handed pitcher and acquired George Herman "Babe" Ruth from the Boston Red Sox. A Golden Age of sports was about to begin. In 1920 Notre Dame football would bloom. Third-year coach Knute Rockne had prayed for the eligibility of restless triple-threat George Gipp.

Principal Brother Bernard Gervais stood outside the school in that fall of 1920 in his traditional greeting role and welcomed two hundred and fifty students into the by-now obviously cramped three classrooms on the upper floor at 1301 North Pennsylvania Street.

The faculty had grown to nine brothers and one volunteer varsity football-basketball coach. Albert G. Feeney, a handsome slicked-back-black-haired furniture store owner, had found Bishop Chartrand's invitation to coach "irresistible" he once recalled. "No one could refuse the Bishop and, frankly, I would have coached if I had to pay for the job."

A graduate of Emmerich Manual Training High School, as has been said, Feeney played center with Rockne on the 1913 Notre Dame team which began the school's national football fame.

The coming of the dapper, mustachioed Feeney to Cathedral extended the school's involvement with Notre Dame. "He picked the school colors, the uniforms (some allegedly were hand-me-downs from Notre Dame) and our style of play," Mark Mooney recalls.

Coach Rockne invited Feeney's Cathedral boys to practice in preseason on the replanted sod of Ireland at Notre Dame's hallowed Cartier Field. So much were the Cathedral boys like Notre Dame in formations, spirit and success that *The Indianapolis News* sportswriter William F. "Bill" Fox (an alumnus of Notre Dame) dubbed them the "Fighting Irish."

But the Ku Klux Klan was already beginning to raise its ugly head nationally, and prejudice was rife; sports was a "contact" area in more ways than one.

Joe Harmon '21 once recalled: "From my playing at Cathedral to playing at Notre Dame and then on into coaching, 'Irish' was the name the newspapers and radio used to refer to us. But down there on the line or under the basket, our opponents called us 'crossbacks,' 'Micks' or even worse.

"Some times it angered us but, mostly, it inspired us to play harder," said Harmon, Cathedral's first son to play in a Rose Bowl game with Notre Dame in 1925.

Just as Rockne as player and coach had vaulted Notre Dame to football prominence, so would Feeney elevate Cathedral to the public's notice. Cathedral had been undefeated under Brother Gregory in 1919. Under Feeney in 1920, Cathedral was also undefeated; in fact, in 1920, Cathedral and Notre Dame both had no-loss records.

Real high school opponents for the first time filled the 1920–21 schedule spots. Cathedral's initial football game against a school opponent was played in 1920 at High School Park in Louisville. The team departed Union Station by train to play powerful St. Xavier College High School. George Sadlier scored the first touchdown in "official" play as Cathedral went on to upset St. X, 20–6. Mark Mooney "kicked goal." The entire Cathedral team had only three headgears and the only other equipment was purchased by the players personally.

The next game featured Mark Mooney setting an individual record that still stands, nearly seven-hundred games later. Playing Boys Prep School (today Park Tudor) at Washington Park, the elusive Mooney scored five touchdowns and kicked fourteen consecutive extra points as the "Irish"—nicknamed for the first time in print—romped to another all-time record, 104–0. Those forty-four points that Mooney accumulated may be an Indiana high school record as well—at least until proven otherwise.

To inspire his former teammate Feeney's first team at Cathedral, Rockne arrived in Indianapolis the day before his own team, Notre Dame, was to play Indiana. With the immortal Rockne on the Cathedral bench, "Feeney's Meanies" defeated Cincinnati St. Xavier, 6–0 to complete a 5–0 season.

The next day, with Feeney reciprocating his friend's loyalty by visiting on the Notre Dame sidelines, Notre Dame defeated Indiana, 13–10, in its closest win of the 1920 season.

While in Indianapolis, the legendary George Gipp also watched Cathedral play St. X; Cathedral players were awed by the warmth of one of the greatest of collegiate football players.

Thirty-three days later "the Gipper," at age twenty-five, died of pneumonia and Cathedral honored his brief but lasting memory at the school with a memorial High Mass for the repose of his soul.

The entire 1920 Cathedral team was comprised of only sixteen players. Brother Theodore was the athletic director. Among those who went on to distinguish themselves were

- Joe Sexton, who coached Cathedral varsity football 1926–28 (won 16, lost 7, tied 2) and one varsity basketball season, 1926–27 (8–12). Sexton was a part-time coach and had a successful law practice.

- Joe Harmon, center for Notre Dame with the "Four Horsemen" team that defeated Stanford in the 1925 Rose Bowl. He coached Cathedral to its first recognized City Football Championship in 1940.

- Rev. Fr. Carl "Dutch" Wilberding of the Indianapolis Archdiocese.

- George Sadlier, a civic leader, president of First Federal Savings & Loan.

- Marvin Brezette, who was to relive Cathedral football glory thirty-nine seasons later in 1959 when his son, Fran, captained Cathedral's 10–0 team.

- Paul Harrington, scholar and athlete, who set the world indoor pole vault record at Notre Dame using a bamboo pole.

Sports, as has often been pointed out, are not the only facet of Cathedral life, and the school early on developed a richly varied extracurricular life.

School spirit evolved quickly and was solidified in 1920 when the Chartrand Club was formed to boost school spirit. It formed the nucleus for all extracurricular activities. Every student joined.

The Megaphone appeared in April 1920. The "Easter Number" had an advertisement from the University of Notre Dame on its inside cover. "Catalogue Sent on Application to the Registrar" it intoned, as Notre Dame, seventy-eight years old but just beginning to be known nationally, sought students.

The Megaphone was a quarterly publication with two hundred subscribers who paid fifty cents per year. Single copies sold for fifteen cents. The first article was accompanied by a photo of Bishop Chartrand "whose paternal care for our spiritual and temporal welfare is ever showing itself in countless ways." Issues featured a certain amount of news, poetry and compositions, mostly fictional. The first poem by J. A. Kelly '21 read:

Poetry Problems
(with apologies to Mr. Dobson)
I started a verse,
But it grew to a sonnet.
It slowly grew worse,
Though I started a verse.
Please send for a hearse,
It's murder, "Doggonit,"
I started a verse,
But it grew to a sonnet.

Cathedral's first major production was on May 10, 1920 at the Athenaeum. Mark Twain's *The Prince and the Pauper* had a cast of forty-eight and a production crew of twenty-nine. Half of the student body were involved. Anthony Manley and James Norton played the title roles and a bearded attendant courier in the cast was J. Corbin Patrick, '22. Patrick was drama and music critic for *The Indianapolis Star* fifty-two years and is revered as an artistic contributor to Indiana's cultural history without peer.

Among the advertisers in the first issue was

John R. Welch & Sons
52 Monument Circle
Real Estate, Rentals and Insurance.

The Welch name would become immortal at Cathedral.

Another highlight as the year ended was news that Paul Harrington had won a one-thousand-dollar-a-year scholarship for four years at Notre Dame for his winning essay contest sponsored by Firestone Tire & Rubber Company.

Baseball came to Cathedral as a varsity sport in the spring of 1921. The schedule was short as was the spring weather. West Newton was defeated; Park School canceled, and the Irish de–

feated Knightstown. The game of the season was played May 20 on Riverside Diamond No. 3, where the Irish defeated Shortridge, 15–9. That set up the city title match with Manual; in that game Joe Harmon pitched a two-hitter as Cathedral won 7–2.

The season ended with a 7–0 record. But Tech's athletic director, "Mr. Fred Gorman, steadfastly avoiding any contest with Cathedral" (as *The Megaphone* reported) refused to play off the 1921 City baseball championship after the Irish baseball team defeated Shortridge and Manual.

Mike Duffecy '22, tinkled the ivories at the school's upright piano and composed a tune that was to arouse Cathedral spirit through the years. "Dear Old Cathedral" was an immediate rallying anthem, and Francis Frey '21, added words of loyalty to what was to become the first original high school song in Indiana.

Cathedral concluded its third year, and, on June 14, 1921, the first graduating class of eleven accepted diplomas from Bishop Chartrand, Brother Bernard and Fr. John Cavanaugh, C.S.C., later president of Notre Dame. Nine continued their education, seven at Notre Dame. Francis McCarthy was president of the first graduating class.

1921–1922

The 1921 football season began with a disappointment. Shortridge canceled its upcoming game with Cathedral without giving a reason.

Cathedral played Sheridan instead of Shortridge, and defeated Cathedral, the school's first varsity football loss, 0–13. "It was my fault," a disappointed coach Feeney told newspaper reporters after the Irish lost the game. The team had trained one week at Notre Dame and Coach Rockne gave the players pointers. Still, they lost. "The Black and White earned the victory at Sheridan," *The Megaphone* reported.

The second game against the Deaf School was called "after the scorekeeper flatly refused to continue on the job when his adnometer blew out after registering seventy odd points for Cathedral."

The season highlight was played at Butler's old Irwin Field in Irvington. Manual's recognized City Champions were defeated,

DEAR OLD CATHEDRAL

Michael J. Duffecy stayed after school often because there was an upright piano in the music room. As a sixteen-year-old junior in 1921, Duffecy tinkled out a tune that was to become the first original high school song in Indiana. Francis Frey '21 wrote the lyrics to "Dear Old Cathedral," which has inspired school spirit and aroused countless Irish athletes to achievements.

"All the high school bands were playing college march songs or 'Boola Boola,' " he said in a 1967 interview in *The Indianapolis Star.* "I thought we should have a song of our own. The bands of sports opponents continued to salute Cathedral with the 'Notre Dame Victory March,' but Cathedral now finally had an original song."

The newly-formed Cathedral Band played it first to open the 1923 grid season against Bloomfield and soon it became an institution.

It was sung by Cathedral-graduate pledges in fraternity houses as a ritual of initiation. Her athlete sons sang it as rookies on college and professional sports teams as they were inducted into the ranks.

"I was never embarrassed," Bob Collier '33 said of the time when he was a pledge of Beta Theta Pi at Indiana University. "The others seemed to envy me because I could sing—or attempt to sing—an original school song."

Duffecy began his musical training studying classical music at the old Metropolitan School of Music, now the Jordan College of Music at Butler University.

After graduation from Cathedral in 1922, Duffecy went to the University of Notre Dame where he again played piano in the school orchestra. One summer he toured Europe as part of a concert group. Duffecy played intramural sports at Cathedral on "the Insects."

He completed his career as an investment counselor for Hornblower & Weeks-Hemphill Noyes in Indianapolis. In 1967, Cathedral alumni honored him at a banquet and presented him the Spes Unica Award. Mike Duffecy remained a loyal son to Cathedral until his death.

Dear Old Cathedral, here's to you
Here's to your colors, gold and blue
We'll cheer you onward everyone,
Whether the battle's lost or won.
So here's to your sons, your fighting team
Let your banners stream
We'll keep them proudly waving to the sky
As we cheer for Cathedral High.

"My only regret," Duffecy said, "is that I called it a fight song instead of a spirit song. We don't like fighting at Cathedral."

87–0. Some claim Manual did not use all its varsity players; others say there was apathy and unconcern as "Feeney's Meanies" defeated his *alma mater.*

The season ended 5–1, with only Sheridan scoring thirteen points against the 241 points scored by the newly-named Irish.

It was in coverage of the Manual game by William F. Fox Jr. of *The Indianapolis News* that the "Irish" name was first used.

Nineteen years later, competing for the first time for the Indianapolis School Board Trophy, the Irish were acclaimed 1940 City Champions. Tech was runner-up.

Coach Knute Rockne spoke at the first football banquet December 15, 1921, in the Riley Room of The Claypool Hotel. While the Cathedral ragtime band whined out a snappy version of "The Notre Dame Victory March," Rockne surprised Feeney, his Notre Dame teammate of 1911–13, by presenting him with a gold watch from the Cathedral Boosters Club.

The yellowed clipping from the October 21, 1921, edition of *The Indianapolis News* shows the increased notice Cathedral High School was gaining in the Indianapolis community and the strong Notre Dame connection the school was enjoying:

FAST CATHEDRAL TEAM CRUSHES MANUAL, 87–O

A youthful Notre Dame drilled incessantly for the last six weeks by Coach Al Feeney, whose notion of teaching football runs right alongside that of K. K. Rockne, the youthful Irish aggregation appeared to be a miniature sports model of the high-powered vehicle of football that Notre Dame swings into action year after year.

Dressed in suits precisely the same as those of the Notre Dame team from the specially-built shoes for the kickers to the massive tan headgears, the kids looked the part and played it also.

It is known that Coach Al Feeney, a graduate of Manual, selected the school colors.

The Senior Class of the 1921–22 year, the first four-year graduates, though, numbered only forty-one. The class had a dropout rate of nearly fifty percent. The reason for this high rate remains unknown and causes one to speculate, especially in view of the fact that the preceding class of seniors had eleven of its original twelve class members earn Cathedral diplomas.

1922–1923

Feeney's undefeated, unscored-on 1922 Irish football team was again saluted at the annual banquet by Knute Rockne. Speaker after speaker lauded a team that is believed to be the state's only unscored-on team (in seven games or more). The first speaker, Mayor Louis Lowe, said Cathedral was the best team in Indianapolis. The next proclaimed the Irish the finest in Indiana. And another called them "the best in the United States."

Rockne retorted, "I'm sure glad my team didn't play them." (In 1922, Notre Dame was 8–1–1 and surrendered twenty-seven points.)

State-wide prominence was a reality.

Cathedral's emergence as an educational institution in Indianapolis had, in general, gained acceptance quickly. Chartrand later recalled that his dream grew and prospered even beyond his expectations, and this early phase of the school's experience confirms his assessment. The enrollment had doubled the year after the school opened, 1919, and now, within five years, it was surpassing five-hundred students. The founding period was over.

The Community of Holy Cross

Jacques-François Dujarie was ordained on New Year's Day 1796. Following the Revolution, France was in educational and religious chaos. The youth of Dujarie's parish, he wrote, were not only in "a state of gross ignorance, but almost in savagery."

Father Dujarie set about building a lay community of female teachers, and after 14 years of turmoil the community was reorganized as a religious congregation: the Sisters of Providence. Their first entry into Indianapolis came in 1859 when a group of Sisters founded St. John Academy at St. John Parish, now near the main entrance to the Hoosier Dome. It was to become the first high school in Indianapolis.

In 1820, about the time the Sisters' community got on an even keel, Dujarie received permission to start a community of Brothers. His plan was to educate and then send them wherever they were needed as teachers, choirmasters or aides to parish priests. Dujarie died in 1838. His successor, Abbe Basil Moreau, began organizing a team of six Brothers who, under the leadership of Father Edward Sorin, C.S.C., sailed from France for America in 1841. The following year they cleared one hundred twenty acres of Indiana woodland and the University of Notre Dame was born. The Brothers targeted their works toward grammar school teaching. Most of the schools, however, had closed by the turn of the century.

In 1909, at the request of the Diocesan bishop, the Brothers opened their first high school—Central Catholic—in Fort Wayne. In 1920 they opened Reitz Memorial High School in Evansville. (Both schools were to become sports rivals of Cathedral.)

At the invitation of Bishop Joseph Chartrand, four Holy Cross Brothers came to Indianapolis and, on September 13, 1918, Cathedral High School was born.

In 1945 the congregation was reorganized into two distinct societies. One was made up entirely of Brothers, and, for the first time, the Brothers could elect one of their own as provincial. The other society consisted of priests and those Brothers who wished to serve as priests' assistants. The societies still share a common superior general and constitution.

(Continued)

Today, there are more than six hundred Holy Cross Brothers in the United States, and their focus is still primarily on education. Along with two colleges, Holy Cross in South Bend and St. Edward's in Austin, the Brothers administer and teach at more than twenty high schools and a few middle schools.

Today, those seeking to become Brothers must first attend a candidate program at St. Edward's, then a novitiate at Cascade, Colorado, then a post-novitiate in San Antonio.

From there, the choice of further education is determined by each candidate's own interest. Some pursue Master's Degrees in social work, teaching areas or administration, others take on anything from law school to medical school. Brothers are prepared professionally for any work they undertake.

—From Summer/1992 issue of *Notre Dame Magazine* by Carol Schaal, associate editor of the magazine. Used by permission.

BROTHER BERNARD, C. S. C.

CATHEDRAL'S FIRST PRINCIPAL

Ss. Peter and Paul grade school was the first home of the free Catholic boys' school established in 1918.

Cathedral's first faculty: Brothers Anthony, Justin, Bernard and Walter.

Joe Harmon

Joe Sexton

Al Feeney

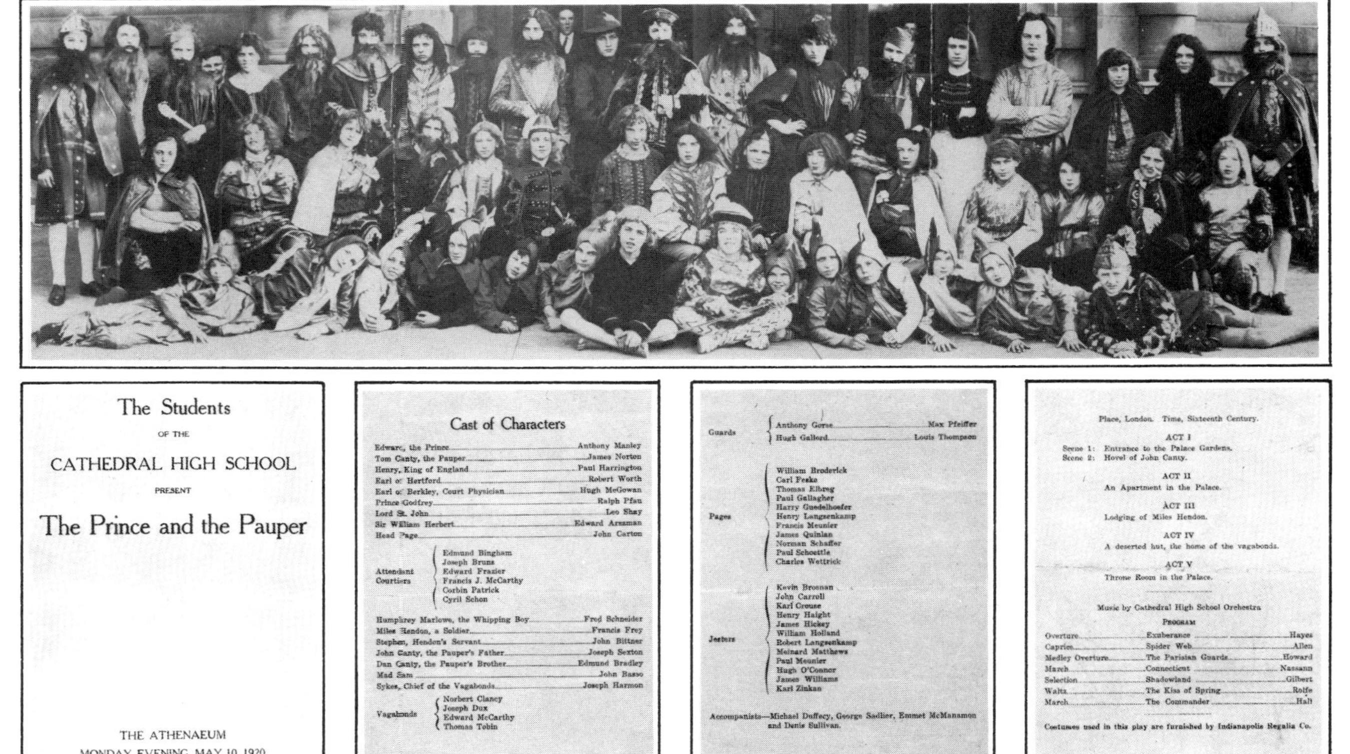

The Students

OF THE

CATHEDRAL HIGH SCHOOL

PRESENT

The Prince and the Pauper

THE ATHENAEUM

MONDAY EVENING, MAY 10, 1920

Cast of Characters

Edward, the Prince — Anthony Manley
Tom Canty, the Pauper — James Norton
Henry, King of England — Paul Harrington
Earl of Hertford — Robert Worth
Earl of Berkley, Court Physician — Hugh McGowan
Prince Godfrey — Ralph Pfau
Lord St. John — Leo Shay
Sir William Herbert — Edward Arssman
Head Page — John Carton

Attendant Courtiers:
Edmund Bingham
Joseph Bruns
Edward Frazier
Francis J. McCarthy
Corbin Patrick
Cyril Schon

Humphrey Marlowe, the Whipping Boy — Fred Schneider
Miles Hendon, a Soldier — Francis Frey
Stephen, Hendon's Servant — John Bittner
John Canty, the Pauper's Father — Joseph Sexton
Dan Canty, the Pauper's Brother — Edmund Bradley
Mad Sam — John Basso
Sykes, Chief of the Vagabonds — Joseph Harmon

Vagabonds:
Norbert Clancy
Joseph Dux
Edward McCarthy
Thomas Tobin

Guards:
Anthony Gorse — Max Pfeiffer
Hugh Gallord — Louis Thompson

Pages:
William Broderick
Carl Feske
Thomas Elbreg
Paul Gallagher
Harry Guedelhoefer
Henry Langsenkamp
Francis Meunier
James Quinlan
Norman Schaffer
Paul Schoettle
Charles Wettrick

Jesters:
Kevin Brosnan
John Carroll
Karl Crouse
Henry Haight
James Hickey
William Holland
Robert Langsenkamp
Meinard Matthews
Paul Meunier
Hugh O'Connor
James Williams
Karl Zinkan

Accompanists—Michael Duffecy, George Sadlier, Emmet McManamon and Danis Sullivan.

Place, London. Time, Sixteenth Century.

ACT I
Scene 1: Entrance to the Palace Gardens.
Scene 2: Hovel of John Canty.

ACT II
An Apartment in the Palace.

ACT III
Lodging of Miles Hendon.

ACT IV
A deserted hut, the home of the vagabonds.

ACT V
Throne Room in the Palace.

Music by Cathedral High School Orchestra

PROGRAM

Overture — Exuberance — Hayes
Caprice — Spider Web — Allen
Medley Overture — The Parisian Guards — Howard
March — Connecticut — Nassann
Selection — Shadowland — Gilbert
Waltz — The Kiss of Spring — Rolfe
March — The Commander — Hall

Costumes used in this play are furnished by Indianapolis Regalia Co.

The Prince and the Pauper seems to have almost the entire student body as the cast, but it was in reality only half the school.

Cathedral's first band was photographed by society photographer Noble Bretzman.

"The Insects" started the tradition of Cathedral sporting achievement.

"Room 2 of the first year of the Cathedral High School Wednesday, May 21, 1919. Top row (l to r) Reeves, Joseph Sexton, Francis O'Connor, Timothy Lenchen, Wm Eich, Schneider, Olsen, Thompson, Stark. (middle) O'Brien, Gavin, Cornet, Cahil, Dux, Schultz, Sherrin, Pfeiffer, Laskey, Moore, Metzger. (bottom) McManamon, McShay, Sharkey, McCarthy, Conway, Bradley, Schilling, Findley, Kelly, Fiddler, Bingham (Desautels, Maddox, Craig and Loftus missing)".

One-hundred-two students, probably 1920, with brothers identified as Bernard, Anthony, and Austin.

The varsity baseball team, 1923.

Baseball Champions 1927 (l to r) Bottom row B. Martin, Al Mueller, J. O'Brien, C Hohman, J. Gorman, C. Commons Second row-E. Miller, L. Sexton, P. Wernsing, V. Willeman, J. Lawrie, V. O'Connor. Third row Bro. Edwin, Coach, F. Mueller, J. Dugan, S. Brown, J. McQuade, Fred Dilger, Coach.

THE TWENTIES

Beginning in the early 1920s, Cathedral first experienced the ugliness of intolerance.

In 1920 the League of Nations had been formed to try to bring about world peace and understanding. The League of Women Voters began to implement the gains of the suffrage movement. But while there were social justice gains on some fronts, there were losses on others. Undercurrents of hatred present since the time of the Civil War and deepened by the xenophobia caused by World War I came to the surface. Indianapolis, and the Midwest in general, were becoming prey to bigotry.

The Ku Klux Klan found in Indiana a fertile land to sow its seeds of hate. Formed in the post-Civil War South, the Klan began to enforce its will on those it believed were not punished enough by Reconstruction laws. Its original purpose was to protect women and children from abuse and to insure the supremacy of the white race, but by the turn of the century its excesses and changing times caused it to die out as an active institution.

In 1920 David Curtis "D.C." Stephenson came north from Texas and Oklahoma, gaining prominence in a re-activated Klan in Evansville, Indiana. After falling out with the Southern Indiana kluxers, he arrived in Indianapolis, where he made a fortune in selling Klan paraphernalia and other interests and bought a home in Irvington. He was the "Independent Klan's" state Grand Dragon.

Stephenson appealed to the typical urban Klan member. Kenneth T. Jackson, in his book *The Ku Klux Klan in the City, 1915-30*, characterized the Klan's appeal to a lower middle-class, blue-collar worker. These Klan-vulnerable Hoosiers had less education and came from neighborhoods whose residential stability was threatened by European immigrants and Negroes moving from farm to city and from South to North. The author's research led him to the conclusion that the Klan was "not a reaction against the rise of city to dominance in American life," but "rather a reaction against the aspirations of certain elements within the city."

Many believe Jackson's assertion that five hundred of the 1,300 delegates to the 1924 Indiana State Republican Convention were loyal to Grand Dragon D.C. Stephenson and that the Klan elected Governor Ed Jackson and a majority of the state legislature.

Stephenson was a fiery orator who could incite a crowd to fever-like intensity, as Adolf Hitler would later do in vengeful

Germany. Both men were the voices of hate and both attacked Jews. However, Stephenson widened his circle of hatred to include Catholics and Negroes as well.

Stephenson's oratory and ire vaulted KKK klaverns to record membership. He was a charismatic leader, a super salesman, a power-mad, convincing liar, and finally a brutal killer. As Grand Dragon he ruled Indiana and several other Northern states. At its height, about one in three white male Protestants, more than 250,000, had joined the Indiana Klan and sworn to work for "One-hundred percent Americanism." Indianapolis Klan membership in the early twenties was second only to that of the membership of the metropolitan area in Chicago.

From 1923–25, D.C. Stephenson was at the peak of his control of the state's political power system, poised to make a run for Congress and, some predicted, the presidency of the United States. Then, in one night, Stephenson's world began to topple. He kidnapped and raped a Statehouse worker, Madge Oberholtzer, taking her on a terror-filled night-time train ride to Hammond. Desperate, she attempted suicide and was returned to her parents' home ill of bichloride of mercury poison and suffering from a life-threatening internal infection.

Stephenson was charged with murder in 1925 after the young woman died. Still, he shouted during the time of his arrest, "I am the law in Indiana." After delays in impaneling an Indianapolis jury the trial was venued to Noblesville, and Stephenson was convicted and sentenced to life in prison. He was paroled twice, first in 1950, and was jailed shortly thereafter in parole violation. In 1956 he was released. He moved to Seymour, Indiana, where he married a wealthy widow. They divorced in 1962 and Stephenson moved to Tennessee and died there in 1966.

But during the 1920s Stephenson and his masked henchmen blatantly ruled Indiana politics, and their contentions that "the Pope would soon take over America" alarmed naive Hoosiers and made all Catholics vulnerable. In 1924 Stephenson ordered his Klansmen to march in front of Ss. Peter and Paul Cathedral, St. Agnes Academy, the temporary site of Cathedral High School's annex and the future site near Meridian Street. The demonstration against Catholics was part of a parade of thousands of white-sheeted Klan members through the streets of downtown Indianapolis.

After commandeering the water hoses of the Indianapolis Fire Department, Cathedral boys disrupted the Klan parade. Ignoring the happening, Indianapolis policemen, many of Irish origin, looked innocently to the sky as Cathedral students sprayed the marching Klansmen.

As if protecting the Cathedral, members of the Knights of Columbus stood on the steps as thousands of cone-headed Klansmen marched past.

After Stephenson's conviction, Klan membership in the U.S. dropped from more than one million to less than 300,000. Its rolls dwindled, and it was universally condemned in later years.

Many still believe it was Klan influence that prevented athletic competition between Cathedral and many schools during the 1920s and into the 1930s. The mystery of the "Invisible Empire" of the KKK is still debated today, and its power has probably been slightly overemphasized in recent depictions. Indiana, after all, was quick to act against Stephenson when it had the chance in the spring of 1925 and to pass legislation which would destroy the power of the Klan. After Stephenson's fall from power, many in the state said they regretted they had been swept up in the hysteria and began to reach out to their Catholic neighbors and in some cases to black citizens. And, if the Klan did have such rural strength, why did many of the high schools in Indiana compete against Cathedral teams and not the Indianapolis City schools? Bigotry was a strong factor but not the only one; Cathedral teams played hard and won, almost invariably, and that truth should not be ignored.

When all that is said, however, there still remains a strong, provable strain of prejudice which is never far from the surface in Indiana history. In Indianapolis, in addition to the Klan, there existed a White Supremacy League, a White Citizen's Protective League, a Capitol Avenue Protective Association and a Mapleton Civic Association; all of which were dedicated to preventing Negroes from moving out of their overcrowded northwest neighborhoods to better housing in white neighborhoods. Moreover, real prejudice against Catholics was a sad reality. Grandparents of present-day Cathedral students tell stories of being treated intolerantly in their Indianapolis suburbs.

The strongest discrimination was, of course, against blacks. After World War I, migration of Negroes from the South to Indianapolis saw more than eight hundred black students enrolled in Shortridge, Manual and Tech, fifteen percent of the student population. In 1925 the decision was made to open an all-black school, Thomas Jefferson High School, which, in 1926, was renamed after the Revolutionary War's first casualty, a black man named Crispus Attucks.

To mask their bigotry, so-called well-meaning Indianapolis School Board members cited a high tuberculosis death rate among Negroes, then ten percent of the city's population but twenty-five percent of the recorded tubercular deaths.

Even though Cathedral was tuition-free and the parishes where blacks lived were established (Holy Angels in 1903 and St. Rita's in 1919), black youth did not attend Cathedral. There were black students in photos in *The Megaphones* in the 1920s and the first graduate is thought to be Edward William Violet '30. Violet, who lived at 2741 Columbia Avenue, was called "Bill." The commencement issue of *The Megaphone* reported:

> *Bill enjoys the distinction of being the only man of color at Cathedral. Endowed with the humor of his race, Bill is a popular member of his class and has a hundred friends. Is he going to college? Indeed yes! And he says once there he will try out for athletics, a thing he wanted to do here, but for which he did not have time.*

Though condescending in its tone by today's standards, the article shows that Bill Violet's acceptance was universal at the school. "I knew Bill well" Dr. Joseph Spalding '30, recalled. "He was a bright, personable guy. I don't think I ever saw him after graduation." Early graduates can offer no reasons why black students didn't attend Cathedral more frequently. "We certainly weren't prejudiced," Spalding believed.

The reality was that from 1922 to 1928, during the Klan's heyday, no city school played Cathedral in football. Washington and Shortridge played the Irish in 1928, Manual in 1931, and Tech in 1933. Broad Ripple became a football rival in 1943 and Howe didn't schedule a football game with Cathedral until 1977.

Irish basketball teams could not compete in the annual City Tournament, which began in the 1928-29 season and recessed in 1942. Crispus Attucks, a city school, was not invited to play during this period either. In 1963 Indianapolis public high schools resumed the tournament and Cathedral and Crispus Attucks were invited to compete and still continue to play in the annual January event. Times do change for the better.

The Indiana High School Athletic Association was founded in 1903, but it wasn't until wartime 1942 that IHSAA invited to membership "parochial, Negro and deaf schools." The first Indiana state basketball tournament was staged in 1911, but the parochial, Negro and deaf schools were not invited to participate. The days of fair and open athletic competition in Indianapolis were for the future, in the 1940s.

In spite of the obvious difficulties with intolerance, Cathedral surged forward in the decade after its founding, and so did the city around it. The Columbia Club began planning its new building on the Circle; Shortridge High School, truly overcrowded, started plans to move north and eventually purchased property at 34th and Meridian; the Indiana and Zaring theatres and the Marott hotel were built, (all in 1925,) and Butler University implemented its decision to move from Irvington to its Fairview campus.

All of these things showed a young and vital city and nation. F. Scott Fitzgerald wrote: "The uncertainties of 1919 were over. America was going on the greatest, gaudiest spree in history." It was an exciting, and perhaps a frightening, time to be young. It was the era of the First Youth Rebellion, the time of the "sheiks and shebas." Once boys had tried to be paragons of gallantry, industry and idealism; girls had aspired to seem modest and maidenly. But that would change. Youth must have its day.

In a refrain that would be heard again in later times a writer named John F. Carter in *The Atlantic Monthly* commented:

> *I would like to observe that the older generation had certainly pretty well ruined this world before passing it on to us.*
> *They gave us this Thing, knocked to pieces, leaky, red-hot, threatening to blow up; and then they are surprised that we don't accept it with the same enthusiasm with which they received it.*

But America's young people didn't care. They went right on in their heedless, narcissistic way, adopting outrageous fashions and singing, "In the meantime, in between time, ain't we got fun?"

Cathedral had launched her first sons at that graduation of 1921. Four, Norbert Clancy, James Collins, Joe Harmon and Eddie Lyons, would graduate in the Class of 1925 at Notre Dame. In changing times Cathedral families were sure to appreciate the strengths Catholic education had to offer in the new school on

Meridian Street. Still, the demands of success would challenge the indefatigable Bishop Chartrand to measure the pulse of his school almost daily.

1923-1924

After winning eighteen of nineteen varsity football games, Coach Al Feeney returned to his family furniture business, 128-130 West Washington Street. In 1923 Cathedral's administrators were concerned about over-emphasis of football. The success and dominance of Irish teams gave Cathedral recognition, built spirit and instilled excellence throughout the burgeoning campus. Still future opponents were wary "of our eligibility problem," *The Megaphone* reported. Success can also breed contempt and, for a variety of reasons, some of which also involved the intolerant climate already discussed, Cathedral was finding it impossible to schedule varsity football games with local schools.

But certainly, as has been pointed out, a large part of the difficulty in finding local opponents was that Cathedral teams were tough to beat. "Our requirements were higher than the public schools'." John Barton '24 recalled. Barton was Mayor of Indianapolis in 1966.

Brother Vincent assumed the coaching job. After a week of training at Notre Dame, the Cathedral team traveled extensively in the state to meet opponents ranging from New Albany to Gary Emerson High School. Cathedral also played Knightstown, Wilkinson, Hartford City and Fort Wayne Central Catholic. Perhaps the lack of success (won four of seven games) proved they weren't invincible, but it wasn't until 1928 that a local school would again schedule the powerful Irish.

Highlight of the season was the opening game win over Bloomfield as the first strains of "Dear Old Cathedral" were played by the khaki-clad, thirty-four-piece school band under the direction of Brother Edwin.

Attired in stiff-collared, World War I type uniforms, the band struck up the fight song. The "Irish" won, 18-0 over Bloomfield at old Northwestern Park, the baseball park which was the home of Indianapolis professional baseball teams, playing as the Indians in the American Association.

Brother Vincent had to scramble for the schedule and three football teams—New Albany, Hartford City and Bloomfield—promised to return in 1924. Dr. Joseph Conley was the "medical attendant" of the squad and served as volunteer doctor many seasons for Irish teams. In defiance of the strong influence of the Ku Klux Klan in Indianapolis in 1923, "Mr. Welbaum of the Chamber of Commerce" assisted Cathedral in staging a downtown homecoming parade which featured a single float. The Chamber also allowed the school use of its Meridian Street window for a display.

Students basked in the celebration of the consecration of old friend and teacher Father Alphonse Smith, who was consecrated Bishop of Nashville, Tennessee, at the Saints Peter and Paul Cathedral. (Bishop Smith had been part of Cathedral life from its beginning and soon would be helping to raise the first $50,000 for the newly-planned school that would be built on Meridian Street.) As winter came on in 1923-24, Brother Vincent also coached a basketball team featuring colorfully nicknamed Captain "Osky" Kelly and "Dashing Dave" Costello to nine wins in fourteen games, all outside Marion County. Other sports were gaining success: the Irish baseball team won the City Championship again, and Thomas Sylvester "Bud" Markey was the City's junior tennis champion. In his senior year, Markey was selected by tennis great Bill Tilden to be his doubles partner. Markey wrote:

> *The week of that tournament was the happiest and the saddest I had ever experienced. We weren't figured to go very far but we got down to the semis. Ahead 2 to 1 in the five-set match and 'Big Bill' said we had to lose on purpose but artfully, as he and Chapin (Alfred his touring partner) had earlier agreed to play an exhibition the next day at Culver. He must have seen tears in my eyes because I was then invited to play in the exhibition with him. We were a sure bet to win in the finals. How sweet it would have been to receive a winners trophy with his and my names on it. But for cruel fate, that cup would now be in the Cathedral trophy case.*

A week later Tilden invited Markey to tour with him, but Bud's father, fearing his son would become a "tennis bum," turned the offer down. John Harrington was the first of many City champion golfers. The flashy clothing of the era was coming to Cathedral, and handsome and elegant Bob "Cameo" Kirby, the band drum major, brought gasps to St. Agnes coeds. Kirby continued to Notre Dame where, as drum major, he led Irish bands onto fields coast-to-coast.

Much of the success of Cathedral athletics can be credited to Catholic Youth Organization sports programs. It was in 1923 that Cathedral teacher Brother Ralph organized the first eleven-team football grade school league composed of Holy Angels, St. John, St. Philip Neri, St. Anthony, Holy Cross, St. Patrick, St. Joan of Arc, Holy Trinity, St. Joseph, Our Lady of Lourdes and Cathedral parishes. Cathedral faculty members and students coached the teams. In 1924 Brother Godfrey took over the renamed "Grade School Football League." As the years moved on and laymen volunteered to coach, Cathedral faculty left the program they had inspired, but the school's alumni remained deeply connected with the program. The Catholic Youth Organization program not only fed Cathedral sports with competition-tested youth, but also provided every high school in the Indianapolis area with soundly developed players.

CYO basketball was added after the fast acceptance of football.

While Mah-Jongg, flappers, dance marathons and flagpole sitting occupied the time of changing America, Cathedral's family was focusing on a more important change. They were drawing plans to build a school of statement. Bishop Chartrand would not be dissuaded from his mission of building his dream school, and talk, thinking and planning began to center around that new school.

The oratory and debate teams were formed and by 1923 both were involved in local, state and national competition and, later on, according to the September 9, 1927, *Indiana Catholic and Record*, "Cathedral teams were undefeated at all three levels."

1924-1925

The opening of the 1924 school year was filled with anticipation, as new Principal Brother Austin Carroll gave the traditional greeting on the front steps to 350 enrollees.

Cathedral was now housed on 14th Street in a temporary building which was precursor to the magnificent structure being planned on Meridian Street. Tapped to direct the one million-plus

"The Rock"

"The Rock," as he was affectionately known through-out the world, possessed a staccato voice, Karl Zinkan '23 re-called. "Coach Rockne would gather us, not just the team but the entire student body, in that tiny yard outside the school building. "His machine-gun-like oratory could be heard on the Circle," Zinkan recalled. The students and faculty listened in awe as the coach who popularized college football would chal-lenge students "to look inside yourself and commit your very being to not only achieve in sport but whatever you have to do." Zinkan continued: "Here we were, a few hundred kids in a little school atop a grade school and this great man found us important enough to make us his audience. "Rockne was big then—and we all knew it—but his legend grew until his death and after that." The coach, with perhaps Will Rogers, became the most admired man in America, possibly the world. "His visits made us feel important," Zinkan fondly reflected.

The Cathedral Site

The Meridian Street school site had an interesting realty history which was traced by Union Title Company of Indianapolis. The tract of land is "L" shaped. It was originally part of Arthur St. Clair addition in 1837, a time when it was outside Indianapolis city limits. St. Clair sold the lots—at $100 per acre—to Edmund Browning for $2,000. By 1925, the price had risen to $500 per square foot facing Meridian Street. The plot had some history. It had been a marshaling area for Union troops mustering for service during the Civil War. The site changed hands several times passing at one time to indus-trialist Eli Lilly and Marian C. Lilly. A Lilly homesite (one of several owned by the pharmaceutical founder) was on the land.

By deed of May 28, 1925 Cecilia M. Stalmaker and her husband, Frank D. Stalmaker conveyed to Bishop Joseph Chartrand all except the north one hundred feet at a consider-ation reported at approximately $150,000. Earlier, on February 28, 1925, Lilly R. Lilly and Josiah K. Lilly, her husband, had sold their residence on the north one hundred feet of the tract to Bishop Chartrand for $100,000, making the total cost of the site $250,000.

—*The Indianapolis Star,* November 6, 1927

campaign to fund the new building was Cathedral parish son the Rev. James Hugh Ryan, whom Chartrand had recruited from his duties at Catholic University.

The duties of an expanding school stretched the work load of the Brothers, who asked Bishop Chartrand for assistance. He assigned the Rt. Rev. Peter Killian as superintendent, the first of six who would serve in that post until 1964, when the Archdiocese turned over governance to the Holy Cross Order.

For the first time, because it was now operating in a school facility not attached to a grade school, Cathedral was approved by the State Board of Education, and graduates were not required to take college entrance examinations.

Americans were whispering about the romance of songwriter Irving Berlin, whose real name was Israel Baline, and Irish socialite Ellin Mackay. Their marriage, and the entry of J. Alfred (Al) Smith as the Democratic presidential candidate in 1927, were encouraging the acceptance of diversity—more particularly of Roman Catholics in every part of the mainstream of American life.

Irving Baline Berlin had already written hundreds of songs and his Music Box Theater in New York City was to resonate to a new form of American music, the modern romantic ballad. While Cathedral was defeating Bloomington, 20-7 in football, not far away, at the world-famous spa at French Lick, Berlin was sitting at a piano in the basement of the hotel. He had a lingering melody in his mind, and he was writing words to his lifelong sweetheart Ellin. The song was "Always."

Brother Vincent would serve as Cathedral's final clergy coach during the 1924 football season. His team was to gain the recognition of the Hoosier Athletic Club as state and city champions, with their nearest foe being Bloomfield, who tied, 6-6. Cathedral and two other teams had a claim to the State Championship as one of only three undefeated teams, outscoring opponents 185-26. Captain Joseph "Mac" McCarthy was First Team All-City and then All-State tackle.

Before the IHSAA football play-offs began in 1973, mythical claims to state championship honors were made by zealous alumni and friends, and the newspaper wire services. Cathedral teams and fans claimed titles in 1922, 1924 (with two other contenders), 1931 and 1952 with Richmond. (Later, in the first

IHSAA-sponsored playoffs Cathedral lost in final games to South Bend Washington in 1973 (19-13), Merrillville, 24-28, in 1976 and to Fort Wayne Dwenger, 27-34 in 1991.)

In 1986 Cathedral won the 3-A Indiana State Championship defeating Northwood High School of Nappannee, 12-0. The Irish won the 1992 3-A title defeating Northwestern, 31-14. Brother William Mang was cultivating local schools to play the Irish, but it would still be four years until the "maverick Micks" as a Klansman flyer referred to them in a circular found near Cathedral High School, would see regular city opponents.

Although football, the grade-school sports program and an expanded offering of extra-curricular activities proceeded in 1924, clearly the school's energy was directed at the all-important building of this definitive Cathedral High School, the landmark which still stands in Indianapolis' downtown as a monument to the pride and confidence of a Catholic community which had come of age in the city and to the inspired leadership of Bishop Chartrand.

The need was clear. The success of the school the Bishop had created had advanced beyond his predictions. Catholics of Indianapolis had been drawn to the unique and effective boys' high school, and the school bulged to the point that expansion was necessitated.

There was really little choice. In 1924, the State School Board of Indiana had issued an edict that Cathedral's commission to teach would not be renewed. This meant Cathedral graduates could not enter a college or university without an admittance examination.

The temporary four-room addition, constructed at a cost of sixty thousand dollars between Meridian and Illinois streets facing on to 14th Street, had become inadequate almost as soon as it was built. Half-day sessions were necessitated to accommodate the swelling numbers of students. (After Cathedral's new home opened in 1927, this older structure was used for meetings, a cafeteria and band practice.) Brother Austin was principal of the enlarged Cathedral. During his term Cathedral was first accredited by the Indiana State Board of Education.

The earliest years of Cathedral had seen students entering from nearby parishes. But with Peoples Coach street car transportation now widely available, soon the sons of immigrant families from all sections of the city were attracted.

Thus, the beginning of the period when Cathedral was to gain its reputation as the melting pot of Indianapolis was underway. Now the Slovenes of Holy Trinity, the Irish from St. Patrick's, the Germans from Sacred Heart and St. Catherine's, the Italians from Holy Rosary and virtually every nationality from a city that was populated by immigrant factions settled in ethnic neighborhoods made Cathedral High School their home.

Stanley Boyle '21, recalled: "We were a mixed collection. We joked about our differences but once we got to Cathedral we became one." The new groupings, however, clearly needed a physical melting pot in which to blend and most of all, that facility needed to be funded.

In 1922, as has been said, Bishop Chartrand had appointed the Reverend James Hugh Ryan to direct the one million campaign for the building of Cathedral High School on North Meridian Street. Ryan had been a teacher at Catholic University.

Impetus for a successful fund drive was generated by the year's gridiron success just described. This should not be viewed as surprising; university development directors attribute contributions in direct proportion to football wins. Perhaps that wasn't true in 1924 but "we were told by Fr. Ritter (a part-time Cathedral teacher) that it helped," commented the late Judge John T. "Cocky" McNelis '25.

Msgr. Ryan was a native son of Cathedral parish, who was later to become the first Archbishop of Omaha, Nebraska. He had been given the monumental task of mobilizing the pastors of the twenty-two parishes to raise the funds and raise the Cathedral building.

Msgr. Ryan led a committee of twenty-three pastor priests to undertake the fund drive. With the strong support of the Bishop, success was assured. Some claim the Bishop assessed each parish based on potential matriculation of students for that parish and set each quota; in any event the enthusiasm and success at the local parish level was made obvious in immediate results.

In only two weeks, on December 10, 1924, the goal had been surpassed; $1,053,296.73 was pledged. Each parish responded and most topped their goal.

The amounts contributed by each parish to the building of Cathedral High School:

St. Anthony	63,000.	St. Rita	10,000.
St. Catherine's	25,044.	St. Roch	6,000.
St. Joan of Arc	74,549.	St. John	36,000.
St. Francis	27,500.	St. Joseph's	38,000.
Our Lady of Lourdes	37,500.	St. Mary's	30,000.
Cathedral	298,000.	Holy Angels	26,285.
Sacred Heart	85,000.	Holy Rosary	6,000.
Assumption	25,000.	St. Ann's	2,557.
Holy Cross	71,727.	St. Bridget's	4,085.
Holy Name	13,000.	Holy Trinity	6,435.
St. Patrick's	67,614.	St. Philip Neri	90,000.

Thus, the foundation was dug and work begun on an Indianapolis landmark.

1925-1926

In the midst of the building enthusiasm, a new year began. The tradition of greeting each student personally fell to the new principal, Brother Ephren, in his fourteenth year as a teacher in Indiana. The line was long again as six hundred students were greeted by the twenty brothers who now comprised the faculty. Chartrand's plans for expansion were obviously going to have to be accelerated.

Football suffered its first losing record, 3-4. The final game was a loss, 3-0, to Fort Wayne Central Catholic. Surprisingly, the opposition quarterback dropped back and drop-kicked a thirteen-yard field goal.

Captain Dave Harmon found joy in a 36-0 win over St. Xavier of Louisville coached by his brother, Joe, Cathedral '21.

Brother Vincent's basketball team was handicapped by inadequate practice time; they could arrange only two nights a week at the Knights of Columbus Hall. The abbreviated season was only ten games, but in spite of the perceived handicap, Cathedral lost but one game.

Another sport familiar to Cathedral life emerged: intramural handball. The sight of wiry and slight students out-pointing varsity lettermen was common and part of the fun of those times.

In the first all-school tournament Robert Wenzel defeated John Connor in six rounds of singles play.

The Cathedral Dramatic Club staged *A Full House* at Murat Theater and took the show on the road to "nearby towns."

The music program was strong, featuring fifty-four band musicians under the direction of Brother Edwin. The twenty-seven-piece orchestra had a section of a dozen violins under the direction of Brother Damian, who played piccolo with the band. From sixty-three aspirants, twenty-eight were selected for the school glee club directed by Brother Finbarr. A vaudeville production starred Joseph Elward singing: "Little Eva, O Death Where Is Thy Sting?"

The big attraction was the excavation of the new school site nearby. Crowded classrooms and people stepping all over each other added to the pressures of the school day. Still, a look around the corner confirmed the building progress. There was no doubt in any student's mind that it would all be worth it. In its Easter issue *The Megaphone* enthused:

> *Another temple to education and virtue will adorn Indianapolis. During the past eight years (Cathedral's) high school curriculum has been taught under terrible handicaps, but despite many material drawbacks the high school has been a wonderful success.*

1926–1927

The distraction of construction noise and interruption nearby was constant as a new year began. "A final capacity of 2,500" was predicted for "someday." That rosy prophecy has never been fulfilled, although with expansion in 1952, the campus in 1963 strained with more than nine-hundred students. The 1990s have seen that figure approached again. The six-hundred students included the first large contingent from the southeast section of the county. The Homecoming parade before the Garfield of Terre Haute game featured two Cadillacs, a Stutz (built nearby on Capitol Avenue), one Reo, one Jordan, a Marmon, a Chrysler, an Oakland, a Pontiac, two Hudsons, an Essex, a Chevrolet, a Star, two Dodges, two Oldsmobiles, two locomobiles, five black "Tin Lizzies" and a Studebaker, seating twenty passengers. Welcomed as a part-time coach was Joe Sexton '21, freshly graduated from Notre Dame with a law degree. Sexton applied himself to his law practice with partner Leo X. Smith in the morning and, as Cathedral's first paid lay teacher, coached football and basketball in the afternoons. Francis Crawford "Tau" Yeazel, Emmett "Mutt" Amsden and Captain Maurice Francis "Bo" Eagan led a 5-2 season. Sexton's basketball team won only eight of twenty games but breakthroughs were occurring, as the Irish played county teams Oaklandon (Lawrence Central) and New Augusta (Pike Township) and Beech Grove twice each. Indiana State School for the Deaf (Silent Hoosiers) defeated the Irish, 40–30.

The Megaphone went to 8x10 four-page format and became a weekly. It also changed emphasis from essays and poetry to school news, with six reporters covering their beats. Another publication was the weekly "Thankee" with news about Holy Cross missions. The 1927 baseball team claimed the City Championship as John O'Brien pitched a 1-0 win over Manual. In recalling his years at Cathedral, William Leppert '27 particularly saluted Brother Austin who created the Specials, football, basketball and baseball teams for students not large enough to play varsity sports and recalled "the discipline and education the Holy Cross Brothers gave to set my life goals."

Construction went on to completion. On Thursday evening, June 9, 1927, an era of anticipation finally ended as the Cathedral orchestra struck up Von Suppe's "Light Cavalry Overture" marking "the first momentous use of the long-awaited new school."

The school chorus offered a rendition of "Drink to Me Only With Thine Eyes" and a beaming Bishop Chartrand conferred honors and diplomas on eighty young men in the seventh graduating class.

On the eve of the event *The Megaphone* gushed:

> *The success of the 1924 Building Campaign is manifested in actualization of the splendid building we are soon to enter. It amply provides for our present needs and has elastic future possibilities.*

The next phase of Cathedral's life as an institution was about to begin. Chartrand's dream was to create a Cathedral that would rival in beauty, academic achievement and athletic success any public high school. Most impartial observers cannot help but

THAT FIRST SCHOOL BUILDING

The original home of Cathedral High School, located at 1350 North Pennsylvania Street, has continued to serve people through its entire existence. It had first served as the elementary school for Cathedral parish and more than 300 pupils, first through eighth grades, were enrolled.

When the school opened in 1918, ninety high school freshmen and sophomores were taught in classrooms located on the second floor of the building which opened in 1912 as Cathedral Grade School.

In 1927, when Cathedral High School relocated to the newly-built building at 1416 North Meridian Street, the former building returned to grade school use.

After Cathedral Grade School closed, the building was used as the office of the Archbishop and provided other service centers for the Archdiocese. In 1981 those offices were moved to 1416 North Meridian Street.

In 1987, the Archdiocese of Indianapolis and the Episcopal Diocese of Indianapolis jointly opened Damien Center in the building. Damien Center is owned by the Archdiocese and both churches provide financial support. It is named in honor of Father DeVeuster Damien, S.J., the famed Jesuit priest who lived and died in the leper colony on the island of Molakai in the Hawaiian Island chain. The center is a comprehensive home for AIDS education, counseling and support. Individuals who are HIV-infected receive services regardless of race, sex, religion or sexual preference. Services are available without regard to the ability to pay.

believe he surpassed that goal: the school created at 14th and Meridian rose as a real triumph, both architecturally and in spirit to the Catholic presence in Indianapolis and to the vision of Christian high school education which the Bishop sought to fulfill.

1927-1928

Bishop Chartrand personally oversaw every stage of Cathedral's construction after hiring J.G. Karstedt Construction Co., 254 N. Capitol Avenue, to build the new school. On September 11, 1927, the day of dedication, Karstedt waxed eloquently in an advertisement in *The Indianapolis Star:*

"By Their Fruits Ye Shall Know Them."

This has been more than just another job.
Indianapolis has just cause to point out that this
new academy is a show spot.
By their fruits—and Cathedral High School is the
fruit of careful planning and honest construction we
stand or fall by it—judge for yourself!

The architect, Adolf Scherrer, contributed many other lasting local monuments in the city. The Georgian colonial-style building was built at a cost of approximately five hundred thousand dollars and proudly displayed the seal of Bishop Chartrand—and Cathedral—in the pediment of the central unit. Its bell tower became the symbol of the school as the Golden Dome identifies the University of Notre Dame.

The dedication Mass was celebrated by two thousand open-house attendees. Presiding was Msgr. James Hugh Ryan of Catholic University, Washington, D.C., the man who had so successfully spearheaded the new school's fund-raising drive in the parishes. Father Joseph E. Ritter, later to succeed Chartrand as Bishop of Indianapolis and then to become Cardinal of St. Louis, deserved recognition in having assisted Ryan in the parish fund drive. Father Peter Killian had chaired the Building Committee with the assistance of Frs. Maurice O'Connor and Albert H. Busald.

The Star editorialized that Cathedral was "a magnificent addition to the educational system of the City."

Many gave generously to the school, including Dr. Vincent LaPenta, who donated the physics and chemistry laboratories, and

Charles Berry, who contributed to the new library. And so, it was a proud, new school, with new steps on which Brother Ephrem stood to greet the six hundred students who matriculated in that fall of 1927. Brother Ephrem had been founding principal of Reitz Memorial High School in Evansville and had served as its head for six years. Two years later Brother William arrived and served as principal until 1934, the longest tenure until Brother Pedro Haering.

Innovations which were to become traditions marked the era in the new school. For the first time in 1927 class rings were found on the fingers of students and their sweethearts.

A Mothers Club was formed in 1928 and "invested" sixteen hundred dollars to have the building corridors, faculty rooms and stairways repainted. The first leaders of the club that was to serve the school for several decades were Mesdames Edward Brennan and Timothy Sexton.

Chartrand had seen his dream, a truly significant accomplishment, materialize. He remained close to the students, saying Mass on game days. He was remembered during this period for little things that spoke of his Christian character as well as his leadership: it was well-known that the kind Bishop would slip a five dollar bill through the confessional to a student in need.

In October, 1927, *The Megaphone* told the school community, "Cathedral has emerged from a little school to a big school, from an unclassified school to a commissioned high school, from a bungalow to a palace."

A palace indeed, and in a year when the new and splendid Shortridge High School was opening its doors, the marvel of the town. But if there was something completely new, the student editors wanted to be certain that an already established sense of tradition would be revered and continued. Eight years had been enough to set the direction of the school in place.

> *The student who does not live up to these traditions soon finds himself out of place . . . . It is tradition at Cathedral that the Freshman has the same rights as the Senior. It is a tradition that the athlete gets no more consideration than any other student . . . . It is tradition that neither wealth nor social standing counts anything at Cathedral; students are judged by character and scholarship. It is a tradition that there are no parish lines at Cathedral, all of the twenty-two parishes have equal footing.*

The new campus also inspired a new song. Brother Edwin, director of band and orchestra, composed the music and words for the Cathedral Victory March:

We're marching down the field to victory!
Our bravest sons, our fighting band.
The Gold and Blue is out to win again;
No foe Cathedral's drive can stand,
Our banners are kept proudly waving high
Our sons are shouting defiance
Come and fight, team! This is Cathedral's day.
And on to vict'ry we will go.

Refrain:
Our banners proudly waving,
Our songs are rising high.
Harken to the roar
As our ranks go marching by.
Proudly we're proclaiming
The glory of her name,
And we'll fight undying
For Cathedral's fame.

A new home, a new song and a new sports season began as the Irish defeated Hartford City at the old Pennsy Park, 2100 Southeastern Avenue. Using a split-T formation, Coach Sexton's charges won seven of eight games. High point of the season was a seven-six win at Jasonville. Irish guard Charles "Chick" McCutcheon's pass interception set up the winning touchdown; all the sweeter because as the Ku Klux Klan had staged a pre-game parade on the field.

The versatile Brother Edwin coached the basketball squad to a record 22-6 season. The dedication game on the shiny new court found the Irish defeating Fort Wayne Central Catholic, 35-23. George "Potsy" Clark, Athletic Director at Butler, was the opening speaker. The first basket in the new gym was credited to guard Thomas Carr, who also led scoring with ten points. New local foes Ben Davis, Park School and Southport were added to the schedule.

The first State Catholic Tournament also sparked enthusiasm. This one was Brother William's baby. It found the Irish, co-captained by Joe Dugan and Larry Sexton, an easy champion, defeating St. Mary's of Anderson, 15-8 in the finals. At the National Catholic Tournament in Chicago, Cathedral defeated teams from Minnesota and West Virginia and lost in the semi-finals to defending and repeating National Champions De LaSalle of Joliet, Illinois.

Basketball was taking its place alongside football as an achievement sport. The Irish would again have a twenty-two-victory season with Shortridge and Washington on the schedule.

The goals had been achieved: a successful and profitable State Tournament and growing recognition. These were things Brother William had dreamed of, and his dreams were evolving.

Thomas Patrick Carey, class valedictorian in 1928, recalled repeat performances on the road of *Peg O' My Heart* as a highlight and the impression left of Brother Killian who "made you think" and taught him how to dance the "Irish Jig." Later, Father Carey commented, "I owe my success as a priest to four grand years at Cathedral."

INDIANA STATE CATHOLIC BASKETBALL TOURNAMENT

CHAMPION	RUNNER-UP
1928 Cathedral	Anderson St. Mary's
1929 Cathedral	Fort Wayne Catholic Ctr.
1930 Decatur Catholic	Jasper Academy
1931 Wash. St. Simon's	Jasper Academy
1932 Cathedral	Vincennes Gibault
1933 Cathedral	Vincennes Gibault
1934 No Tournament	
1935 Huntington Catholic	Fort Wayne Central Catholic
1936 Anderson St. Mary's	Evansville Memorial
1937 Anderson St. Mary's	Evansville Memorial
1938 Anderson St. Mary's	Evansville Memorial
1939 Ft Wayne Ctl. Cath.	Cathedral
1940 Ft. Wayne Ctl. Cath.	St. Joseph's Academy
1941 Evansville Memorial	Huntington Catholic
1942 Ft. Wayne Ctl. Cath.	Cathedral

1928-1929

A year after Lindbergh's thirty-three-and-a-half-hour flight to Paris from Roosevelt Field, Long Island, N.Y., the world began to grow smaller.

Indianapolis was an aviation city. One of its own, swashbuckling Colonel Roscoe Turner, set up an airline that ran from Los Angeles to Reno, the city renowned for its quick divorces; Turner's route became known as the "Alimony Special." After this venture folded, Turner convinced an oil company whose trademark was a lion that it could attract enormous publicity if it hired him to fly around the country with a lion cub as his passenger. Flying didn't bother the lion, but the Humane Society insisted that Turner strap a parachute on the beast.

Dance marathons were still flourishing and a wild, carefree America was singing "Anything Goes." Cathedral parents and teachers constantly reminded their boys that anything *didn't* go.

Those who could afford to were dressing "collegiate" and even though Indianapolis was not considered a "college town," Cathedral boys blended when they could with Shortridge youth to try to convince those they hoped would watch them that they were frat guys from Butler.

In spite of that sort of grand-standing, the madness of the era was beginning to wane. Ominous signs should have alerted the nation that "boom" could soon go "bust." Dismal notoriety and poor moral conduct of movie and sport stars filled the sensationalistic columns of newspapers. Still, celebrities were in vogue. Cathedral lured one of sports Big Three, Harold "Red" Grange, the famed "Galloping Ghost" of the Fighting Illini.

During promotion of a film about his gridiron career, Grange witnessed the first Cathedral-Washington football game.

Cathedral won, 31-6, and Grange presented Irish captain and All-City Emmet "Mutt" Amsden a football helmet on the old Lyric Theater stage.

Shortridge returned to the Irish schedule after five years and the City champions swamped Cathedral, 25-6.

Coach Joe Harmon, Cathedral '22, brought his Louisville St. Xavier team to Indianapolis and defeated his Alma Mater, 13-0, thereby becoming the first alumni coach to defeat the Irish.

After a successful 16-7-2 record that final year, Joe Sexton went into law practice full-time, making way for Joe Dienhart.

One of the city's greatest golfers-to-be, knicker-clad senior William A. Heinlein won the City Golf Championship.

The brilliant athlete Kenny Dugan captained the Irish basketball team which defeated St. Andrew's of Richmond In the first game on the shiny new court. Dugan was killed in a tragic automobile accident that ended what might have been a professional baseball career.

On June 7, 1929, the day before forces of Chiang Kai-Shek seized Peking and ended the Chinese Civil War, the largest senior class of nearly one hundred went off to a complacent world. A high (for that time) thirty-six percent went on to college.

Five months later The Crash would occur and confidence plummet resulting in a new, sober era of sizing down.

Cathedral's Only Fraternity

There wasn't much to do after school in those early months of the new Cathedral High School. There was no gymnasium, no recreational yard as yet, no area to pass the time.

"Some guys would hang around the Herron Art Institute, just up the street at 16th "Louis Thompson, '22, recalled. That's where J. Hugh McGowan and several others conceived the idea of a secret club to be patterned after the college Greek groups. Now joined by lyricist Francis Frey (co-author of "Dear Old Cathedral") the trio asked Brother Anthony for assistance.

Shortridge had Beta Beta Sigma and Tech had its Ace Club. It was reasoned that Cathedral's club was a way to have inter-school social exchanges, since city schools didn't play Cathedral in sports. The Owl Club had its own pin, song and "The Screech" was its newsletter. Members were selected and had to survive an initiation. Its elitist foundation was counter to Cathedral's family tradition "but it was okayed by the faculty, sort of tacitly, which surprised us since Notre Dame didn't allow fraternities there," Thompson reflected.

During the 1931 Christmas holiday season the Owl Club sponsored a dance at the Knights of Columbus Hall, 1315 N. Delaware Street. "It got pretty rough. There was drinking (the Prohibition Act was in effect) and a fight got started," John Ford '32 recalled.

The melee brought police to the scene. Bootleg "hooch" was confiscated and there was publicity that embarrassed Cathedral. Word of the ruckus reached Bishop Chartrand. Permission to allow an elitist club was lifted and the Owl Club disbanded.

On Recruiting

The Indiana High School Athletic Association describes recruiting as "using undue influence." IHSAA officials, perhaps for at least seven decades, were asked to investigate charges of alleged tampering by Cathedral.

From its inception, the recruitment of students to attend Cathedral has been an element of survival. All private schools, be they Ivy, Stanford or Notre Dame, proselyte, bringing youth to their campuses.

The success achieved by recruitment is the "rub," as Shakespeare would say. Those schools which attract the best become the best, be it scholastic, athletic or the potential for funding purposes. Private institutions—unlike public—are not automatically at the end of the funnel of matriculation.

Among the criticisms of Cathedral the word "tampering" has been heard, mostly in attracting those of skills for competitive sports.

When Bishop Chartrand's pastors directed (as forcefully as possible) a graduating eighth-grade pupil should enroll at Cathedral, critics were not heard. But as Cathedral's athletic success grew, there were those who wished to staunch the pipeline, as impressionable teenagers sought a school of success which was building tradition.

Charles Maas, the late former Tech and Butler athlete and assistant IHSAA commissioner, challenged critics in the 1980s to "bring us proof. If they've got the facts and are willing to back it up, give us the names." None did. Instead, to retaliate some stopped competing against Cathedral teams.

The cry was not new. In 1954 some Indianapolis schools attempted to ban Cathedral from their schedules. Shortridge and Washington refused to participate. Two years later, in February of 1956, the Indianapolis Public Schools, led by Edgar Stahl, principal of Manual High School, unveiled its plan for a City (public school) Athletic Conference which would not include Cathedral, Sacred Heart or Scecina. This raised much concern and many arguments and "side taking." The Catholic schools objected to being shut out of competition with other city schools. Editorially, the Indianapolis newspapers also took sides: *The Star* and *The News* opposed the exclusion of the Catholic schools while *The Times* supported the proposed conference. Two weeks later the Board of School Commissioners settled the argument by vetoing the plan for the proposed conference.

In 1980 an athletically-gifted student allegedly was "tampered" with by Irish Coach Tom O'Brien, prompting Washington Principal Thomas J. Rosenberger and athletic director Gene

(Continued)

Robertson to drop Cathedral and urge other schools to prepare a list of public school players recruited to Cathedral.

Arlington Coach Ed Ward entered into the controversy. "The circumstantial evidence is heavy" said Marshall basketball coach Roger Schroeder. "It is not a coincidence that so many black, non-Catholic kids are going to that school. You know they are doing it but you can't prove it." Lawrence Central dropped Cathedral in basketball charging, "Cathedral is almost immune to recruiting penalties."

"People say we are turning our heads," countered Maas. "But wrongs have to be substantiated. We can't go to court on a phone call." "I don't think there's much to it," said Coach O'Brien. "It doesn't bother me at all."

Charges of athletic recruitment increased. From its first varsity sports seasons in the early twenties, Cathedral faced criticism from others, but by the 1980s, parochial school officials became part of a new chorus that was formed. Some criticism was hurled by former students, alumni and teachers.

"The whine (wine) of their gripes—or grapes—was mostly sour," the late Bob Welch '45 recalled and added: "Sure, we had to recruit students—and that included athletes. Our student body enrollment base would be changed by the move so marketing was necessary."

A particular target was basketball Coach Tom O'Brien. The personable, energetic O'Brien produced successful teams including the 1982 state finalists and a wealth of outstanding players, many of whom went on to achieve collegiate success.

Many were black, non-Catholic boys from the traditional Crispus Attucks, Shortridge and Tech high school districts (prior to open enrollment) seeking opportunities for college scholarships. But there were other reasons. Carl Daniels '84, recalled:

> *Coach O'Brien offered me and others a chance to leave the neighborhood and broaden my scope of possibilities. I enjoyed my friends and schoolmates, but I could still play against them while at Cathedral. What I found at Cathedral was a new family; people I could not have met otherwise and who remain, to this day, good friends.*

Now on the staff of the National Collegiate Athletic Association, Daniels equated his opportunity to attend Cathedral to the open enrollment plan. In the 1950s, Supreme Court decision on Civil Rights mandated open public school enrollment.

O'Brien reflected:

> *I always related to kids well and I wanted to see them come to the school I loved as a student and teacher/*

(Continued)

coach. The charges hurt as I never promised financial support, only a chance to attend a great school—the melting pot of the city—that could prepare them. To my detractors I always challenged them to prove their accusations. So did the IHSAA. Their charges proved unfounded.

Cathedral athletes set a high-performance record. There were few drop-outs and most went on to attain collegiate degrees. They now have successful, productive lives; some did gravitate to careers as professional athletes. I am proud to realize that I had a hand in helping dozens of young men go on to worthwhile lives.

O'Brien is now Chairman of the Democratic Party in Marion County. "Proper recruiting was always a Cathedral reality. Feeney did it, so did Dienhart and so did I," Joe Dezelan recalled.

The feeder system for Cathedral students has mostly been through parish grade schools. Conversely, there is much evidence of City school coaches luring Catholic athletes for seventy years. That has been true since Indianapolis school sports re-started and flourished in the early twenties.

The fields and courts of the Catholic Youth Organization, founded in 1923 by Brother Ralph, a Cathedral teacher, as has been said, have been the richest spawning arenas of athletic development in Indianapolis.

"I used to referee as many as four games on Sundays," Dezelan recalled. "I never offered a potential player a scholarship or any inducement except to remind him that, at Cathedral, he would receive a good education."

The most successful high school coaches, public and parochial, witnessed CYO sports, Indianapolis' only pre-high school athletic incubator in early days.

"While some coaches waited for them to come to their schools and go out for sports," said Dezelan, "we encouraged and watched them as they were part of the CYO programs."

In the early 1980s much criticism of Cathedral's coaches came from a former teacher-administrator at Cathedral, then the principal of Chatard.

"They (Cathedral representatives) are openly recruiting and it was wrong," he charged.

"He seemed to forget that Cathedral, an independent school, did not receive funds from the Archdiocese and was operating without parish boundary restrictions," Dezelan said.

The disgruntled administrator led a boycott to move to ban games with Cathedral teams and also enlisted the support of Scecina Memorial, Roncalli and Ritter high schools.

(Continued)

After the administrator departed Chatard to work away from Indianapolis, the athletic director at Chatard contacted Joe Dezelan and athletic relations resumed in all sports and have continued. Scecina has not resumed regular-season play with Cathedral teams in football and basketball.

In 1961, when Indianapolis city schools athletic officials moved to ban Cathedral after the Irish had won nine city titles in eighteen seasons, newspaper criticism and public reaction ended that effort.

Another attempt by city schools was thwarted in the 1970s. Today, recruiting of students is from several sources. The reputation of the school and the achievements of its sons and daughters are the endorsements.

It should be emphasized that Cathedral's mission of diversity and her actual ability to exist has been dependent on telling the Cathedral story. For some the word "recruiting" denotes unduly influencing students to come to Cathedral. The reality is that every student who has chosen Cathedral has been recruited. For seventy-five years no student has automatically matriculated from a "feeder school." Students and their parents have always voluntarily chosen Cathedral as their school, based on the school's ability to offer their sons (and now daughters) an outstanding program. The staff and loyal supporters have, naturally, been dedicated to helping tell the Cathedral story. Most importantly, while Cathedral has achieved an enviable record of athletic excellence, that same excellence has been evident in academics, drama, music, and all other endeavors of Cathedral students.

Recruitment should be looked at as it is in all other independent schools and colleges—as presentation of the program. It has allowed parents to make an informed choice about what is best for their students—no more, no less.

Cathedral parents host casual gatherings in their homes to offer testimonials. Cathedral representatives visit schools, solicit the assistance—and accept recommendations of public and parochial teachers. The messages of alumni in paid advertisements in local newspapers, a campaign conceived of by teacher Jim Obergfell, have been effective in drawing students to the school.

Even though not all freshman applicants are accepted into Cathedral, the paid advertisements instill a feeling of pride and tradition.

In a free society choice is an individual right. An editorial in *The Indianapolis Star* in 1980 addressed the issue of recruiting. It read in part: "the move to bar competition between schools and Cathedral is wrong. It smacks of jealousy. Let the kids play."

The Growth of Tolerance

The saga of school segregation began with the entry of the Klan. In 1920, to protect white children the Indianapolis School Board established a black school—but it "should be modern and well equipped"—the Indianapolis Chamber of Commerce excused.

When Crispus Attucks opened in the fall of 1927 at 11th Street and Northwestern Avenue, segregation of the city was absolute. As a student the late Attucks football coach, Graham Martin, Attucks '37, walked 5.2 miles to attend school. Shortridge was two miles from his home.

Butler University admitted only ten black students each year. In February, 1943, Cathedral competed for the first time in the Indianapolis sectional played at Tech gymnasium. Cathedral's 5-13 season record, third worst in the school's history, showed they were no immediate threat, as the Irish lost to Washington.

Cathedral's two sport coach in 1942-43 was Milt Piepul, former Notre Dame All-America fullback.

Although it went almost unnoticed at the time, the IHSAA actually was ringing a bell for freedom. Competing for the first time in the basketball tournament were Indiana black schools, including emerging power Crispus Attucks High School. A dozen years later the Tigers would win back-to-back State championships in 1955-56.

Also getting into the tournament was a long-time Cathedral opponent in sports, the Indiana State School for the Deaf. Affectionately known as the "Silent Hoosiers," traditionally they were the sentimental favorites at Sectional tournaments. Friendships formed at Butler University between Irish coach Cleon Reynolds and long-time Deaf School coach Jake Caskey found the Silent Hoosiers regularly on basketball schedules, and the schools played a football game in 1943.

Another unrelated event spurred Cathedral's sports relationship with Crispus Attucks. On the night of October 4, 1944, vandals—perhaps from Shortridge and Cathedral high schools—painted the front entrances and columns of each other's schools. The sports rivalry between Shortridge and Cathedral had been long and intense, as many Cathedral students resided in designated Shortridge neighborhoods. (There were very few open districts in Indianapolis. Public school students were usually required to attend their nearest school with the exception of blacks who, though they lived throughout Indianapolis, were required to attend Crispus Attucks until 1953.)

Angered by the incidents, officials of Shortridge and Cathedral mutually agreed to suspend playing each other in football in 1945. It was the only interruption of a series from 1928 that continued until 1980 when Shortridge closed its doors.

(Continued)

Crispus Attucks seized the opportunity to fill Cathedral's open date. The Attucks athletic director, Alonzo "Lon" Watford, called his long-time friend, Cathedral coach Joe Dezelan, and begged Attucks be added to Cathedral's schedule. Watford, like Dezelan, had been a football star at Butler where both had played for Coach Tony Hinkle. Watford was also a Catholic and probably laid a little guilt on Joe. He agreed and took the request to athletic director Brother Giles Martin. He too approved the invitation and they cleared it with Principal Brother Benedict.

Watford had pleaded for Cathedral to give his school a chance to break a barrier they had faced since the school opened in 1927. To find opponents, Crispus Attucks' teams traveled even more than Cathedral. There were only three black high schools in Indiana so the Tigers were bussed to Gary and Evansville and competed against black school opponents in St. Louis, Louisville and Dayton to assemble a seven or eight game schedule. "Cathedral did us a great favor we never forgot," Watford said in an interview.

Watford and Attucks principal, Dr. J. Russell Lane, also a Catholic, came to Cathedral, and signed an agreement. The game was played at Tech field November 9, 1945. More than six thousand fans watched, little knowing that this was to be a breakthrough event in Indianapolis' sports history. Even though Cathedral's student body numbered several races, including blacks and many nationalities, it was classified as "white" to most.

The Irish of 1945 were en route to their first City championship under Dezelan coaching in his second season. Undefeated Crispus Attucks, coached by Watford, featured the running of All-City halfback Orville Williams.

To launch the series, exchange visits to school pep rallies were arranged as Coach Dezelan and Irish Captain Mike Carr visited Crispus Attucks.

Early in the game Cathedral scored on a dive play by All-City fullback Vincent "Bekie" Gatto. Perhaps Cathedral's greatest passer-receiver combination of all-time, Jimmy McLinn and "Jekie" McHugh, moved the game out of reach. McLinn and McHugh were both named to the All-State team. McLinn threw a forty-yard touchdown pass to the fleet Rudy Bayt, brother of Phil Bayt, former Indianapolis mayor. (Judge Bob Bayt, Phil's son, later played basketball at Cathedral.) Attucks scored late, but Cathedral prevailed, 20-6.

Cathedral alumni of earlier years, in an informal poll, voted Shortridge its favorite rival, reflecting the heated sports rivalry and friendship built by Shortridge's long-time coach and athletic director Bob Nipper. Shortridge had been the first Indianapolis school to play Cathedral in football and basketball during the 1920-21 season.

Both Crispus Attucks and Shortridge were converted to junior high schools in 1980. The first basketball meeting between a

(Continued)

black and white school took place February 15, 1947 in Tech gymnasium. The much-traveled Tigers were anxious to play a city team having gone undefeated through their first thirteen games under the coaching of Fitzhugh Lyons. An assistant Tiger coach that night later became perhaps Indianapolis' greatest high school basketball coach, Ray Crowe. Crowe coached the Oscar Robertson-led teams to State titles in 1955-56.

The rivalry moved to the hardwood with Cathedral playing Attucks during the 1946-47 season under Coach Cleon Reynolds, who also was a Butler letterman and friend of Coach Watford. Attucks was led by Lively Bryant and Reggie Cross. Cathedral countered with two-hand set shot artist captain Paul "Duke" O'Connell. Duke hit a late long-shot and a lay-up by Norm Muller, who later played at North Carolina State, clinched a 49-44 win, one of sixteen recorded that season. Another Irish regular was big Bill Frohliger who later played at Annapolis and coached Cathedral and Bloomington basketball teams.

Even though the first football and basketball games between Crispus Attucks and Cathedral are remembered as the games that opened inter-racial high school team competition, the Tigers and Irish had met years before in another sport—baseball.

Charley Hill, of that great Class of 1932, recalls a game played on Riverside Park Diamond #2. Charley remembers: "We didn't think too much about it. The Klan was after both of us so it seemed right that we were playing each other. We won and I don't remember too much about the game except the Attucks catcher never stopped chanting to his pitcher, 'Hit me in the belly, Charley'.

In 1949 the Indiana State legislature passed a law to eliminate racial discrimination in public education at all levels. North Central High School opened in 1956 and thus began the end of segregated schools. Black enrollment at Shortridge rose to twenty-eight percent in 1957.

The shadow of D.C. Stephenson was gone.

The Songs We Played and Sang

From the time that skinny junior Mike Duffecy sat at the upright piano in the music room at the original Cathedral High school and tinkled out the tune that was to become "Dear Old Cathedral," music has been a part of Cathedral.

The early tunes were played by Cathedral students on banjo, violin and piano in trios who whined the music of Sigmund Romberg and the Tin Pan Alley tunes of Cohan, Berlin and Gershwin. At honors awards programs, dances, theatrical productions and athletic events, music was always featured.

Later, the strains of Rogers & Hart or Hammerstein, Mercer, Carmichael, Kern and Porter songs were played and sung in Cathedral musical productions and dramas.

Violin soloists were popular, and J. Emmet McManamon (later Judge McManamon) fiddled at Cathedral sports banquets and student musicals which also featured a new form of American music, the jazz dance bands.

Tom Tobin warbled "Mighty Lac a Rose" and of the production of *The Prince and the Pauper* prompted *The Indianapolis Star* critic to note: "for a school production Cathedral's first is a smash."

A member of the cast (a bearded attendant courier) was J. Corbin Patrick '22 celebrated critic of *The Star.* "Pat" recalls: "Half the school was in the cast or production crew. We were an optimistic, if not terribly talented bunch parading around in medieval costumes."

And who played the role of girls in these productions?

The boys. Anthony Manley was the prince and James Norton the pauper in John Lane O'Connor's dramatization. It wasn't until the 1930s that the sisters at St. John, St. Mary's and St. Agnes academies relented and allowed their girls to participate in productions on the Cathedral stage. From Cohan to Garth Brooks and M.C. Hammer, Cathedral has played, sung and interpreted the music of great and popular composers in hundreds of productions.

Class of 1921.

Bud Markey was Cathedral's first tennis champ.

THE TENNIS SQUAD
Tom Quinn, Bud Markey, Bill Rickey, Bill Krieg.

The Harrington classic today takes its name and inspiration from early golfer John Harrington.

1923 varsity football team.

LADIES FAIR. Back—J. T. Fogarty, E. Gallagher, T. Carey. Front—T. Quinn, L. Jordan, F. Shine, M. Sweeney.

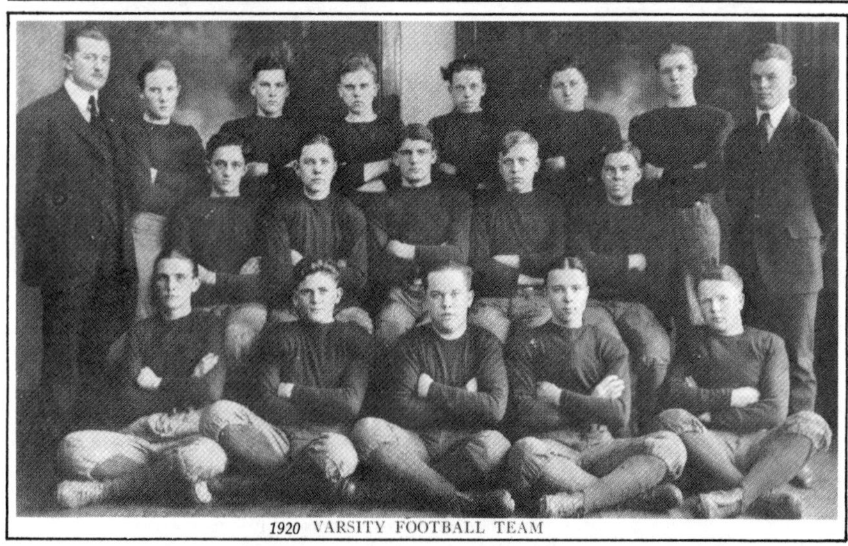

Back Row: Coach Feeney, Captain Sadlier, Joseph Harmon, Alvin Royse, Frank Roth, Joseph Sexton, Paul Harrington, Brother Theodore, Manager.
Middle Row: Marvin Brezette, James Kelly, Tom Ruckelshaus, Carl Wilberding, Tom Madden.
Front Row: Tom Hartnett, Matthew Laftey, John Glaska, Mark Mooney, Robert Gavin.

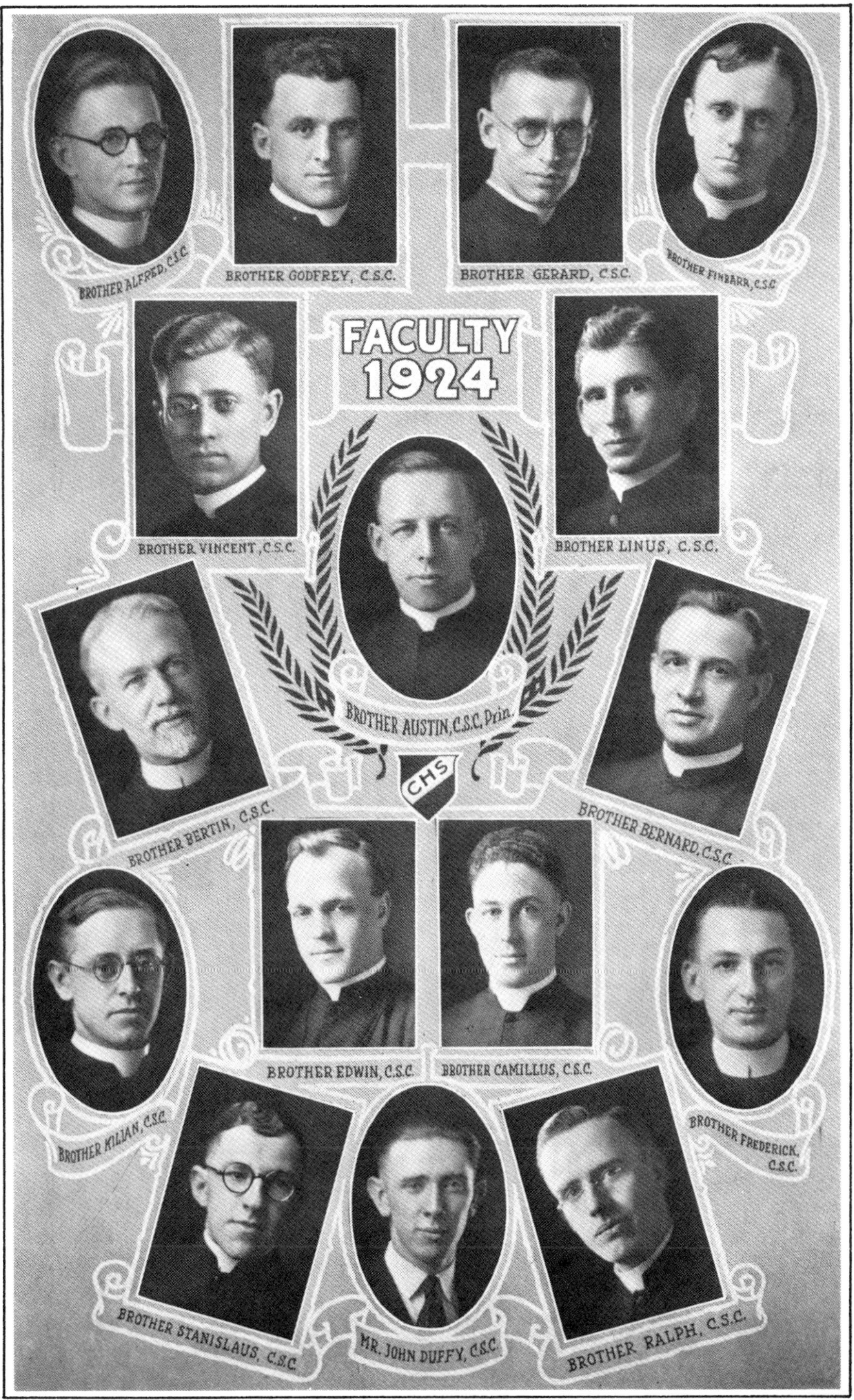

BROTHER ALFRED, C.S.C.
BROTHER GODFREY, C.S.C.
BROTHER GERARD, C.S.C.
BROTHER FINBARR, C.S.C.
FACULTY 1924
BROTHER VINCENT, C.S.C.
BROTHER LINUS, C.S.C.
BROTHER AUSTIN, C.S.C., Prin.
BROTHER BERTIN, C.S.C.
BROTHER BERNARD, C.S.C.
CHS
BROTHER KILIAN, C.S.C.
BROTHER EDWIN, C.S.C.
BROTHER CAMILLUS, C.S.C.
BROTHER FREDERICK, C.S.C.
BROTHER STANISLAUS, C.S.C.
MR. JOHN DUFFY, C.S.C.
BROTHER RALPH, C.S.C.

The Month
BRENNEN'S HOMECOMING
THE BASKETBALL SEASON BEGINS
THERE'S A GROWING DEMAND FOR THE NEW CATHEDRAL BELTS
CATHEDRAL
BOOKS WANTED FOR THE NEW LIBRARY
THE NEW HIGH SCHOOL LIBRARY IS OPENED TO THE STUDENTS
BVD SIGNING OFF
RADIO CONTINUES TO BE THE POPULAR INDOOR SPORT AT CATHEDRAL
THE ELOCUTION CONTEST WENT OFF BIG
THE NEW CAFETERIA CATERING TO THE NOON-HOUR RUSH
RUMORS
A NEW GYM
NO SCHOOL DURING THE XMAS VACATION
CAPT KELLY'S MEN WILL WALLOP FT WAYNE AND GARFIELD
A FIFTY PIECE BAND BY EASTER
JORDAN'S FLOAT MADE A HIT IN THE SCHOOL PARADE

Joseph P. McNamara   William J. Broderick   Lawrence A. Fitzgerald   Thomas E. Elbreg

Cathedral's first debating team.

THE THIRTIES

The song of the year—"Happy Days are Here Again"—
was played, martially and melodically, but it was not prophetic. It
was 1929 and on October 29 of that year, The Crash happened on
Wall Street. At Cathedral students had seemed insulated from
problems, secure in the prosperity and elegance of their shining
new school. They little knew at that moment the impact the Great
Depression would have on their lives.

On October 28, at the beautiful French Lick hotels south of
Indianapolis, millionaires were taking swan dives from their
suites to the marble floors beneath. It was estimated that nearly
ten thousand Americans committed suicide over the loss of their
fortunes.

On the good side, the Klan seemed to have fallen upon
hard times, with their Grand Dragon in prison for murder, and
tolerance was a slightly more acceptable attitude than it had been.

Dienhart coached his first football team, and a 2-5 record
concealed the coaching genius of a man who got so much out of
his athletes later. It was, as they say, a building year for two seasons ahead. A sophomore quarterback, John Ford, was being
groomed.

Dienhart's basketball teams began a program that would
bring the school strong recognition. His teams were eventually
destined to take twenty-two of twenty-eight games overall and
would repeat as State Catholic champions and advance to the National Catholic Semi-Finals in Chicago. In Chicago, they would
defeat teams from Clarksburg, West Virginia and Detroit and lose
to DeLaSalle of Joliet, Illinois, the eventual champion.

Cathedral students felt brotherhood with other minorities;
our first black student, Bill Violet, graduated in 1930. In the spring
Charley Hill was shortstop on the 1930 baseball team that played
in an athletic breakthrough: the first game in Indiana between a
white and a "colored" school.

The record reflects that with Joe Bear pitching, Cathedral
defeated Crispus Attucks, 7-3.

"Little did we know that was the first time a so-called
'white' school played Crispus Attucks. They were good guys,
good athletes, but they didn't have much equipment," Hill said.

Later, according to black historian Stanley Warren of
DePauw University, Cathedral handed down to Crispus Attucks
athletes their used baseball uniforms which had been handed

down to them by Cathedral friend Owen J. "Ownie" Bush, general manager of the Indianapolis Indians baseball team.

A campus visitor was the distinguished scientist Father Julius Niewland, C.S.C. Credited as the inventor of synthetic rubber, he inspired a favored student of his, Knute Rockne, to continue his studies at Notre Dame. He was disappointed when "Ka-nute chose football over chemistry," he told Cathedral students.

Another sportsman member of that class, Carl Hindel, is considered "Mr. Bowling" in Indianapolis.

Crispus Attucks lost to Cathedral, 2-1 in 1931 when Carl Kiefer hit a bases-loaded double. After Cathedral suspended baseball in 1932, the schools did not compete again until a football game in 1944.

Joe "Babe" Lawrie '30 played third base and was the hitting star in the Attucks win. "You know, I don't even remember that game," recalled Babe, a retired Indianapolis fire-fighter and for years one of the foremost amateur actors in Indianapolis.

"What I do remember about Cathedral was the strict discipline. I transferred from Sacred Heart and was stunned by the punishment those Brothers delivered. It was a sudden change from the Sisters of St. Joseph."

Depression budgets impacted sports; only seventeen basketball games were played. Cathedral won eleven and, in losing in the Catholic Championship final game, saw its string end at the Armory.

On May 31 the Cathedral band made the first contact at the five-year-old Ladywood School, offering a friendship which was not reciprocated.

The versatile thirty-five-voice Glee Club enchanted crowds with selections "Mighty Lak a Rose," "River Shannon," and the orchestra's trombones slid through Hoagy Carmichael's "Old Rockin' Chair's Got Me."

Cathedral's tradition of Christian service was continuing. Louis Dezelan '34 sold the most Bengal Mission drive tickets (thirty-seven dollars) and the Dezelan name was established at Cathedral.

Class poet Robert Maloy concluded:

"Let us remember to be true always to God, to Country, to honor and our school," as ninety-six graduates departed Cathedra. As a fortunate class none would die in the war ten years hence.

1930-1931

Joe Dienhart wanted his players to get a head start. After the disappointment of the 1929 football season (the Irish won two of seven games), he looked to find a camp where Irish athletes could tune up for the approaching season. Each player had to come up with the funds (fifteen dollars) for his two weeks of intense concentration with some extra-curricular fun. Though not a member of the Indiana High School Athletic Association, Cathedral was inordinately concerned about football infractions.

Coach Dienhart recalled:

After that bad season when we lost our last four games, I checked to see if Cathedral could participate (in pre-game football camp) and not be penalized.

Hell, I found out that many teams were doing pre-season workouts so I contacted Mr. H.A. Pettyjohn, athletic director at Muncie Central High School, and director of a camp at Little Tippecanoe Lake. There were about a dozen schools training at Camp Crosley including Gary Roosevelt and Chicago teams. In fact, as we left camp, Shortridge came up to use our space.

Living at the camps (Cathedral moved to Camp Gridly on Bass Lake near Knox, Indiana later) was not deluxe, but the camp proved so popular and effective that it was continued for years, becoming a Cathedral tradition.

Football Camp at Cathedral

"We slept on cots over a concrete slab with a tent over-head," Harry Caskey '39 recalled. "We swam in Bass Lake, practiced twice a day and Coach Dienhart set up boxing matches for all of us."

Caskey, a two-sport player, later coached football and basketball at Sacred Heart High School. In 1939 Caskey was high scorer with six points as the Irish basketball team defeated Tech, 27-19—the fourth consecutive win for Cathedral over the Greenclads at Tech gymnasium.

Later Harry Painter, Manual coach and athletic director, became camp coordinator. It was Painter who revived Manual's playing Cathedral in sports. That was in 1930, nine seasons after an Irish football team had trounced Manual's recognized City Champions, 87-0.

Teen-aged boys had their share of fun at camp. John Sage, 1941 All-City lineman, recalled: "We carried one particularly cocky guy, bed and all, to the middle of Bass Lake. It was so shallow we could wade a long ways from shore. He was so exhausted from practicing he slept through it all. Next morning he woke up and stepped into the lake."

The townspeople of Knox liked Cathedral's teams and at the conclusion of camp invited them to play an intra-squad scrimmage on a softball field near the center of town.

"Camp Gridly was not only a place where we prepared for the season ahead," Kenny Geiman '41 recalled, "but it was where we grew up. Those practices were intense and, I think, gave us momentum, but it was also the setting in which we matured and came together as a team."

During two football seasons that followed, 1930 and 1931, Cathedral was 8-0-1 and 9-0. Sportswriters hailed the Irish as state champions after the Irish defeated brawny Clinton there, 7-6.

Cathedral's athletic record in those two years is blazoned in the records of Indianapolis high school sports. In basketball, in 1930-31 the Irish were 20-6, runners-up in the State Catholic Tournament and earned fourth place in the National Catholic Tournament in Chicago.

1931-1932

The 1931-32 Irish basketball five won twenty-one of twenty-five games, won the State Catholic Championship and finished fourth in the National Catholic Tournament.

These impressive achievements were sparked by one of Cathedral's greatest athletes, two-sport man John Ford. While leading four varsity squads, Ford's teams combined won sixty-eight, lost ten and tied one.

(Ford went on to play three varsity basketball seasons at Notre Dame, and was captain of the 1936 team which was proclaimed National Collegiate Athletic Association Champions after a 22-2-1 season. NCAA post-season basketball tournaments began in 1939.)

His high school exploits were extolled in a book, *Captain Johnny Ford*, written by Cathedral teacher Brother Ernest.

One of Ford's evergreen memories was the Clinton game, the finale of the 1931 season.

> *We went to the coal mining town by bus. They had great fans and when we got off the bus they were chanting: "Where's number 44 (Ford)?"*
>
> *Coach Dienhart was a master at mind games. Before the game he had me change jerseys with Jim Carson. Near the end of the game the fans were still asking Coach Dienhart to put in No. 44, not knowing I had quarterbacked the entire game.*

"The game was so exciting," Charley Hill '32, recalled: "Our All-City end, Nick Connor, wet his pants when he lined up for the kickoff."

Cathedral scored its only touchdown on that kickoff when Cathedral's Bob O'Neal (later Marion County sheriff) booted the ball into the end zone. Confused, Clinton players stood by and watched as Russ Sweeney fell on the ball and claimed a touchdown.

A heated argument ensued before Coach Dienhart produced the latest rule book and read a new rule that stated the ball was "alive" and the touchdown was allowed. Bernie Breen swept end for the extra point and the Irish held on to claim the city's first Indiana state football championship.

Ford's grandsons Terry '92, a defensive back on the football team, and Brian '93, one of the state's finest receivers and punters, also starred at Cathedral.

Our Catholic Tournament

When Cathedral wasn't invited to play in the Indiana State High School Basketball Tournament, Cathedral Principal Brother William Mang called together officials of the eleven parochial schools to make plans for the first state-wide Catholic Tournament March 9-10, 1928.

Brother William, a native of football hotbed Massillon, Ohio, was a pioneer in athletics. He not only established the State Catholic Basketball Tournament but he also personally broke barriers, inducing Indianapolis high school officials to schedule games with Cathedral teams. The shiny-new Cathedral gym was to be the setting for the tournament, with radio coverage on WFBM featuring Blythe and Ted Hendricks.

Coach Joe Dienhart's team won the initial two championships in 1928 and 1929, defeating Anderson St. Mary's and Fort Wayne Central Catholic. In 1930 Decatur Catholic took the crown with "Hoosier Hysteria" peaking, and the 1931 tournament moved to the larger National Guard Armory on the City southside.

In 1929, Cathedral's Leo Gallagher, a three-sport star, won the A.G. Feeney diamond-studded medal for sportsmanship in Tournament play. In 1931 John Ford won the award.

Cathedral won four of the first six Catholic State championships but none after 1933. The Irish lost in title games in 1939 and 1942, the final year of the event. In 1934, the Tournament moved to Fort Wayne and was held there until Catholic schools entered the IHSAA tournament in 1943.

The Depression was beginning to take its toll in 1930 through '32. Students rode to school on bicycles, and if they could afford a seven-cent token, hopped the street car that clanged up Illinois Street to Cathedral.

An ad in *The Megaphone* by lawyer Leo X. Smith reflected the somber mood of the times:

> *Write Your Will Now*
> *Tomorrow May Be Too Late.*

Watching the Fords Go By

John Ford '32 recalled of his years playing football:

We had some wonderful rivalries and grand friends. The Klan had lost steam after Stephenson (D.C., Klan Grand Dragon) had been sent to prison. In the early '30s we played all the city schools except Tech. Broad Ripple was a smaller school and not considered at a competitive level. [Cathedral began playing the Rockets in basketball in 1934-35 and won the first nine meetings.] Brother William tried to schedule games but it wasn't until 1933 that Cathedral would play Tech, the year after I left.

Ford was preceded at Cathedral by his brother Joe who, John claims modestly, was the better athlete. Joe captained the 1929-30 basketball team (11-6) and was recruited to play two sports at Notre Dame. While a student at Notre Dame, on January 23, 1932 Joe suffered a burst appendix and that night, in St. Joseph's Hospital in South Bend, died of peritonitis. Joe Ford's funeral at the Cathedral was a community event. The crowd of more than 1,500 poured outside onto Meridian Street. Joe's teammates and coaches from Cathedral and Notre Dame attended. Indianapolis city officials, school officials and coaches and players Joe had played against mourned the loss of a young man whose life would probably have been spared today by a single injection of penicillin.

The News printed the poem "Young Lycidas" in tribute to a young man mourned. "He was much better," John demurred. Perhaps, but no single Cathedral athlete ever led his football and basketball teams to greater success than John Ford.

Cathedral abandoned varsity baseball in 1932 because it was anxious to be accepted in the Indiana High School Athletic Association.

"Principal Brother William called the team after seeing the names of most of them in baseball box scores in the newspapers," Charley Hill recalled. "I was playing for the South Side Turners and was paid five dollars a game which helped my family. Stop playing semi-pro sports, Brother William demanded, but it was already too late," Hill recalled. "Playing sports helped our families. These were lean times."

Other athletes played on a football team sponsored by Joseph James Canning, owner of Canning Plumbing Company. Canning's team, the "J.J.C.s," was composed of mostly Catholic players but had at least one black, a Jew and a native American.

"The Klan was still strong," Hill recalled "and the kluxers referred to the J.J.C.s as 'Jigs, Jews and Catholics.' "

Thought thoroughly offensive today, cruel nicknames and ethnic slurs were still common in the thirties, firing the flames of bigotry. Cathedral youth, along with other Catholics in the city, learned to grow accustomed to the slurs, but to this day many of that generation recall the pain the name-calling inflicted.

At graduation, Father John Cavanaugh of Notre Dame returned as Commencement speaker. The venerable priest had spoken to Cathedral's first graduating class eleven years earlier. A powerful orator, he was president of the university in its years of great growth.

Another record class, 124, including more than fifty who matriculated, was graduated from Cathedral in 1932 and has remained one of the all-time great classes through alumni years.

1932-1933

In 1933, however, Cathedral enters a period of legend. The 1933 basketball season, viewed from the vantage point of today, seems to transcend reality. While Fred Astaire and Ginger Rogers were dancing into American hearts and talking movies in general were creating new stars every week at the local cinema, Charley Shipp was a shining star who brought the school its finest glory.

His career is shrouded in myth. Even his size is disputed. Chicago newspapers described him as "one-half inch under six feet four inches tall." Yet in professional basketball records he was listed as six feet one inch and his weight at 190 to 205 pounds.

Shipp is considered one of the state's greatest high school players ever, even though he played only eighteen high school games. In the game for the National Catholic Championship, Shipp's seventeen points outscored all of St. Rita High School of Chicago as Cathedral defeated Illinois' Number One-ranked team, 31-10.

Charley was voted into the Indiana High School Basketball Hall of Fame in 1985. (The 1932-33 Irish squad were honored in 1983 at the annual Hall of Fame Banquet for their greatest accomplishment, winning that National Catholic Championship in 1933—the first Indiana team to win a national title.)

Shipp was discovered while Coach Dienhart was refereeing an amateur game at English Avenue Boy's Club on the city's South side. St. Patrick's grade school coach Bill Rosengarten introduced Dienhart to Shipp. Rosengarten was married to Charley's sister, Dorothy, and knew the boy's talent well.

Shipp was then a sophomore at Tech but was not playing for the Greenclads. Dienhart invited him to Cathedral and, with the encouragement of Bishop Chartrand, Charley enrolled as a junior. Many characterized Charley Shipp as "the George Gipp of Cathedral." Shipp was a brilliant, natural athlete, "one of the first to perfect a one-hand fall-back shot from the key that was virtually unstoppable," team-mate Bob Collier has said. Yet Shipp didn't always use his full potential, many thought.

Southsider Shipp preferred to pal with older men and found pool halls more to his liking than classrooms. He could not play sports as a junior at Cathedral because of the transfer. That year Shipp was observed in Garfield Park punting a football, barefooted, sixty yards and soon was acclaimed as a phenomenal kicker. He didn't play varsity football, although at football practice in the spring of 1933, he was shown to be a powerful and skilled runner who laid out potential tacklers.

Finally his hour came. In mid-season Shipp was eligible for the center post. He was flanked by the O'Connors, Eddie and Johnny, as forwards, guards Jimmy Carson, Larry Broderick (later Marion County Sheriff) and Maynard "Red" Theobald. The Irish were inconsistent in early season play until Shipp joined the team; then they won their final nine games.

Only one shadow clouded the horizon; during his time as an active player, it was learned that Shipp was born in December 1913. It was then that the IHSAA imposed a nineteen-years-of-age limitation that came to be called "the Charley Shipp rule."

Meanwhile, in November 1932, Coach Joe Dienhart put on the floor what was to become one of the most smooth-working and well-balanced teams in the school's net history. The State Catholic Tournament proved to be easy for the Dienhart men. Cathedral defeated Gibault School for Boys of Terre Haute in the final game, 27-21.

Practice sessions were long and arduous as Dienhart groomed the aspiring Irish for the most prized goal of all. The team was heading for the National Catholic Title.

The climax of the year occurred on March 22, 1933, as the team boarded the train from Union Station for Chicago, and even the most ardent Irish fans believed they would come home losers for the sixth time.

Chicago newspapers began to take notice at practice, though:

> *Cathedral of Indianapolis took to the floor this afternoon with an impressive lineup of six-footers. After a slow start, the Indiana champions stepped out to a 28 to 10 victory over Our Lady of Victory, Lackawanna, N.Y. Charley Shipp led Cathedral scorers with five baskets.*
> *—Tourney Times.*

The tournament at Loyola was a set-up for Shipp. In Indiana, rules prohibited a center to play with his back to the basket so Shipp was often used at guard. In Chicago, he could take a pass and pivot to the hoop or fall back and shoot.

Second Round

> *Cathedral regained its position as the lower bracket favorite by defeating Cretin High School of St. Paul, Minnesota, in the final afternoon game 42-18. The Indiana champions trailed 4 to 3 at the quarter, only to step out in the next three periods and run up an impressive total. Charley Shipp led the Cathedral attack.*
> *—Tourney Times.*

Third Round

The big, fast Cathedral team from Indianapolis held the Augustinians (Carthage, N.Y.) in check by a slim margin throughout the game, leading 4-1 at the quarter, 10-6 at the half, and 14-10 at the third quarter. Augustinian came up with a rush in the closing minutes and brought the spectators to their feet cheering, but just failed to catch up.

—Chicago Tribune.

Fourth Round

Surprising as it may seem, De Paul Academy unbeaten Chicago Catholic High School League Champions, and regarded as an outstanding favorite, will battle for only third place honors. The rangy, husky Hoosier champs, all except one player towering six feet or better, found the De Paul warriors 'out on their feet.' Bewildering the Chicagoans with a speedy, tricky attack and even interrupting many of their passes, the Hoosiers stepped out to an 11 to 2 advantage in the first quarter. Tracy of De Paul registered his only basket goal of the game, but Cathedral then registered 15 consecutive points before the Academy made another. Charley Shipp, the center who lacks only half an inch of being six foot four inches and tips the scales at 195, sank eight baskets and a free throw. Besides this, he passed beautifully in the pivot play, which accounted for many points. The O'Connors, performing at the forward posts, were next in the scoring, Johnny sinking nine points and Ed hitting for six.

—Herald Examiner.

The Championship Game

Indiana, the state where a basketball uniform is an indispensable part of every layette, boasted possession of the National Catholic prep title for the first time in history. Cathedral High of Indianapolis the new champion (and what a champion!) was the only outside team

> *a Chicago quintet (St. Rita) was asked to beat and*
> *didn't. Charley Shipp was named captain of the All-*
> *Tournament team that was named by officials and news-*
> *papermen.*
>
> *With Shipp catching passes on his fingertips,*
> *pivoting away from guards and scoring field goals from*
> *every angle, Cathedral rushed into a commanding lead*
> *in the first quarter and kept increasing it till the final*
> *gun. At one time they scored 17 consecutive points,*
> *while holding their opponents scoreless. Twenty-two*
> *minutes of play had elapsed before St. Rita was able to*
> *make a field goal.*
> *—Chicago Daily News*

They came, they saw, they conquered. The adulatory newspaper coverage showed the surprise Chicagoans felt at the upstart Indiana victories, but did not withhold the praise the exceptional Indianapolis team deserved:

> *Somewhere, someplace, there may be better*
> *teams than the Cathedral High stalwarts of Indianapo-*
> *lis, who last night captured the 10th annual National*
> *Catholic interscholastic basketball tournament at Loyola*
> *University. And maybe there are better losers than the*
> *gallant St. Rita team, which absorbed a 31-10 beating.*
> *but if there are, they never played in any of the meets at*
> *the north side gymnasium. (Loyola University.)*
> *—The Chicago Daily News*

On returning to Indianapolis, the team was greeted with a tumultuous celebration, class dismissal, a pep rally and a caravan to Monument circle. The public appreciation was held in the Cathedral gym and a special guest of honor was newly-consecrated Bishop Joseph Elmer Ritter, long-time Cathedral supporter. Bishop Chartrand, in ill health for two years, had left his post.

The Class of '32

That Great Class still numbers more than fifty who have gathered every month for years to renew old ties and enjoy each other's company. A member of what they describe as "the Great Class of 1932," John Ford and his classmates still get together every month at the Indianapolis Knights of Columbus Council at 13th and Delaware streets.

"We wear Class of '32 caps," former Indianapolis Fire Chief Charley Hill recalls "and as a group travel together to watch Cathedral teams."

The group journeyed to New Castle in 1982 to see their classmate, John Ford, be admitted to the Indiana Basketball Hall of Fame. They were also part of the nine thousand wild fans who watched the Number One-ranked Irish defeat New Castle for the second time that season. In spite of Steve Alford's thirty-seven points, Cathedral, led by Scott Hicks, endured to win the Hoosier Classic Basketball Tournament. "We always begin our dinners by singing 'Dear Old Cathedral,' " Hill recalls.

"One time a group of Indiana University alumni who were meeting in the next room, asked us to hold it down. Can you imagine, there were five hundred of them and twenty of us and we were too loud."

Cathedral is a school where only boys can go,
But right across the street you'll find some girls you
*   know.*
Now at Cathedral High the boys work very hard,
And many times amongst them you'll find a sturdy guard.
When playing basketball they're certainly tough cus-
*   tomers;*
On football fields they form a mighty line of shoulders.
While on the campus too they play this game of foolball
In every way I know.

At noon each day they gather noisily in the "cafe,"
And there they buy some hot-dogs, talk things over and
*   laugh.*
And in the classroom too they like to talk and play,
But when they're called upon they don't know what to
*   say!*

And then each year we find a certain number gone
Their happy faces missing from the school they loved so
*   long.*

*   —Eugene Dockter '32*

And, of course, the world rolled on. To the strains of "Happy Days Are Here Again" Franklin Delano Roosevelt in November of '32 had been elected by a landslide over a crippled Republican administration. When FDR began thirteen years of service as President, the country was frightened, more frightened than ever in its history, with even the President of Bethlehem Steel, Charlie Schwab, remarking that "everyone is afraid." By March the new administration's plans to stimulate a recovery were underway.

The basketball championship game date was March 26, 1933, six days after a snarling Guiseppi Zangora shouted "push the button" and was electrocuted for assassinating Chicago Mayor Anton J. Cermak.

While civic officials in Indianapolis lauded the National Champions, President Roosevelt was moving to implement his campaign promise; he signed the beer and wine repeal ten days later.

For their efforts in the tourney, Cathedral received temporary possession of the Cardinal Mundelein Trophy, and permanent possession of the Loyola University Trophy, now on display in the school's trophy room.

At the conclusion of the 1933 season, in that hard-times Depression era, a benefit game was conceived of to match Cathedral and the Martinsville Artesians, 1933 Indiana State Champions. Wayne "Blondie" Patton, sports editor of *The Indianapolis Star* proposed the game be played at Butler Fieldhouse, site of the Indiana championship matches. Fans and politicians, including Indiana Governor Paul V. NcNutt, favored the post-season benefit.

"We really wanted to play the Glenn Curtiss-coached champions," John O'Connor '33 recalled.

"Arthur L. Trester (commissioner of the IHSAA) wouldn't hear of it. We could have raised fifty thousand dollars to help the unemployed and both teams were disappointed."

Shipp never graduated from Cathedral. Notre Dame Coach George Keogan visited his home and salivated over his talent, but was wary of his scholastic ability. Coach Lenny Sachs of Chicago Loyola dreamt of a way to get Shipp on his team, but it was not to be.

Shipp played amateur basketball after leaving Cathedral and in 1935 became a starting guard and player coach on the Akron Goodyear Wingfoots team of the National Basketball League.

The NBL preceded the National Basketball Association which began play in 1949.

During thirteen seasons Shipp starred for the Oshkosh All-Stars, Fort Wayne Zollners, Anderson Packers and the Waterloo Hawks, where he also was player-coach. Irish teammate John O'Connor recalls: "For eight of nine seasons Charley was first team all-NBL."

Shipp played professional basketball with another Indianapolis great Leroy "Cowboy" Edwards who, while at Tech, led his team to the 1935 State Championship final game.

Shipp scored 2,174 points in more than four hundred professional games as a play-making defensive swarmer who pressed opponents in a style not seen before in the 1930s and forties.

Bobby McDermott, one of the last great two-hand set shot artists, recalled of his teammate Shipp: "Shipp was one of the greatest players I ever played with or against. He was strong, quick and could ball handle, rebound and shoot."

McDermott added: "He had one failing, his temper. Charley was intense and temperamental and was prone to fouling out of games. Sometimes when we needed Charley he was on the bench."

John O'Connor recalls Charley as being impoverished. "At least two or three nights every week he stayed at our home at 1423 North Pennsylvania Street. My Mom loved Charley. He never spoke of his father (who died in 1919) and his mother worked in the Cathedral cafeteria."

McDermott continued: "Charley had no peer when he wanted to play hard. Many times he could take over a game on talent and strength. But have one call go against him and he would rampage. Opponents found an uncontrolled temper was his Achilles heel. They would bait him and soon the torment would release itself through personal fouls that sent him to the bench."

Shipp and Coach Dienhart were reunited years later when Joe, Purdue's assistant athletic director, hired Charley to work in the athletic department.

Shipp was plagued by diabetes, which eventually affected his extremities. He suffered through two leg amputations and died in March of 1988 shortly after being recognized by the Indiana Basketball Hall of Fame as one of the greatest high school players of his era.

And so Charley Shipp remains an enduring legend. His National Catholic Tournament trophy still stands dominantly in the trophy case in the present-day Cathedral trophy room. It spans the years to remind the school community of a past great: iconoclast at times, fun-loving, a practical joker with an incendiary temperament and a basketball talent that God seems to give only a few times in a generation.

Earlier in 1933 the death of its beloved Bishop Joseph Chartrand (1870-1933) had saddened the Cathedral family. He had been ill two years and succumbed to a heart attack December 8, 1933. His remains were interred in the Cathedral and moved to Calvary Chapel Mausoleum in 1976. "He was a part of our lives," Bob Collier '33 recalled.

The Catholic and Record (December 11, 1933) best expressed the school's reaction to the loss of its founder and inspiring spirit:

The Human Side of Bishop Chartrand

Cathedral High School boys were astonished at the stories about Bishop Chartrand that filled the newspapers from the moment he died. They had not realized that he was a famous theologian. They had, boyishly enough, not known that he was a great churchman.

Their big brothers had told them that Bishop Chartrand taught religion to Cathedral seniors each Friday. They understood that he had done that from the first day of the school's existence. He was a part of Cathedral High School to them. When, as freshmen and sophomores, they dreamed of being seniors, he was part of their dream; and when as juniors they patiently awaited their final year, his Friday class was a natural and important part of that year.

It is never easy for the boys to settle down for class. They seem especially filled with restless energy, with boyish impulsiveness, perhaps because only boys attend their school. Teachers realize the situation and have learned what to expect when the boys enter the classroom from street or campus But the boys were quiet on Monday morning, December 11.

The few minutes between the first bell that calls them to their room and the second bell which begins the class were not filled with the usual chatter. The boys sat quietly at their places, and, if they spoke at all, did so in whispers. Teachers describing them would say, perhaps, that they seemed frightened. It was their first class since newspaper streamers had informed them three days before of the Bishop's death.

For in spite of the papers, Bishop Chartrand was not even yet to them a famous churchman and a great theologian whose death might be taken with quiet respect. A very dear friend was lost to them. A simple, kindly man who seemed always in some mysterious way to be wishing them well was gone.

It was also the habit of the Bishop to present each senior with rosary beads of sterling silver. Time and again had been told the story of the non-Catholic boy who hurried breathlessly into the school office with the word that he had not received his beads. That boy knelt in the Cathedral from 2 to 3 o'clock Wednesday morning.

The Bishop's interest in athletics undoubtedly resulted from his interest in boys, but he always had questions for the coach, Mr. Dienhart, or for the players, concerning the coming game that showed intimate knowledge of the matter.

"Don't come back if you lose," he told a football player before one game. And when the athlete shot back "We'll be back," the Bishop enjoyed that answer so much that this story too became a favorite. During the National Catholic Basketball Tournaments in Chicago, Father Dunn had the continued assignment of telephoning the Bishop immediately after the Cathedral game.

The Bishop habitually showed the boys the human side of the personality. His talk with them in the school corridors and even in the class room was filled with laughter. Even on graduation night when, before the exercises began as he walked among the boys in the locker room or dusty backstage, his remarks were always humorous and he was quick to reward with a bright smile the swift reply as humorous as his own.

But his primary influence on the boys was intensely spiritual. His famous four points for seniors are known the city over: (1) never commit a mortal sin; (2) never commit a venial sin; (3) never miss a Communion you can possibly receive, and never miss Mass on Sunday.

Through all of his vast learning and intelligence and humor there ever burned the bright light of a heart given utterly and simply to God, and the boys of Cathedral High School never lost the sense of that love. There was indeed that in him which they could not fathom and which lent all to their admiration of him. As an alumnus expressed it, "You don't know how much Bishop Chartrand did for you until you're out of school three years." It was inevitable that the prelate's unusual educational endowment should find early expression in efforts to promote the standing of Catholic schools. He did much to coordinate the work of the various parish schools and in 1918 opened the first free Catholic boys high school in Indianapolis. The enrollment increased steadily and need for larger quarters resulted in the completion of the imposing Cathedral High School on North Meridian Street. The Bishop's zeal also was responsible for initiating the practice of daily Communion among his parishioners, for which he received special commendation from Rome.

Cathedral entered into a period of mourning. School closed as students, faculty and alumni he served celebrated the life of the man whose dream it was to create a Catholic boys high school.

One year later, on the first anniversary of his death, a Requiem High Mass was held. Cathedral singers and voices from every parish in the Diocese joined in a chorus directed by Brother Ernest.

Chartrand's passing brought to an end the beginning chapter of Cathedral's history—no longer would the daily shepherd minister to his "beloved Cathedral boys."

A movement began to rename the school in his memory, in spite of the fact that he had requested that the Cathedral name he chose not be changed. In the mid-sixties, a new school was opened named Chartrand. Kennedy High School (the old Sacred Heart) closed and its students merged with the students of Chartrand to form Roncalli High School, the family name of Pope John XXIII.

Chartrand's passing did not alter the support of the Diocese to Cathedral, however. A long-time friend of Cathedral, Joseph Ritter, was named Chartrand's successor.

Ritter was consecrated Bishop in March, 1933 and his first public appearance after was in the Cathedral gymnasium as he joined thousands in a salute to Cathedral's 1933 National Catholic Championship basketball team.

The newly-installed Bishop Joseph Ritter, was another honorary son of Cathedral. He appointed Rev. Peter Killian as the school's first superintendent in 1934. Under Fr. Killian, needed tuition was assessed for the first time. The fee of fifty dollars per student remained for more than twenty years, with a reduced rate for multiple family members.

Fr. Killian served until January, 1939 when Rev. Thomas J. Finneran succeeded. Brother Bernard returned as principal in 1934-35 and Brother Richard assumed the position for 1935-37.

In 1937, William J. Hurrle, father of athletes Ott, Bill and Ray "Ike,", formed the first Boosters Club to provide special assistance to athletic teams and other school organizations.

The full force of the Depression was being felt in Indianapolis, as elsewhere. The strained budgets in the Diocese, which necessitated the establishment of a fifty-dollar tuition at Cathedral effective at the end of 1933, were also affecting the families who had to pay it. The fifty dollars per student fee would remain for twenty years, along with the strong belief that Cathedral should be financially available to any qualifying student who wished to attend.

Bishop Ritter, formerly a Cathedral ethics teacher, also spent time at Cathedral, though his visits were less frequent than Chartrand's because of the demands of an expanding congregation. He presided at official Cathedral functions and was a staunch supporter of the school. In 1944, the Indianapolis Diocese was elevated to the status of Archdiocese and with that came the Archbishopric.

Joseph Elmer Ritter was transferred to St. Louis in 1946 and was elevated to the cardinalate by Pope John XXII on January 16, 1961. Joseph Elmer Cardinal Ritter, a native of New Albany, died June 10, 1967 and is buried in St. Louis.

Archbishop Paul C. Schulte became the sixth spiritual leader of the central Indiana congregation in 1946 and served until 1970. He died in 1984 and is interred in Calvary Mausoleum. It was Archbishop Schulte who conceived of and supported the establishment of Cathedral Latin School.

Schulte was succeeded by Archbishop George J. Biskup, who served until his death in 1979. He is interred in Calvary Mausoleum. Archbishop Biskup presided over the reformation of Cathedral in 1973 and the amalgamation of Ladywood-St. Agnes and Cathedral in 1976.

Edward T. O'Meara was named fourth Archbishop of Indianapolis in 1979. An active supporter of Cathedral, the popular Archbishop died in 1991 and is interred in Calvary Mausoleum.

The fifth and current Archbishop of Indianapolis is Daniel Bucchlein, a native of Jasper. He was formally installed in the Metropolitan See of Indianapolis in 1992 and has been a friend and supporter of today's Cathedral.

Each of these servants of Christ has contributed to the growth and success of Cathedral High School. Cathedral is indebted to the tradition begun by Bishop Joseph Chartrand of care for the young of the Catholic community.

1933-1934

It was, or should have been, a new era. The combination of the loss of influence of the Klan, the success of Irish athletic teams and the statesmanship of Principal Brother William prompted the sports editor of *The Indianapolis Star* to write a column urging the IHSAA to admit Cathedral.

W. Blaine ("Blondie") Patton wrote: "Their (Cathedral's) eligibility rules are practically the same if not more severe." He urged admission to the State Association. Commissioner Trester and the Board of Control were not ready. It would take nine years and the unifying spirit of the wartime era to force an invitation. Brother William did persuade Tech to play the Irish in football, and the Greenclads won 19-14 at Perry Stadium baseball park. Though they finished 4-6, the team fought Clinton's State Champions to their closest margin, 0–19.

Nineteen-thirty-three, then, was the last year of a tuition-free Cathedral. A record 124 seniors hurried to get on with their lives after graduation.

One of the returning two-sport lettermen, John O'Connor, recalled: "We had to help our families by working or getting a degree as fast as we could." O'Connor, a starter on the National Championship team the year before, would captain Cathedral's seventh consecutive winning basketball team in 1933-34. That group won twelve of twenty-one games and bowed out in the second round at Chicago after a victory over St. Catherine's of Dubois, Pa.

O'Connor would continue his allegiance to Cathedral as a volunteer who was instrumental in building the new Cathedral.

Another graduate of the Class of 1934 who would distinguish himself in the legal profession was John Tinder, longtime, hard-driving Marion County prosecutor.

1934-1935

On August 22, 1934 gangster Charles Arthur "Pretty Boy" Floyd was killed by "G-Men." (The Government-Men later became the Federal Bureau of Investigation—FBI.) John Dillinger was still loose (probably visiting his Mooresville, Indiana, home) and America was swept in the craze of bullets and death.

The most noticeable change on campus was the altered appearance of the venerable and by now old fashioned-looking

The Megaphone. "Irish Strength Defies Techmen" and "Irish Champs Play Noblesville" were banner headlines that reflected a remake of the softer styles of *The Megaphone* of the past fourteen years. No longer would its first eight to ten pages be filled with student sonnets, rambling narratives or poetry. This was journalism, perhaps reflecting the restless new era of Charles MacArthur's *Front Page* on Broadway or the movie renditions of tough, effective newspapers.

The name atop the masthead was senior Frank Widner, later to hold top editorial positions at *The Indianapolis Times* and *The Indianapolis Star.*

"We had a wonderful English teacher, Brother Leonard, who told us to do what we wanted." (Brother Leonard Zuber, an innovative and inspiring teacher, is later mentioned in the 1938-39 period in this book.)

Body (reading) type size was increased, and illustrations were used. The format was newspaper: inviting, easy-to-read. That revision would continue as the publication moved from creative writing content to news. *The Megaphone* was issued bi-weekly. Widner served as News Editor of an investigative series on the Indianapolis Police Department that won for *The Star* a Pulitzer Prize in 1975.

In football big (six feet one inch, 170 pounds) John McMahon was a latter-day John Ford. He captained the football team to a 7-1-1 record including victories over Tech (31-6) and Shortridge, 35-0. (Shortridge was the recognized City Champion.)

The Irish defeated the Millers at Noblesville, 14-6, before eight-thousand fans to claim the "Central Indiana Championship." One week later the Blue and Gold reached too far in a State Championship showdown at Clinton. The Miners' passing game blasted the Irish, 26-0. At the season-end Victory Banquet a special guest was the powerful Arthur L. Trester, commissioner of the IHSAA, whom the Irish were courting.

Cathedral's first principal, Brother Bernard, returned to succeed popular Brother William, who retired after six years of principalship at the school, expressing his wish to spend time earning a graduate degree at the University of Chicago. Bill Connor, one of four Connor Cathedral sons, was elected Senior Class President and captained a 7-12 basketball team, the school's first losing season in eight years. There were two highlights: a 19-18 upset of Shortridge at Butler and a 20-21 loss to City Champion Washington. Reflecting the hit song of the day a *Star* headline read: "Irish Almost Do the Continental."

The graduation class of 116 heard a distinguished graduate, Paul J. Harrington '22. The eloquent and educated American record-setting pole vaulter had an alphabet of degrees—Ch. E., M.E. and was a researcher for Standard Oil Company, Fanwood, N.J. Still close today, the Class of '35 meets monthly. "We're not quite as active as the Class of '32," reported Widner, "but we try to hang together."

1935-1937

Armed with the new wonder from Europe, the fast 35mm camera with its revolutionary capacity to deliver candid pictures, photo journalists began exposing people and events as never before. Cathedral's football season in '35 was 6-1-1 under Captain Jim McNamara. *The Megaphone* stretched pennies to present a more graphic Cathedral in photographs and illustrations.

The world peeked at a Royal affair. Vivid photos of Britain's Edward VIII with socialite divorcee Wallis Simpson, shocked Britain and forced his abdication as heir to the throne.

The year 1936 at Cathedral marked the further growth of student theater featuring all-boy casts. It would be a few years before academy nuns would allow their girls to appear at Cathedral .

After two successful seasons on the gridiron, Captain Bob Fitzgerald's team began optimistically, as the blue and gold jersey-striped Irish swarmed Shelbyville, 52-0. The following week more than two thousand fans traveled to Louisville to meet the perennial Kentucky State champions from Male High School. There was excitement and curiosity about the exaggerated stories of the barefoot Kentuckians. The rumor was true—at least partially—as the Male kicker, sans footwear, boomed a football more than fifty yards in pre-game warmup. Cathedral controlled the game until their taunts of "barefoot Kentuckians" backfired. The game ended in a 12-12 tie. Male went on to another State Championship and Cathedral would only defeat Manual to finish 3-4-2 (including a tie with Elwood).

Cathedral's drab-painted, cream-and-brown halls were patrolled by Brother Patrick. "At six feet four inches , 220 pounds, no one challenged him," mused Bernie Broderick '37. Broderick's brothers, Larry and Charley, also stared on Cathedral teams. Bernie captained the 13-8 basketball squad and went on to lead Butler's 1942 baseball team as an infielder-outfielder. Still strapped by the Depression, Catholic schools decided there would be no State Catholic Tournament and the team couldn't afford a trip to Chicago to play in the National tournament.

"Our basketball team was pretty good," Broderick recalled. "We beat a good Tech team and were peaking at the end when we rolled over (69-22) Windfall. I wish we could have played on, as we had size and speed."

Big (six feet four and a half inches) Joe Gillespie played pivot in the first season after the center jump had been eliminated following every successful field goal. Joe went on to letter at Notre Dame, where both centers were from Cathedral—Gillespie and "Effy" Quinn '38.

On June 4, 1937 (the day the first supermarket cart rolled down a grocery-store aisle in Oklahoma) 126 sons accepted diplomas.

Nearly half of the class sought degrees. Nine would become medical doctors, and four would not survive the war.

1937-1938

The jitterbug, the rage of 1937, quickly caught on at newly-instituted CYO dances. Popular Brother Agatho Heiser continued the tradition of fine English teachers and was elevated to principal. Though there wasn't much athletic success—2-5-1 in football and 13-10 in basketball—outstanding players went on to collegiate careers.

The back-to-back 3 and 2 victory seasons marked Cathedral's worst showing in seventy-four years of football competition. All-City tackle Nick Scollard, a six-foot two-inch, 215-pound strong boy, would become Cathedral's first professional football player. Scollard was one of the early great kickers and for years held the NFL's record for field goal distance. The 1937-38 season would be Dienhart's last; he went on to coach St. Joseph's College.

The first of four Hurrle brothers, Bill, Jr., captained the basketball squad. Bill's dad began the Booster's Club, formed to assist Cathedral teams which had been kept from participating in the National Catholic Tournament in Chicago for four seasons due to lack of funding.

The first contribution of the 375-member Club was the purchase of a "classy-looking machine with a General Motors chassis," a seventeen hundred-dollar bargain that would transport Cathedral athletes, singers and musicians for fifteen seasons.

Lanky Francis "Effy" Quinn, the son of immigrant Irish parents, was All-City and All-State and was the city's leading scorer with a thirteen-point average. In many basketball games, the six-foot two-inch center scored more than half his team's points. Quinn went on to star at Notre Dame and was 1942 team captain. He and his wife had thirteen children, and their eight sons all graduated from Cathedral, a one-family record.

The 114-member graduating class sent fourteen of its group to Notre Dame. "I was told Cathedral sent more people to Notre Dame than any other high school," Quinn says. Today that fact has been reaffirmed by Notre Dame administrators who still compliment the school for the quantity and quality of her sons and daughters choosing Notre Dame.

Another 1938 letterman at Notre Dame was Bernie McKay, a lettering fullback on Elmer Layden's Irish.

In the outside world, the year was notable for Italy's conquest of backward Ethiopia and Emperor Haile Selassie's impassioned, but ignored plea for help from the League of Nations. Hitler repudiated the Versailles Treaty, and another ogre of power, Josef Stalin, was murdering millions of Russians. Americans danced the "Big Apple."

A young comedian was being noticed, and his theme song, "Thanks for the Memories" was the hit song during Cathedral's twentieth year.

1938-1939

In 1938-39, the popular song "Cathedral In the Pines" might have interested students, but it didn't catch on like the classics "A Tisket a Tasket" and *"Bie Mir Bist Du Schön"* or Gershwin's last song, "Love Walked Right In." The Nazis began conquest, first by annexing the Sudetenland, but America ignored the ominous move and laughed in movie theaters featuring Mickey Rooney as Andy Hardy and his new heart-throb Frances Gumm (Judy Garland).

One of the school's great servants, Rt. Rev. Peter Killian, left Cathedral in March due to ill health after a record fifteen years as school superintendent. In a letter to Bishop Ritter from his Holy Name parish, Killian praised the work of the Brothers and defended them against his fellow priests who felt the Brothers were too slow to collect tuition.

He said that frequently salaries could not be paid. "We divided the available money between bills outstanding and the salary due."

Joe Harmon '21 became Cathedral's sixth football coach.

Captained by All-City fullback Joe Fitzgerald, one of three brothers who played between 1934-39, the 7-2 team won its first five games, slipped to Tech before six thousand in its new stadium, and lost to Shortridge. In the season finale, ten thousand fans filled Manual's Delavan Smith Field to watch the Irish play undefeated North Side of Fort Wayne, Indiana's Number One-ranked team. Captain Fitzgerald scored two touchdowns even though he was knocked unconscious at least once. Halfbacks Paul Moxley and the fleet Harry "Rabbit" Caskey also led the Irish to hand North Side an 18-6 defeat, their first loss in three seasons.

The News' William F. Fox Jr. proclaimed the victory "the Upset of the State in '38!" In basketball, Caskey led the Irish with six points, as Cathedral defeated Tech for the fourth consecutive time at Tech. In a game against Greenfield, the first quarter ended 0-0. Cathedral went on to win, 29-15, and held the Tigers without a field goal.

Captain John Mattingly led the basketball team to the State Championship game only to lose to Fort Wayne Central Catholic. The Fort Wayne team won two consecutive national Catholic titles.

As state runner-up Cathedral qualified to return to the National event, its first visit in five seasons. At the National Catholic Tournament Cathedral defeated Chicago's Messemer and lost to another Chicago team, St. Ignatius. The final record was 14-14.

The current glamorous news in 1938 was David 0. Selznick's signing of Vivien Leigh for her Academy Award-winning role of Scarlett O'Hara in *Gone With the Wind.*

An advanced sell-out of Stephen Foster's operetta *Beautiful Dreamer* was dedicated to Josiah K. Lilly, the pharmaceutical giant whose Foundation would later benefit Cathedral. Mr. and Mrs. Lilly were "guest guests" of the school at the premier performance. *The Megaphone* reported the Lillys, who once lived in a home on the Cathedral school site, were "most enthusiastic in their praise of the fine student production."

Brother Leonard Zuber, producer of the show and organizer of student theater at Cathedral, died three months later at age thirty-nine.

Ninety-two seniors graduated with the Class of 1939, and six would lose their lives in the conflict that was fomenting and would soon engage the United States in another war.

1939–1940

When "Dorothy" was singing the haunting "Somewhere, Over the Rainbow," the weekly "precious little creature" publication *The Memo* was first circulated.

Returning to Cathedral from Fall River, Massachusetts, after six years came Brother Marcian as principal.

In 1940 Brother Marcian became president of the Indiana Catholic High School Athletic Association. Joyfully, the ICHSAA disbanded after three years. A war-united nation was evolving socially, and Cathedral and the other Catholic schools would soon be invited to membership in the IHSAA.

The tradition of rigorous academics continued into the new decade. "Marcian, like memorable Brothers including Sylvan, James, Bruno, Regis and Charles, prepared us well intellectually and morally," wrote Thomas Beechem '40.

White-maned handsome Indiana Governor Paul V. McNutt, a friend to Cathedral, was on the cover of *Life Magazine.* FDR had just appointed him as the United States governor of the Philippine Islands. Many thought it was a canny move to get the popular Democrat out of the way so the President could seek an unprecedented third term against Elwood's Wendell Willkie the following year.

Another Fitzgerald, Jim, captained a Cathedral football team his junior and senior seasons. It was Cathedral's first ten-game season since 1933. Next year the Irish would play ten games, but the schedule "was shortened to nine as the faculty opposed too many games," *The Memo* reported.

The gold-helmeted Irish team won its first six games, including a comeback win over a taunting Muncie Central team. They lost their final four to end 6-4.

It was a strong year for city football featuring Boris "Babe" Dimancheff of Washington, Kenny Smock of Shortridge and Chuck Howard of Tech. When Cathedral played the City Champion Blue Devils, a Shortridge receiver caught a tipped pass to beat the Irish, 6-0.

All-City lineman Herb Seidell went on to play at Purdue before joining the service and later captained the 1950 Fordham team. He would be named All-East.

The versatile Kenny Geiman co-captained the basketball team as a junior to a 8-17 basketball season and third place (a consolidation game win over Central Catholic of South Bend) at the finish of the State Catholic Tournament.

The season opener pounding by Tech (15-37) was Tech's first win over the Irish in five seasons. The most forgettable game, a real humbler, was a 39-34 loss to Noblesville in the Cathedral gym. The Millers had lost thirty-one consecutive games. Just days earlier, Cathedral had upset Manual's City Champions.

Jim Fitzgerald was president of the graduating class which for the first time since its move in 1927, slumped below one hundred in number.

War-consciousness was swelling. Tom Beechem editorialized for neutrality wrote: "If only more writers had the courage . . . the pro-ally grip would be broken . . . . True neutrality means helping neither belligerent. Only in this manner, can the United States remain outside the great catastrophe spreading over Europe."

Beechem was one of many who protested America's inevitable entry into the war. In speaking against U.S. involvement, he upheld the independence of thought and voice that are Cathedral traditions.

In 1940 Cathedral was allowed to compete for the coveted Indianapolis School Board trophy for the first time. On a cold November afternoon Kenny Geiman kicked an extra point to defeat Shortridge, 7-6, and win Cathedral's first recognized City Championship.

1932-1933 (Won 20 Lost 7)

Cathedral	42	Noblesville	19
	47	Elwood	28
	36	Manual	27
	30	Cent. Catholic Fort Wayne	34
	38	Lebanon	37
	25	Greencastle	34
	??	Shortridge	18
	32	Danville	15
	??	Cent. Cath Fort Wayne	35
	28	Brownsburg	23
	16	Delphi	25
	24	Jeffersonville	22
	21	Ben Davis	29
	28	Flora	24
	30	Southport	22
	23	Beech Grove	17
	38	Washington	32
	25	Connersville	31
	28	Huntington Catholic	20
	29	St. Simon's, Washington	20
	34	Cent. Catholic, Ft. Wayne	17
	27	Gibault High, Vincennes	21
	28	Our Lady of Victory Lackawanna NY	10
	42	Credtin High, St. Paul, MN	18
	40	De Paul High School Chicago, IL	19
	31	St. Rita High Chicago IL	10

NATIONAL CATHOLIC CHAMPIONS!

Coach: Joe Dienhart   Captain: Eddie O'Connor

CYO Leaders From Cathedral

Cathedral—and the youth of Indianapolis—owes its gratitude to hundreds of men and women—volunteers all—who devoted time and personal sacrifice to coaching youth sports. A CYO coach himself, Joe Dezelan mined the football fields on weekends to scout talent for Cathedral teams. A stalwart of the CYO program was Rev. Fr. Richard T. Kavanagh who, later served as Cathedral assistant superintendent and superintendent, 1943-56. The contribution of volunteer coaches to CYO athletics is appreciated. Two men who directed CYO stand out, and although both are deceased, they are not forgotten. Bill Sahm, CYO Director, was an ardent follower of his brother, Walt, one of Cathedral's greatest—and tallest—athletes at six feet ten inches. Walt, '61, was Cathedral's first Indiana All-Star and went on to a distinguished career as Notre Dame's center and was, up to that time, its tallest athlete.

Of course the mention of CYO brings to mind Bill "Smiley" Kuntz '46, long-time director for whom the CYO Soccer Field is named, the site of Cathedral's "home" football field from 1949 to 1976.

Big, affable "Kuntzie" was an All-City football guard on the 1945 City Championship team and later a Butler team captain.

Among many outstanding coaches, the accomplishments of John Schmutte deserve recognition. Schmutte, whose sons Frank, Joe, Charley and Sam played football at Cathedral, coached St. Joan of Arc for more than twenty years. Schmutte sent many athletes to Irish teams as his 1934, 1941, 1944, 1945 and 1948 teams won CYO titles. John Schmutte died in 1948.

Football was King when this 1934 team picture was taken.

1932-33 National Catholic Basketball Championship team: (l to r) Jack Sweeney, Jim Carson, Dave Connor, Larry Broderick, Ed Barnhorst, Ed O'Connor, John O'Connor, Dan Royhans, Charley Shipp. Not pictured: Maynard Theobald, Bob Collier and Hugh Baker.

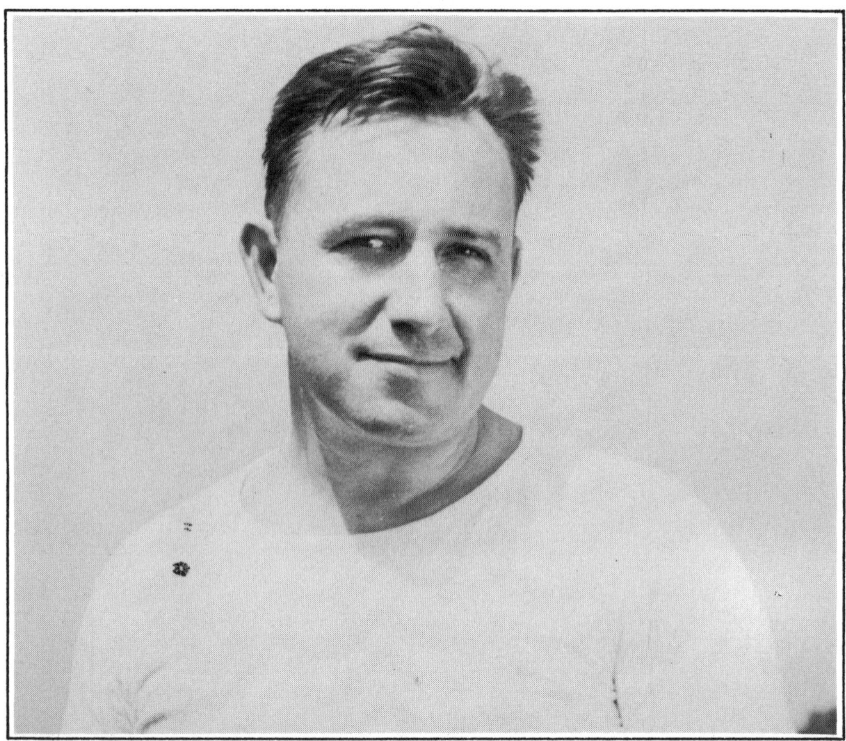

Joe Dienhart

The cast of Clarence dressed up as ladies for the performance in 1932.

Three Fords: John, Class of '32; Brian Class of '93 and John, Jr. Class of '60.

(foreground) Charley Shipp; Back row, John O'Connor, Jim Carson, Bob Collier, Ed Barnhorst, Bill Connor and Hugh Baker with the shining basketball trophy of 1933.

Cathedral High School Football team 1937

Marie Ferris was the devoted and well remembered "mother figure" of Cathedral through four decades.

1940 football team

THE FORTIES

The effort for full recognition was rewarded in August, 1940, when the Indianapolis Board of School Commissioners voted to allow Cathedral to compete for the coveted City Championship football trophy they had been denied for so long.

It will be remembered that after wins over Manual in 1921 and Shortridge in 1922, Cathedral teams were not scheduled by Indianapolis City schools until 1928. Had the Irish been granted official participation, the teams of 1921–22, 1930–31, 1934–35 and perhaps, the undefeated, mythical State Championship team of 1924, might have earned City Championship recognition.

This admission did not reflect bitterness; still the 1940 team, captained by Ott Hurrle, sought respectability. In spite of an embarrassing record (0–49) loss at Evansville Reitz Memorial (Memorial lost only two games in seven years) Cathedral won three of four City games and won the School Board Trophy in its first year of competition with a grand assist from Shortridge.

A big Tech team, led by Frank Budenbaum and Frank "Hoot" Meyer, defeated the Irish, 6–0. A victory over Manual and a 7–6 victory over Shortridge, gave Joe Harmon's team a mathematical chance. Tech, a two-touchdown favorite over Shortridge, was upset 20–0 and Cathedral defeated Washington, 13–0, to win the trophy.

After the Cathedral teamed had received a call at the Irish locker room that Shortridge had upset Tech, pandemonium broke out. Coach Harmon stopped the celebrating to offer a prayer for the Blue Devils and Coach Bob Nipper to have a joyous Thanksgiving.

Seven years later another Irish team would upset Washington, giving Shortridge a City Championship to return the favor.

Hurrle and Tom Broden, Kenny Geiman, Jim Dilger and John Sage were All-City and big Ott was All-State. After service in World War II, Hurrle captained the 1947 Butler team and was named Collegiate All-State center over Notre Dame's George Strohmeyer, a first-team All-American.

Veteran Indianapolis radio announcer Joe Pickett ("Piggott") '41, a rangy member of the squad, recalls Coach Harmon's giving the team a pregame Rockne-style pep talk.

"It scared the hell out of me. He was on a tirade—a lot of go-go stuff at the top of his lungs."

The official championship gained the attention of IHSAA Commissioner Arthur L. Trester, who attended the victory banquet. And at the banquet, handsome Otis Bryant, one of the most popular seniors, received a small block "C" as a running back with the champions. Thus, he became the school's first African-American letter winner. Two years later the powerful mogul of Indiana athletics would encourage the Board of Trustees to admit Cathedral and the "Negro" schools to full membership and the opportunity to compete for all varsity championships beginning with basketball.

In 1940–41 Brother Marcian Karsky was principal. He came to Cathedral High School with good credentials, based on his previous experience as principal of a high school out East.

United Parcel advertises: "We operate the tightest ship in the shipping business." This saying could be applied to Marcian's operation.

Even though Marcian was well organized and demanding, the atmosphere was relaxed. Twenty-two Brothers of Holy Cross, with the lay teachers and other staff, joined the principal in doing what schools should do: teach. Brother Lawrence Miller wrote:

> *Among the students there was a spirit that was high on academics: history, music, art, languages. The athletic spirit was there also; we were champs in football.*
>
> *Most of the staff was made up of Brothers, and the relationship with students was excellent. It was excellent in my view at the time because I did not have Brothers as teachers in my high school days.*
>
> *Shortly after the school year got under way, one of the veteran teachers told me, "You are giving too much home–work!" This was good news to my young ears. Brother Majella, my "Techniques of Teaching" teacher, emphasized: "It is easier to let up than tighten up."*
>
> *The students were of a caliber that even a young teacher could learn from them. I learned to understand youth. Some students came to class dirty. One of the first things I learned in Indianapolis was that these same students left home clean an hour earlier. Consider the times—1940—Indianapolis was a city that was still to learn about smoke abatement programs. The janitor would clean the classroom the night before, but I often found myself cleaning my desk top first thing in the morning.*

At prom time the seniors cavorted to the melodies of "Warpy Waterfall and his popular Indiana University orchestra" at the Country Club of Indianapolis. One hundred and two left Cathedral on a warm June Sunday in 1941 and nearly all were to be consumed in the horror that began five months later. Nine would not return to the Indianapolis they loved.

The 1941 fall season was to be the final football camp experience, as World War II restricted travel and Cathedral was admitted into the IHSAA.

Much help was provided over the years to Coach Dienhart by burly Frank Welton, a former All-City star at Manual who opposed John Ford's 1931 Irish team in that memorable Irish 13–6 win.

The late assistant football and basketball coach to Dienhart went on to coach Westville High School in Illinois. In the 1942–43 season Cathedral hosted Welton's Westville basketball team and won, 25–21.

1941–1942

Cathedral's basketball team was underdog to Fort Wayne South Side at Butler Fieldhouse. Led by Leo Barnhorst (he scored twelve points), they upset the Burl Friddle–coached Archers only days after America was ambushed into war. Though world conflict was inevitable, the extent of its tragedy in December of '41 was unknown at that time. That tragedy, of course, would affect the American character forever.

Just before the bombing of Pearl Harbor, in pre–war bliss *The Megaphone* wrote of Glen Gray's Casa Loma orchestra. Cokes were sipped through long straws at the "Harvest Hop," and in the shortening days of peace living was innocent and serene. Cathedral's blue and gold uniformed eighty-four-piece band had high-stepped in white shoes leading the city's Armistice Day parade (with a dozen Academy majorettes).

"Barney" Barnhorst, one of the school's most interesting athletes, had a noteworthy career after his graduation from Cathedral. After WW II he played at Notre Dame and was a member of the 1949 All-Americans playing a series of games pitted against the Harlem Globetrotters on tour throughout the United States and Europe.

He began a five-year career in 1949 in the National Basketball Association, playing with the Chicago Stags (now Bulls). From 1950–53 Leo was a favorite player with the Indianapolis Oympians. He was a two-time member of the NBA All-Star teams in 1952 and 1953 and was elected to the Indiana Basketball Hall of Fame. He concluded his career with Baltimore and Fort Wayne teams, averaging 9.4 points in 344 games. Leo is past president of the Notre Dame Monogram Club.

And then came December 7, 1941, with its inevitable shock, disruption, and patriotic enthusiasm in the school community.

The January, 1942, issue of *The Megaphone* editorialized, calling for tolerance of nationalities whose homelands brought war to America. Cathedral still showed that it knew a little more about tolerance than most. Still, the school began to mobilize.

Good news arrived from the war front. Fr. John Duffey, a member of the Cathedral faculty in 1923–24, had been honored by General Douglas MacArthur for "singularly meritorious action" when he was wounded in the Philippines.

Gasoline and tire rationing began and, as the war rolled along, women's silk stockings, food, candy and sugar were among the curtailed items.

The discordant muffles of conflict were a backdrop to almost all events; ninety-two members of the Class of 1942 accepted diplomas and left into an uncertain world. Nine would pay the full sacrifice.

As the tramp of marching feet echoed across the gravelled yard, Cathedral's new unit of the ROTC marched in answer to the commands of their officers. It was the only time Cathedral boys would train in the Reserve Officers' Training Corps program that had been conducted in public schools since World War I. Under the command of a retired Army lieutenant colonel and assisted by student officers from Shortridge, more than seventy Cathedral lads marched with dummy wooden Springfield rifles.

The pace of war support was heightened during 1942. Scrap metal drives were held on the old tennis court, and the bookstore opened its successful campaign as agent to sell United States Savings Stamps at ten cents each and War Bonds.

Coach Joe Harmon departed to war and twenty-four year-old Milton John Piepul, Notre Dame's 1940 All-American fullback and linebacker, came as coach. Poor vision kept the granite-like, bespectacled, 207-pounder from military service. Though an industrious driver, Piepul led a team that was plagued by injuries, the draft and early enlistments and won three of nine possible games.

> *God of our fathers, known of old,*
> *Lord of our far-flung battle line,*
> *Beneath whose awful hand we hold*
> *Dominion over palm and pine—*
> *Lord God of Hosts, be with us yet,*
> *Lest we forget, lest we forget.*
>   "Recessional"—Kipling

Black-bordered obituary notices appeared. The first reported death was Second Lieutenant Hubert Pryor '36— killed in action somewhere in the Pacific.

1942–1943

Private Thomas Fish '39—Member of the Army Air Corps died in the service of his country near Tucson, Arizona, August, 1942. Before the war would end several sons were to die in the nation's service.

The football team opened with a 26–0 victory over Noblesville, as handsome Jerry Blackwell scored one touchdown and passed for another. On November 17, 1944, PFC Blackwell was killed in action in a German woods.

Al Obergfell was voted the "Ideal Cathedral Man" by his peers at the end of the year in 1942. He attended Notre Dame but left after his freshman year to fight the war in Europe. He returned after the war to finish his degree. When he was in Germany, he stumbled onto a grocery store named Obergfell's, not far from where his father grew up. Surely this experience was happening to other second generation immigrants who had attended Cathedral and suddenly found themselves in the land of their fathers.

The beloved Brother Marcian Karsky, who began at Cathedral in 1924 and was school principal in 1939 until illness forced retirement in 1941, had died in late 1942. Bob Burns '43 said

Brother Marcian "knew the name of every student and he commended or paddled every person with perfect impartiality and always with a smile."

Reflections of 1939–1943
by Larry Connor '43

We entered as lambs and left four years later to a slaughter that took the lives of five classmates and scattered the rest of us all over the world.

We were the Cathedral High School Class of 1943. Among the last survivors of the Age of Innocence, we were a tight little island of Catholics in a world of Protestants. In that time and place sex was the major sin, though missing Mass on Sunday carried the heavier penalty.

Although Cathedral was a haven for the innocent, we didn't realize it then. We thought that life meant little more than books, girls, dances, sports, and trips to the Parkmoor, the TeePee or Al Green's. Our interests were reflected in *The Memo*, the weekly newssheet, and *The Megaphone* that came out whenever the copy and editors could get together.

Even the war seemed distant; fought in places with strange names—Bataan, Corregidor, Monte Cassino, Guadalcanal. It touched us only when we heard that a relative or friend of the family had been killed or wounded.

For those of us who grew up in Cathedral's neighborhood, the school had been our playground, especially during the summer months when the Brothers had returned to Notre Dame. We were allowed to play in the schoolyard as long as we didn't break a window to bring Mr. Kern, the janitor, from his quarters in the northwest corner of the grounds.

We played baseball there, hit tennis balls against the gymnasium wall when we weren't playing handball. We even tried netless tennis on the run-down court that became the resting place for the surplus airplane Brother Bruno lodged there during the war.

As children we assumed the school had been there forever, though it had been open less than ten years. In those days Cathedral athletes Johnny Ford and Charley Shipp and Johnny McMahon had become legendary figures to us, though they were still in their twenties. We read and reread *Captain Johnny Ford*, the fictionalized account of Cathedral's Jack Armstrong that Brother Ernest wrote about the school's star athlete.

On cold winter nights I sat with my parents in the stands in the gym to watch my older brothers, Bill and Bob Connor, play varsity basketball. After the games while waiting for them to come out of the locker room, we took off our shoes, and shot baskets with our stocking caps.

The gym was very special. On some Saturday mornings our grade school basketball team was allowed to practice there; a treat for boys who usually practiced on an outdoor court on baskets without nets.

We sat in the gym when Cathedral boys teamed with St. Agnes girls to produce operettas such as Sigmund Romberg's *The New Moon*. We came out singing "Stout Hearted Men," while the adults hummed "Lover, Come Back to Me" and "Softly as in a Morning Sunrise." Louise Argus and Bill Croker and my cousin, Rita Connor, often had the leading roles. On winter evenings Brother William, the soft-spoken principal, sometimes ate dinner with us at our home in Hampton Court a half block north of the school.

If we didn't know most of the Brothers personally, we knew enough about them from our older brothers and their friends so that they were not totally strange and forbidding when we enrolled as freshmen. Could any of those cassock-clad Brothers have been any more fearsome than Sister Rose Elvire, the diminutive disciplinarian who ruled the seventh and eighth grade boys at Cathedral Grade School in a manner that General Patton would have approved?

For most of our families coming up with the fifty-dollar annual tuition was a real hardship and, indeed, some of our friends went to Shortridge or Tech for that reason. This was the tail end of the Depression when gasoline cost seventeen cents a gallon and streetcar fares were seven cents or four tokens for a quarter. My brother Bill often said that the difference between being rich and poor in those days was having a five-dollar bill. But because none of us ever had much more than a quarter in our pockets, we were unaware of the difficult times our parents faced.

Our tight little world expanded slightly as freshmen. Our new friends continued to be Catholics, though we began to realize that there was a world beyond 14th Street. Most of our activities revolved around the Catholic Church. The kids who attended Tech and Shortridge were distant and mysterious to us. In time we broke free of our ghetto mentality, at least free enough to admire some of the girls at Shortridge and Howe.

At Cathedral we began to learn how other people lived. As we grew older we visited classmates in all parts of Indianapolis. We knew them by their parishes. They didn't live on the North, West, East, or South sides; they lived in Joan of Arc or Lourdes or St. Catherine. While we weren't conscious of it, those parish designations were offering us a demographic picture of the economic, social and even cultural backgrounds of our friends.

Cathedral in those days was something of a melting pot, attracting boys from all over Indianapolis. But the pot had the aroma of Irish stew. The Class of 1943 had a preponderance of Irish. Most of the Slovenian Catholics from the Westside chose Washington High School. Cathedral had very few blacks, though I remember Otis Bryant, an affable kid who took more punishment from a few teammates in football practice than he ever did in a game. Otis made untiring efforts to be liked and accepted. Could any of us imagine the difficulties he faced? Did we even give it a thought?

In those days, twenty years before Vatican II, we had few doubts about our Catholic faith. We would have expected Cathedral to be staffed by Holy Cross Brothers forever.

And what a group they were: there was Brother Marcian, the stern but fair principal; a strong man seldom seen outside his office that was guarded by Marie Ferris.

I can still see Brother Dunston standing on the second-story window sill, threatening to jump because we showed more interest in clowning than in conjugating a verb or appreciating Wordsworth. One of the school's favorites was Brother Pierre. He thought that if we could understand and appreciate and, yes, even memorize Browning's "My Last Duchess" maybe, just maybe, we'd begin to appreciate poetry.

Has anyone since those Cathedral days been addressed as "Mr. A-4" or "Mr. C-5" as we were labeled by seat and row by Brother Cassian? Was there ever a teacher more formidable than Brother Bruno (had he really been a cop?) who taught physics and aeronautics? Anyone who sat in front of his desk faced the threat of a heavy paperweight being dropped on his feet should he be foolish enough to prop them against his desk.

"Costello, up to board," he would bellow at Ed Costello. I can still see Brother Bruno grabbing my cousin Jim Connor for whistling in the hall, booming out, "What do you think you are, boy, steam engine?"

Costello and I sometimes relieved the tedium of memorizing flora and fauna in biology classes by leaving notes or pieces of candy in the recesses of a desk that we shared at different class hours. Biology was taught by shy Brother Christian, who chastised errant students by bringing his right hand out of the muff he fashioned from his cassock and dipping a finger at the miscreant.

Typing classes were fun, perhaps because they were an elective. You knew that if you typed a perfect paper you would be commended by gentle, goateed Brother Bertin, for "hitting a home run." Brother Bertin patrolled the aisles encouraging his charges with little taps on the back. Did any of us ever conquer Brother Paul's Latin or Brother Etienne's French ("Ooey, ooey, monsur")?

Brother Fidelis tried to jam chemical formulas into thick heads, often shouting, "Tousands and tousands of times I've told you!"

What has happened to those selfless servants in the fifty years that have passed? Did many of them leave the order to join the service in World War II? Did Vatican II deplete their ranks? It never seemed to occur to us that the Brothers were religious—that they had joined the Holy Cross Order to serve God and man. In the day-to-day effort to force-feed education into us, they seemed rather more as formidable adversaries than servants of the Lord.

Did they spend much of their free time in their residential quarters wondering if it was all worthwhile, after spending the day dealing with boys more interested in handball than chemistry? In four years at Cathedral I can never recall being in the Brothers' quarters. But I got in there on a recent visit. Only now it is part of the Catholic Center that houses the offices of the Indianapolis Archdiocese.

Many of the Brothers' bedroom cubicles are now counseling rooms for Catholic Charities. When the school was opened in September 1927, a story in *The Indianapolis Star* reported that the quarters consisted of thirty bedrooms; a chapel, community room, living room, dining room, kitchen and pantry, trunk and laundry rooms, plus a suite of bedrooms and a parlor for a housekeeper and assistants.

On that return tour of the school it was difficult to locate the different classrooms and the study hall because the rooms have been sliced into offices. The ancient band room and cafeteria that sat along 14th Street behind the school were gone—probably leveled when an eight-room annex was added to the school in 1952.

The Indiana Catholic Conference occupies space on the lower level where we had our lockers. Desmond Ryan, who heads the conference, says old grads occasionally pop into his office looking for the spot their lockers occupied. Across the hall are spotless restrooms—a contrast to the old shower rooms that once were there. I half expected to hear lockers banging shut.

Up two flights, walking along the hall's terrazzo floors (now carpeted), I had a similar sensation, expecting the class bell to ring out and see a stampede of boys bursting out of the classrooms.

The gym looks much as it did in those glory days of 1942 when the Irish basketball team went something like five and fourteen and even the parents stopped coming to the games by season's end. The floor is still lined for basketball but the baskets are gone. So are the bleachers. The stage is hidden by a frayed maroon curtain; the rigging in the ceiling is gone, and the stage is piled high with unused desks and file cabinets.

Standing in that gym brought back memories of imposing Milt Piepul, who tumbled from his pedestal as an All-American fullback at Notre Dame to coach football and basketball at Cathedral during the dismal seasons of 1942–43. One year was enough for Milt. We thought him a fearsome figure with his thick glasses and deep, guttural voice. An adult figure to us, he couldn't have been half a dozen years older than his players.

Our class was embarrassed to do so poorly in athletics after watching Ott Hurrle lead the Irish gridders to the City Championship in 1940 and Leo Barnhorst star on the outstanding basketball team of 1942. That was avuncular Joe Harmon's last year as coach. The outside wall of the gym that served as the handball court now is blocked by a garage. In our class the handball courts were ruled by short, agile guys like Gene Hindeliter, Tony Rene, Mike Raimondi, George Jennings and Ed Roney.

The old schoolyard is now a parking lot. On most mornings in the early 1940s the only car parked there was a massive LaSalle that brought the McNamara brothers to Cathedral from their farm at Carmel. Very few students owned cars then and gas rationing during the war years kept them idle most of the time.

You could still get a double-dip ice cream cone at Tompkins at 16th and Meridian streets for a nickel or a hamburger at Gay Dan's for a dime. Did a steak sandwich, fries and shake—all for seventy-five cents—ever taste better than those served in Harry and Al's Diner on Illinois Street behind the schoolyard?

Wandering through those halls, I began to wonder what it was that made Cathedral special; why it was able to turn out so many graduates who later achieved success? Surely it wasn't the academic curriculum that demanded so little of its charges. A good memory usually meant good grades.

Still the Brothers must have done something right. The Class of 1943 produced at least four physicians, two optometrists and a chiropractor; lawyers and engineers, actors, artists, authors, editors, and a dozen or more graduates who took over family companies. The Class of 1943 was no different than others of that era.

Perhaps it was the religious training. We were reminded regularly that our roles in life were to serve God and our fellow men; that we were expected to be honest and fair and work hard. As Catholics, we were expected to set good examples; our faith and education were gifts we dare not squander. The charge we were given at school and at home in those days was SACRIFICE. So it is not surprising that business owners felt safe in choosing such men to run their companies.

In those days Catholics lacked the boldness they display today. We were drilled that materialism was evil. Perhaps that's why Cathedral produced so few entrepreneurs. Better to get a steady 8-to-5 job than get out there and chase the almighty dollar. Or could it have been that our parents inadvertently had passed on the uncertainties that lingered from Ku Klux Klan days that as Catholics we were still outsiders in a Protestant world; that we'd better not get too pushy and vocal.

With the shortage of help during the war years, most students were able to find part-time jobs. We ushered in movie theaters and worked in restaurants, drug stores, department stores, bowling alleys, gas stations and hardware stores. Many students were up before dawn delivering *The Star* or hauling fruit and produce to grocery stores from the South Street produce markets.

When we became upperclassmen, we began to pay attention to the girls at St. Agnes, Ladywood, St. John and St. Mary's, as well as those at the public high schools. Those were the days when every girl had to wear bobby sox and saddle shoes and the boys wore corduroy car coats that hung to midthigh. We listened to Glenn Miller and the Dorsey brothers records on 78 rpm discs and stuffed nickels into juke boxes to hear Sinatra sing "I'll Never Smile Again" and "I'll Be Seeing You." We danced— after a fashion—at the proms at the Severin Hotel and Westlake to the music of Louie Lowe and the vocals of Bill Croker.

It was a time to fall in love for the first time. By the time we were seniors the war had intensified. The Allies finally went on the offensive and the songs reflected it: "I Left My Heart at the Stage Door Canteen," "Coming in on a Wing and a Prayer," "I Came Here to Talk for Joe." The movie theaters were showing *Mrs. Miniver, Casablanca,* and *Thirty Seconds Over Tokyo.*

We began smoking Chesterfields and drinking Calvert's and ginger and CC and Seven when we could get it. We spent a lot of that final year discussing which service we'd join or whether we'd wait for the draft. Some left early to enlist and others got permission to move on to college after the first semester. It was all so exciting and we were anxious to be part of it.

But we soon learned there was a heavy price to pay. Ed Roney, Jerry Blackwell, Phil Scott, Jim Pritchard, and Phil Carmody were killed in action. The rest of us spent three long years in places far from home. Life was never the same for any of us after 1943. The Age of Innocence had come to a close.

1943–1944

"With hardly time for a word of farewell, without even a party, jam session or innocent blowout on Cokes, nineteen Seniors last month exchanged the ancient halls of CHS for the equally ancient and harrowing halls of higher education," *The Megaphone* reported in March, 1943. The V-12 Naval program allowed seniors to jump-start their education to become Navy officers at Notre Dame, Indiana, Butler, Wabash, St. Joseph's and Purdue.

Patriotic fervor grew as the band played "The Stars and Stripes Forever" and the glee club crooned "When the Lights Go on Again" and "America, the Beautiful."

Brotherhood was the national theme, and the 1942 admit–tance of parochial and Negro schools and the Deaf School into the Indiana High School Athletic Association described earlier, cred–ibly recognized all competition.

First Lt. Bob Grothaus '31 was Cathedral's first graduate to earn a high military honor, the Distinguished Flying Cross, during action in North Africa.

The classic film *Casablanca* was released about the time Americans stormed the North African shore and the offensive against the Axis powers of Europe had begun. Publications bannered "Buy War Bonds and Stamps," and Cathedral did so in amounts that earned her the first Minute-Man Treasury Flag presented to a local school.

"In Union There Is Strength" was the theme in a *Megaphone* editorial and the national commitment was epitomized as Felix "Doc" Blanchard and Glenn Davis, "Mr. Inside and Mr. Outside," led West Point to wartime gridiron glory.

Another Irish coach arrived as Piepul moved on to Dartmouth College. Cathedral's new coach was John "J.D." Janzaruk, a former star end at Indiana University. Shortages continued, and the 4–4–1 season was cut short because of scarcity of gasoline. Cathedral and Washington played each other twice, with the Irish winning both games. On the opening play of the season, Captain John Grande broke his wrist, but returned to play later in the season. The football rivalry with Broad Ripple began.

The glee club boomed "Oklahoma" along with patriotic and armed forces songs as patriotism swelled. Twenty-seven seniors were missing when the Class of 1944 graduated on May 21, fifteen days before D-Day and the invasion of fortress Europe.

For the first time Cathedral published a yearbook. *The Cathedran* debuted in a brown, hard cover edition during the summer. It contained 149 pages; editor-in-chief was senior Tom Jordan.

1944–1945

A new school year brought a new coach, one who was to leave his mark as indelibly as any man who ever came up the steps of Cathedral High School.

The move to hire the twenty-nine-year-old Joe Dezelan, who had coached Holy Trinity's championship CYO team, was not met with universal enthusiasm. He was the fourth football coach the Class of 1945 had to experience, and several questioned the administration's decision. "After all," Jack Baker '45 recalled, "we had had two Notre Damers and an IU man and Dezelan hadn't even graduated from Butler."

Dezelan sensed the unrest. "The first week of practice I was going to call a team meeting before the Shelbyville opener," Joe said. He even informed Fr. Thomas Finneran that he was bringing the issue to a head. "Look, if you guys don't want me, I'll leave. We have to be in this together, but you will practice the way I want," he told the team. They listened; eventually they came around.

"I had no contract, no teaching license and a bunch of unsure players," Joe recalled. "If we had lost the Shelbyville game, it was back to the bowling alley for me."

In addition to Baker, two others who would figure in the school's future—Bob Welch and Bob Collins—were on the team. "Bob Collins was my lawyer," Dezelan chuckled.

Shelbyville was defeated 19–0 at Victory Field, now the Indianapolis Indians baseball park. And win they did over Sacred Heart, Southport, Noblesville, Broad Ripple, Tech and Shortridge: Cathedral's longest win streak since 1938–39. It ended, surpris–ingly, at Manual, 0–14. But the Irish still could win the City Championship by defeating Joe's alma mater, Washington, the next week at Shortridge Field, rented as Cathedral's home field. The Irish missed several opportunities and lost, 6–0, to Joe's former coach, the legendary Henry Bogue. Dezelan's teams won 182 and lost sixty, "but none was harder than the Washington game," Dezelan recalled.

American and Allied troops were inching towards Berlin and confidence was building as Cathedral's delightful Season's Sing brought happiness as one of the school's most successful student productions.

On December 19, 1944, Indianapolis rejoiced as Bishop Joseph E. Ritter was elevated Archbishop of the new Metropolitan Province of Indianapolis. The newly-decorated Cathedral gym was the setting for the civic celebration attended by Governor Henry F. Schricker and Indianapolis Mayor Robert H. Tyndall. The Cathedral family basked in reflected glory; Archbishop Ritter had been a close friend of the high school from its inception.

With a new Archbishop and a new football coach, the world seemed warmer as Jodie Baltz and Jimmy Dicks sang with the swingin' Cathedral orchestra led by Jim Traub.

Some claim Joe Dezelan read a handbook on basketball coaching while directing the Irish varsity to a record of 8–11 including a 30–26 win over Washington. Captain Paul Murray left for service in the Navy. "I think it was our Navy," Dezelan now laughs.

Sprucing up Cathedral

After six years, Fr. Finneran was assigned to a parish and Father Richard Kavanagh became Cathedral's third superintendent February 12, 1944.

During the summer of 1944, Coach Janzaruk resigned to coach at New Castle and young Joe Dezelan began his long career as a three-sport coach.

The gravel-covered school yard, seldom used by student automobiles, was paved with asphalt, and suddenly students noticed the structure on the northwest corner of the lot. It was home to Leo Kern, a school custodian who, during one cold Christmas, forgot to turn on the coal-fed boilers that heated the building, and disappeared.

His old hang-out looking like a mysterious edifice out of "Psycho" was an old home, origin unknown. At one period it served as a classroom for Brother Albert's mechanical drawing students and later was home to *The Cathedran* staff. It was razed in the 1950s. Possibly today it is best recalled as the place where Cathedral Grade School parked its bus.

Kern's inaction, as a matter of fact, caused Superintendent Monsignor Richard Kavanagh to decide to replace the boilers with gas heaters provided by the Indianapolis Power & Light Company. IPALCO set a high rate on its installation and heating bills until Brother Bruno intervened. Perhaps it was the bull-like appearance of the legendary Cathedral teacher, an authority on aero-dynamics, algebra, geometry and other sciences, that steered IPALCO officials into a reduced financial package. "Big Butch" as Dezelan affectionately referred to Brother Bruno, "dazzled them with his knowledge and intimidated them into an adjusted financial agreement."

Dezelan was particularly impressed when the gymnasium was painted, presumably for his debut as basketball coach.

"That's not for your team," athletic director Brother Giles intoned. "It's for the celebration honoring the establishment of the Archdiocese" and the elevation of Joseph E. Ritter on December 19, 1944.

The war in Europe ended in May. The anticipation of victory spurred bond and stamp sales to an average of thirty-one dollars per student, the highest percentage in Indiana. Money from the 1945 year sale alone had purchased a B-25 Mitchell bomber (125,000 dollars), a F6F Navy Hellcat-fighter(92,000 dollars) and an artillery Weasel (4,815 dollars).

Three months later the Enola Gay led a formation of bombers on an atomic bomb mission that brought about the end of the war with Japan. Victory was declared in August and at Cathedral—and music switched to the happier "On the Atchison Topeka and the Santa Fe" and the Academy Award-winning song of 1945, "It Might As Well be Spring." The new version of the wartime hit had warmer lyrics. "The lights went on again, all over the world."

1945–1946

Postwar America was a wonderful, giddy place. A new gadget named television appeared, and new politicians and entertainers emerged who molded themselves to this new phenomena. Suddenly, we had gone from shortage to indulgence. Cathedral boys, who would have been marshaled for the conquest of Japan, rejoiced. It was a time for winning the peace and accommodating returning servicemen.

President Truman promised over two and a half million new houses by 1948, and the most significant act of social change was legislated: the G.I. Bill of Rights, which meant that more Americans than ever could now attend college.

And Cathedral herself was livelier as a new personality came to campus, the irrepressible Cleon "Goofy" Reynolds. For the first time Cathedral would have two full-time, paid varsity team coaches. Reynold's colorful style complemented the strident coaching techniques of Joe Dezelan. Perfectly suited in temperament and talent, they would rebuild Cathedral's war-damaged varsity won-lost records.

Perhaps the greatest passing and receiving team in Cathedral's rich history were 1945 All-Staters halfback Jimmy McLinn and end John Joseph "Jekie" McHugh. But beyond their athletic skills, the tricks they inflicted on coaches Reynolds, Dezelan and others are still recalled with amusement and some exaggeration. Exploits such as tieing up "Goofy" and placing him, upturned in a trash barrel, of water pistol fights in the school halls, of pushing Dezelan's cherished automobile to a used car lot and placing a "for sale" sign on the hood have become apocryphal.

Reynolds, a member of Butler's national basketball championship team in 1929, accepted and returned pranks in-kind with many of the six hundred or more students. He placed twenty-five cent bets on college football games before he would sell ten-cent tickets in the cafeteria line.

Following the success of the 1944 football season, optimism plunged, after the Irish absorbed a 0–26 thrashing at Evansville Memorial. The Irish would go on to win eight consecutive games and the City Championship. The most historic happening of all, however, was the beginning of athletic competition with nearby Crispus Attucks.

Friends from the first grade at St. Patrick's, the brother-like McLinn and McHugh reflected on memories of a grand, frivolous time, one that resulted in a laughable paddling incident for McLinn from principal Brother Benedict. "Old 'Indian Joe' cracked me so hard the paddle broke," McLinn laughed. "You know, Cathedral never cared who you were. It was a great lesson."

Led by captain Jimmy Doyle, the Irish basketball team adapted slowly to Reynolds' disciplined offense which contrasted with the flamboyancy of the coach's persona. "No one–hand shots, no hook shots; pick, pick, pick was his philosophy," Jekie HcHugh recalled. In a Sectional game win over Southport, the right-handed McLinn arched a left-handed hook shot from the corner baseline. As the shot was launched, Reynolds jumped to his feet and screamed "McLINN!!!" As the ball ripped through the cords, his ire melted and the coach intoned, "Good shot."

It was Cathedral's first taste of heady tournament wine (in 1944, the team had won two Sectional games) and a 25–26 stall offense loss to Tech in the Sectional Championship game ended a 14–10 season.

Except for the Sectional defeat, the Irish would have swept City championships that season. Doyle went on to star for Butler in basketball and baseball and was an All-America shortstop, invited to play in a national series for high school baseball stars in New York City.

1946–1947

As in the year before, football opened with disappointment (Cincinnati Elder) and ended with eight straight victories and a City Championship. The title at first was shared with Tech and then awarded to Cathedral, due to a Tech player's ineligibility. Shortridge returned to the schedule after a one-season interruption caused by school pranksters, and would remain our strongest rival (according to alumni ratings) until it closed after the 1980 football meeting. The Shortridge series began in 1922 and ended in Shortridge's final year of football—1980. Against the Blue Devils CHS won its most games against an opponent, thirty-three, and suffered its most losses, nineteen.

Tech severed football competition with Cathedral in 1946, but returned for three seasons only to drop the Irish again from 1950 through 1958. Joe Dezelan explained it this way: "Tech's athletic director didn't like us and played us in basketball at their place only because they would win. He had the backing of the Tech principal in this."

To move into the future a little, the only meeting during eight seasons was by draw, when the 1952 City Football Jamboree matched the rivals. During the Jamborees format, schools were placed on North and South "teams." Location of the football after one quarter had expired was inherited at the point of placement.

"Tech took the ball from Howe on our two-yard line and, four plays later, we stopped them on the twenty," Dezelan proudly recalled.

Some credit for the ease in handling Tech goes to former Washington coach Henry Bogue (1927–1951) who helped his former player's team.

"Pappy had an old eight millimeter-movie camera film of his last game against Tech. We took twelve defensive players to his home on Rockville Road and he had his living room set up like a movie theatre. From that film we knew every Tech move. Coach Bogue also gave us tips on playing Evansville Reitz, which was our biggest swin (18–13) to earn state recognition," Dezelan recalled.

The 1952 Irish team (acclaimed mythical State champions) went on to score fourteen points in the twelve-minute quarter assigned to each team in the Jamboree. Pressure from newspaper sports columnists forced Tech officials to schedule the Irish in 1959, and Cathedral won twelve of the next thirteen games, with a tie game in 1968, the only blemish in a 9–0–1 season.

But in 1946 nine Irish were named All-City and three—Rudy Bayt, Bill O'Laughlin and sturdy Flavian "Skeets" Weidekamp—were All-State selections.

Student production's offering was the *Band Fanfare, An American Rhapsody*. The Lenten Mission Crusade and clubs occupied extracurricular hours. The "Reynoldsmen," as *The Cathedran* called them, won a Holiday basketball tournament.

Competition with Crispus Attucks in basketball began (a 45–41 Irish win) and, in the Sectional at Butler Fieldhouse Irish Captain Paul "Duke" O'Connell hit a two-handed set shot to defeat Tech, the first win over the Greenclads since the 1938–39 season.

A new sport—bowling—came to Cathedral this year, with the influence of Joe Dezelan rumored to be a factor. The intramural bowling teams rolled at Dezelan's Bowling Alley, Holmes Avenue and West l0th Street.

Bill Worcester '48 drove to Cathedral in a flashy 1923 Model "T" Roadster. When it was driven into the school gymnasium during pre-game pep rallies, the "Cannon-Ball" created roaring response and Cathedral didn't lose after the excitement.

It was a grand time to be young.

1947–1948

Cathedral's gym was the scene of another civic celebration October 11, 1947, the day following installation of the Very Rev. Paul C. Schulte as Archbishop of Indianapolis replacing the departing Elmer Ritter. One of Cathedral's strong supporters since her opening, Ritter was transferred to St. Louis where he would become Cardinal.

Bob Hope serenaded Jane Russell with the Academy Award-winning song "Buttons 'n Bows," and in 1947 Brother Regis became principal. *The Cathedran* was dedicated to Marie Ferris for her eleven years of service. Former Irish football Coach Alfred G. Feeney was mayor of Indianapolis and Joe Dezelan's team lost their opening game to Crispus Attucks to start a disappointing 4–5 season. It was Joe's first losing season, one of only three in twenty-six. Cathedral's upset win over Washington gave the City Championship to Shortridge, a repayment to the Blue Devils for defeating Tech in 1940, a win which gave Cathedral a recognized City title.

It was the age of innocent dances. Coke–sipping Cathedral boys and academy girls with corsages pinned in their hair shuffled through the Grand March at the Harvest Hop, the Easter Ball and other dances under the traditional canopy festooned with blue and gold crepe paper. "It was big time," Senior Class President Jack Bradshaw noted. Mrs. Ferris carefully inspected corsage boxes—hiding places for forbidden refreshments.

The City Basketball Tournament restarted and, for the first time, Cathedral was invited to participate. Cleon's stalwarts won fourteen of twenty-one basketball games. In one of the season's more memorable moments, the incomparable Coach Reynolds propelled himself off the bench to object to Referee Roland Baker's call. "So excited was he," *The Indianapolis News* sports writer Wayne Fuson wrote, "his dentures came flying out of his mouth. In one quick reaction Cleon caught his flying teeth, put them back in his mouth and, without interruption, continued his harangue."

It was again a time of peace but old men were beginning to argue once again and, soon, in a place called Korea, American servicemen, including eleven from Cathedral, would make the final sacrifice.

1948–1949

In 1948 an orchestrated promotional campaign of Eden Abbey, a conspicuous ascetic, rocketed the poetic song "Nature Boy" to Number One on the Hit Parade. And Cathedral found its own version of a real nature boy in the gladiator-like George Eng–land, fullback extraordinaire. A bruising battering ram, England scored fourteen consecutive Cathedral touchdowns, as the Irish won six of nine games and lost in the City Championship game to Broad Ripple.

Led by captain Mike Radkovic, among the last who fired the two-hand set shot, the basketball Irish won sixteen of twenty-two games including wins over Martinsville and Greencastle to win the Artesian's Invitational Tournament.

There was no yearbook in 1949. As nearly as can be recalled, *The Cathedran* had lost money in the previous years, and the students were given a sort of ultimatum early in the 1948–49 school year that there would be no yearbook unless they supported it financially *before* it went to press. How much money they were to raise in advance isn't known, but it wasn't raised, and so principal Brother Regis and advisor Brother Etienne decreed there would be no yearbook. And there wasn't. There was a "COMMENCEMENT ISSUE" of *The Megaphone* which contained the pictures of all the graduates.

"They were a rotten class," Bob Brown '50 laughed. "There are varying reasons but, according to John Knoerle '49, we didn't get enough advertising."

One of the features begun at Cathedral in the early fifties was the introduction of "Open House," usually the third week of October. The idea was to invite parents for an evening in which the school's daily schedule was telescoped into periods of ten minutes each. The parents followed the same schedule their sons followed during the school day, going from room to room and listening to a brief presentation by each teacher of the goals and means to those goals (as well as problems and road blocks, and so on).

OPEN HOUSE THROUGH THE YEARS

Open House has had several forms. In the forties it was initiated as a parent-teacher interaction to inform the people who paid the tuition, and cared a lot about what Cathedral had to offer their students.

The program gained increasing acceptance from the parents. In October of 1956 a record 519 parents attended, and it grew to 625 parents in 1957 and 750 in 1958. The number 750 was very close to the number of students in school. If anything, characteristic of Cathedral in the fifties the faculty and parents enjoyed nearly one hundred percent cooperation in the interest of the students.

"I doubt it would be possible today to do what we did back in the fifties," Brother Pedro commented. "As is said so often, life was simpler then. And it really was."

(Other forms of Open House include the very successful form initiated during the eighties, a highly organized "hands-on" visit with students, faculty, and actual learning experiences, which was one direct cause of the phenomenal enrollment growth during the early nineties.)

Another long-awaited Cathedral wish became reality in 1949 when CYO Athletic Field was dedicated and Cathedral football would have its first "home" field. The teams played there for twenty-eight seasons. On September 12 a football double-header matched the Irish and Westfield, followed by Sacred Heart Central vs Plainfield Charlton. The dream of a stadium was launched by Archbishop Joseph Ritter at a banquet honoring the 1945 City Champions, and a committee of fifty was formed. Banker Frank E. McKinney, Sr. was asked to raise two hundred thousand dollars. The group selected 13.6 acres on West 16th Street. After Ritter departed for St. Louis, the new Archbishop, Paul C. Schulte, was equally enthusiastic about the stadium project.

The stadium committee overcame zoning problems and trimmed seating capacity to five thousand. Proudly participating in the dedication ceremony was silver-haired Al Feeney, mayor of Indianapolis and coach of powerful Irish teams from 1920–22. During the next twenty-seven years, Cathedral teams would win more than eighty percent of their games played at CYO, beginning with the opening win, 14–0 over Westfield.

To Irish halfback Gene Mangin went the honor of scoring the first touchdown at CYO, on a nine-yard first quarter sweep.

Fr. Bill Munshower, the 1950 class president said, "By today's standards we were a tame generation and our big action was a cheeseburger at the TeePee or a tenderloin at Al Green's."

The present-day chaplain of the Cathedral Board went on to recall that these were the days building to civil rights unrest, and a somewhat unpopular confused "police action" involving Americans in Korea.

"I recall Evelyn Thompson, a black coed at St. Mary's (Academy) She endured embarrassment one night at Al Green's drive-in. A bunch of us went there after a school play rehearsal. We were refused service because, the manager said 'we don't serve coloreds here.' We all left."

Evelyn went on to become Sister Francesca Thompson in the Franciscan Order. She has had a distinguished career in national and international minority issues, including apartheid. Evelyn Thompson's mother, Sadie, was a Republican party leader in the Indiana Avenue area.

Appeals Court Judge Pat Sullivan '50, reflected a feeling many entering students experienced about the continuing "melting pot" affect Cathedral had. "When I first enrolled, I was somewhat fearful that the guys from Haughville, the Eastside or Irish Hill might make things a little rough for a freshman from the stuck-up Northside. Wrong again, Sullivan. I found that lasting friendships were easily formed.

"I also found it was okay to study hard and get good grades without being thought of as a wimp. I am proud that Cathedral represents the finest in private Indiana education."

Dean Cuningham (later to play at Michigan State) captained a 7–16 Irish team that bowed to Sectional Champion Broad Ripple in the afternoon semi-final. A budding sophomore who starred in two Sectional basketball victories, was Bob Springer, future Washington High School basketball coach.

1949–1950

During the ever-changing 1950s, Americans quickly accepted new heroes. A Baptist minister, Martin Luther King Jr., helped organize a bus boycott in Montgomery, Ala. and emerged as spokesman of the burgeoning black civil rights movement. Hoosier actor James Dean stirred our national conscience in *Rebel Without a Cause* and became a symbol of his generation.

Dwight Eisenhower replaced cantankerous Harry Truman in the White House and Bobby Thompson would shock baseball, and the Dodgers, with a dramatic "shot heard 'round the world" home run in the 1951 playoff game to decide the National League Championship.

It was The Holy Year, and the 1950 Cathedran was dedicated to His Holiness Pope Pius XII, "in recognition of his unceasing efforts to bring the world into lasting peace."

Peace on the football field was the last of Joe Dezelen's goals for Cathedral's football opponents—his 1950–52 teams would win consecutive City Championships, a mythical State title and twenty-seven of twenty-nine games. The Irish lost only to 1950 State Champion Lafayette Jefferson and shut out eight opponents. After losing its 1951 opener to Hammond Noll, Cathedral won nineteen consecutive games. The nine victories in 1950 established a school record which was tied with the 1986 and 1992 State Championship teams' twelve victories each season.

The year 1950 was to see the arrivals of Msgr. James P. Galvin and Brother Eugene Weisenberger and the departure of Cleon Reynolds. Galvin replaced Msgr. Richard T. Kavanagh who had served Cathedral for five years as superintendent.

Irish-faced Msgr. Galvin would direct the school four years and remain a supporter and friend throughout his life. In 1986 he received an honorary degree from Cathedral. "It's hard to evaluate the good things Msgr. Galvin did for Cathedral," John Riddle '51 said. The music of Brother Eugene would entertain and inspire Cathedral for the next twenty-three years until he and the Brothers would leave Cathedral. His precision-stepping bands, numbering two hundred musicians and performers, would earn dozens of musical honors, participate in "500" Festival parades and build wondrous memories from glee clubs to student productions that furthered the school's artistic reputation.

Reynolds, later to be fire chief at the Indianapolis Motor Speedway, would coach the basketball team to a mid–season 6-5 record and turn the team over to his protege' Jimmy Doyle '46, recently graduated from Butler University.

The lovable "Goofy" Reynolds left Cathedral for Shortridge and its pension security. His Irish teams were 73–60, but it was the intangible, good-natured fun that endeared him and for which he is remembered.

At Shortridge, Reynolds produced great teams, yet he could not win a Sectional. Crispus Attucks was the King of Hoosier basketball and proved a continuing nemesis to Shortridge's fortunes in the Sectional.

Doyle's first game as coach was against Shortridge in the Blue Devil gym and the formerly rebuffed Irish won by twenty points. They would win three of nine games in the Sectional semi-final, before they were swamped by Crispus Attucks' first state contender.

Paul Farrell, a member of the Class of 1951 was Cathedral's "Mr. Tennis." He would later write: "In my long association with Cathedral tennis, I would coach more than one-hundred student athletes, including my six nieces. Many of the jobs at Cathedral are performed with volunteers, and that is why so much can be accomplished in the face of unfavorable odds. Cathedral is a family."

The Senior Class president and All-City halfback was Joe Lutz who, as Army major general, would command America's special forces during the eighties. In 1982 General Lutz, wearing his paratrooper beret and shiny jump boots, would receive a Distinguished Chartrand Award for career accomplishments. Lutz in his student days had played the title role in the production *The Fire Prince*. His classmates won't let him forget the comic opera costumes he wore for the production.

Class of 1943

Three members of the Class of '43 were among several who sacrificed for their country in World War II: Corporal Philip J. Carmody (center) met his death December 19, 1944; Jerry Blackwell (right) was also killed in action; John Smith (left) was a German Prisoner of War.

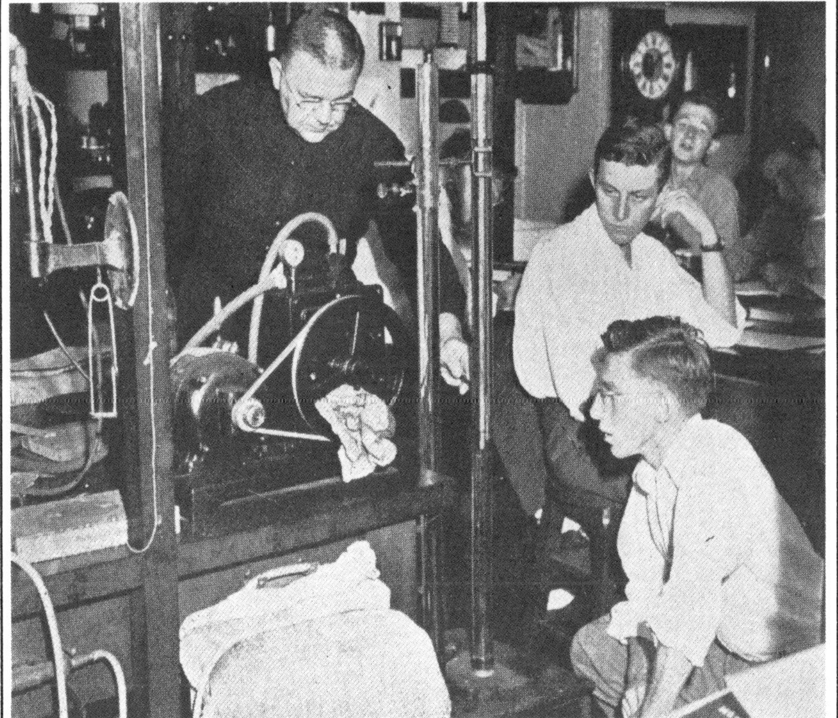

(upper left) Brother Etienne was sponsor of many extra curricular activities like drama as well as teaching French; Brother Marcian was a respected principal of the forties; the unforgettable Brother Bruno demonstrates an experiment in the physics labo for Hagner and McIntosh.

Archbishop Paul. C. Schulte succeeded Archbishop Ritter in 1946.

Father Richard Kavanagh became third superintendent in 1945.

Spring practice 1946, Joe Dezelan.

Study hall was jammed in the forties with people who seem to be doing homework.

Cathedral's greatest passing combo ever: Jeke McHugh and Jim McLinn with team captain Mike Carr, '45.

Football star Bob Welch, not yet a senior, with Coach Janzaruk.

Tony Hinkle was the speaker at the CHS football banquet in 1946. With him are Joe Zore, CHS captain, Rudy Bayt, All-State halfback, and Coach Joe Dezelan.

Academy girls were pretty members of the Mikado's Court in 1948.

A page from the '48 Cathedran shows dapper Cathedral boys and glowing dates, mostly from the Academies.

Bill Worcester's car went everywhere at the end of the forties--even into basketball games. Here it is shown in the parking lot with Brother Bruno's plane as backdrop. (on the back fender) Phil Roney, Bill Dietz,(on the front fender) Charlie Patrick, (back, left) Ed Mackell and Dick McNamara. Willie Worcester is the driver and Charlie Schmutte rides shotgun.

THE FIFTIES

1951–1952

Dwight Eisenhower was winning the White House as the first Republican President in twenty years; Henry Schricker was Indiana's governor again and 3-D movies were the latest fad. Frank Sinatra was making the film *From Here to Eternity*, marking his comeback. *I Love Lucy* began and was to become a television legend, and the 1952 *Cathedran* was dedicated to another legend, Brother Damian. Eight classrooms were added on the west portion of the building and 759 students bulged inside Cathedral's walls.

Repeating the pattern of the years 1945 and 1946, Cathedral would lose its opening football game and then go undefeated with nine consecutive wins. State Champion Hammond Noll defeated Cathedral, 21–0, and began a twelve-game rivalry the Irish would eventually dominate 9–3 in victories. Coach Dezelan doubled as coach of an undefeated reserve team.

On that varsity team were the Mahoney brothers, Tom and Leo. Leo Mahoney would later assist as Irish football coach and become the school's first wrestling coach.

At Cathedral's football banquet, Butler Coach Tony Hinkle and *The Indianapolis News* sportswriter Wayne Fuson praised the 1951 City Champions.

Coach Jim Doyle's 13–6 basketball team played two physical battles with emerging Crispus Attucks only to lose each by three points. One of the city's strongest drivers to the basket, Bob Springer, pushed Coach Ray Crowe's Tigers. "As competitors," Attucks star Hallie Bryant reflected, "the Cathedral team was as tough as we played all season. That Springer was mean and rough," recalled the 1952 Indiana "Mr. Basketball."

In a regular season game against Attucks at Tech, more than six thousand fans jammed into the gymnasium by climbing through bathroom windows to join the sellout crowd. Bruising forwards Springer and Tom Catton formed one of the school's better rebounding tandems. Doyle left coaching at season's end.

Student Council President Jack Miller was given an airport sendoff by Indianapolis Mayor Phil Bayt as Miller headed for New York City as a 1952 representative to the United Nations.

On stage before the student body, Cathedral's "Quiz 'Em On the Air" team defeated Shortridge in the current topics program heard over radio station WIRE with Quizmaster Tom Carnegie. The Cathedral team was composed of Henry Herpel, David Harper, Ray Vurpillat and Don Walz.

In Korea the "Conflict" ended the lives of eleven Cathedral sons, including Norman Clapper, who left his Cathedral class before graduation to join the Marines. Clapper was the youngest Leatherneck killed in the Korean Conflict and was honored at a Marine ceremony at the school in 1991. His portrait hangs in the school today.

1952–1953

Brothers began to take on their family names and there were changes when a record 826 boys were greeted by thirty-seven faculty members. The study hall, library and Brothers' chapel were remodeled, but the most noticeable change was the south addition of eight classrooms, a cafeteria, a freshman locker room, two counseling rooms and a shower room for visiting athletic teams.

The latter addition was saluted by former Lebanon star Dave Richey who recalled, "When you played at Cathedral, you were threatened by the student body, lost the game and took a bus home without a shower. But, as you were about to leave, a Brother got on board, thanked you for losing and gave you an apple."

After two successive football City Championships, Cathedral felt assured of another. And so it occurred; the powerful 9–0 Irish were co-State champions with Richmond, and played only two close games.

Ten veterans led that team to its third straight City title—co-captains Kenny Stroud and Ron Battreall, Ken Mattingly, Bill Schmutte, Jim Gormley, Bob Kirkhoff, Jack Furgason, Don Stuhldreher, quarterback Jake Kiefer and the fleet and strong All-State halfback Dick Roseman. Stroud, Stuhldreher and Battreall all played in the first North-South All-Star football game.

It was one of the school's and city's finest teams. Before seven thousand shirt-sleeved fans in the Evansville Bowl, the Irish passed their toughest test, a 18–13 win over the perennial Pocket City Champions from Reitz High School.

The News sports writer Wayne Fuson counted his bet winnings and partied the night with Coach Dezelan. It was a light, quick team with only two players over two hundred pounds, both

Brother Bruno Klusewitz— "Big Butch"

Of the hundreds of men of the Holy Cross who taught at Cathedral none conjures more memories than Brother Bruno. At every reunion of a class which attended Cathedral during his years of teaching, students from those years tell tales of Brother Bruno.

"Big Butch," as he was affectionately called by Joe Dezelan, was a brilliant mathematician who could curdle blood with a look. To some he was Erich Von Stroheim; to honor students he was Einstein; and to those who cracked that hard surface, he was a friend, counselor and model of self-denial.

The mind-picture is vivid today: the crew-cut, bull-necked linebacker standing outside his classroom door watching the seconds tick off as he held that timepiece connected to a chain under that mountain of cassock cloth.

There were those who believe he enjoyed closing the classroom door on a tardy just seconds late. His commitment to punctuality was another lesson he taught us that carried us through the rest of our lives.

Leo Klusewitz was born in Reading, Pennsylvania. Contrary to rumors he had not played professional football, nor wrestled, nor served as a Chicago cop. He was not a terror in the Ardennes. It only seemed that way.

The respect he earned radiated outside Cathedral. He had a lifetime pass at General Motors' Allison Engineering Division in Speedway as advisor. His knowledge of engineering saved thousands of dollars IPALCO planned to charge when the original coal-burning school boilers were converted. He confronted and dazzled utility officials who, like bewildered freshmen, were awed by his brilliance. He also had a pilot's license. Ignatius "Nish" Dienhart, (Joe's brother) arranged for Butch to have a free rein as a pilot and aeronautics authority at the old Stout Field.

He negotiated from the War Surplus Property Commission a P-47 Thunderbolt Fighter plane for classroom use. During the war the plane served as a reminder that America was at war. Perhaps this symbol in the schoolyard caused the sale of United States Savings Bonds and Stamps on the Cathedral campus, bringing it recognition as the first school in Indianapolis to earn the Minute-Man Treasury Flag which flew from the flagstaff.

Brother Bruno was devout to his God, attending Mass regularly at the Cathedral and counting collections on Sunday along with his friend Brother Damian.

Beyond his exceptional commitment to teaching, Brother Bruno lived a rather solitary life. He was not a mingler. Reading—and learning—consumed his hours. He didn't attend school events

(Continued)

or games. When he did leave the school on a rare social visit, he was dapper in a black Homburg.

Loath to yield his trust to anyone, Brother Bruno was surprised when young Joe Dezelan crept into his confidence. At one time Coach Joe was hopeful Brother Bruno, the teacher, would grade-wink one of his players and was rebuffed. Dezelan never again asked a favor for one of his players, because he knew it would be denied. One student, Mike Mooney '52, tried to ply Brother Bruno with a box of his favorite tobacco chew, Horseshoe. That, too, was in vain. "Big Butch was a 'pussy cat', one of the finest men I knew, and I could say, he was my friend," said Joe Dezelan. As he stood by his door I would ask him, `How ya doin', Butch?' He would answer, `None of your business.' This was our ritual every morning."

The Brothers of the Holy Cross and dedicated lay teachers at Cathedral provided the foundation for educating young lives. And of these brothers, no one ever gave more of himself to his students and Cathedral High School than Brother Bruno.

The young Brothers who came to the school each September held Brother Bruno in awe. They were afraid of him just like the students.

He disdained vacations and spent his summers living alone at Cathedral as a "super." He loved Cathedral and refused requests to transfer. A daily communicant, Brother Bruno was missed at the altar rail two consecutive mornings. There was concern. School secretary Marie Ferris went to his quarters and found him dead, the victim of a heart attack.

Legends are formed in the experience by personal impressions and by the gifts one leaves behind to help others improve their lives. Brother Bruno Klusewitz lies in a quiet setting on the fringe of the campus of Notre Dame, but his memory is evergreen.

sophomores. The line averaged 176 pounds and the backs 162. Cathedral's only other close football game was with Broad Ripple, but the Irish won by six points. In the final season tabulation Cathedral outscored its opponents 205–58.

Professor Ken Stroud of Indiana University Law School, a product of this era, reflected about the fifties: "The memories of the whole school stand out in a way that they do not when others think of their schools. There was just something about the closeness that still has the same effect on me today."

The season was also the debut of Dr. Tom Brady who, as a volunteer physician, tended to Irish athletes until retirement in the fall of 1988. The role of volunteer coaches, trainers, and doctors cannot be over-emphasized at all times, and Brady's devotion highlights their roles.

An outstanding moment of Dr. Tom's career came "when, after five or six years of begging, Coach Mike McGinley allowed me to call one play. It was against Warren Central. Cathedral was on the one-yard line. I called a quarterback draw and it worked."

Dr. Brady was made an honorary graduate of Cathedral in the spring of 1989. In a letter to the author he vividly recalled the speech given by champion wrestler Lance Rhodes on life after graduation, when he praised the value of a humanities education.

Dr. Brady concluded: "There will always be a part of Cathedral in me and there will always be a part of me in Cathedral." His sentiments reflect the view of many.

Boosters Club President Don Stroud predicted one thousand members. Raymond "Pete" Winegard of Rushville succeeded Jimmy Doyle as hardwood coach. Winegard's 1952 first basketball squad was also small, with only two juniors (Bob Early and Dan Meyer) reaching six-foot one. After a 10–11 season, the Mother's Club prepared and served the Irish a banquet. Msgr. Galvin exclaimed: "This is one of the finest meals I've had in attending three years of banquets at Cathedral."

Baseball finished 5–5.

In May Brother Regis ended nine years as religious superior and principal in accordance with the rules of the Congregation of Holy Cross. He had seen the development of the CYO Stadium, the expansion of the school, the creation of the guidance program, the reorganization of the Mothers Club, the Boosters Club, and the Student Council. His grand service was saluted at a farewell banquet.

Senior Class President Kendall Carll led 135 seniors down the front steps, and 121 of the graduates sought higher education as U.S. involvement in the Korean "police action" ended.

Brother Pedro Haering, one of the greatest contributors to Cathedral's life as an institution, arrived in 1953 to begin his years as teacher, administrator, production director and discjockey emcee at the "sock hops." Pedro's phlegmatic yet peripatetically creative mind would leave a lasting impression on Cathedral.

1953–1954

The thought of winning a fourth City Football Title predominated as the school year of 1953 began. Unlike the circumstances of the previous three seasons, this year the Irish were well sized and had experience. An opening win over Anderson stretched the winning streak to nineteen and Crispus Attucks looked towards another victory. The Tigers had not defeated Cathedral in eight meetings. Coach Graham Martin devised a trick pass play and the Irish string ended, 20–18. Shattered, the Irish would lose twice more and finish, 6–3.

One cold morning in January, 1954, Brother Pedro was teaching a geometry class when he was told Archbishop Paul C. Schulte was in the principal's office and awaiting him.

"It was the first time the leader of the Archdiocese had called on me and I was excited to talk to him," Pedro recalled.The messenger said not to hurry and not to dismiss class early.

The imperious-looking Schulte wasted little time saying to Brother Pedro: "I'm thinking of starting a school for boys interested in the priesthood and Cathedral seems like the place it should be located."

"I was pleased with at the suggestion and offered full cooperation," Pedro said. He wondered about the rationale.

"The church has reviewed its practice of taking boys from their homes and wants to take a new approach. This will give students an option to always studying at a seminary," Schulte explained.

The curriculum followed the traditional college preparatory plan: science, mathematics and social sciences with particular emphasis on Greek, Latin and modern languages.

In a week or two the Archbishop sent the Rev. Joseph Brokhage, whom he had named as Latin School director. Now a retired monsignor, Joe Brokhage (as he prefers to be called) arranged a two-year program for the entering freshmen that September 2, 1955.

Father Brokhage, a graduate of Gibault High School in Vincennes, was pastor of St. Leonard's Church in West Terre Haute and had at that time taught at St. Mary-of-the-Woods. He had been a counselor at Cathedral (1948–51) while he served as assistant pastor at St. Joan of Arc and St. Thomas Aquinas parishes.

The first class of twenty-eight Cathedral Latin students, though housed at Cathedral, never actually felt a part of the school.

"Our studies were apart and, even though Cathedral guys were friendly, we didn't do much together," recalled a former student. They shared some classes, notably physical education, but could not try out for sports teams or participate in other extra-curricular activities.

The school was administered by Schulte as its regent with Frs. James Galvin, superintendent of Archdiocesan schools, Bernard Gerdon, Cathedral's superintendent, and Brokhage as its governing board.

With the closing of Holy Rosary grade school on the city's southside in 1952, that campus was converted to the Cathedral Latin School. Its name was changed to Brute (pronounced Brewtay) Latin School, named for Simon Gabriel Brute, the first bishop of the Vincennes (the future Indianapolis) Diocese (1834–1839). The name as might be supposed was unfortunate.

"The inference was bad and subject to joking references," Msgr. Brokhage recalled, "so we picked another name, the Latin School of Indianapolis.

"Enrollment grew from twenty-five to 253, and its high academic standards earned LSI immediate acceptance in the accrediting body the North Central Association.

"Our largest entering class was 103 freshmen and we had varsity basketball and baseball teams," Brokhage recalled with pride. "Several graduates entered the priesthood, one became a religious Brother. We had ties with Cathedral as Brother Edgar taught part-time and Brother George Kovatch and Brother Robert Leamnson were assigned faculty."

Declining interest in the vocations led to the closing of the school in 1974. Msgr. Brokhage fondly reflected, "In my seventeen years at Latin we produced wonderful candidates who now serve the Church. I shall always have grand memories of Cathedral High School."

Msgr. Brokhage retired in 1992 and lives in an apartment near downtown Indianapolis.

Joe Mattingly

Perhaps no one person gave more volunteer time to Cathedral than Joseph "Moose" Mattingly. When affable Joe played at Tech in 1944–45 his teams lost twice to Cathedral but he was respected as an unrelenting opponent.

Mattingly began helping Joe Dezelan in 1954. He assisted with varsity teams and coached champion freshman and reserve teams for more than twenty years.

The success of Cathedral varsity teams has been well documented in the book and in the annals of Indianapolis sports reporting.

Through the years Irish freshman and reserve teams also attained success—a winning percentage of 84% against all comers and, like the varsity, they played most of their games on opponents' fields and floors.

In 1990 Joe Mattingly was honored as an honorary graduate at Commencement, along with Dr. Brady and Father Kelly. Though he never spent a day in a classroom as a Cathedral student, Joe Mattingly of Tech, like Joe Dezelan of Washington, was recognized as a true son.

1954–1955

The terrifying Richmond football team, claimants to state titles and Cathedral's chief challenger in a grid power, opened the 1954 season. Years of frustration were over: two teams which had undefeated seasons and had never met would clash now! The massive Irish line stopped the high-scoring Red Devils as Thomas "Jo-Jo" McGinley scored both touchdowns and the Irish won, 14–7.

The inevitable talk of a State Championship following that game ended the next week as 1954 co-champion Evansville Reitz defeated Cathedral, 19–7. The 7–2 season saw the other co-champion, Lafayette Jefferson, beat the Irish.

The City Championship game against Broad Ripple ranks as one of the great comeback demonstrations. A standing-room-only crowd of 7,500 watched at CYO Stadium as Broad Ripple, aided by four Cathedral fumbles, led 7–0 at halftime. At the half Coach Dezelan was honored by more than one hundred of his former players with a plaque to commemorate his one hundredth game as Irish coach.

While this was taking place on the field, assistant coach Lyn Lynch read the inscription on the plaque to fire up the Irish for a comeback.

On the third play of the third quarter, another Cathedral fumble set up the second Rocket touchdown and a 13–0 lead.

At this point, the late Joseph "Tank" Farrell, the 230-pound All-State center and co-captain (with "Jo-Jo" McGinley) blocked the Ripple PAT effort. Ripple led 13–0.

With a minute left in the third quarter, quarterback Ray "Buzzie" Oyler combined with slippery junior halfback Pete Shuppy on a twenty-eight-yard touchdown pass. Senior guard Tom McFadden booted the extra point.

Then, late in the final quarter, Oyler pulled a great fake that fooled three Ripple tacklers who mangled him, while fullback Jim Fralich exploded for fifty-three yards and the tying touchdown. Again, McFadden was perfect and a Dezelan team had won its sixth title in eleven years. The celebration continued as Dezelan was honored at the K of C Hall.

A slightly unusual sport, one that was gaining adherents nationally, took the spotlight. Cathedral had a spotty record in forming varsity swimming teams but in 1953–54 five students (Bob Bowers, Tom Moynihan, Tom Lord, Tom Moran and Frank McKinney, Jr.) swam with the team of the Indianapolis Athletic Club. In the following year Frank McKinney swam in the Pan-Am games and won the backstroke title.

"Hodge Podge" drew SRO crowds. Brother Etienne assembled talent including the hilarious "Four Aces," perhaps the tallest (six-foot four-inch average) singing quartet ever—topped by basketballers six-foot five-inch Bernie Sergesketter, Bob Early and Dan Meyer and "Swimmer" Tom Lord. *The Megaphone* reported "the harmonious quartet sang 'Honey in the Horn' in a fashion strangely similar to that of the original "Four Aces."

The tall (six-foot two-inch average) basketball team opened Manual's new gymnasium, with Cathedral winning 56-39. Spindly Sergesketter, who had a front tooth knocked out in a victory over Broad Ripple, scored thirty-four points (one shy of Bob Springer's record) in defeating Ben Davis. He also was the tallest band drum major ever at Cathedral.

"Hoosier Hysteria" peaked, and the "Miracle of Milan" unfolded as Bobby Plump's last-second shot plumped through the Butler net. The impossible had happened: Milan 32, Muncie Central 30. The movie *Hoosiers* had been born. Plump's son, Jonathan, later would play varsity basketball at Cathedral.

Brother Pedro directed *The Passion Play.* Dr. David Latz, reflecting on his years, said he regrets turning down the part of Jesus. The thirty-fourth graduating class entered a world at peace.

Senior Tom Finn of that graduating class would be injured a year later as a passenger in a one-car traffic accident and would, tragically, become paraplegic.

He wrote: "Like many young people certain facets of the education available were taken for granted. Especially so in the religion classes, yet it is this fundamental background which has been the 'keystone' to my adult life: it has enabled me to accept the cross God gave me. Faith was also my family's salvation in the period of hardship."

Brother Pedro recalls:

In 1954, athletic director Brother Casper Molchan and I were invited to a meeting of principals and athletic directors to discuss the problem arising from the fact that all Marion County schools were assigned to one (sixteen team) Sectional at Butler Fieldhouse. This amounted to a considerable disproportion since Marion County had ten percent of the high school population in the entire state, yet was represented by only one of sixty-four Sectional Champions. 'Parity' would have provided five or six sectional sites for the Indianapolis area. But we had ambitions for only two—possibly three later on.

I was appointed to a committee to meet with the Indiana High School Athletic Association to discuss the matter.

On the surface we seemed not to get anywhere— however, I am sure we broke some ground, because the Indianapolis area has had four Sectionals, and Cathedral, moved from site to site, is the only school to win a championship at each site: Hinkle, Southport, Ben Davis and Franklin Central.

Oyler was as good at baseball as he was at football, probably more so, as later events proved. He first gained fame three years earlier when he was selected winner of a contest as Indianapolis Indians' batboy. He starred as a Cathedral shortstop and went on to play major league baseball for five seasons. In 1968 he was starting shortstop for the pennant-winning Detroit Tigers and became the first Cathedral graduate to play in a World Series that same year.

The affable Msgr. Galvin left Cathedral after four years as superintendent. He was succeeded by Fr. Bernard Gerdon who would serve two years.

The largest graduating class of one hundred and ninety were granted diplomas, and college scholarships were awarded to thirty-seven, including nine to athletes.

Americans prayed for full recovery for President Eisenhower, stricken by a heart attack, and in Philadelphia, Wilt Chamberlain received his diploma from Overbrook High School.

1955–1956

During the school year the world experienced the end of domestic tranquility. Suddenly, it seemed, a lot of people were mad at a lot of people.

In Montgomery, Alabama, the arrest of Rosa Parks for refusing to yield her seat to a white person triggered a black boycott of the city's bus line. That successful strike triggered civil rights protests throughout the South.

In Europe Hungarians rose against their Soviet oppressors and fell bloodily.

There were 722 students (down 47 due, perhaps, to the opening of Scecina, a new Catholic high school on the East- side.) Those who came found a new handbook prepared by the faculty. Senior Class President Joe Wade would complete his record as class president all four years. He, along with six-foot five-inch Delbert Schoening, would co-captain a 5–5 football team that got off to the worst start in Cathedral history at 0–5. The team won its last five to avoid a losing season. Slick Pete Schuppy and Schoening were All-City.

Wade went on to Notre Dame for a year and later wrote a history of Cathedral. Facts he uncovered are included in this work.

A new football opponent was Ben Davis. The first game went to Cathedral, 19–6, and the winning pattern was repeated for the next four contests.

"The Meg," self-defined little brother to *The Megaphone* appeared. It was initiated by staffer Neil Martin. Brother Eugene's bandsmen won thirty first- and second-place medals, more than any other school, in the City Solo contests, and an Irish orchestra, " The Headliners," played school dances throughout Marion County.

Mel Woods led the Irish basketball team with support from Jim Kervan, Rick Tingle, Jim Noe and Packy Cunningham. In a Sectional semi-final game the Irish led Crispus Attucks but lost, 57–49. The Oscar Robertson-led Tigers were enroute to their second straight State Championship.

A special appearance of the world-famous Salzburg Marionettes was arranged by the Mothers Club on the Cathedral stage. Children from throughout the county saw the three-and-a-half-foot-high dolls perform as characters in selections ranging from "Rumpelstiltskin" to *The Fledermaus.*

In May two years earlier, *The Megaphone* had bannered: "McKinney Pan Am Swim Champ." Sophomore Class President Frank E. McKinney Jr. was in the process of shaving a tenth of a second off his world backstroke record. The sixteen year old would later claim many medals including a bronze, silver and gold medal in two Olympic games. Fr. Gerdon remarked that McKinney was true to the CHS name—"Champions Have Spirit."

In light of his achievements, Cathedral awarded a varsity "C" letter sweater to a non-varsity athletic team performer. At a school assembly senior Frank E. McKinney Jr. was honored by his school for winning a bronze medal at the 1956 Olympic games in Melbourne, Australia in the 100-meter backstroke. Four years later in Rome, "Mickey," as he was known to his classmates, led the American team to a gold medal in the 400-meter medley relay and also won a silver medal in the 100-meter.

In an interview for this book with student Chris Abriani

'91, McKinney said: "When students went to Cathedral as boys, they were all thrown together and had to make it. It didn't matter if you were from the Northside and were a great football player you had to make it on your own. The school spirit was amazing. It was a very close group."

Along with his friend Bob Welch '45, McKinney perished in a tragic airplane accident September 11, 1992.

The seniors went big-time for their Ball at Westlake Country Club. For the sum of eight hundred dollars they contracted Buddy Morrow, a big band disciple of Tommy Dorsey. The Ball was preceded by a reception hosted by Wade and the class officers at the old Antlers Hotel.

Two seniors reflected on this period. Indiana State Representative John Day said, "I learned (at Cathedral) there was life beyond my own neighborhood. I had models of public service . . . who encouraged me and my classmates to strive toward excellence, to exercise self-discipline, and to be well-organized."

Veteran Channel 8 newsman Mike Ahern commented: "Among the things I learned at Cathedral was never to get a burr haircut on the day before the yearbook picture is taken.

"The competition, the daily joshing with fellow students, the discipline, all combined to keep a student's feet squarely on the ground. There was little time for flights of ego at Cathedral. Someone was always there to shoot you down."

In June of 1956, Brother Damian Daele was moved to South Bend after twenty-five years of service to Cathedral (which followed several years of service to the missions in India). A number of farewell parties, receptions, and an open house were given in his honor at the end of the school year.

Brother Damian, a native of LaPorte and of Belgian ancestry, was one of Cathedral's most colorful characters. Most alumni of the period can remember sessions in the biology lab when, with Bunson burners burning, Brother Damian would regale (and replenish) with tales of his days in India. What student of those times could forget the story of Brother being caught in a bathtub with a slithering cobra?

The Brothers were challenging teachers and inspirers. If one wants to truly appreciate the men of the Holy Cross Order who gave their lives to their students, he can visit one of two cemeteries near Notre Dame where they are interred.

Row upon row they lie in peaceful order under the simplest headstones, which identify them only by their Order names, dates of birth and death. If the Brother ever served in a branch of the armed services, that is noted. The cemeteries are located in a country-like setting down a road not far from the Brothers' retirement home at Colombo Hall, near the northern entrance to the campus, off Highway 31.

A newer cemetery is located at Dujarie Center across Highway 31—near the Holy Cross campus, and it, too, is from time to time the scene of sentimental pilgrimages of grateful Cathedral alumni.

Chowder and Marching Society

In the mid-fifties, Jake Kiefer, Joe Qualters '46, and Coach Joe Dezelan concocted the idea of forming a purposeless Cathedral Chowder & Marching Society.

With short notice the members met monthly at the Westside Outing and Social Club, 710 N. Warman Avenue, in the heart of Haughville, for general fellowship and to exaggerate the experiences of their years at Cathedral. Most of the "members" were Cathedral graduates but others, such as Washington football Coach Joe Tofil and Shortridge basketball Coach Cleon ("Goofy") Reynolds and Indiana Central's Angus Nicoson swelled the crowd.

It was during the uncertain time that Scecina was emerging. "The club held Cathedral alumni spirit together," Dezelan recalled. Annually, the group hired a bus to attend a football game at Notre Dame (tickets were plentiful then), Indiana or Purdue.

One of the more memorable events was a charter from the club to attend a Butler football game at Butler Bowl. The members left hours before the kickoff and took a circuitous route to Butler, frequently stopping for refreshments. The usual twenty-minute trip lasted hours and the Cathedral Chowder Club arrived after the kickoff.

1956–1957

Ten new faculty—four priests, six Brothers—opened the school year, including alum Brother Francis Davis '28.

A promotional story on the 1957 *Cathedran* was featured on page one in *The Megaphone*. To remind recalcitrants of the fate of the no-yearbook Class of 1949, National Merit Scholar James Carter '57 wrote: "All financing of the yearbook will be under the dollarly, I mean scholarly, supervision of Brother Just."

Replacing Fr. Bernard W. Gerdon as superintendent was dimple-cheeked, curly-haired, blond Fr. James P. (Jim) Higgins. A Southsider (St. Catherine's parish), Fr. Jim would serve Cathedral through 1964 and would be remembered for his sparkling spirit, for his enchanting Irish humor and for awful-smelling cigars. On the sideline at every Cathedral football game, Fr. Jim would run alongside a breaking Irish back. Though ever the booster, his comments could agitate officials and Coach Dezelan always feared forfeit. "He knew how to chide officials . . . just enough," said Dezelan. His death in late summer of 1993 saddened the Cathedral family.

During his tenure, Fr. Jim, Dezelan, Brother Pedro and Marie Ferris were the embodiment of Cathedral. The school they served, however, was changing, as new Catholic high schools were finally coming into their own in Indianapolis.

Fritz Bloemker crooned to co-eds Mary Anne Glynn and Linda Kurkey in the blythe *Happy Days* production. The days *were* happy. Dwight Eisenhower would stay in the White House and Junior Bob Bayt's dad Phil was the mayor of Indianapolis. In the summer of 1956, Brother Pedro was assigned, as usual, to direct Notre Dame Camp for Boys at Lawton, Michigan—a summer apostolate of the Holy Cross Brothers.

Brother Pedro:

> *We had 125 to 140 boys (ages six to thirteen) for eight weeks (in periods of two weeks each) of fun and games from, roughly mid-June to early August. The camp staff was made up of Brothers from our various schools, always a fair number of them from Cathedral. (After camp was the time for the Brothers' vacations.) Cathedral's assistant Principal, Brother Viator Grzeskowiak had been assigned to teach summer school*

*at St. Edward's High in Cleveland. No one (except
Brother Bruno) was at Cathedral from mid-June to mid-
August. I would make out the master schedule, by hand
(not by computer) and send copies to Brother Viator and
perhaps one or two others for suggestions. By mail or
phone or both, Brother Viator and I tried to work out the
problems and other kinks. Then I would begin to schedule all the students individually, starting with the seniors—and taking about a week for each class. I would
return to Indianapolis around August 10th to work out
any other problems. Usually I would find other problems. This year, for example, there were two Brothers
removed from the faculty and sent elsewhere in late August. and I did not find out until August 28th who
would replace them.*

*Finally, when I did get two other Brothers as
replacements, neither of them taught in the same areas as
those Brothers who had been changed. A lot of flexibility
was demanded of everyone.*

There were joyous times on the football field in that fall of
1956. In one of the most tenaciously-fought games Cathedral ever
played, Dezelan's Irish defeated Scecina, 7–6. On one key play, a
vicious hit by Lee Grimm of Cathedral on Scecina's Dave Poetz
held up the game while physicians attended both injured players.
Impatient and anxious to get the game re-started, Dezelan
shouted to the writhing Grimm, "While you're lying there,
Grimm, do some pushups." Both players were taken to the hospital with traumatic injuries. It was Scecina's first senior football
squad and Coach Bill Sylvester, Cathedral '46, assembled a team
of size and attire that looked collegiate. The Crusaders outweighed the Irish sixteen pounds per man.

The Scecina president, Fr. Harry Hoover, Cathedral '31,
prayed a novena for football victory to launch the Scecina era.
Assisting Sylvester was another Dezelan protégé Bill Kuntz '46.

The game was played October 18, 1956. One sportswriter
described the game as "the finest, most spirited high school football game in Indianapolis in the last decade." Nearly ten thousand
fans filled every seat, including temporary end zone bleachers.

Beyond the game, it was the challenge of the New Irish versus the Old Irish: thirty-eight-year-old Cathedral against emerging Scecina. Many Cathedral graduates and fans had switched their allegiance. It was a "Catholic civil war," *The Times* reported.

After a scoreless first half, the Irish marched sixty-eight yards on the ground in thirteen plays. Jim Crossen scored on a twenty-yard inside reverse run set up by the adept ball-handling of quarterback Phil Long. Dan Gallagher kicked the extra point.

Irish blitzer Dave Scheper sacked Crusader quarterback Dave Oberting six times for sixty-three yards lost. Scecina scored with 2:20 remaining in the game. An aggressive charge by the Irish line caused the Scecina kicker to miss the PAT.

With twelve seconds left and Cathedral at fourth down on its one yard line, the versatile Leo Braun punted out of his end zone and the win established for Cathedral a supremacy over Scecina. In twenty-six games played, Cathedral holds a 20–6 series lead. In 1984, Scecina discontinued the football rivalry.

Perhaps no football game was to have more impact on Cathedral than that one played October 18 at CYO. Shiny Scecina, then in its promotional period, had recruited city-wide in areas including the south and west side grade schools, once considered Irish "territory."

Sons of Cathedral were sending their sons to Scecina, as the Scecina president, coaches and faculty, justifiably as far as they were concerned, felt Cathedral was aging and ripe for takeover. Cathedral's 1953 freshman class was small, heavily depleted by Crusader proselytizing. Scecina had lured freshmen from Holy Trinity, St. Catherine's and other parishes.

Two years earlier, in 1954, the Irish football team had only six sophomore class varsity players. "It was dismal," Coach Dezelan recalled. "I contacted Brother Pedro to call a meeting of sophomores who did not go out for the team. It produced results. Ironically, one of the returnees was Jim Crossen, who scored the touchdown that won the 1956 game, 7–6. The hard-fought win stemmed the tide of defection and Cathedral was saved.

The momentum of the great Scecina win died one week later as the emotionally-spent Irish were upset by Broad Ripple for the City Championship. Perhaps the greatest single-game performance ever played against the Irish was that of Rocket halfback Byron Broome as he scored a record four touchdowns in a 25–6 romp at CYO.

Basketball's new coach, Bill Frohliger '47, began a coaching career that started modestly, a record of 8–13 and a first game upset loss to Wood in the Sectional at Butler Fieldhouse.

"Froggy" played at the Naval Academy and produced fine teams at Cathedral. Frohliger, big and affable, later in his coaching career led Bloomington High School to a State Final appearance.

Hoosier author Ross Lockhart wrote the book *Raintree County*, which was made into a top film, starring twenty-five year old Elizabeth Taylor. At the same time Fr. Bill Munshower '50 was ordained at St. Meinrad's. Fr. Munshower, who was later to serve as pastor at Holy Spirit Catholic Church, had been editor of *The Megaphone* in his senior year.

Fifty-two freshmen and sophomore students attended Cathedral Latin School where a faculty of nine, led by Rector Fr. Joseph Brokhage, prepared them for religious life. It would be another year before CLS teams would be formed to play varsity sports.

1957–1958

In 1957 young, pug-nosed Brother Douglas Roach came to Cathedral to begin a career that would continue until the end of the school's association with the Brothers of Holy Cross. He came to teach journalism and religion and would leave as its last Holy Cross principal.

Now teaching in Tennessee, he wrote of his days through 1973:

> *One of the unique factors was the geographical location of the school. Because it was a downtown school, young men attended from all over the county. I, as well as other faculty members, learned about the four corners of Indianapolis via the student population, who brought a special flavor to the school. Cathedral, being located at 14th and Meridian was never a neighborhood school, unless of course, one considers all of Marion County as a neighbor. When students attended Cathedral they tried to bring a little bit of the atmosphere of their section of the city or respective Catholic parish, but that was not enough. Once the students enrolled, the school took on its own unique features: students from all over the city merging into a school that had a special feature all of its own. We could not be*

referred to as the east, west, north, south school. We were Cathedral and we learned and appreciated the uniqueness of each person and where he lived. Many young men had never met other young men from the different areas of the city. Students at Cathedral made friends with fellow students, who then that took them to different areas of the city and county.

I would be remiss if I did not pay tribute to the faculty people who taught at Cathedral. The faculties were strong each academic year, which in turn had an effect on the students. The religious faculty of the Brothers of Holy Cross continually raised the standards (academic). In '57 Sputnik impacted the educational system in the U.S. and Cathedral aligned itself with the educational pursuits of that event. Cathedral's English, math and science departments were outstanding. As principal I had a difficult time keeping these departments from becoming overcompetitive: a compliment to the faculties of these departments.

Cathedral had great support and backing from parents of the students. Parents were vitally interested in their sons as evidenced by the monthly teacher/parent conferences. The Mothers Club and Dads Club were very active and very supportive of all school activities. On the lighter side, I was always intrigued by the traditions that were passed on from one school year to the next. One was that no one used the main entrance to the school, the one facing Meridian Street. To my recollection there was never a school rule forbidding students from using that entrance. The main entrance, though, was sacred and was a taboo. I do not know how that tradition started. The one exception was graduation. Seniors went out that entrance as graduates and returned via same entrance as alumni. Even today, the building at 14th and Meridian, now The Catholic Center, uses the entrance only in case of emergency.

Cathedral Latin School now had classes for three year students and an enrollment of seventy-five.

Irish football skidded, and a 27–14 win over Sacred Heart in the finale assured a 5–4–1 season. Highlights were victories over Broad Ripple and Scecina. The drain of talent from the Eastside was noticed, and then it passed. After the 1958 season, Dezelan's team would win a record five City titles in six seasons and, from 1959–64, would amass a 53–3–4 record—one of the most successful string of seasons in Indianapolis history.

One of the finest after-dinner speakers Cathedral football players had experienced, Illinois Coach Ray (Nuspickel) Eliot, spoke at the football banquet. It was emceed by Leo Barnhorst '42, Notre Dame All-American and National Basketball Association veteran.

Brother Eugene's excellent band earned a record eight first place ratings awarded to Jim Sullivan, John Gee, Mike Rollins, Gus LeFebre, Ronnie Garvin, Fred Koss and Charles Collet. Rollins was the first Cathedralite to be awarded two first place awards.

The word most frequently used to describe the 1957–58 basketball team was "surprising." With unkempt Jim Berg, jersey shirt untucked, bespectacled Neil Chloupek, four-sport star Leo Braun (who earned a record eleven block "C" letters) Bob Bayt and Tom Schrader, Cathedral won ten of eleven games and a top ten ranking. Scecina shocked them in the Sectional opener, but the team finished, 13–4.

At one game the 1933 National Catholic Champions were honored at halftime on the occasion of their twenty-fifth anniversary. Cathedral high hurdler Dave Shoemaker's :14.9 time reset a twenty-year-old Indianapolis record.

1958–1959

Deservedly, the 1959 *Cathedran* was dedicated to Brother Pedro who was leaving Cathedral after serving the longest term as principal, 1953–59.

A native of Evansville, Pedro Haering would return to be part of the dramatic change and would again serve as principal during the critical days of 1975–79. Now semi-retired at Dujarie Hall, Pedro contributed much to this history. Two other stalwarts from the Congregation—Brother Joseph Walter and Brother Edgar—celebrated Silver Jubilee anniversaries. Thirty-six men of the cloth and five lay coaches—Joe Dezelan, Leo Mahoney, Raymond (Pete) Winegard, Tom O'Brien and Bill Frohliger— coached a total of 715 active young men during this period.

How the Time Flies was an appropriate name of the fall musical and tunes "Once in Love With Amy" and "It's a Big, Wide Wonderful World" ushered patrons out humming into chilly November nights.

Dezelan was honored as recipient of the John Bosco Medal

for outstanding work with Catholic youth. Dick Dullaghan, in the nineties coach of Ben Davis' perennial football champions, starred on the City Championship freshman team, as in the real world "Dear Abby," Pat Boone, and the book *Dr. Zhivago* starred as modern celebrities.

On October 31, 1958, the first internal heart pacemaker was implanted by Dr. Ake Senning in Stockholm, but the big event that week for Cathedral was the big game against invincible Manual at CYO Field.

Manual Coach Noah Ellis assembled perhaps that school's finest football team—one that had averaged forty-point plus wins over nine opponents. Playing one of the state's tougher schedules, Cathedral was co-captained by Tim DeCroes and All-Catholic, All-American center Mike Galbreath, who went on to star at Air Force Academy.

Though the Irish's record was 6–3, many predicted they would continue to dominate Manual. On the opening kickoff Manual recovered an Irish fumble and scored to begin the rout of Cathedral, 35–0, before the largest local crowd in more than twenty years. Dezelan was furious at the poor mental preparation of the team, almost as angry as he was at Manual's Coach Ellis for running up the score. One year later, in retaliation, Cathedral defeated Manual 41–7. "We did it by winning big—as they did to us the year before. It was the only time I allowed my team to run up a score," Dezelan reflected.

The Sweethearts' Ball was attended by two special guests, John Russell and Peter Brown, stars of ABC-TV's *The Lawman.*

Dave Armstrong (winner of the first Father Higgins Scholar-Athlete Trophy) was the only letterman on the varsity basketball team, which was building. Sophomores Walt Sahm, Ron Keller, Mel Blaycock, Garry Donna and Vic Sahm gained experience that would bring winning seasons later on.

City championships were won in tennis, golf and baseball. In 1958, at the urging of sportswriter Jimmie Angelopolous, Cathedral began a wrestling team which would become one of its most successful endeavors.

Coached by Leo Mahoney '52, wrestling was first considered to be a strength-development program to aid the football program.

"I was surprised," recalled Mahoney, "how quickly the kids and the student body took to wrestling."

It wasn't until 1960 that Cathedral had its first Sectional champion, Steve Evan, in the 127-pound Class. Since that day when Evan '61 won the school's first award, Cathedral has dominated Indianapolis high school wrestling.

Former Notre Dame "Four Horseman" Harry Stuhldreher, vice president of United States Steel, praised the football team at its banquet. Stuhldreher, who had coached at Wisconsin, was the uncle of Don Stuhldreher '53, a mainstay on the 1952 State Championship team; and Bill '49.

In his welcome address to students, School President Fr. Jim Higgins intoned: "Anyone who isn't happy to be a part of the Cathedral spirit isn't worthy to be here and shouldn't be here."

An accompanying editorial bannered, "The sports spirit at Cathedral is unbeatable."

The envy of all was the 1929 Hudson automobile of senior Joe Niesse. The 4,200-pound, super-six, town sedan boasted stock-bodied gasser with its 123-inch wheelbase, suicide doors and dual side-mounts. It reminded admirers of the car Chicago gangster Al Capone used. Niesse claimed he had to dig three .45 caliber bullet slugs out of the radiator.

The candidacy of Senator John Kennedy for the presidency stirred a *Megaphone* editorial debate over the specter of Kennedy's religion. Seniors Bill Brower and Jeff Klaiber took opposing positions with Klaiber maintaining prophetically that Kennedy's religion would not hinder him.

The end of the Fabulous Fifties was here and Camelot was about to dawn.

In 1959 one of Cathedral's better cross-country teams finished sixth in the State championship meet. Scrappy John Wirtz (now a teacher and baseball coach at Roncalli) had six points as Cathedral defeated Hammond Tech for the championship of the Pike Invitational. Still building, the team finished 16–6.

"It was always a rush to the bus after school to try and be one of the lucky few who got a ride to the CYO practice field," said Bob Perry '63. "The Orange Demon," the bus that had transported Irish athletes and students for seventeen years was retired. "TOD" was removed from service after the principal, Brother Giles, observed the dual wheels revolve through a hole in the right fender.

Proudly, Cathedral drum major Ray Fox received the Band Recognition Award on behalf of the Irish band. The "Music Man" himself, Meredith Willson, presented the award.

What at first appeared to be a setback to the evolution of tolerance in Indianapolis occurred about this time. In 1958, a group of athletic directors of Indianapolis public high schools met to discuss forming a public high school league such as that which existed from 1920–1939.

Led by Howe's athletic director Sam Kelley, Tech's Charley Dagwell and George Farkas, IPS athletic director, the group announced a plan to form their own sports league. Parochial football teams could continue playing city schools but would not be eligible for their "City Championship." To some it appeared *déjà vu*. In 1940, IPS had opened competition after nineteen years of excluding Cathedral.

Howls of protest were heard and ugly discrimination reared its head. One newspaper, *The Indianapolis Times*, supported the idea of a public league and proposed that the public and parochial "champions" meet in a finale to determine a grand champion, a tradition in many cities, such as Chicago.

The Indianapolis Star editorialized against the plan and the writings of Bob Williams, who had covered Cathedral since 1943, and Sports editor Jep Cadou, Jr. (a Shortridge graduate) prevailed. The behind-the-scenes influence of *The Star* Managing Editor Bob Early '22, also was influential in causing IPS officials to drop the ill-conceived idea. To their credit the athletic directors of Shortridge, Washington and Broad Ripple had not favored the plan.

The Star threatened to present a trophy to the "true" City Champion. Among the reasons for this questionable proposal was that parochial schools held an advantage, as evidenced by their success against public schools because of the Cathedral–inspired feeder system produced by the Catholic Youth Organization. Since 1923, as has been shown, CYO programs were incubators of excellence in athletic competition. The reasoning was spurious. Many boys and girls from CYO went on to play on public school teams, too, and take prominent roles in defeating Cathedral teams, so the system impartially produced seasoned players.

1959–1960

Brother Giles Martin, the man who opened the door to scheduling Crispus Attucks, returned to Cathedral as its principal in 1959 after an absence of sixteen years. He has described "going home:" "I served the congregation at many schools but there was not another place such as Cathedral," he stated from retirement at Columbo Hall. "The spirit of the student body was unmatched. The enthusiasm of the faculty, the participation of the parents; it was just a marvelous place to me."

Another testimonial of the period came from France from Andre P. Verbert '60. An exchange student, Andre wrote: "I was interested in science, and during my year at Cathedral my natural curiosity was stimulated. Here again, I found the importance of responsibility and the willingness to find help in yourself first. When I returned to France, I was different, different forever, and I am still under the influence of my year at Cathedral."

Dr. Verbert today is chairman, Department of Biochemistry, Université des Sciences et Techniques de Lille, Flander-Artois, France.

Dominance in football returned as at the end of the fifties the Irish went 10–0 and won the City Championship. They finished second in state rankings and were the first Irish team to tally double-digit victories. (To date, six Cathedral teams have won ten or more games. The eleven and twelve back-to-back victory seasons of the 1991 and 1992 squads is an all-time record). "Iron Mike" McGinley, a square-jawed, crew-cut, All-State halfback was the star of a balanced team. "Michael," Joe Dezelan recalled, "was as tough a kid as I ever coached. He had the tools and we had the line to spring him."

McGinley would go on to star at Butler and to guide Cathedral as coach and President of the School in key years of its growth. An "Extra" edition of *The Megaphone* proclaimed the 10–0 Irish football team City Champions and boasted "Dezelan's finest." Phil Richart and Fran Brezette co-captained the team ranked Number Two in Indiana in final polls.

Scholarship was heralded as well; George Bifano and Steve Roesinger, later an All-City quarterback, advanced in National Merit Scholarship competition.

Enrollment soared (tuition was sixty dollars with a one hundred-dollar fee for two family members) and the independence of the student was awakening as the Student Council strengthened its Constitution to gain more responsibility in school affairs. The election of John Kennedy stimulated youth to wider participation. It was a time of awareness that the status quo would no longer be accepted.

The Megaphone probably surprised some of its reading community with an editorial: "Is Catholic education really necessary?" It affirmed the importance of what Cathedral was doing, but the question was worth asking.

Dan Cunningham '60 observed in a letter reflecting on those times: "The traditional strength of Cathedral was discipline (whether we are talking about the discipline of church doctrine and/or personal discipline in the form of corporal punishment). CHS did not make excuses for its strong discipline policies."

Still building, the basketball team would finish 16–6 and names like Gary Donna, Sahm (Vic and Walt), Mel Blaylock and Ron Keller were heading for what would be a fine senior season.

Varsity wrestling posted its first winning season and Learmon Blaylock, Dave Carr and Ron Doxsee qualified in the Sectional semifinals.

Life With Father attracted sold-out audiences. Nancy Stipher of St. Agnes was crowned queen of the Sweetheart Ball. Her date was tall, blond, crew-cut Gary Tofil, a junior football and basketball letterman.

Those Academy Girls

From the first football game in 1919 until St. John and St. Mary's academies closed and St. Agnes merged with Ladywood, academy girls were a part of Cathedral life. Were you one of the freshmen who paid five dollars to the seniors for a pass to the non-existent secret tunnel under 14th Street leading to St. Agnes?

"I remember looking out our second floor windows into the Cathedral school yard hoping to spot one of my boy friends," wrote Margie Cutshaw, St. Agnes Class of 1954. "I was dating several guys, including Harry Steffey, who happened to be a Cathedral cheerleader. I always thought I was hot stuff wearing his letter sweater to the Sectional ball games," recalled the mother of five who lives near Kokomo.

"We would gather at the St. Regis Grill on our way to school. Cathedral was a big deal with athletes like Dick Roseman, Ron Battreal, Dave Foley and others," Margie Cutshaw Dezelan wrote.

Mary Margaret Cutshaw was typical of thousands of academy coeds who were smitten with Cathedral boys. Cathedral boys respected and loved the girls who cheered their teams and participated in student stage productions.

And, like more than a thousand others, Margie Cutshaw married a Cathedral boy—Dick Dezelan '53, nephew of Coach Joe.

"It was sport to work on the stage crew. During the day we'd pull ropes or do whatever looked important so that we could peek through the stage curtains and watch the St. Agnes girls work out in gym classes," recalled Sal Punterelli '45. "We always had plenty of volunteers for stage crew."

Those who thought Cathedral boys lacked female contact never watched the happenings across the "38th Parallel" as 14th Street was called. St. Agnes girls were dismissed fifteen minutes earlier than Cathedral boys—a plot conjured by the Sisters of Providence. "Some of us just dawdled around our lockers and stalled for time until Cathedral let out at 3 p.m." remembers Margaret Ann Roesinger Crisp, St. Agnes '58. "Sometimes we'd change out of our blue skirt-white blouse uniforms and then rendezvous near our schools or at the St. Regis Grill at 13th and Pennsylvania.

(Continued)

"Sure, we dated guys from the public high schools, but Cathedral was, to most of us, our school," Crisp said. "Cathedral was so much a part of my life. My uncle, Leo Gallagher, was a star athlete there in the late 1920s. My brother (Steve Roesinger '60) was a star end of a City Championship team."

From the 1920s until St. Agnes closed and moved to the Ladywood campus in 1970, the meeting of St. Agnes and Cathedral students after school was a blending of friends, some from grade school associations. Other familiar gathering places after school were the upstairs at Hook's Drug Store at Illinois and Ohio streets, Gay Dan's at 14th and Illinois, where delicious hot dogs and "green rivers" could be consumed, and when affordable, the Wm. H. Block Co. Tea Room.

It wasn't until the late 1930s that the nuns allowed academy girls to take part in Cathedral student productions and wear blue skirts and block "C" letter sweaters as cheerleaders on the sidelines. Academy girls competed for positions as cheerleaders and drum majorettes, and a highlight of every school dance was an academy girl crooning alongside the Cathedral soloist.

Ladywood girls also were asked to participate in Cathedral activities but "never felt as close to Cathedral because of the driving distance," said Chris Zinser, Ladywood '70. Chris Zinser Lavelle is now Feature Editor or *The Phoenix Gazette.*

Though all-male until 1976, Cathedral never lacked support or companionship from those wonderful "Academy girls."

What We Looked Like to the Rival Side

A former student at Broad Ripple High School recalls her impressions of Cathedral at a football game during the early fifties, more than forty years ago.

The experience wasn't like any other. Cathedral students and fans seemed to literally invade our campus unlike any other rival. Those were daytime games, before we had lights. Sitting on our (Ripple) side of the field I watched with surprise, anger and, I admit, some jealousy, the Cathedral stand.

They were swaying with emotion. It was like a wall of spirit. Their band, cheerleaders, the banners, the music and roar were like a wall. Then their team came onto the field. They seemed so fierce as they pounded each other during warm-ups. I also recall that they all seemed so red-cheeked and healthy-looking. The players huddled, held hands and made the Sign of the Cross. There was something a little scary about the experience. I asked my friend if she thought they were praying against us. It is hard to describe my wonderment at this all-boy's school. We probably had more students and fans but they screamed louder. And the worst memory of it all: they always beat our football teams.

Rivalries with Cathedral were always ultra-intense during the period of renewed athletic play. This same girl from Broad Ripple, Nancy Niblack Baxter (recently teacher of Senior English at Cathedral) had the supreme satisfaction in 1952 of beating the Cathedral team on "Quiz 'Em On the Air." In that year the Broad Ripple team took the Indianapolis championship, and she cherishes a picture of the awards banquet, with a young Bill Shover sitting across the table from her representing *The Star.*

Bob Williams Writes About Cathedral Sports

One of the cornerstones of the Golden Era of high school sports was Cathedral football. Joe Dezelan was Cathedral football coach for most of that period. Cathedral didn't win every game with Dezelan calling the shots from 1944–69. It only seemed that way to most of us.

The Schmuttes and the Hurrles and the Rosemans and the McGinleys took on the state's best in those days. Dezelan still put together one of the Hoosier state's best football records before he retired in 1969. Joe wound up with 182 wins and only sixty losses with twelve City Championships and five unbeaten teams in his pocket. Not bad for a guy who ran the dive play more than Ohio State.

Best high school football game I ever saw? No contest. Cathedral and old rival Tech got together before an overflow crowd of 13,800 at the Indianapolis Indians baseball park in 1962. It was billed as a battle for the City Championship and nobody would ask for a refund.

Cathedral was stopped on Tech's one-yard line with only 2:02 to go in a scoreless tie. Cathedral fullback Bob Romberg was carried off the field with a broken ankle on fourth down. Tech tried to run it out of the end zone but Dan Quigley and Dan Hasbrook made the tackle for a safety. Cathedral went on to win, 2–0.

Mike McGinley coached a 3A state champion in 1986 under the IHSAA tournament format now in its 20th year. Four other Cathedral football teams advanced to the final game in 1973, 1976, 1991 and in 1992 won the 3A title again.

It wouldn't be fair to say Cathedral's clippings have been limited strictly to football. Walt Sahm helped Joe Sexson, Willie Gardner, Hallie Bryant, Oscar Robertson, George McGinnis, the VanArsdale twins, Billy Keller and Louie Dampier pump up the basketball. Frank McKinney Jr. was an Olympic gold medal winning swimmer and nobody will ever surpass Lance Ellis' 4-year unbeaten record in wrestling.

(Bob Williams covered high school sports for The Indianapolis Star from 1943–84. He reported more games of Cathedral teams than any other writer. Now retired from The Star, Bob is the public relations director of the IHSAA.)

Freshmen had important experiences in activities and on sporting teams. Here Father Courtney breakfasts with a freshman team.

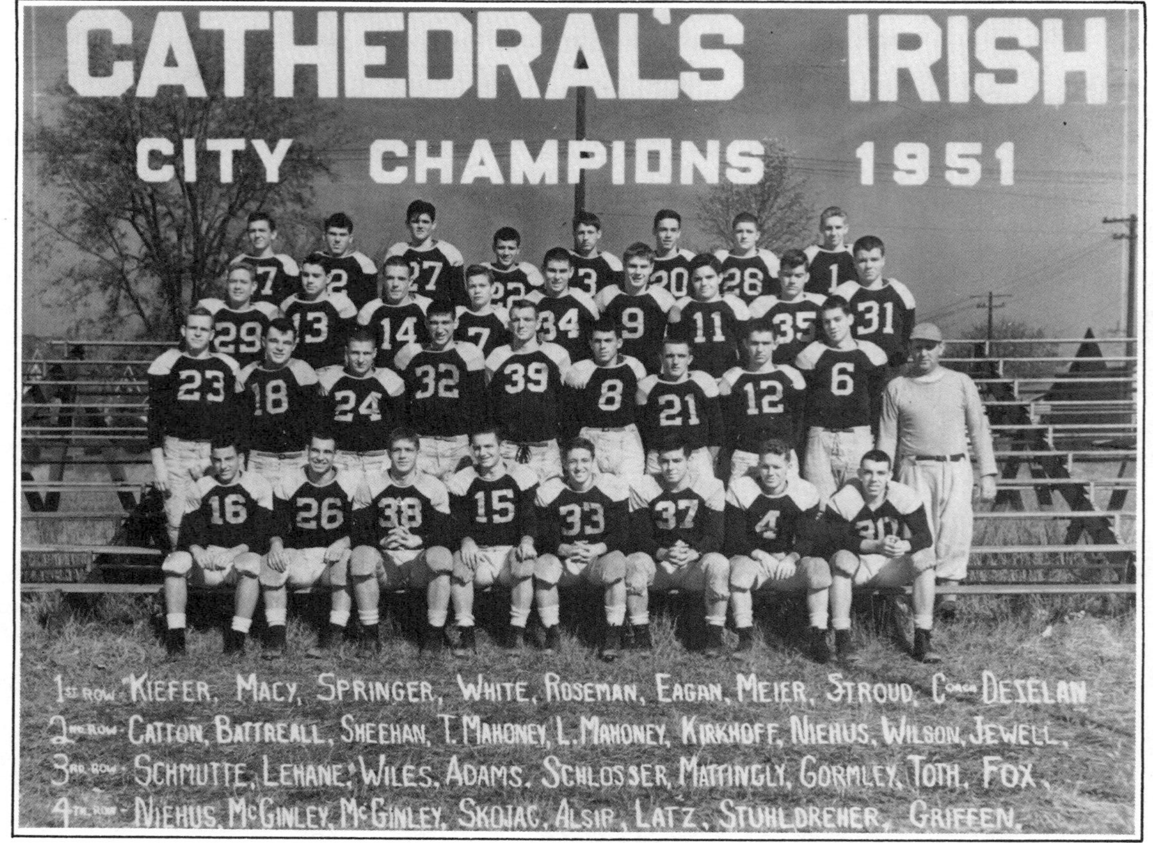

Cathedral's Irish City champions, 1951.

Cleon Reynolds, Bill Shover and Joe Dezelan holding a Chowder and Marching Society blanket.

Perhaps the finest Indianapolis All-City basketball team with Bob Collins (foreground) Cathedral '45, former Indianapolis Star Sports Editor. (l to r) Hallie Bryant, Crispus Attucks; Joe Sexson, Tech; Willie Gardner, Crispus Attucks; Dick Nyers, Manual; and Bob Springer, Cathedral. The occasion was Springer's June 4, 1991 induction into Indiana's High School Football Hall of Fame.

Father Higgins, Fifties swim star Frank McKinney and Brother Pedro.

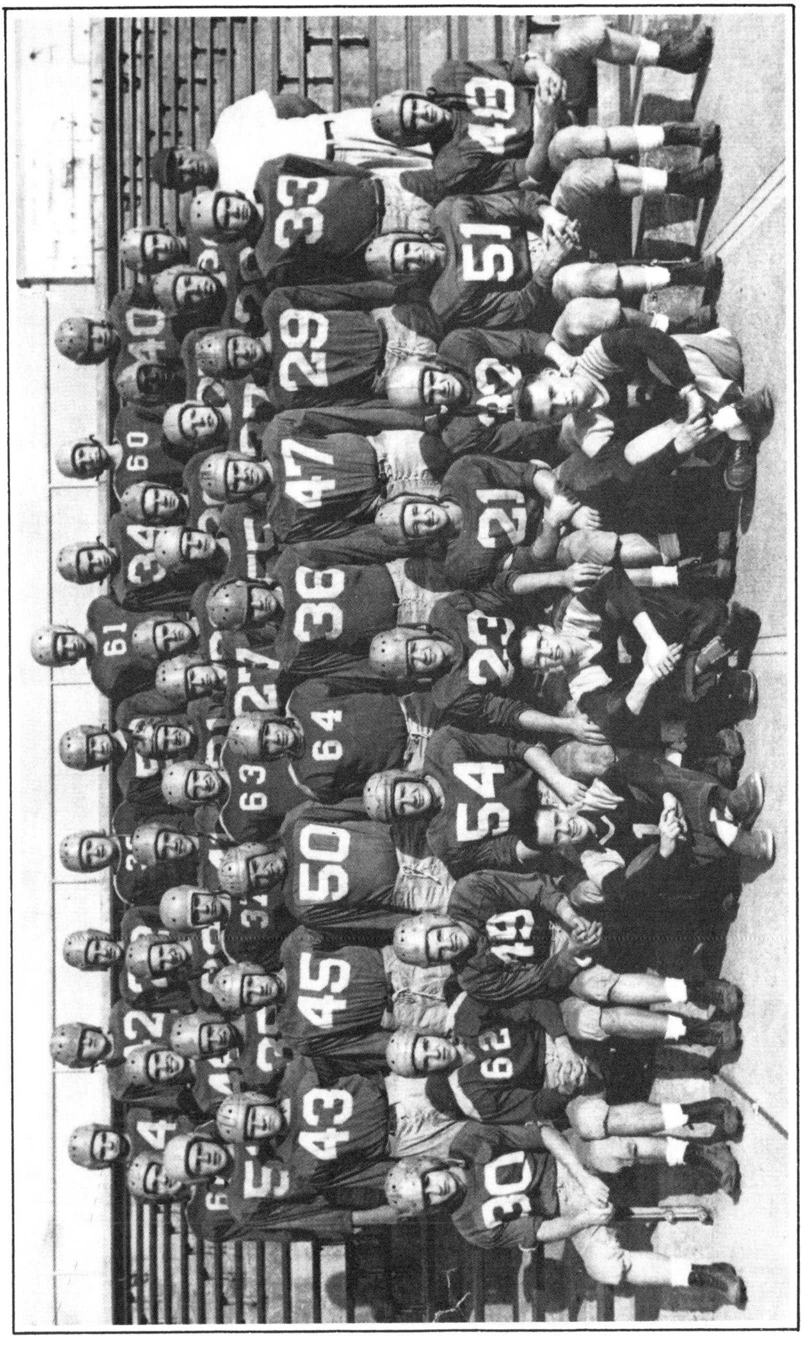

1952 Champions

TOP TEN PERSONS OF DECADE

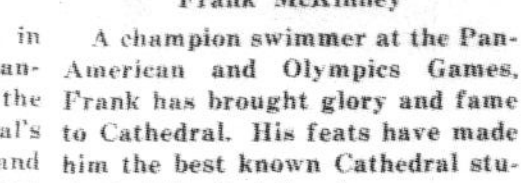

Monsignor James Galvin

Becoming superintendent of Cathedral in 1951, Father served until 1955 when he left to become Superintendent of Archdiocesan Schools. His promotion in rank was due to his capable and efficient administration of Cathedral affairs.

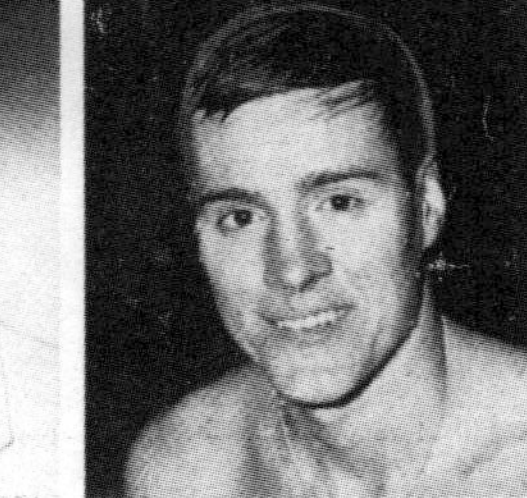

Father James Higgins

Well known and popular, Father became Cathedral's superintendent in 1956. His spirited vitality and energy and his devotion to Cathedral mark him as one of the outstanding personalities of the last decade.

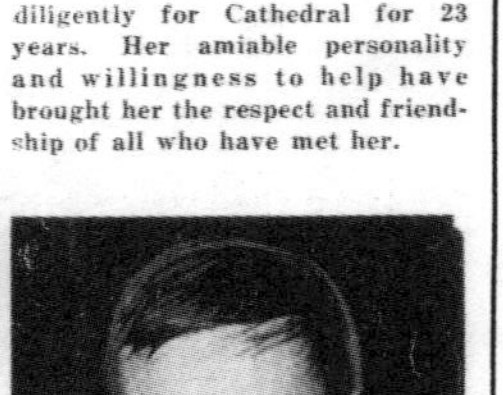

Brother Pedro, C.S.C.

Brother served as principal of Cathedral from 1953 to 1959. Honored and respected, this dedicated man made many profound and lasting changes in Cathedral while he served as its principal.

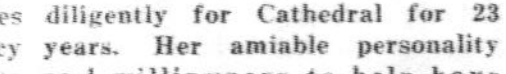

Brother Giles, C.S.C.

Newly installed as Cathedral's principal this year, Brother Giles has already shown his competency and ability to serve as one of its ablest administrators.

Mrs. Marie Ferris

She has worked devotedly and diligently for Cathedral for 23 years. Her amiable personality and willingness to help have brought her the respect and friendship of all who have met her.

Brother Damian, C.S.C.

In 1956 after serving 29 years at Cathedral, Brother left us to teach at Notre Dame High School at South Bend. Though he is not here now, his long years of service at Cathedral make him a prominent personality of the 1950's.

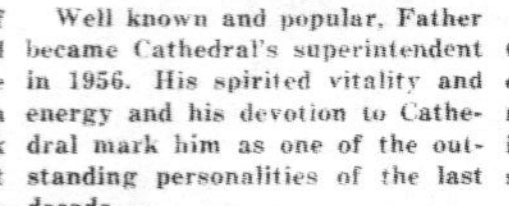

Brother Bruno, C.S.C.

For 25 years Brother has served Cathedral faithfully and unselfishly. He has guided and instructed so many Cathedral men over the years, that he has become a living legend and a part of Cathedral's tradition.

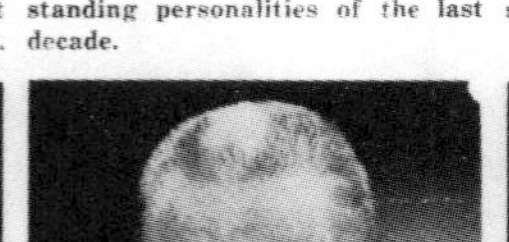

Brother Eugene, C.S.C.

Here at Cathedral since 1950, Brother has gained renown for his supervision and formation of one of the finest bands in Cathedral's history. The pep band, orchestra, and musicals are a few of the many contributions Brother has made to Cathedral.

Mr. Joseph Dezelan

Since he became head coach in 1944, Coach Joe Dezelan has managed and produced some of the finest football teams in Cathedral's history. He has brought honor and glory to Cathedral by his untiring efforts and work.

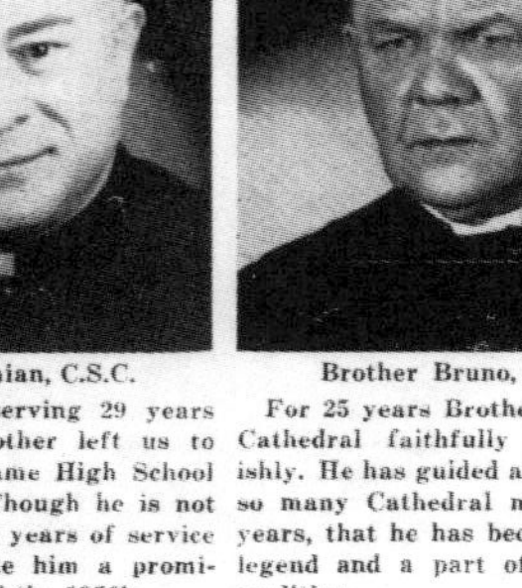

Frank McKinney

A champion swimmer at the Pan-American and Olympics Games, Frank has brought glory and fame to Cathedral. His feats have made him the best known Cathedral student of the last decade.

Alex Yovanovich, '59, All-City, All-State.

'59-'60 City Champions. Walt Sahm is smiling broadly on the left.

THE SIXTIES

The serious scholastic emphasis that Brother Pedro had implemented was having its effect. More students were Merit Scholarship winners, and Cathedral challenged Shortridge High School as the city's center of learning.

In that Class of 1961 was James E. Muller, a four-year Honor Roll student, a finalist in State Math competition who eventually went to Notre Dame and studied Russian. Jim Muller, now James E. Muller, M.D. was recipient in 1985 of the Nobel Peace Prize for his work as a co-founder of the organization International Physicians for the Prevention of Nuclear War. Dr. Muller was so trusted by Russian scientists that he was the first American allowed to assist in the Soviet Union following the nuclear disaster at Chernobl.

In later days a frequent visitor to Cathedral, Dr. Muller was a participant in a spirited extemporaneous debate at the school in 1982 when he received the Distinguished Chartrand Award. Also receiving the Award that evening was Maj. Gen. Joseph C. Lutz '51, then commander of Army Special Forces Delta Force, and the other end of the Red Telephone in case of national emergency. The friendly byplay was classic, as the man of war and the man of peace vigorously exchanged differing views.

Dr. Muller, staunch opponent of violence and its potential for nuclear response, challenged Gen. Lutz who responded: "Jim, no one hates war more than I, for I will have to fight it."

The character of the school was captured in one moment as two of its alums of such diverse opinions argued their viewpoints in an atmosphere of mutual respect and tolerance.

Today, Dr. Muller is affiliated with Deaconess Hospital, Boston, at the Institute For the Prevention of Cardiovascular Disease.

Gen. Lutz was honored by President Bush for his service to the nation, and is retired and living in Florida.

Nineteen-sixty was an outstanding year. The football team, co-captained by Tom McGinty and Roy Smith, was 8-1-1, losing only a controversial 12-7 game at Muncie Central. An offensive holding call canceled what would have been a winning touchdown run by Bill Perry. Sacred Heart and the Irish slugged out a scoreless tie but gained another City Championship trophy for Cathedral's case. Smith, now Brother Roy of the Holy Cross Congregation, also was a pillar of strength of the 20-4 basketball team. Another outstanding player for the Irish was Doug Lawrie.

Lawrie, triumphing over the difficulties of playing football with one arm, was named All-State along with Roy Smith,

Before a record crowd of more than fifteen thousand at Butler Fieldhouse, the Irish overcame a fourteen-point deficit to defeat Number One-ranked, and previously unbeaten, Crispus Attucks, 65-58.

Led by the eighteen points of center Walt Sahm and a dozen by Garry Donna, Cathedral created what Bob Williams of *The Star* called, "a night to remember."

The veteran Shortridge athletic director Bob Nipper said: "Cathedral has the most fired-up coaching staff (Bill Frohliger and Tom O'Brien) and athletes in the state." The next week the 16-2 Irish were rated Number Two behind Kokomo's eventual State champions.

It was a grand era for Indianapolis basketball, too. Ranked behind Cathedral at Number Three was Crispus Attucks, followed by Manual at 18-2. The Redskins, led by the VanArsdale twins, Dick and Tom, would defeat Attucks in the Regional and lose in overtime to Kokomo in the State Championship final game.

Early in the season, the Irish defeated Manual by ten points, a frustrating, second consecutive season loss for the twins to the Irish.

Sahm went on to play three years as varsity center at Notre Dame. At 6´-10´´ he was, at that time, the largest athlete to play for the Irish. Sahm became Cathedral's first Indiana All-Star player in the annual series against Kentucky. Sahm also was a pitcher on O'Brien's baseball squad, perhaps the tallest hurler in city history. Basketball co-captain Donna, a sharp-shooting guard-forward, played at Butler, and is now publisher of *Hoosier Basketball* Magazine.

An outstanding pitcher, Ron Keller, led the baseball team to the City Championship and went on to play in the Minnesota Twins organization.

Athletically, the Irish couldn't be topped. The cross-country team was City Champion and third in the state meet. The emerging wrestling team had four City Champions—Steve Evan, Stan Kremp, Mark Steinmetz and Randy Qualitza. The reserve and freshman teams won City titles. The patience of Coach Mahoney was rewarded, and the climb was under way.

After winning fifteen of sixteen baseball games and another City Baseball Championship, Cathedral received the *Indianapolis Times* All Sports Trophy with a record number of accumulated points. Cathedral would win the award four times—more than any other school.

A Message From The Twins: Tom and Dick VanArsdale

The Cathedral athletes were such competitors. We always knew we were in for a battle, win or lose. During our era, players like Sahm, Donna, Blaylock, and Smith were excellent basketball players. Each year we would begin the season by playing Cathedral. In 1961, when Manual was 28-3 and runner-up to Kokomo in the State Finals, Cathedral gave us a wake-up call by defeating us in that opening game. Our good friend, Bill Shover, still reminds us of that occasionally. For a school that was known primarily for its strong football teams, it was also pretty good at hoops. We can't help but mention, however, that in 1958 Manual won the mythical State Championship in football and thumped Cathedral pretty convincingly in the closing game of the season at CYO Field.

During the summer, we used to play basketball all over the city of Indianapolis, and as a result, became pretty good friends with the Cathedral guys. The games were intense and we feel our basketball skills were enhanced by that competition. To this day, we still have fond memories of those battles and the Cathedral athletes.

(Stars at Manual, 1961 State Champion Runners-up, the twins played thirteen seasons in the National Basketball Association.)

1961-62

L.S. Ayres reported that all Cathedral sweatshirts were sold out to academy girls. In a letter to the editor of *The Megaphone,* "The Bitter One" wrote: "The girls come to football and basketball games and take up all the space saved for the Cathedral (which the girls call theirs) cheering block."

He went on to complain, "they buy up reserved seats on football bus trips before we have a chance to." St. Agnes girls continued to be a dominant force in the lives of the Cathedral boys from across the street. Joining the boys before and after school at the local high school hangouts, working together on stage productions and cheering at the sporting events, the girls formed close friendships that often developed into romances and marriages.

Bill Perry was an outstanding athlete of this era. He starred as quarterback, running back and kicker. He was honored in his junior season as the All-City quarterback and the only underclassman to be selected for the team that year. (Bill died in early 1993.)

Another Dezelan, Joe Jr. "Butch," centered on another undefeated City Championship football team. With Gary Tofil and Mark Steinmetz, the three co-captains led the Irish to nine wins and a tough 6-6 tie with Broad Ripple.

Tofil, son of Joe, long-time Washington coach, received the Father Higgins award as the scholar-athlete of the year. He was All-City end and filled in as quarterback in the Irish's 36-0 win over his dad's team in his junior year and quarterbacked as a senior. In basketball, he played varsity four years; in track he set a school record in the pole vault and was on the record-breaking mile relay team along with seniors Mark Steinmetz and Steve Tudor and junior Bob Perry. Gary was vice-president of his freshman class and president in his sophomore, junior and senior years.

Indianapolis high school football came into its own and Cathedral was queen. Before 7,500 wild fans, the Irish defeated Manual, 13-0, at Victory Field. Speedy Dick Dullaghan gained seventy-two yards on nine carries to lead the team.

Co-captains Harold McCullough and Sam Schmutte were named to the All-City team along with halfback Dullaghan.

Depleted by graduation, the basketball team finished 14-9. The cheerleading team of Helen Quiesser, Joanne Ford and Provy Tantillo of St. Agnes, Nancy Cerne and Toni Page of St. Mary's, and Bob Desautels of Cathedral, won the Kiwanis Club award as the city's finest.

With a new wrestling coach, Carol Purichia, the Irish were

undefeated in ten dual meets.

Another emerging sport which began to engage Cathedral's serious interest was tennis. The first team in years was undefeated in fifteen matches, losing only fourteen sets.

Under the advising touch of Brother Ronald, Cathedral publications—"The Memo," "The Religious Bulletin," *The Megaphone,* and *The Cathedran*—took on a new, professional look and earned awards. Student Manager Jack Woelfel attended a worthwhile workshop at Ohio University.

Commencement found 160 seniors earning diplomas. A record for that time, $64,000 in scholarships was awarded to eighteen seniors.

1962-1963

Returning students found Cathedral had experienced a loss. Brother Bruno Klusewitz had died in his residence late in the summer. He had taught mathematics at Cathedral with style, wit, and brilliant ability. His sense of dedication and rigorous discipline instilled those qualities in Cathedral students for years to come.

Brother James Sullivan became the twelfth and next-to-last principal from the Holy Cross Congregation. He would serve four years. The Cathedral Varieties student production again featured the song and dance talents of St. Agnes' Sue Rutledge and senior Jack Calabrese.

Our first football loss to Scecina in six years, 12-7, marred a 8-1-1 football season and the only non-City Championship title year in five seasons. The highlight game of the season, considered by veteran *Star* sportswriter Bob Williams "the finest high school game he ever covered," was against Tech. Coach Dezelan was elated when officials moved the game to Victory Field, where he had always triumphed with a 9-0 record.

Bob Perry remembers, "When two-a-day practices concluded, Coach Dezelan huddled the team and said to the sophomores: `You can go home now and tell you dads that you are men. If they don't believe you tell them to come out here and go through two-a-days with you.'"

A crowd of 13,800 turned out to see a scoreless tie going into the fourth quarter. With 2:30 left to play, Irish fullback Bob

Romberg was stopped one yard short of the goal line and was carried off the field with a broken ankle. Romberg was named scholar-athlete of the year and winner of the Fr. Higgins Award. With 2:02 showing on the clock, Tech took over and Cathedral put in an extra lineman to go for the safety. On the first play, blitzing 180-pound guard Dan Quigley and Dan Hasbrook met Titan halfback John Smith in the end zone. Quigley and Hasbrook body-slammed Smith, and Cathedral won 2-0, its only victory ever on a safety.

Before a packed stadium at CYO, the Irish then lost to City Champion Scecina. Devastated by that loss, Cathedral tied a weak Washington 13-13 to end the season.

Co-captain Sam Schmutte, one of five Schmuttes to play for Dezelan, was All-City. The heart of the line, rugged Harold McCullough, earned All-State honors.

Another City championship was earned by the Irish harriers.

Vatican II and its sweeping changes for Catholics worldwide ended, and *The Megaphone* editorialized:

A long-range effect of the Council is yet to be seen; but, nevertheless, the Second Vatican Council will mean one thing—a renewal of the Catholic Church to better enable her to carry on the work of saving souls in this modern, ever-changing world.

The number of men and women entering religious life was dwindling. Its effect would take ten years to reach Cathedral and the Brothers of Holy Cross, but a most significant process was beginning. The continuance of celibacy and the strictness of Catholic doctrine would remain.

Cathedral's young basketball team advanced to the Sectional semi-final game but, again, emerged with no title. The squad finished 12-11 to keep Coach Frohliger's winning record intact. Cheerleader Jim Alerding '63, recalling his teachers at Cathedral, said: "Brother Joseph Zutelis and Brother Raymond Harrington made my college teachers seem easy." He sent his own son and three daughters to learn first-hand the "Cathedral Experience."

Also on the cheerleading team was Rosie Thomas, now Rosie Houk, the present mainstay of Cathedral's office staff.

Irish wrestlers won nine of twelve matches with junior "Julie" Peebles a mainstay. Peebles, later to become Cathedral president, was elected King of the Junior Class Ball.

The golf and tennis teams won City championships and the big news was the third straight City Championship in baseball.

The sports year marked the play of another Roseman family member. It had begun earlier, in 1949 with Dick, All-City and All-State with the 1952 State Championship team. "Dynamite Bill" followed, earning the same honors as Dick. Not as naturally gifted in the sport, Mike earned the praise of Coach Dezelan who said: "Mike made use of what he had." Mike served his country during the Vietnam War and was one of the many young men who died there. Steve began as a freshman in 1963 and competed through 1966: seventeen years of Roseman athletes.

The Forty-fifth and the school's largest graduating class—146 seniors—were presented diplomas by Brother George Kovatch, senior class sponsor. Advancing to college were seventy-three percent of the graduates.

1963-64

The joy of another City Championship football team was shadowed on November 22 by the news of President Kennedy's shooting in Dallas. The report of his death brought an eerie quiet to the halls that had recently reverberated to the cacophony of victory. Another undefeated Irish team won the school's fourth City title in five seasons—an unprecedented string.

Another death noted was that of Brother Bernard Gervais, a member of the original school faculty in 1918. Some recalled that Brother Bernard had returned to Cathedral in 1934 and implemented the school's first tuition fee—fifty dollars.

The Shoes of the Fisherman headed the book best-seller list and the drug cult was capturing Americans, first with marijuana. Dr. Timothy Leary was a convincing if illogical advocate, and drug use increased from 300,000 to 8,000,000 American users in a few years. "Puff, the Magic Dragon" wasn't written about pot smoking, but it could have been the anthem of an epidemic.

Cathedral's enrollment was an all-time high of 860 and the need for Brothers to teach and administer the school was stretched. Twenty-one came from Notre Dame, augmented by nine priests and ten lay teachers. The surge in interest in Cathedral, buoyed by a baby boom in the late 1940s, prompted the Brothers of Holy Cross to purchase the school. Scecina and the new Brebeuf Preparatory had not, as predicted, caused a chronically declining enrollment at Cathedral.

Msgr. James P. Galvin, Archdiocesan superintendent of schools, said the school would be operated by the Order beginning in September, 1964. The reason for the sale, Galvin stated, was to "provide more efficient administration under a single authority. The Rev. James Higgins, superintendent of the school, and other priests assigned by the Archdiocese will be reassigned. An increase in tuition will be necessary from $120 to $180," he announced.

Msgr. Galvin praised Father Higgins, former principal Brother Pedro Haering and present principal Brother James Sullivan for the work they had done in raising the academic level of the school.

The departure to the new Bishop Chatard High School of Father Jim, who had been at the school since 1956, was viewed by the school community with regret. During his tenure he contributed greatly to the students' educations and lives and still is regarded as one of its most popular administrators. Until his untimely death in 1993, he served on the Cathedral Board of Trustees, most recently as its vice-chairman.

Football had been spectacular in 1963. The squad was led by co-captains Mike Harrison and Julian Peebles, both All-City. At center, Peebles anchored a line that would surrender only three touchdowns in ten games. A 12-12 tie to Wood shocked the team that went on to score 244 points by season's end, the widest point margin in Irish history. Time expired with Cathedral on Wood's six-inch line.

The basketball squad had a disappointing 10-11 season. Still, the final breakthrough of acceptance was achieved when Cathedral was invited to play in its first City Tournament. The Irish defeated Northwest, but lost to Washington. It was one of the taller squads with 6´-8´´ Jim Goodin, 6´-5´´ John Rohm and Clarence Hupfer and Tom Westfall, both six-feet, three-and-a-half.

Coach Frohliger resigned at season's end and moved on to Bloomington High School. His replacement was red-headed Bill Green, athletic director and head basketball coach at Sacred Heart Central High School. Green had begun coaching at Park School.

He played at Manual. One of more than thirty applicants from four states who sought to come to coach at Cathedral, he went on to coach at Washington and Marion High Schools, where his accomplishments earned him Hall of Fame recognition.

A second Sectional Championship was achieved by Coach Purichia's wrestlers.

The largest graduating class of 225 said farewell and eighty-five percent continued their education, including nine who received athletic scholarships.

1964-65

A change of leadership occurred both at the school and in the world. The Brothers had full authority over the management of the school for the first time.

On the international scene, a kaleidoscope of developments heralded change. Nikita Khrushchev was forced off the world stage and became a non-person. The Warren Commission's painstakingly reasoned conclusion that Lee Harvey Oswald had acted alone in killing President Kennedy would alarm opportunistic theorists, who capitalized on findings that even today remain clouded.

And at Cathedral there was sadness as senior Jim Cross was killed when lightning struck a shelter he had sought at the Indianapolis Motor Speedway.

Gene Carpenter Gardner '67 reported in *The Megaphone* the drama of the Republican National Convention, while Barry Goldwater swept the nomination and the dubious challenge to an incumbent Lyndon Johnson. And in the ranks of that senior class was smiling Daniel J. O'Malia, whose noble service to Cathedral would extend from student to teacher, to major volunteer and Chairman of the Board of Directors.

Joe Dezelan's warriors would fail but once in ten games and win their fifth City crown in six seasons. That loss, the first ever to Sacred Heart, would end Cathedral's dominance in the fifteen games against the spunky Spartans. It wasn't even close, 39-12.

Scecina defeated Sacred Heart, so another title loomed as the underdog Irish met the Crusaders. *The Star's* Bob Williams wrote:

Frank Countryman, 182-pound senior left end, took his place among Cathedral football's finest ever in last night's 19-13 upset victory over Scecina before an overflow CYO Field throng of 8,000. Cathedral scored all three touchdowns following blocked kicks—breaking a tie with only thirty-six seconds left on the clock— and if Countryman lives to be 100, he'll never play a better football game.

The 6´ -2 ´´ Countryman blocked two punts, caught two touchdown passes from quarterback Joe Martella and set up the winning score with a one-handed circus catch on the one-yard line. All-State tackle Mike Haley blocked another punt to set up the title touchdown.

It was Dezelan's eleventh City Championship. Countryman was named All-City, All-State and Catholic High School All-American while Haley was an All-State selection.

On December 11, the first public induction ceremony of the Aquinian Chapter of the National Honor Society was held. It was conducted by Dr. J. Russell Lane, principal of Crispus Attucks High School. An anonymous alumni donor (it was John "Jake" Schaler '46) paid to sand-blast the facade of his school. Cathedral also assumed operating CYO Field on a low-cost lease basis to eliminate a $20,000 loss by the CYO.

Coach Bill Green's young Irish basketball team (9-15) advanced to the Butler Sectional championship game with three upsets, only to lose to Ben Davis. Cathedral amassed twenty-four fouls to ten by the Giants.

Cathedral's band won twenty-five first-place medals to win the State Championship and was selected to play at President Johnson's campaign stop in Indianapolis and the Circle Theater premiere of the film *My Fair Lady.* Brother Leonard Leary filled in for the ailing Brother Eugene Weisenberger and directed the ninety-six-piece Marching Irish. Brother Leonard, Cathedral '39, was observing his twenty-fifth anniversary in the Congregation.

The City Baseball Championship—the fifth consecutive— was claimed by Coach Raymond Powers' team, undefeated in sixteen games, to begin a record string of twenty-seven victories.

Junior Dan Carpenter, later of *The Star*, by-lined an article asking for input to *The Cathedran.* Of his days at Cathedral, Carpenter wrote:

Unique in this century, my Cathedral class graduated on 6/6/66. I didn't know anybody in high school who smoked marijuana or who believed the U.S. was wrong to be in Vietnam. We had a sociology teacher named Larry Bowman who had us primed to picket the American Opinion bookstore over on Pennsylvania Street until Brother

James Sullivan, the principal, got wind of it. Not just no, but HELL NO. It was a different epoch. The Beach Boys were our rap, even jocks hauled armloads of books home, notebooks were graded for neatness, Shakespeare was memorized, themes were marked down for grammar and spelling—God, the indignities we acquiesced in. Virtually every year they threatened us with uniforms; and why they didn't make good, I'll never know.

A lot of guys couldn't hack the regimentation and/or lack of females and moved on to Sacred Heart or Scecina by the end of sophomore year. I suppose many of the free spirits endured the workload and the harassment and the detentions because Cathedral enjoyed a certain cachet in youth circles, thanks largely to its football and its Northside mafia.

A poor kid from Fountain Square who didn't even know where they bought those Madras shirts and penny loafers, I nevertheless identified with the institution right away. I lived and died with the football scores, and I went on to choose "The Cathedral Man" (gack) as the yearbook theme when I was editor in my senior year.

This tradition stuff was partly personal. I enrolled in Cathedral because my Dad had gone there, and it barely occurred to me I couldn't afford it. The Brothers made it easier than it should have been financially, letting me slide by on scholarships and after-school jobs. Their classroom rigor was an even greater gift, for which I was no doubt even less grateful. Outside of some obvious personal passages, I doubt I've had an experience more valuable than English (Brothers Ronald LaLonde, Raymond Harrington, Carl Shonk and Gerard Mason) at Cathedral High School. I was a runt with no car and no social life, so I don't have the store of memories the lettermen can dip into. I do remember the pep rallies with homegrown rock music, the WIFE Radio "Window on the World" next door in the days when AM was king, the City Championships in football, the pre-dawn Saturday drives to debate tournaments, the old yearbook office in the fine arts building across the parking lot, the rush of seeing my name on that mimeographed honor roll.

I remember I was in biology class on the afternoon of Nov. 22, 1963, when the announcement came. The next day was my fifteenth birthday. My son, at ten has seen more, done more and spent more than I had at fifteen, plus, he has a harnessed radical for a father. Can I imagine him at a place of the Old Cathedral's temperament and standards? In a minute. Literacy is worth four years in prison, which Cathedral was not, even for freshmen, much.

1965-1966

It was a dramatic year—the cauldron of hate, arson and death boiled in Watts, and Malcolm X was felled in a fusillade of bullets from Black Muslim members' guns. Free people mourned the passing of Winston Churchill and the film *Those Magnificent Men in Their Flying Machines* brought joy to the world. Soviet cosmonaut Leonov was the first to walk in space, while transplanted organs led off a revolutionary frontier of medicine.

Crew-cut John MacLeod left Smithville High School to assist Bill Green in basketball and succeed Carol Purichia as baseball coach. MacLeod went on to coach Oklahoma University and then to a distinguished career as one of the most successful coaches in the National Basketball Association. In 1993 he was basketball coach at Notre Dame.

False promise set in as the Irish won their first three football games but slipped to a 5-4-1 record. Plagued by injuries, the squad compiled the worst record in eight seasons but, nonetheless, a winning record. Homecoming was spoiled by Scecina, 21-13.

Something was missing on campus: the fine arts building at the northwest corner was razed and black-topped for parking.

A new opponent, named for Cathedral's founder, Bishop Chartrand High School bowed to the Irish, 20-6. Cathedral would defeat Chartrand in three of four varsity football games, before the school later changed its name, in 1969, to Roncalli, in honor of Pope John XXIII.

A rebuilding basketball team was 9-14, again with upset wins in the Sectional against Attucks and Ben Davis. Wrestling coach Lou Hurrle, in only his second year as coach, directed the matmen to a 12-0 dual meet record and won the Sectional.

The Young Christian Movement was created as a Catholic Action group for adults. At a unique Mass sponsored by YCM, seven Cathedral Latin School students played banjos and guitars in folk music instead of the usual hymns. It was the beginning of a trend; still, in the face of change, many things at Cathedral remained the same.

Attorney Bill Hasbrook '66 reflected: "Our strength was our diversity. Cathedral had white students and black students from rich families and poor families. Our friends' parents were auto mechanics and doctors, factory workers and lawyers, barbers and insurance agents. But at school we were all student—and we were there to learn about life and to prepare for college. It was expected. Everyone knew it."

For the first time scholarships to twenty-two seniors topped $100,000 in value. The growing prep school reputation was enhanced as eighty-four percent of the seniors went on to seek university degrees.

1966-67

In Vietnam, "escalation" was the word; at home, "Black Power" and a new meaning for the word "trip." The world was restless and "peaceniks" inserted flowers into rifle barrels pointed at them.

Every issue of *The Megaphone* carried a box: "Pray For Peace."

For the Holy Cross and Cathedral it would mark countdown to disassociation. The Congregation tapped the driven and dedicated Brother Douglas Roach as its fourteenth and last principal to deal with declining enrollment. The enrollment problem had causes larger than the school's own situation; Catholic education was eroding. Cathedral Grade School was in its final year, and only twenty pupils graduated.

The football team fell to 5-5. Kennedy Memorial (formerly Sacred Heart) would fall to the Irish as would old foes Tech, Shortridge and Broad Ripple. Washington Coach Bob Springer '52 got revenge for the first time over his former coach, Joe Dezelan. In a televised basketball game, Cathedral defeated Bishop David High School of Louisville. Highlights were few and far between, though, as the team lost its season finale to Southport by a record fifty points, 90-40. The final record was 4-16. The student body gave little support.

The basketball program had dropped to its lowest level in spite of two excellent men—Green and MacLeod—who would go on to great coaching careers. Coach Green resigned—he couldn't win basketball games at Cathedral. He went on to Indianapolis Washington and then Marion where his teams won an unprecedented three consecutive State Championships.

But the wrestling team finished third in the Sectional. Cross country could finish no higher than fifth. As seasons go, the records of 1966-67 were disappointing.

Baseball was coached by Paul McCoun, and the 15-4-1 Irish lost their first game in the new State competition. Social events and student productions helped to compensate for the athletic defeats, and the Varieties of 1966 featured tunes of the time, "Somewhere My Love" and the Academy Award-winning "Strangers in the Night."

Forty-two scholarships were awarded to thirty seniors as scholastic effort fostered success. Dr. John A. Lawrie, '67, an All-City tackle, now a physician in Yardley, Pa., wrote: "I continue to use my lessons learned at Cathedral every day." Dr. Lawrie was graduated from Princeton and is a Fellow of the American College of Emergency Medicine.

1967-68

A new concept of studying, one which gave the pupil more individual freedom and a home-like atmosphere in which to learn was adopted at Cathedral.

In the fall, students found their old library had been completely remodeled and renamed the Learning Research Center. It was nearly doubled in size and provided private areas to study.

In a national tragedy Apollo 12 ignited on the ground and astronauts Ed White, Roger Chaffee and Hoosier Gus Grissom perished. The space program was halted, temporarily.

Campus anticipation built as Principal Brother Douglas and Student Council President John Guy reviewed blueprints for a proposed science wing to be built and ready next year.

The school was on the eve of the Golden Anniversary year, and the hopes were high that the somewhat discouraging year before could be forgotten. A new teenaged reality hit Cathedral as the seniors sponsored the "Purple Haze" dance, with music provided by the Dawn Five and the new, reverberated stereophonic sounds of keyboards and electric guitars. The juniors sponsored a formal "April Love" prom; but it was the new rhythms and "Light My Fire," "Alice's Restaurant" and every Beatle composition that changed Cathedral's music.

Detroit glowed from the fires of civil rights unrest, but Indianapolis, thanks in part to the cooling influence of legendary Crispus Attucks coach Ray Crowe, remained an island of calm. After retiring as coach, Crowe went on to serve as a respected City Councilman.

Two less-than-great football seasons would be stretched to three as Joe Dezelan—JOE DEZELAN—would watch his lads suffer their first losing season in eighteen years. The tie game in the opener warned of some difficulty, but three consecutive victories were comforting. And then losses to Kennedy (formerly Chartrand) (20-42), Shortridge (6-39), Scecina (0-19) and a 6-44 romp by Washington gave locals the revenge they had been waiting for.

There was no talk of Cathedral recruiting or of forming a public school league: Cathedral in 1967 had a 4 and 6 record and vengeance was everybody else's. The wheel was wobbling and Dezelan's detractors chortled that the dean had lost his touch in the new, wide-open offensive football scheme of things.

But the Irish reserves and freshmen again won City titles. Could help be on the way? It couldn't come fast enough for Cathedralites.

In the middle of this despair light shone as the cross country team had a 47-4-1 record in '67 and a City Championship. Wrestling boosted school spirit with a 10-2 record. Hopes for basketball shot up as Cathedral sons Tom O'Brien and assistant coach Garry Donna took the Irish to a 14-10 record—the best since 1961—against stern competition. It was a little more than a glimmer, but there was at least forward motion.

Tennis suffered as well—a 3-11 record—but on that team was senior Chuck Kriese, who won fourteen of his seventeen matches. Kriese is now tennis coach at Clemson University, where he took a virtually unknown program into the national limelight. He has been College Coach of the Year three times and is the author of *Total Tennis Training*.

Cathedral's baseball team won the Sectional, only to be defeated by Pike in the Regional final game, finishing 17-12 for the season.

Still, the shadow loomed. Enrollment was declining; there was no doubt about that. As times changed and Catholics in Indianapolis had other choices for high school: Chartrand, Kennedy, Ritter, and Scecina were drawing students now in different parts of the city from a diminishing pool. Scholastic achievement continued to rise, however, as eighty-six percent of the 120 graduating seniors continued their formal education.

1968-1969

It was the Golden Jubilee year and Cathedral planned additions to its plant. A science wing was opened, along with a band-Glee Club room, a physical education exercise room and a lobby in back of the gymnasium, containing a bookstore and athletic office. Bob Welch '45 was general chairman of a fund-raising campaign to assure Cathedral's central city continuance.

Grumbling was heard as five diocesan-owned high schools each needed $100,000-plus to augment their income. Parents paid tuition of $200 each while average cost per pupil was $430. The forty-six parishes were assessed amounts ranging from $31,320 (Little Flower) to $720 (Fortville) to subsidize operational losses at the Diocesan high schools. Independent Cathedral struggled to go it alone, but the belt was tightening.

Broad Ripple was selected as the foe for Homecoming and "The Memo" reported confidently, "Mayor Lugar will give a talk following the Irish victory."

It was prophetic. At the Homecoming bonfire, Mayor Lugar, a Shortridge graduate, praised Cathedral's fifty years of service to the community. Then Cathedral won, 13-6, to highlight another undefeated season of nine wins and a 13-13 tie with Tech.

Dezelan's team captured his twelfth City crown in twenty-five coaching seasons. Tech principal (and former football coach Howard Longshore) presented the trophy to Joe and co-captains Dave Weimer (All-State) and Jim Casey. In the final statewide poll, Cathedral finished in fourth place.

LBJ would not run again in the presidential race, and Bobby Kennedy won Indiana's delegates. Frequent presidential candidate Eugene McCarthy kept the Vietnam political pot boiling.

Classes were jointly held with St. Agnes girls and some of the Brothers donned black suit, white shirt and black tie attire. St. Agnes and St. Mary's coeds played a curtain-raiser football game before the Homecoming clash (St. Mary's won). Times were moving on in America and at 1401 North Meridian Street.

Coach Tony Ardizzone's wrestlers won ten of twelve dual matches including a rare shutout of Crispus Attucks, 46-0. David Kern, at 138 pounds, became CHS's first state wrestling champ.

The O'Brien-Donna coaching tandem returned pride in Irish basketball. The season record was 17-4, all four losses against teams ranked in Indiana's top four. It was the most successful team since 1961. John Gorman, a 6´-2´´ guard, scored a record fifty-one points as the visiting Irish blasted Battle Ground, 102-65. Gorman, a senior, hit twenty baskets and eleven of fourteen free throws.

Swimmer Pat O'Connor, later one of the top swimmers in the country involved in competitive swimming at Indiana University and a team-mate of Mark Spitz , won the State 200-yard individual medley event.

The varsity track team, coached by the versatile alumni returnee Mike McGinley, was the school's finest, winning thirteen of seventeen dual meets.

The highest college matriculation ever was achieved as ninety-five percent of the 192 graduating seniors went off to college.

1969-70

The 1969 season began with disappointment and ended with drama. The Irish were rated Number Two in pre-season polls after their undefeated, City Championship year of 1968, when Cathedral outscored ten opponents 226-59.

For Joe Dezelan, the 1969 team would be the twenty-sixth and last he would coach. Big, tough and fast, the Irish were co-captained by Pete Weber and Steve Schaefer. Both were selected All-City and All-State.

Weber later played at Indiana and Schaefer at Purdue. Also on the '69 squad was Jim McLinn, the son of 1945 All-State selection Jim McLinn, Sr. He is today Cathedral's Junior Class counselor.

Other regulars included six feet four, 240-pound junior tackle John Jordan (All-State in 1970), speedy Mike Waugh, Mark Maley, Charles Lyons, Jim Curry, Greg McGinnis and Tim McCalley.

To add to the anticipation, the opening game opponent was the defending mythical 1968 State champion Elkhart High School. Sportswriters tabbed the meeting "the game of the decade" as the Irish headed for Elkhart field.

In the city where Alka Seltzer is produced, Dezelan could have used a double dose of headache remedy. The Elkhart game turned out to be its worst nightmare of 699 varsity games in which

Cathedral's sons have competed. Whatever could go wrong, did.

"I've never seen a Cathedral team—as a coach, opponent or spectator—ever collapse as we did that awful night in Elkhart," Dezelan recalls.

Julian Peebles, who had now graduated from Butler and was an assistant Cathedral coach said: "When they (Elkhart) ran onto the field I thought they would never stop coming. It looked like the Chinese Army." Elkhart had the reputation of being a traditional football powerhouse, and that reputation was obviously true. (In 1972, Elkhart would split with the opening of Central and Memorial high schools, thus diffusing its manpower base and also its mystique.)

The 0-52 shellacking is Cathedral's largest loss margin, the only game in which a Cathedral opponent would score fifty points.

On their return from a forgettable experience, Dezelan's final team committed itself and went on to win eight of nine games, losing only to Broad Ripple, 0-6. They dominated opposition 210-62 in points to wash away the memories of that nightmarish September night in Elkhart.

Elkhart went on to win the mythical 1969 Hoosier State Championship as voted by state-wide sportswriters and broadcasters.

Julian Peebles coached Irish reserve football teams to five straight City Championships. Through his tenure the reserves had a thirty-nine-game winning streak which was not broken until the following year—after forty-six games.

Dezelan's coaching career—and the '69 season—ended dramatically as the Irish defeated Joe's alma mater, Washington.

It was the 250th game Dezelan would coach the Irish and ranks high in the competition for most emotional. Washington, young and talented, was favored, but the CYO scoreboard blinked: CHS 26 GWHS 16

Cathedral's players carried Dezelan on their shoulders off the field and to lifelong admiration after coaching Irish teams in more than one-third of the school's varsity football games. Competent Michael McGinley took up the tradition and prepared to coach varsity football in '70.

Life Magazine published the photographs of 242 United States servicemen, each of whom had been killed in Vietnam in one arbitrarily selected week (May 28-June 3, 1969).

Many publications were beginning to change to a "dove" position; mounting casualty lists reflected the futility of a war that could not be won. President Nixon, still arguing American involvement would stem Communist aggression, ignored appeals and even the factual disclosure of the Mai Lai Massacre did not alter his determination to continue the war.

In *The Megaphone,* an editorial bannered "Awareness" called for the removal of American troops in 1970. Co-editors John Short and Chris Crockett were criticized for carrying too much political comment. "Give us school news," a reader demanded.

With the assistance of Julian Peebles, Coach Ardizzone's wrestlers won a second consecutive Sectional Championship.

A swimming team (5-5 in dual meets), coached in its second season by Larry Bowman, featured Senior Class President Pat O'Connor, later one of the top fifteen swimmers in the world in the 200 and 400 meter individual medleys.

Coach Garry Donna's baseball team featured fastballer Jim "Big Daddy" McLinn, who held Ben Davis hitless for six innings in a 6-4 victory. Varsity baseballers won twenty-one of twenty-three games, including eleven shutouts. A one-run loss to tough Ben Davis ended their Sectional hopes.

Frank Venezia, "Cathedral's own stick of dynamite" at ninety-eight pounds, won a State wrestling title. Swimmer Pat O'Connor was the only swimmer at the State finals to win two firsts: the individual medley and the butterfly.

From his home in Wilmette, Illinois James McKenna '70 commented: "I am thankful for Cathedral. I live near one of the finest public high schools, New Trier. In looking at their class syllabus, I was gratified that what they are teaching today, I had the advantage of learning in my days at Cathedral only they did it in the more simplified form of electives."

Handsome Jim Curry, a three-sport star, hit a desperate one-handed shot at the buzzer as the 17-4 Irish defeated Brebeuf, 61-60. Coach O'Brien's well-balanced team featured three sophomores who would gain many court victories. Combined, the varsity, reserve and freshman teams would win forty-six of fifty-nine games. *The Megaphone* was regularly circulated and took on a "Memo" (mimeographed) look under co-editors John Short and Chris Crockett. Consistent with the times, youth was taking itself seriously and the paper railed against Governor Ed Whitcomb's policies on education and President Nixon, warning Americans to get out of Vietnam. Conversely, it thanked the Indiana Pacers for acquiring Lebanon-Purdue star Rick Mount.

Joe Dezelan's last Irish team had been cheered by a squadron of Academy coeds led by his daughter Cathy.

Simon & Garfunkel's haunting melody and words to "Bridge Over Troubled Waters" sounded the theme of social consciousness which dominated the end of the decade as draft-dodgers headed for Canada, the Students for Democratic Action invaded some schools and the first Earth Day was observed. A stunned *Megaphone* staff voiced its tribute to the assassinated Dr. Martin Luther King Jr. on the front page.

The tragic and sudden death of Dr. Martin Luther King Jr. was reported in "The Memo" with his words: "I've been to the top of the mountain and I've seen the promised land. I may not get there with you, but someday, WE SHALL OVERCOME. Mine eyes have seen the glory of the coming of the Lord."

Thinking people all over the world mourned.

However, there was happiness—Joe Dezelan was named athletic director in March—and sadness; the news that St. Agnes Academy would close and merge with Ladywood School.

A mountain of canned food—45,000 cans—was collected during the "People of Cathedral" drive for the hungry-poor of Indianapolis.

Vietnam was winding down and 206 seniors entered a new phase of their lives in an America which had weathered the storm, but which would never be the same again. Cathedral High School, of course, was no exception.

Marie Thompson Ferris: The Only Lady On Campus

Marie Ferris couldn't be fooled. In her years as secretary at Cathedral, she heard every excuse for tardiness, absence and request to leave campus. Thousands of alibis were pierced by her sharp intuitiveness.

"She could handle all of us," Msgr. Richard Kavanagh recalled.

From superintendent to student, Marie Ferris was the constant. She seemed to create tradition by her understanding and compassion for young, impressionable and sometimes desperate men. Never fooled, she might make it appear that she was deluded by a calmness she could bring to what seemed to be moments of panic.

She was supposed to be the school secretary, but she also was a notary public, a doctor and a nurse, a chaperon, a time-keeper, a stenographer, a teacher, a matron, a tailor and a dress-maker, a designer, a decorator and a myriad of other people in one kind personality.

Marie graduated from St. Agnes Academy in 1916. Her "baby brother," Louis Thompson '22, was a member of Cathedral's first four-year graduating class. Marie spent twenty-six years at Cathedral (1941-67) and left when Rev. Fr. James P. Higgins (former Cathedral superintendent from 1956-64) was assigned to become principal of the newly-opened Chatard High School.

She remained at Chatard until retirement in 1971. "Mrs. Ferris" as she was known to thousands, had two daughters, Mary Frances, married to Joseph C. Lyons '43 and Betty Lu, married to Edward J. Galm, also of the Class of 1943.

She died in 1988. Her passing was noted for her service to Catholic education. The slight, sly smile that could detect exaggeration was only one of the gifts Marie Ferris brought to work with young people.

Marie Ferris, the only lady on the campus for more than one-third of Cathedral's years, will always be remembered as another personality who gave much to making the school the institution it was and is.

A mass in the Cathedral opens school traditionally.

Father Jim Higgins in the early sixties.

Mayor Richard Lugar (center) with the 1968 City Champs, including (l to r) Steve Schaefer, Jeff Lawrie, Peter Weber, Coach Joe Dezelan, Jim McLinn, and Mike Waugh

Some members of the 1961 City Champs (l to r) Gary Tofil, Butch Dezelan, Star Sports Editor Jep Cadou, Mark Steinmetz and Coach Joe Dezelan.

Roy Smith, now a Brother of Holy Cross

Standardized testing is a feature of modern education. Here Mr. Edward Nelson and Brother Douglas Roach help the Readak man administer tests.

Pep bands were big during the sixties. Here is one of several that pumped up the Irish or played for events.

The football squad in the fall of '68.

Dave Kern was Cathedral's first State Champ in wrestling.

A group of Cathedral charitable givers presents a check to the Little Sisters of the Poor.

Governor Matt Welch and Brother Douglas Roach at a recognition breakfast in the cafeteria.

The Brothers, Christmas '63.

Mayor John Barton '24, receives the first check to Cathedral's alumni banquet from Chairman Jack Redmond.

Harold McCollough tackles arch-rival Scecina's quarterback Terry Rogers in the fall of 1962.

Julian Peebles hikes the ball to quarterback John O'Conner with Mike Harrison, Butch Hawkins and Larry Mervar in the backfield of the '63 City Champions.

CATHEDRAL HIGH SCHOOL
Board of Directors

Current Board of Directors

Michael G. Schaefer - Chairman
Paul P. Farrell - Vice Chairman
Richard K. Leighton - Treasurer
John Davis - Secretary
Rev. William G. Munshower - Chaplain

John W. Adams III
R. James Alerding
John I. Bradshaw
H. Jack Baker
Harry L. Bindner
William T. Brady
James R. Cain
Joseph A. Caito
Matthew A. Cohoat
Kevin Davey
Joseph F. Dezelan
G. Christopher Duffy
John F. Ford
Michael L. Harrison
Mrs. Jack Harvey
Rev. Msgr. Richard T. Kavanagh
Rev. Patrick J. Kelly
Michael A. Kiefer
Hugh B. McGowan
Mrs. Frank Mossbrugger
Patrick J. O'Conner
Daniel J. O'Malia
Julian T. Peebles
Joseph F. Quill
John J. Quinn
Lyman B. Rhodes
Steven Schaefer
John D. Short
R. Joseph Stark, Jr.
Rev. Mark A Svarczkopf
Joseph P. Wade
Mrs. Carolyn Welch
Gerald Zore

Original Board of Directors

Robert V. Welch-Chairman
Frank E. McKinney Jr.
Rev. Msgr. James P. Galvin
Rev. James P. Higgins
Dr. Fredrick R. Vanabeele
Dr. John W. Courtney
William S. Sahm
Michael G. Schaefer
Thomas R. Keating
David W. Foley
John C. O'Conner
Robert C. Robisch
Edward J. Gaughan
Joeseph H. Broecker
Thomas J. McShane
Robert E. Kirkhoff
Thomas F. Redmond
John L. Davis
Joseph F. Morris
Mrs. Mary Lou Roberts
Fred G. Johnston, Jr.
Rev. Patrick J. Kelly

Former Board Members

Michael P. Alerding
Joseph M. Areddy
Rev. Clement Davis
Michael Browning
Rudy T. Mueller
Leo A. Barnhorst
George M. Bindner
Rev. Thomas E. Chambers
Mrs. Edward Drew
Joseph L. Flynn
Bro. Pedro Haering C.S.C
Daniel T. Hasbrook
Mrs. Joesph Kennedy
William H. Krieg
John E. Leahy
William L. Lyons
M. Joeseph Maginn
Leo P. McNulty
John E. Moran
Rev. James Moriarty
G. Joseph O'Malia
Stephen J. Roesinger
F. Joseph Viehmann
John W. Courtney, M.D.
Michael A. Maio
Ronald Renner
Robert V. Elson, Jr.
Joseph R. Clarke
Patrick J. Fisher
John W. Flynn
James L. Kennedy
Jacob E. Kiefer
Lloyd R. Mattson
Michael D. McGinley
Frank M. McHale
John J. Pearson
Sr. Mary Pius Reigner, S. P.
Robert C. Robisch
Charles E. Q. Stuart
Arthur J. Sullivan
Mrs. Howard Young
Karl Zinkan

THE SEVENTIES

1970-1971

Although they had been around for a long while, all the big issues seemed to converge as the world headed into the '70s: Black Power, women's lib, the sexual revolution, the "drop-out" youth culture and the war in Southeast Asia, where Americans had been enmeshed for half a decade.

Activism exploded on all fronts. The raised fist was everywhere, even at the Miss America contest. And when National Guardsmen, who had been issued "live" ammunition, fired not warning shots but lethal ones into the crowds of stone-throwing Kent State students protesting the war, four were slain.

But trying to channel the newly rising social consciousness was only one of the problems Cathedral faced. In a few years Cathedral's high enrollment had dropped nearly three hundred and action was necessitated.

Uncertainty abounded—the administration tried to pare a $200,000 debt by firing teachers. Unlike other parochial high schools (except Brebeuf) Cathedral could not seek financial support from the Archdiocese that assessed parishes for losses incurred by its five Catholic high schools. The enrollment which had dropped from 750 to 610 between 1970-1972, caused classes to be cancelled and careers at Cathedral to end for seven teachers.

By spring, reflecting the restlessness of the times, there was a sense of uncertainty and discontent that had probably never been present at the school before. Jeff McKenna, valedictorian of the Class of 1971, in a letter to *The Megaphone*, wrote:

I feel that Cathedral has regressed throughout the past four years, and at this point the school seems on the verge of despair. The firing of various teachers and the so-called repression of student objectives by the administration are just two alleged manifestations of this bleak situation. However, I question the validity of these charges—for who is responsible for this degradation, if it exists at all, but everyone involved with Cathedral . . . particularly the students, Seniors included.

Youth everywhere were calling for change, seeking empowerment. The Student Council told the administration:

In essence, our goal is to establish and maintain STUDENT power; we mean not necessarily total disregard for faculty or administrative policies, but rather giving the students an influential voice in school affairs. We realize that in past years the Cathedral student has not had a true voice in determining school policies. We will have at least one open meeting per month, hopefully on school time.

The students were delivering an ultimatum, but they were also pleading for responsiveness to change.

That year a special meeting was called by Brother Douglas to review the structure and activities of the school and to study the changes which Cathedral could make for the foreseeable future. At Student Rap Day the student body was divided into groups. The most important result of the meeting was the attitude in the school that favored progressive change. A second meeting, one month later, explored ideas for that change further.

Mutton-chopped sideburns, worn by teachers and students alike, were a visible sign that evolution rather than revolution was taking place, all over America as well as at Fourteenth and Meridian.

Destiny placed Brother Douglas at Cathedral. He was a progressive, and his attitude smothered fiery student unrest.

1971-1972

An obvious indicator that financial stress was showing on The Old Girl was the fact that *The Megaphone* began cost-cutting procedures itself. Cathedral's stalwart oracle, *The Megaphone*, had appeared in many formats from its first issue in 1920, but the new, cheaper format sent a loud salvo that the till was getting dusty.

Only 154 freshmen entered in the fall, and *The Megaphone* urged students to respond to a readership questionnaire. A "gripe box" was set up; presumably there was plenty of paper to fill the box.

Mike McGinley had come back to his alma mater and began the formidable job of following in Dezelan's footsteps. The football team slipped to 6-4 and was upstaged by the basketball and baseball teams, both of whom won Sectionals (Cathedral's second in basketball) and its first Regional championship.

Four "Irishmen," reflecting the continuous ethnicity of

Cathedral—co-captain John Wise, guard Lou Angelicchio, linebacker Chris Svarskopf and tackle Mike Heim—were named All-City football players.

Losses to Chatard and Brebeuf were included as Cathedral played four Top Ten teams. The highlight was an 8-7 homecoming win over Number Eight-ranked Shortridge.

Senior Mark Skehan, one of Cathedral's finest distance runners, was the individual City Champion in the City Cross-Country Meet at Riverside in a fast 9:42 time over the two-mile course. In dual, triple and individual meets the cross country team's record was 63-20.

Down by seven points to Attucks with 2:46 left to play, the Irish basketball team rallied to win the Regional. Steve Willis, later to star at Nebraska, led the Irish with thirty points. A proud Brother Douglas clipped the nets at Butler for Cathedral's trophy case.

The following week Connersville defeated Cathedral, 76-68, the closest win for the Spartans as they went on to take the 1972 State Championship.

All Irish varsity teams were successful and the wrestlers lost only to Scecina in eleven matches, including a 33-17 upset of perennial powerhouse Mooresville.

Golfer Jim Russell won his fourth consecutive City Championship. The Irish baseball team, led by slugging Steve Bohnert, won another City Championship.

And, perhaps prophetically, the Cathedral drama department presented two all-male-acted plays—*Twelve Angry Men* and *The Mouse That Roared.* They took the shows to the new girls' conglomerate—"LSA," Ladywood-St. Agnes.

A Cathedral Senior Class that led city high school seniors in a Walk for Development for financially-poor Americans, accepted diplomas in a year that eighteen-year-olds were given the right to vote. America was responding to its youth and Cathedral rode the wave. But more troubled times yet were ahead.

1972-1973

It was October 18, 1972. In a statement to parents, students and alumni, Principal Brother Douglas Roach announced: "Cathedral has been no exception to a decline in Catholic school enrollment reaching thirteen percent nationally in the last three years, with conservative estimates that enrollment will drop forty-two percent by 1980.

"The problem is not a lack of religious personnel: Cathedral has sixteen religious personnel on its staff. Rather, the problem is the declining enrollment over the past five years. Presently, the school is 220 students below its 760 capacity.

"There's no place I'd rather be than a hundred miles away from this microphone," Brother Douglas told 540 stunned students. "But if this announcement has to be made, then I want to be the one to make it. I've been here sixteen years and this is not an easy thing to do."

What he was saying was that the Brothers were departing, preparatory to closing the school. After the morning assembly, one faculty member said he saw "easily fifty to one-hundred kids crying" as the student body silently left the gym, shattered, confused and doubtful about their futures.

"I remember when I was a kid and I heard that John Kennedy had been killed. I felt the same way I do now," one student was quoted as saying. Most of the members of the school's fifteen-man advisory board were not informed of the decision until the board meeting that afternoon. Some of the members decided not to take the decision sitting down.

Bob Welch '45 and Tom McShane '46 responded to *The Indianapolis Star* and, on page one of the October 19 edition, vowed to seek financial support to quick start their ailing school.

Uncertainty shrouded Cathedral like a hovering fog. The distractions were constant as students pondered and fretted, and alumni, parents and friends volunteered to Welch forms of support beyond anticipation.

The Brothers had tossed a gauntlet. It reminded one in reflection of Japanese Admiral Yamamoto's prophetic words hours after the attack on Pearl Harbor: "All we have done is to arouse a sleeping giant." The giant, which had for a while seemed like a mouse, roared.

The mobilization of the new Cathedral had actually begun a few days earlier, when word from South Bend of the Brothers' desire to close had reached Welch. What that mobilization portended was in the realm of speculation and dreaming at this early stage.

The reality was that Brothers were leaving. The Brothers would be saluted in departure: the 1973 *Megaphone* would soon be dedicated to the sixteen men who formed the final Holy Cross faculty.

There would be, at the end of the year, a special tribute to Brother Eugene Weisenberger, Cathedral's "Mr. Music Man" for twenty-three years. He served as organist and choir member at the Cathedral parish in addition to creating of one of the state's strongest music departments.

His marching, symphonic and jazz bands were acclaimed and, as *The Megaphone* reported, "he had always maintained a beautiful rapport with his students."

These sixteen were, like their more than four hundred predecessors, dedicated servants of God who performed assignments long and far beyond those of traditional teachers. As was expressed in hundreds of alumni memories, the Holy Cross brothers created and hand-molded Cathedral High School in their own likeness, and this deepened the sense of loss at their leaving.

The Brothers were: Principal Douglas Roach, Leon Gnenuch, James May, Charles Drevon, Glenn Rousey, William Dygert, John Ptaszek, William Dusseau, Richard Smith, Roland Driscoll, Raymond Harrington, Richard Fischenich, Eugene Weisenberger, Thomas O'Malley, Dennis Calsin, George Klawitter and Chaplain Rev. Fr. Bernard Survil. After leaving the congregation, Glen Rousey would return to serve as vice-principal in the late seventies; most left Cathedral forever.

The final year would not be a wind-down year for the Brothers; they worked in their usual fashion to the last day on blood drives, charity campaigns, protest marches around pornographic book stores, and, of course, intensive instruction in academic subjects.

Mike McNulty, 1973 class vice president, recalled "the Brothers never let up in their commitment. It was tough on them, tough on the students. I admire them for their diligence." But that is really ahead of our story. What occurred in the fall was that the school community accepted the reality of the departure of the Brothers. What Cathedralites were not willing to countenance was the second part of the decision announced on that bleak day in October of 1972. The Brothers were not going to be allowed to close the school. "It was unheard of," said Tom McShane '46. "I thought, Cathedral is my school, not theirs."

The Brothers of Holy Cross had been the faculty, administration and, in the early years, coaches of Cathedral students for fifty-three years. But they were not the school itself. The October announcement was made; now events would move rapidly. Carolyn Welch was in Methodist Hospital and husband Bob '45 at her bedside when a call came from Tom Keating '57, the late columnist for *The Indianapolis Star.*

"Bob," Tom said, "several Cathedral men want to meet with you tonight." It was then after 7 p.m. and Welch said he would meet them at the Indianapolis Athletic Club at 8:30.

"Several had worked up a mad before I got there," Welch recalled. "They wanted to fight the Brothers publicly. I advised that we keep calm, say the Holy Cross have every right to do what is in the best interests of the Order," Welch recalled. Ever the reporter, Keating was facing a deadline and wanted Welch to comment on behalf of the group that several alumni were banding together to keep Cathedral open. Robert P. Early '22, *Star* managing editor, was holding the press run for Keating's story.

Keating reported, in the October 20, 1972 edition, of *The Indianapolis Star:*

"The Holy Cross brothers have every right to leave the school if they so desire," Welch said, "but they do not have the right to close the school. My phone has rung off the hook all day and there is a huge outpouring of support on the part of the sizeable Cathedral alumni in this area that the school should not be closed. A group of Cathedral supporters has already been formed and meetings have been arranged with the Archbishop to discuss the best way for Cathedral to continue as a topflight academic school. Cathedral's financial picture is not all that bad" Welch continued. "There is a debt but it is not one that can't be handled with a little thought. The school is, in effect, breaking even on its yearly operation." The Brothers' decision to leave was based on the declining enrollment rather than financial distress.

Cathedral's enrollment over six years had been down about two hundred from what it had been, but still 540 pupils paid a yearly tuition of $475.

The group assessed damage. What needed to be done was to right the capsizing ship of state, plan for a real future, infuse new capital, and keep the students and their parents from panic.

There was, of course, more to the Brothers' decision to leave the city than the announced declining enrollment. The Brothers' decision to leave Cathedral after 1972 was made against the background of feeling that they were not really wanted in Indianapolis anymore. The earlier importation of a Jesuit high school (Brebeuf in 1963) and five Archdiocesan high schools was a major blow to enrollment and they doubted the support of the archdiocese.

In considering a future for Cathedral, Bob Welch thought that there wasn't simply one decision to make, there were two. One was could, or should, the Brothers continue to operate a school in Indianapolis? The second question was should Cathedral continue, even possibly without the support of the Brothers? The answer to the first question had to come from the Brothers and their answer was clear—NO. They would not continue to operate the school.

The answer to the second question had to come from the Cathedral people of Indianapolis, and that answer wasn't so clear. To secure the school's re-establishment and future would take academic excellence in the tradition the Brothers had solidified. The Cathedral of the future would need a diversified enrollment which would reverse the enrollment decline, an infusion of capital the school had never sought before. The Brothers had not been paid their full stipends for years. The budget had been running around $200,000 and the tuition of $475 per year was not keeping up with the cost of operation. A new basis for financial operation would have to be undertaken.

At this point squabbling among some of the clerical participants confused the issue. It was then that Msgr. James P. Galvin, former Cathedral superintendent and director of Archdiocesan schools, was enlisted as consultant to effect an orderly changeover.

The early 1970s were a time of transition for religious schools. Just months earlier a similar transfer from religious to lay management had taken place at 130-year-old University of Notre Dame. So there was a path to follow.

"I will give you full support," Archbishop Biskup stated, "but not financial aid from the Archdiocese," he told the incorporators.

Soon after the original announcement, more than half of the Cathedral student body joined Cathedral alumni and friends in the gymnasium to conceptualize a strategy for the new Cathedral. Welch and Msgr. Galvin sat on stage. The non-religious faculty sat in the audience. (There were five lay teachers at the time.)

Most of the student body, which had dwindled to an enrollment of just over five hundred forty, attended. The crowd was more than eight hundred, far beyond anticipation, and the message was unanimous. "Cathedral must be saved," read the banners.

Bill Sahm '73, a senior and a halfback on the football team, addressed the meeting and told the gathering there were several purposes. "First of all we want to try to discourage any premature transfers out of the school until such time as we definitely know the school is closing," Sahm said. "Right now we feel our alumni won't let us down and will be able to keep the school open.

"Also we want to organize ourselves to help recruit grade school pupils to our school," Sahm added. "We feel Cathedral is the best school in the state and we feel we can sell this idea to potential students.

"As for the seniors, we don't want to be the last graduating class from Cathedral," Sahm said. "Even those students who are usually apathetic are saying today that they really didn't realize how much the school meant to them.

"The main reason for our meeting," Sahm concluded, "is that we want the alumni to know we're here and ready to help and that we do care."

"I am going to do everything in my power to see that Cathedral remains open," Welch responded. "I think this can be the beginning of a new era at the school rather than an ending and there are many others who share my feeling."

How prophetic he was.

Welch implored Brother Rex, assistant to Brother Philip, to help see that Cathedral could not close. There was plenty of support, he said. "If they are so supportive now" Brother Rex questioned, "where were they when we needed them?"

Brother Rex agreed to come to Indianapolis to meet with Brother Douglas Roach to set a mood for negotiated compromise. The two Brothers, Welch, Keating and Bill Sahm, Sr., former director of the Catholic Youth Organization, met for dinner at the Indianapolis Athletic Club.

The discussions failed to reach a satisfactory solution. Sons of Cathedral would accept no compromise: Cathedral would remain open, they vowed.

Again, the loyal and concerned Cathedral parents met with administrators to urge them to remain. The Brothers insistently declined; to keep Cathedral open was sheer folly. Welch had asked the Brothers not to be adamant, but his request went unheeded. Brother Rex presented a well-defined position: the Order of Holy Cross had taught and managed schools nearly 150 years and they were capable of evaluating a dying institution.

Their firmness only hardened the resolve of the parents and alumni that Cathedral would not close. The call to rally round the institution was sounded, and in places such as McShane's Tavern on Michigan and Emerson streets pledges were mounting. Owner Tom McShane '46 challenged his patrons and an estimated $200,000 was pledged (but actually, as a matter of fact, never materialized).

Attorney John O'Connor '33, a member of the National Catholic Championship basketball team, formed a separate corporation with Welch, Keating and Bill Sahm, Sr. as original incorporators.

It was a traumatic time, and these were perhaps the darkest, most desperate days in Cathedral's history. She had seen her sons not return from wars; had survived the hatred of the Ku Klux Klan, had endured a Depression, but now the lights were about to be turned off. But the switch was never allowed to be thrown.

Welch took the lead and set up a Board of Trustees made up of men from every part of Indianapolis who could build support and, quite frankly, write a check.

On October 21 Fr. Patrick J. Kelly was dressing to offer ten o'clock Mass. Kelly was associate pastor at St. Luke's Catholic Church after having served as Principal of Sacred Heart High School and Superintendent at Roncalli. On that chilly October morning Fr. Kelly recalls, "Bob Welch literally burst into the sacristy and exclaimed: 'They can't do this to Cathedral.'"

Father Kelly, a respected rival of Cathedral for many years, calmed Welch by offering to help in any way he could.

He joined Welch, Keating, Sahm and O'Connor as they formed a strategy. O'Connor volunteered to research the legal ramifications of a lay board operation to keep accreditation with the Indiana State Department of Education. Several priests who had taught and administered at Cathedral volunteered to pitch in. The Board decided to try to hire Brother Pedro Haering to re-form a faculty. He would serve as head of the school in its new form. Then the decision was made: it wouldn't be easy, but they decided to give it a go. Welch announced that the newly formed Board of Trustees would operate Cathedral High School and take it into the future.

The new plans needed to be presented to the school community at large. "We were asked some tough questions", Brother Pedro said "and were told by our critics our answers were vague. Our critics were right."

And so the Board was formed, choices made mostly to balance educators with business and professional people who could help financially and represent the different parts of the city.

The school had to have a wide appeal; it could not look like a neighborhood school.

In-depth plans began to be immediately formulated and it is well to take the time to survey them in detail because they set the course for the school for the future.

Brother Pedro informed the Board early on that we had a huge responsibility, and needed to think about what we must accomplish. One of the departing Brothers had described Cathedral as a building made up of a lot of bricks, with the Brothers as the mortar for the bricks. The Board had to find the new mortar."

Brother Pedro recounted that the Board determined Cathedral had been:
- an academically superb school
- a Catholic school
- a catholic (small "c") school in that it was for the entire city not a neighborhood or district
- a spirited school, expressed in associations such as sports.

The Board decided that Cathedral would:
- Continue to be an academically superb school by providing the resources to recruit and maintain an outstanding faculty
- Continue as a Catholic school with four years of required religion classes and the promotion of a Christian atmosphere among faculty and students. While the school would be a private, independent one, it would work with the Archbishop
- Continue as a small catholic school by providing $100,000 a year in scholarship funds with a scholarship in each of the Catholic parishes in Marion County. This was especially unique because Cathedral didn't have the $100,000
- Provide the resources to continue the fine spirit of Cathedral.
- Take Fiscal Responsibility and "pay-as-you-go "
- Increase tuition
- Pay salaries
- Provide suitable facilities.

The budget for 1974 was $200,000. [By 1989, it would exceed that amount more than ten times. Today, the current annual budget is $3,800,000.]

"While there were differences at times," Welch said "I honestly believe the Board did not make one decision that wasn't best for the students and the school." As this intensive planning went forward Brother Pedro, however, was denied permission by his Order to return to Cathedral.

It was a desperate situation; time was essentially running short. The Brothers were to leave Cathedral in less than six months. An important meeting to reassure the school community was scheduled for the next day to outline the future.

Fr. Kelly was immediately informed of the decision of the Brothers not to release Pedro. He agreed as an experienced school administrator to shepherd the journey.

Without appointment, Fr. Kelly went to the office of Archbishop Biskup. Fr. Kelly waited in the Archbishop's outer office until 3 p.m., when the Archbishop could squeeze minutes into his packed schedule.

"Why are you here?" Biskup wanted to know. "With all due respect, your Grace, I am here to advise you, not ask your permission. I intend to involve myself in solving the dilemma Cathedral High School now faces."

The Archbishop seemed mystified. "If I ask your permission, you then become a part of the matter," Fr. Kelly explained.

The Archbishop demurred, thought it through and agreed. The long day had left Fr. Kelly with a splitting headache, and he was unable to attend the reassurance meeting that evening. Still, they announced he would be heading the transition. [He took the awkward title of "Interim Transitional Coordinator Pro-Tem" to serve as liaison between the Brothers and the lay volunteers.]

At the meeting of the school community, sincerely and diplomatically, Welch announced plans for a Board and a interim coordinator. He praised the Congregation for fifty-four years of noble and effective service at Cathedral. The crowd cheered and the healing began.

Or so it seemed.

There were doubts after the cheers died down. Could a group of emotionally-charged alumni and friends organize a competent faculty and set an approved curriculum?

One strong consideration was the hiring of Fr. Kelly to serve as coordinator. The choice of the wise, articulate and tactful Kelly was a sound decision.

As the school year wound down there was high anxiety, but mounting skepticism was usually more than balanced by the fervent confidence that Cathedral would rise again. Joe Dezelan and Larry Bowman served as especially effective cheerleaders assuring one and all that Cathedral would be stronger than anything in the past.

The Brothers were to depart on a Saturday morning and turn the school's keys over to the Archbishop, who would transfer them to the Board. Welch declined to be at the scene.

"About 11 a.m. the doorbell rang at my home," Welch recalled. "Standing there was Archbishop Biskup who had just spent three hours overseeing the Brothers' move to be sure that Cathedral's furniture, books and all properties remained."

Cathedral faculty member Melinda Bundy was present after the school re-established itself on its own and is still a teacher at Cathedral. "I'm still amazed by the turn-around that occurred as the Cathedral family launched a journey we never envisioned," Mrs. Bundy said. "The simple, remarkable truth is that school arose like the Phoenix Bird of Egyptian mythology, from the ashes and sprang forth anew," she concluded.

On a cold November evening Cathedral's Irish dressed and wrapped for what many nay-sayers thought would be the final time a Cathedral team would charge onto a football field.

The Irish took a 7-2 record to Washington High School's field that night. Long one of Cathedral's respected opponents, Washington was undefeated with a 9-0 record, a Number Two statewide ranking and with a mythical State title looming.

Tom Keating wrote in the 1973 edition of *Down Through the Years With Cathedral Football:*

The tradition and emotion was thick enough to cut with a knife, as the Irish proceeded to do what they had done so many times before— fire up sky high and win a game they were supposed to lose.

All-State end Joe Weber scored on a 19-yard pass from All-City quarterback Dave Zapp and tough cornerback Jim Loughery fell on a blocked punt in the end zone for the second score as the Irish entered the fourth quarter in a 13-13 deadlock.

Late in the fourth quarter, the Continentals faced a fourth down situation on their own fourteen yard line and Coach Bob Springer (Cathedral '52) decided to gamble and go for the first down. The gamble failed as Washington fumbled and three plays later Cathedral halfback Bill Sahm (that same Bill Sahm) crashed into the end zone behind the blocking of All-City end Tom McShane (son of Tom '46) and fullback George Lauck for the winning touchdown. The score was Cathedral 20; Washington 13.

There was a grand celebration at McShane's after the game.

Many have commented that the upset win over Washington was the launching pad that was needed to escalate Cathedral to her next stage on the road to recovery.

While Cathedral's future was evolving, Coach Jean Ancelet's basketball team was driving to another Sectional basketball championship at Ben Davis. In his first year as varsity coach, Ancelet's Irish, fashionable in new lightning-bolt jerseys, won twenty-one of twenty-seven games, including three over Crispus Attucks and four games in which they scored more than one hundred points.

It wasn't the last football team, basketball season or year at Cathedral. Cathedral wasn't dead, not by a long shot. Brother Douglas did not complete his term; he was appointed Province Personnel Director of the Midwest. Brother Thomas assumed the final days as school principal.

With Brother Pedro unavailable, the Cathedral loyalists launched a search for a principal, and Bernard Melevage became the school's first lay principal for the school year 1973.

BOB SPRINGER

One of Cathedral's finest athletes, Coach Springer was All-State in football and All-City in basketball on what many believe was the finest All-City team ever. Joining Springer were Crispus Attucks legends Hallie Bryant (1953 Indiana "Mr. Basketball") and Willie Gardner; Joe Sexson, perhaps Tech's greatest athlete, and 1952 "Mr. Basketball," and three-sport star Dick Nyers of Manual.

Springer has the winingest Indianapolis high school football coaching record for his combined seasons at Sacred Heart High and at Washington. Springer's record of 242 victories is third highest in state coaching history. He is a member of the Indiana Football Hall of Fame.

In recalling his memories of Cathedral, Springer said, "Cathedral has always stood for the best in everything. As a student athlete I wasn't treated any differently. Some of my greatest friendships were formed at Cathedral.

"As for coaching against Cathedral," the former Purdue football star recalls, "No school has given me tougher games and sadder defeats. I still have nightmares over the 1972 and 1977 games," he added.

1973-1974

Melevage brought strong educational credentials to Cathedral, but he proved not to be what the Board needed for the delicate, emergency necessities of reformation and transition. He remained only three months in the fall.

Mike McGinley was appointed Acting Principal in December and served in that capacity for two years.

Instead of closing Cathedral's doors, the large and loyal alumni had assumed operation of the school. The Brothers who had served Cathedral's sons well during fifty-four years, were no longer our teaching community. Nine faculty members returned to open Cathedral's fifty-fifth school year. The reformed teaching staff came from as far away as Canada.

Familiar names on that newly-organized Cathedral faculty included Dan O'Malia, past Chairman of the Trustees; Coach Joe Dezelan; Sister Jeanne Moore and teacher Glenn Mauger. A new use was found for the abandoned Brothers' residence rooms. The Commons was the setting for the Common Hour. Here students could exchange thoughts and ideas with teachers, each other and community leaders.

The faculty that opening day in September, 1973, consisted of three priests, two new Brothers, two Sisters and twenty-two lay teachers and coaches. Enrollment numbered 537, something of a miracle, but well below the 913 who attended the school ten years earlier.

The relatively strong enrollment was a tribute to the Cathedral students who had recruited eighth grade classes, and loyal alumni and friends willing to take a chance with their most precious possession—a son seeking a fine education.

Cathedral's halls were strewn with gold and blue. "Dear Old Cathedral" was played and loudly sung but there still lingered an unspoken fear that this effort, though sincere and dedicated, would fail. To quote *The Megaphone,*

. . . the transition year brought not only a new administration but innovation, transition, and inevitably, chaos following. The novice administration was a sapling best described by the attitudes of its keepers. Many believed that support for the young tree was the key to its subsistence. Only by nourishing the sapling—by giving it a chance—would it grow firm and yield fruit.

The Old Cathedral: Today The Catholic Center

The building that remains Cathedral to thousands of sons still stands looking much the same as it did when it opened in September, 1927.

Since its re-opening in 1982, The Catholic Center has been the home of central services for the Indianapolis Archdiocese and the office of the Archbishop. It contains most of the Catholic agencies ranging from education and social services, to public relations and purchasing. After Cathedral High School moved to the Ladywood-St. Agnes campus in 1976, the building was closed while a feasibility study was conducted for its future use.

Archbishop Edward T. O'Meara announced after the conclusion of the study that it was in the best interest of the Archdiocese that services be coordinated and officed together. In doing so, Archbishop O'Meara reaffirmed his commitment to Indianapolis' center city. He also believed that the Cathedral church—as well as the former high school building—should be preserved as the hub of the Catholic community.

Remodeling of the high school building took place over two years at a cost of two million dollars. The former Cathedral gym where every freshman drudged through physical education, the basketball games, wrestling meets, pep assemblies, sockhops and those memorable school dances were held, is now the Assembly Hall.

Cathedral class reunions have been held there and the echoes of the sounds of old Cathedral may be heard if one strolls through the halls in quiet reflection. The classrooms, locker rooms, study hall, library and the thirty tiny cubicles where the Brothers lived were remodeled into offices. Sal Punterelli '45 paid his Cathedral tuition by mopping floors in the gymnasium. Sal retired recently as Director of Purchasing for the Archdiocese. "Everyday I have a memory of my days at Cathedral," Sal reflected.

"Often, we'll have a former Cathedral student stop at the reception desk and ask if he could walk around the building," commented Chuck Schisla '55, director of the Communications Center for the Archdiocese.

Fifty years of Cathedral life, two-thirds of the history of the school, were formed inside that hallowed building.

To use the same flowery metaphor, in spite of good intentions at re-birth, Cathedral almost withered that first year after the Brothers left. *The Megaphone* chronicled,

Perhaps the administration could have bloomed into awesome red wood. Yet, cynicism acted as a tourniquet upon the tree's system. The indifferent passively sat back and let it be.

These were troubled years for youth everywhere, and it just happened that Cathedral was trying to reconstitute a school in a time of national uncertainty. Certainly that added to the problems within the school.

Long hair was the rage, whether long and stringy or page-boy bob. LBJ was dead and the foreboding years of Richard Nixon were beginning. America was retreating from Vietnam and a happy, though shamed, nation was welcoming POWs as singers whispered "Killing Me Softly with His Song."

Cathedral Mothers Club instituted Tuesday afternoon bowling to comfort, console and interact with a youth that seemed to be slipping into pipe dreams, questioning values that had been strong for generations in Catholic Indianapolis.

The opening football game was the first public demonstration of the new school in the fall of '73. Again, the opponent was Washington. The 5-0 victory was not as dramatic as the one ten months earlier, but it heralded a season that was to produce the school's first eleven-victory season and an appearance in the first IHSAA championship game.

Coach Mike McGinley never coached better; the team outscored its opponents 230-67 in a 10-0 season. The first official playoffs found Cathedral placed in the upper division. Other schools surpassed Cathedral in enrollment, but obviously not in spirit, as shown by the football team of '73.

Misfortune struck as Cathedral's finest runner, George Lauck, was injured and missed the final two games of a season that probably would have produced for him an all-time rushing record and All-State honor.

The final game of the regular season was played before an overflow CYO Stadium crowd. Halfback Bob Willis ran for 215 yards in a 29-22 win over Scecina. It was Cathedral's fifteenth City title since 1940.

The victory also earned the Irish the dubious honor of an invitation to travel to Bloomington to play South High School, the State's Number One-ranked team and owner of the nation's longest winning streak of sixty games. Facing this difficult challenge, Coach McGinley reached back into the tradition and inspired the players, speaking of their heritage and destiny.

The week before the meeting, South Coach Tom Sells asked Washington Coach Springer what to expect from Cathedral.

Springer laughed and said, "Just wait until you see how fired-up they get for a big game. You'll find out about Cathedral." It was a 32-27 victory of which legends are made. There are those who still believe that victory was Cathedral's greatest ever.

From the opening play on, Cathedral seized the moment. Senior halfback Vince Gaughan, who set a school record by starting thirty-two straight games, began the scoring as he ran back the opening kickoff ninety-five yards for a touchdown. Less than two minutes later quarterback Dave Zapp tossed a thirty-yard touchdown pass to rangy end Rodney Burns.

Zapp was to receive the first Football Mental Attitude award ever presented by the IHSAA one week later. Bloomington's lightning-like offense was smothered by strong defense; Coach Sells' players fumbled five times.

Only Cathedral and South Bend Adams, pre-season Number One team, remained to settle the championship.

Following a three-hour bus ride to South Bend, the Irish were poised. They had had only six days of rest. Their pre-game meal was held at Notre Dame's Morris Inn, where they were to be again infused with a deep draught of tradition—as if they needed more adrenalin. What they needed was luck.

More than nine thousand fans and a statewide television audience watched a 13-13 tie head into the fourth quarter. Games may be won or lost through fate, but this night it was punting which led to poor field position. Playing on its home field, Adams won the game 19-13 but Cathedral won a larger victory as the football momentum moved the school, literally and figuratively, to a higher plateau.

The next two years were full of anticipation and wonder. Could a school at 1416 North Meridian Street continue to serve a population that was moving out to the suburbs? The answer was yet to come.

1974-1975

The first women teachers had come to Cathedral, part of the trend of real change in the school. Some were not Catholic, but their teaching credentials were outstanding.

In 1974, Melinda Luckey—"Miss Luckey"—began teaching at Cathedral, a chauvinistic institution that had never endured a woman teacher for more than six weeks.

"Mr. McGinley called us [four new women teachers] into his office and told us not to smile or be nice until January. And there was another problem—short skirts. So we were to wear longer skirts as much as possible."

She described a fight in the second-floor hall which she knew better than to try to break up. "When I went out in the hall, the boys were much more concerned about my safety than about breaking up the fight and did everything in their power to get me to leave. So I decided that the boys had finally decided that I was going to spend the year with them."

Mrs. Melinda Luckey Bundy, who has continued to teach at Cathedral ever since, went on: "The seventies were a period of change. I don't think Cathedral could have existed downtown. I don't think we could have gone coed downtown because parents were not going to send their daughters downtown. I was a little frightened at times going back downtown for after-school events. The year that we went coed, Brebeuf went coed and in a time period of two or three years all the one-sex schools closed. St. Agnes was the first to go. St. Mary's was gone. Most of the girls schools closed. They didn't even have a chance to go coed. The last hold-out was Latin School."

Some teachers reflected the dress and hair styles of the era: English teacher and senior class moderator Dan O'Malia wore his hair in a page-boy, *a la* Prince Valiant. O'Malia would leave teaching for his family grocery business and, in 1987, would be elected Board Chairman of the school's trustees.

The Mothers Club and the Fathers Club, led by president Leo Barnhorst '42, conjured up schemes and membership to keep a swirling school afloat in a world of change.

The Senior Class of '75 had been tested, and loyalty prevailed. They encouraged—and recruited—entering freshmen. The final year on 14th Street—and its rapid change—was dawning.

1975-1976

It was the Bicentennial year of the United States and the Fiftieth anniversary of the start of construction of the building at 1416 North Meridian Street. *The Cathedran* recalled that on the school site in 1861, Indiana Governor Oliver P. Morton's administration established Camp Carrington for the marshaling of Hoosiers into the Union Army.

The 1976 Cathedran cover featured a swaggering Irish leprechaun and on the subject of the resurging school spirit, *The Megaphone* bannered:

Maybe we've got spirit because we have an all-male student body. Maybe we've got spirit because of our academic and athletic prowess. Whatever the reason, the important thing to remember is that we do have spirit, and it makes us what we are.

In spite of all the bravado, the actual physical placement of Cathedral was still uncertain. Should it remain where it was, move and build, or merge? In the spring its destiny would be decided.

Still, school continued. A dynamo of spirit, teacher Dan Wellman buoyed students with his restless enthusiasm and his commitment to learning.

"Cathedral and I met at a fortuitous time," Noblesville native "Doc" Wellman recalled. "I think the school has given me far greater than I gave to her."

Band director Larry Everhart changed the uniform style to black shoes, white spats, black tuxedo trousers, gold waist sashes with tassels, blue and gold shirts, and black bear hats. A multi-talented musician, Everhart could stir the soul with his bagpipe rendition of "Amazing Grace."

Coach McGinley's football squad lost its first two games by a total of five points and won its next eight including a 28-12 Homecoming win against Number One-ranked Washington.

Indianapolis high school basketball featured three top ten teams, but Cathedral wasn't among them. It would be the final season Cathedral would play on the floor that had been its home court for forty-nine seasons.

The Old Cathedral Gym

Cathedral opened play in the gymnasium on December 7, 1928, defeating St. Andrews of Richmond, 27-26. In the forty-nine seasons on the shining floor with its tight sidelines, Cathedral teams won three State Catholic Championships, eleven Holiday and Invitation tournaments, 322 basketball games and achieved a seventy-four winning percentage over eighty-three rival schools.

Perhaps no other school used its gymnasium/auditorium more than Cathedral. Every able Cathedral student took physical education there; St. Agnes Academy girls used the gym; it was the site of three installations of Church leaders, Bishop Ritter and Archbishops Schulte and Biskup. Thousands attended Mass, received communion and accepted diplomas there

For nearly fifty years Cathedral boys strung streamers of multi-colored crepe paper as they tried to transform the gym into an exotic escape for dances and parties. The rhythms of Romberg and Dylan made the rafters resonate.

Singers, dancers, thespians performed on the stage and hundreds of parties and receptions were celebrated beneath the ceiling that was finally punctured by the high-flying baton of 1972 band drum-major Dan Walker.

Still used for Archdiocesan functions, the old Cathedral gym will always bring memories of that first date, the reverberations of pep rallies, and the thoughtful silence of Retreat.

To return to that empty gym, even in memory, is to live again the sights, sounds, and feelings of adolescent youth gone by.

The film *All the President's Men* documented America's greatest scandal, the Watergate affair, and Cathedral was readied for its final sentimental school event. On Sunday, May 16, 1976, Cathedral's 56th commencement, 126 graduating seniors heard Principal Brother Pedro Haering reflect on the school's glorious past, commenting on the struggle of youth for independence and the search for identity.

To football captain Terry Woehler would go the honor of receiving the final diploma of old Cathedral.

Proudly, the seniors strode into the night, the school lights were clicked off and the old Cathedral ended. Months later, the new Cathedral would arise on a wooded campus only six miles away, but a world apart in setting and atmosphere. Something revolutionary had occurred.

The Sisters of Providence had contacted Bob Welch during the spring of 1976 while he was in Florida vacationing.

I met with the Sisters at their request; they wanted to know if we could work out an arrangement for Cathedral to take the Ladywood–St. Agnes campus, become coed and whatever. Ladywood-St. Agnes had determined that the Sisters would not continue and no one had made a serious effort to continue it under different auspices.

My first reaction was no—I need no more headaches. The Sisters had me visit the school. It was and is a marvelous plant, a beautiful campus. The main building is extremely well built with up-to-date classrooms, labs, etc.

At Cathedral the Brothers had done practically no maintenance on the buildings for the last few years. Upkeep had been allowed to slip. Even before the Sisters called, the Board had felt we would have to spend about two million dollars on the 14th and Meridian facility to keep up with the academic and athletic needs. And after spending all that we would have a little less than two acres compared to thirty-nine acres at Ladywood-St. Agnes. In the final analysis we decided it was best for Cathedral to do it. Cathedral got a real plus in the campus.

If Cathedral was ever going to be coed this was as good a time as any to do it as the increased enrollment—from about 425 to 675 as projected—made for better budgeting and long-range planning.

There were negatives—our faculty and staff was not attuned to a coed school. None of the nuns had planned on staying, although some did *and have. Ye gads, new faculty recruitment—again. We decided to do it. The American Fletcher Bank (now Bank One) and its Chairman Frank E. McKinney, Jr. '57 and President Harry L. Bindner '35, were very helpful in arranging a loan to pay the Sisters the $1.8 M we had agreed on.*

The announcement was not handled well at all. The Sisters in Terre Haute were saying that we had worked out an agreement that meant the facilities could be continued to educate in a Catholic atmosphere in Indianapolis. The Sisters at Ladywood-St. Agnes were saying it wasn't going to happen.

The transition took place and the school obviously has survived in spite of some terrible scars.

Ladywood

Founded by the Sisters of Providence in 1925, Ladywood was a country-day and boarding school for "ladies of educational and expressive interests," a 1930s school brochure intoned.

The earliest inter-school contact on record was in 1930 when Cathedral's seventy-piece band "its best ever," according to *The Megaphone,* participated in an outdoor pageant on the Ladywood campus.

The band members, then attired in World War I-styled uniforms replete with leggings, high collars and stiff-brimmed, mountie-style caps, were "concealed in the woods, on either side of the stream, playing Indian music," reported *The Megaphone.* The ladies were not impressed.

"Most of our dates for dances and games were from the academies and Shortridge, but a few 'ladies from Ladywood,' as we called them, came to our events," said Jim Bugher '46.

It wasn't until the 1940s that cheerleaders, singers and actresses for Cathedral productions came from the three girls' academies and Ladywood School, and, of course the relationship grew much deeper, if problematic, in the seventies, when the Ladywood campus became Cathedral's new home.

The August 25, 1976 edition of *The Indianapolis News* bannered: "GIRLS? They're NO Big Deal." Featured were comments of Mary Huffman, Eric Timmens, Mike Ruwe, Anne Kennedy and Kevin Kernel.

Sporting a broken nose from a football practice forearm, Ruwe said: "It's not like we've been cut off from girls. I went to coed schools until the ninth grade. This will be just like grade school—except the girls have grown up a little." And so the improbable became the possible and then transformed into the reality. Three fine Catholic schools in Indianapolis joined traditions and the new Cathedral was born.

It was not easy, and that is an understatement. On April 19, 1976 a group of angry parents met at Ladywood-St. Agnes to protest the action of the Sisters of Providence to sell to Cathedral's Board of Trustees.

The parents reportedly had offered the Order a higher price than the $1.8 million they had accepted from Cathedral. In a front page story in *The Star* April 20, Bob Welch said the Board would sign papers for a cash loan from American Fletcher National Bank, where he was a member of the board of directors, and the Windridge Development Company, which he owned, was to provide collateral. (Welch had purchased the Windridge land and the former Stoughton Fletcher mansion, all a portion of the original Ladywood campus, three years before and later developed it.)

The angry parents questioned whether the new school would be coeducational or just for boys. One woman attending told the gathering that Welch's daughter (Maura) was a sophomore at Ladywood-St. Agnes, so the school would be coed. "I can't see him throwing his daughter out," she opined.

Parents and students were angry that the Sisters had declined their unsecured two million dollar offer. Robert L. Smith, president of the Ladywood-St. Agnes Parents Club, commented: "We made our two million dollar offer ten days later and it was subject to a ninety-day closing so we could get financing together. You can't go to banks until you have an offer that's been accepted."

Rancor followed, with vandalism occurring on the campus. Neighbors protested the imagined specter of the building of a football stadium—lights, blaring bands and thousands of cars in the neighborhood.

Even Sister Ann Casper, the principal, suffered from the wrath that marked that three-month period. On returning from a meeting to finalize the sale to Cathedral it was rumored she was locked out of her residence because the locks had been changed.

The Order was in financial distress, supporting many elderly nuns, and also was selling school property they owned in Chicago, Washington, D. C. and California, Smith said. His final comment was, "We need another coed high school in this city like we need a hole in the head."

To acquaint the student bodies with each other, Cathedral arranged buses to transport its student body to visit the Ladywood-St. Agnes campus.

"They came in like invading Huns," one parent stated. "Those boys were smoking and urinating in the woods. It was a disgusting sight."

As if protecting their girls from invading marauders, teachers and parents gathered the girls together in the gymnasium and they huddled together, singing the school song over and over.

For some, the transition—though necessary for both institutions—was simply not going to be accepted. Thankfully, time has erased the most traumatic memories.

Brother Pedro, who had finally been granted permission to head the school, remembered that time: "I'm not sure how long it took to make the decision to move to the present location, but when I came back to Cathedral in 1975 that was to be the last year to be at 14th and Meridian. There were continuous rumors about the availability of Ladywood-St. Agnes, that they would have to sell out. Or . . . we were going to expand downtown, we were going to build a stadium. We didn't have the property [to expand] but there was property available near the Spaghetti Bowl, where I-70 and 65 come together around 9th street. It was going to cost three million, including a band building. We were going to try to raise three million to try to accomplish that.

"Then this place opened up for $1.8 million and one point eight million was a song for this property. It was a steal, so why enlarge downtown when enrollment would continue to decline when you could get this beautiful thirty-nine acres for one point two million less? Many of the nuns lived at Loretto Hall for many years. If we hadn't bought it, it might have wound up a barber college.

The school buildings needed a little work, but women take better care of property than do men."

To be accommodating, Pedro recalls: "We came out here with our faculty. I offered Ladywood-St. Agnes faculty jobs. However, only one nun and five lay teachers responded. All the rest didn't want to have anything to do with Cathedral. I came out here a number of times in the spring after the deal was closed, and I never was in any atmosphere with such hostility ... but I can't blame them.

"I may sound prejudiced," Pedro continued, "but I think the boys were a little more generous about attending girls sports and coming more than half way."

The newly-formed Cathedral had no dress code, just what was reasonable, but reserved the right to tell students if they dressed unacceptably again that they would be sent home. "In the early days I had contact with fifty percent of the parents, so all I had to say was that the dress was inappropriate and they would take care of it. From 1972-1980 the parents would say 'well that's your problem.' Levis were not permitted and shirts with collars had to be worn. The parents would have been pleased if there was a uniform," Pedro reminisced.

"One of the problems with the drinking was we were at the beginning of the other drugs—pot, cocaine etc. and the parents adopted the attitude, let them get drunk . . . it is better than pot. We had the constant problem with more parents who were gone on weekends so a lot of the kids would have all-night parties. We were somewhat tolerant, as drinking has always been a part of CHS—as far as I understand it. "

BROTHER PEDRO WRITES OF THE MOVE

There were many problems to relocation. First off, moving a school six or seven miles to another part of the city is not only a physical problem, but the Sisters of Providence were very attached to the school and rightly so. They had been there since 1925 and had been involved for a half-century. It was traumatic, and the Sisters of Providence and the girls were unhappy.

Many of the girls would not accept the change and thought they were holding out for the old Ladywood by making it as difficult for Cathedral as possible, but that was not true of all of the girls though many transferred to other schools—many to Brebeuf.

The neighbors were also Cathedral enemies. They feared that we would build a big football stadium and that there would be a lot of people in and out of here and that we would have lights at night.

An organization of the residents brought legal action, and the Board of Trustees signed papers saying that Cathedral would not have varsity football games played there. Some of the boys did not want to move and neither did the parents. They wanted to keep an all-boys school. My theory for operating a high school was to get involved with the parents, and they have to want to be involved in the school. When I was at Cathedral in 1952-59 the cooperation was there and we would talk about the school. From 1975-80 it seemed like the parents thought the furthest thing from their minds was being involved in the school. They seemed to believe, "If we come to a parents meeting we want to be entertained! Get a Notre Dame football coach to come and talk to us. Nothing to do with the kids—the kids are your problem for six hours a day and we don't want to hear about it."

In the old days if a student was a discipline problem we'd call the parents and they wanted to help to get the student back on track. When we had a discipline problem out here I had three people, the two parents and the student who perhaps wasn't telling the truth—the parents simply would not believe that their kid would cause trouble. It didn't make any difference what the evidence was, so it took us a while to get through that.

1976-1977

Over the summer arguing subsided, the adjustments were being made and CHS-LSA became CHS. Enrollment reached 675 with 250 coeds on August 23 when the new Cathedral began at 5225 East 56th Street, the school's third location. Principal Brother Pedro said all but two Cathedral teachers from downtown would be retained. Eight LSA teachers were continued and Pedro said the school could handle eight hundred students but stressed: "We are not interested in being crowded."

In spite of dire predictions, the move cost Cathedral few students: four seniors, six juniors and twenty-five sophomores elected not to move. "Perhaps only four or five left because Cathedral was becoming coeducational," Pedro recalled.

Cathedral operated two or three buses. "One of the biggest obstacles the school has to overcome was distance," he explained. "Some students were making daily trips of more than fifty miles."

"One of our important fears was that we would lose too many students from the south and west," Pedro observed.

Cathedral's program in religious studies was revised and a matching grant of $2,500 from the RasKob Foundation of Delaware helped fund significant religious studies.

The move also afforded the opportunity to expand in such areas as drama, arts, crafts, athletics, home economics and music.

Joe Quill '39 represented Cathedral in a zoning case to allow the school to erect lights on its practice football field. As its volunteer lawyer, Quill plead the case, but angry neighbors, still aroused by the entry of more than four hundred boys into their pleasant, wooded neighborhood, won out.

"There was just no reasoning with them," Joe recalled. "I was even charged with conflict-of-interest because I was a member of the Metropolitan Development Commission. These were ugly days."

The neighbors demanded a 1,700-foot fence, six feet high, be erected around the perimeter bordering private property. It was ruled an unreasonable request. The court granted rezoning January 19, 1977 to allow a field area for band practice and athletic activities.

A lawsuit filed in Boone County was dropped when the zoning was changed from residential to "limited use." Even though Ladywood had used the field more than twenty years for sports, Cathedral was initially denied use of the field until the decision was overruled by the Indiana Supreme Court.

Cathedral had no field for practice or games; the lease on CYO Field expired October 31, 1976, but the success of the "Spirit of '76" football team was to cause an extension.

That team won its first dozen football games with only one close decision during the season (21-20 over Tech).

Only sixteen teams were selected to compete for the State Championship in the fourth year of State Championship play. Cathedral drew North Central, the state's largest school in enrollment, in the opening round.

North Central, which opened in 1956, was supposed to be the visitor but, because Cathedral was without a stadium, CYO officials were asked to intervene. North Central's stadium seated 8,500 but Cathedral wanted to play at CYO—and North Central didn't criticize the Irish desire.

Boasting a team of players of college-size proportions, the Panthers outweighed the Irish thirty pounds per player on the line.

"When I scouted those guys," Coach McGinley recalled, "I thought they were Notre Dame."

More than seven thousand fans jammed into enlarged CYO. Tough Tom Bowling rammed over from the one-yardline, and Chris Cullina's kick was even and over. North Central was driving late and Vince Lorenzano blocked their field goal attempt with thirty-three seconds to play in a 7-6 victory.

The topper was yet to come. Playing on Prescription Athletic Turf in Reitz Bowl, Cathedral defeated Evansville Reitz, 7-0, on a Jimmy O'Hara to Gerry Leahy thirty-yard touchdown run. Reitz had a sixteen-game winning streak and was ranked Number One in Indiana.

Nearly ten thousand spectators in frigid weather in Evansville were stunned, as the Hilltoppers were shut out for the first time in nine years. It was Cathedral's twentieth consecutive win, the longest win streak, although 1960-61-62 teams went twenty–four games without a loss including a 6-6 tie with Broad Ripple in 1961.

While San Francisco publisher Randolph A. Hearst posted $500,000 bail for his missing daughter, Patty Hearst, sought on charges of kidnaping, robbery and assault, Cathedral prepared for its second shot at a State Championship. The stage was readied—

CYO Field's final Cathedral game there. Merrillville was 10-1, Cathedral 12-0 going into the match.

Cathedral would have moved the game to Butler if the IHSAA could have guaranteed $500 from concessions, Coach McGinley said. Merrillville's Pirate linemen outweighed Cathedral twenty pounds per man.

Tom Keating wrote a column describing Coach McGinley's analysis of the character of the Cathedral team.

"Forty-three boys accepted the fact that they wouldn't be able to do a lot of things their peers were." Quarterback Jimmy O'Hara (now coach at Hamilton Southeastern) worked eight hours each Saturday and Sunday at a parking garage to pay his Cathedral tuition.

Because the game could not be televised, due to low-wattage field lights, the IHSAA lost $4,000 in rights fees. "The move to the Ladywood campus had disproved a theory of some that Cathedral would no longer be a tough football school." Wayne Fuson wrote November 19, 1976 in *The Indianapolis News:* "Nostalgia was thick," Fuson wrote, as more than eight thousand fans gathered for the final game at storied CYO Field, Friday, November 19, 1976.

With 1:33 remaining, a third Merrillville touchdown pass turned what seemed victory into another Irish disappointment. Cathedral led 10-0 and 19-7 at the half.

As the clock expired, Cathedral end Gerry Leahy grabbed what looked like a touchdown pass, but officials ruled his foot was inches outside the end zone. Final score: 24-28.

Leahy also was denied a seventy-yard touchdown after plucking a fumble out of the air and racing in. Officials ruled the ball was dead. A *Star* sportswriter reviewed the play as "a quick whistle."

In giving credit to Cathedral, Pirate Coach Ken Haupt said: "I used to coach at a Catholic school. So I know all about how you can make a 170-pounder play like a two-hundred pounder."

Though the new Cathedral didn't resemble the old, the spirit and tradition had made the seven-mile journey.

Among the changes: girls sports. Through 1977-78, Ladywood athletes had distinguished themselves in sports competition. Beginning in the 1970s inter-school competition began for the girls. Among the many fine athletes at LSA was Cecilia Mimms '77. Her basketball talents took her to the Indiana All-Star basketball squad, first ever to play Kentucky in the annual series which benefits the blind.

The beginning of Cathedral's eighth decade would be Brother Pedro Haering's twelfth and final year as its president-principal. A native of Evansville and a graduate of Reitz Memorial High School, Brother Pedro served the old school from 1953 to 1959 and the new Cathedral from 1975 to 1979.

Now living in semi-retirement at Dujarie Hall on the Holy Cross College campus near Notre Dame, Brother Pedro assumed many roles including deejay for the post-game "sock hops" in the 1950s.

An outstanding educator, sports booster, disciplinarian and humanitarian, Brother Pedro's busy life today includes hosting a good music program on WNDU, Notre Dame's radio station. Brother Pedro owns a collection of American music standard tunes and is recognized as an authority on pop music.

Under his direction, a staff and faculty of fifty conducted the school into her sixtieth year. The new campus offered nature as a laboratory. Many classes were held outdoors and Fall Creek became a test tube for George Kovatch's biology lab. The wooded glens and meadowed lawns near a bubbling stream became the inspiratory setting for creative writing and English poetry classes in the spring, when occasionally, they might convince their teachers to "meet outside."

While spider-like Barry Manilow belted out his hit "At the Copa," Cathedral students romanced to "Just the Way You Are" and played the controversial song "With a Little Help From My Friends."

Ann Seidensticker Wendroff '79, wrote from her home in San Diego, "Cathedral not only gave me a good educational foundation but life-long memories like teacher Julia Birge, the pep rally with Adam Smasher and the sports wins." Like others, Ann Seidensticker had been unsure how she would gain from the merger, but she was happily surprised by the results.

1978-1979

Not only would the 1978-'79 school year be Brother Pedro's last year, but it also saw the last graduating class which featured individuals from the old Cathedral, Ladywood-St. Agnes, and Our Lady of Grace schools. Even though most of these individuals came together as sophomores, animosity still persisted among various factions as long as they were still together. The boys from the old school still had some difficulty in accepting that they were not in an all-boys' school, and the girls had just as much difficulty in not being in an all-girls' school. Discontent and misplaced anger within the Senior Class marked the year. Nevertheless, everything came together and Baccalaureate and Graduation ceremonies went off without a hitch.

English teacher Kevin McDowell, a 1968 graduate of Cathedral High School, was the faculty member chosen to speak at Baccalaureate ceremonies that year. Mr. McDowell sternly warned the Class of '79 that their discontent might shape their future. Students listened to him, they respected him, and they appreciated his genuine and sincere comments, not to mention his quick wit.

He had enjoyed and challenged the Class of '79 throughout their years on the new campus. McDowell left Cathedral in 1981 and currently serves as legal counsel to the Indiana Department of Education. While at Cathedral, he taught English, journalism, and math and was moderator of *The Megaphone*. He also served as Cross Country and Track coach. Among his students were Jon Schwantes '82, political reporter for *The Indianapolis News* and Letitia Miele '81, reporter for WISH-TV News.

The significance of girls attending CHS was particularly obvious with the Class of '79. The two most prestigious awards given at the end of the school year were received by females. Although the valedictorian and the salutatorian were both boys, Pete Zoog and David Hoffman, the Al Feeney Award (now the Joe Dezelan Award) went to Mary Hession as the most outstanding student athlete, and the Board of Trustees Award went to Denise Clark for her leadership, dedication and commitment to Cathedral High School. Mary went on to play college and professional golf, and Denise went to law school at Georgetown University and is currently practicing law in Washington, D.C.

Almost no year can go by in Cathedral history without mentioning football, and the 1978 season is no exception. Fans witnessed a devastating loss to Scecina on the Lawrence Central football field and saw coach Mike McGinley keep his players on the bench after the game until almost everyone filed out of the stadium and the field lights were shut off.

A note concerning that 1978 Scecina game seems important to recall. Scecina warmed up for the game wearing their white uniforms. When they returned to the field from the locker room to start the game, they were wearing bright new yellow uniforms, with even the cheerleaders in new outfits. According to assistant coach Jim McLinn, Scecina had a good team that year, but the switching of the uniforms *a la* Notre Dame gave the Scecina team and their fans that something extra which may have made the difference.

The following week, Homecoming night of 1978, the CHS football team played third-ranked Martinsville. The Irish clobbered Martinsville with Mark Clayton on a mission to repay all the insults he suffered the year before in Martinsville. (When Cathedral played at Martinsville in 1977, Clayton and other black players were called "niggers" throughout the game.) Martinsville had always been a stronghold of the KKK, and even in 1977 the Klan legacy was evident. It must always be remembered that the KKK and those who were sympathetic to it were as much anti-Catholic as they were anti-black. For that reason the Cathedral team and the fans were more than a little apprehensive while in Martinsville and could not wait to get out of there.

The Martinsville game in 1978 took place at the Lawrence Central field. Clayton absolutely exploded for touchdown after touchdown, to show the stunned Martinsville fans just who it was they were dealing with. Assistant coach Jim McLinn said he believes that the Martinsville game was one of the top five wins in Mike McGinley's career. "He wanted to win that one very badly," McLinn said.

McLinn noted that the Martinsville coach had been taunting Cathedral all week long in the press about coming up to the big city to play the team his boys had beaten the year before. McLinn also noted that Mike McGinley did the most "un-McGinley"-like thing he has ever seen—he had ordered fireworks to go off when the team scored. Moreover, when the football team returned to the field to start the second half, McGinley sat his players down at the south end zone. Very little was said, and then an all-green fireworks display of the word IRISH lit up the opposite end zone as it hung from the goal post. The crowd was thrilled. When the fireworks were over, Mike turned to his team and simply said, "Let's play football." According to McLinn, the game was over at that moment. Martinsville didn't stand a chance, and Mark Clayton had the game of his life up to that point in his career.

Clayton went on to star at Louisville and later was an all-pro wide receiver in the NFL while with the Miami Dolphins, holding the record for the most touchdown receptions in a single season. Currently, he is with the Green Bay Packers.

The 1978-79 school year marked the beginning of the end of the turmoil of the seventies, the transition to 56th Street, Brother

Pedro's term as president-principal, and memories of the old days.

In retrospect, one can see that change marked the seventies not only at Cathedral, but also throughout the country and world in profound ways. The seventies witnessed American students killed by American soldiers at Kent State and later watched a President (Richard Nixon), win a second term by a landslide only to be forced to resign in disgrace within a year and a half. It also saw an interim president (Jerry Ford), defeated two and a half years later, and yet another one (Jimmy Carter), serve only one term. Powerful political leaders were prosecuted and imprisoned, only to return to make millions of dollars through speakers' fees and royalties from books about their crimes, marking the beginning of the realization that white collar crimes did indeed sometimes pay. The seventies also marked the beginning of the realization of America's dependence on Second and Third World countries for natural resources when it witnessed OPEC—an organization of Arab countries who banded together to develop more economic power. The results—the Arab Oil Boycott.

As the seventies evolved, Watergate came to an end, inflation was staggering and self-doubt began to creep into the American psyche. The Ford Administration passed out WIN buttons to "Whip Inflation Now." Drug and alcohol abuse grew worse and people were still dying from lung cancer caused by cigarette smoke, despite all the warnings. The world lost Pope Paul VI, Pope John Paul I, Elvis Presley, and Bing Crosby. Nine hundred religious cult members in Guyana, South America, committed suicide on the orders of a former Indianapolis minister named Jim Jones.

While the kidnapping of Patty Hearst by the Symbionese Liberation Army, (SLA) dominated the news, micro-chips, digital electronics, personal computers atari and video arcade games were being talked about on back pages and slowly crept onto the scene. The impact of the electronic and computer age in the next decade was far greater on American society than anything that transpired as a result of Patty Hearst's kidnapping, though few realized it then.

The seventies saw the end of the Vietnam War and of the Shah of Iran. In their place it witnessed the Killing Fields in Cambodia, the taking of hostages in Iran, and the height of terrorism worldwide.

The seventies watched disco music come and go, along with bell bottom pants, fly-away shirt collars, and polyester leisure suits. As all these things happened, the American Bicentennial came and went in a flash in 1976.

Archie Bunker, Mary Tyler Moore and Bob Newhart dominated the TV ratings along with the ever-popular "M*A*S*H" and the often decadent "Saturday Night Live." *Star Wars, The Godfather* and *Jaws* were smash hits at the movies. The military draft came to an end, abortion was legalized, and the death penalty was reinstated. Famine began to rule in the middle of Africa, and civil war in Afghanistan and Central America continued to keep the world divided. The killing of hundreds of children in Soweto, South Africa, followed by the torture death of activist Steven Biko focused world attention on apartheid in South Africa.

The seventies saw Notre Dame win two national football championships in 1973 and 1977, and Indiana University beat Michigan three times in the same season, including once in the final game of the tournament to win the 1976 NCAA Basketball Championship. They won thirty-two games while registering no losses.

Some have said that cynicism marked the seventies and infected American youth, turning them into the "me" generation. Others could counter that the example shown by those who grew up in the fifties and sixties set the stage for all the negative happenings which transpired in the two decades that followed. After all, teenagers were not involved in Watergate in the seventies, nor were they involved in Iran/Contra or the Wall Street scandals of the eighties. Ivan Bosekey and Michael Milliken were not teenagers; they were the products of the fifties and sixties.

Historians may debate forever which generation brought about the cynicism, skepticism and self-centeredness which began to dominate American society in the late seventies, but one thing was certain: at Cathedral in the 1980s, times were changing, and they were changing in a very positive way.

THE FIRST FUND DRIVE

The 1976-85 Campaign to Raise Five Million Dollars

Cathedral's leadership plotted an action to retire the school's mortgage and establish an endowment. Local newspapers gave editorial support to the campaign. *The News* commented: "It has been only a relatively short time that it seemed impossible that this respected high school might close its doors forever, but the enthusiasm and loyalty of its alumni and friends prevented that possibility from becoming an unhappy fact."

"Its halls (on Meridian) and rooms are filled with the ghosts of happy memories and they are the kind which will inspire alumni to make Challenge II a successful drive."

The goal and the dream of the campaign was laudable but the results were less so. The newly-formed Cathedral was still a road show playing Hartford and wasn't ready for Broadway and the big time.

From Boyle to Woehler to Baker

When Stanley Boyle received his diploma as Cathedral's first graduate in 1921, until Terry Woehler accepted his diploma at the Cathedral in 1976 as the last graduate of the all-male school, 3894 young men completed four years of high school education.

It was fitting that the first graduate of the re-formed Cathedral be a female, Linda Baker '77. Stanley Boyle died in 1991 after a distinguished career as an engineer working on projects world-wide. He was graduated from the University of Notre Dame and received his doctorate at Massachusetts Institute of Technology. Boyle gave three interviews for this book and his comments can be read in the sections on the school's early years.

Boyle was a writer and editor on the first *Megaphone* staff, played piano for the school's first orchestra and was a member of the school's successful Debate Team.

It was Boyle who coined the promotional line: "If you see it in *The Star*, it may be true: if you see it in *The Megaphone*, it is so."

"Last grad" Woehler was captain of the 1975 Irish varsity football team playing tight end and went out for basketball his freshman and junior years. As a freshman, he was shocked to hear the Brothers planned to leave and Cathedral would probably close. "In my sophomore year there wasn't as good classroom instruction. By my senior year, the school was stabilized and we were proud and sentimental about being the last class at the old school."

Terry attended Indiana University-Purdue University Indianapolis and received his bachelor's degree from Indiana University. He still lives in Indianapolis and is security manager of L.S. Ayres Company, Glendale.

Today, Linda Baker is Mrs. Steven Hullett. She is a registered nurse and a graduate of Indiana Central University (University of Indianapolis). She also studied at IU-PUI and currently is doing occupational contract health work for Indiana Bell.

Linda spent her first three years at Ladywood-St. Agnes and, like other LSA students who decided to stay, was unsure about the merger.

"I had an open mind because my Dad (Jack Baker '45) was a Cathedral graduate. I knew a few of the guys, but we (LSA) were closer to Brebeuf. There were things to adjust to like working on our appearance. We still had a dress code and the class instruction continued strong.

"The most visible resistance to the move was when some of the girls burned the letters 'LSA' in the front lawn.

(Continued)

252

There were other manifestations of protest," Linda recalled. "Some of the girls collected 'For Sale' signs and placed them on view alongside 56th Street."

She continued, "We knew how to drive up the ice-covered hill but the guys didn't. Some girls poured water on the hill. It was really harmless fun."

Cathedral's administration was more strident and structured than Ladywood's had been. The nuns had allowed LSA seniors to leave the campus. Cathedral did not, so some girls left the campus in cars and even went over the hill on foot to have lunch off-campus.

Linda Baker Hullett recalls her graduation at the Cathedral and is proud to be the first female to receive a Cathedral High School diploma.

Staring at Woods on a Snowy Afternoon

The grounds of Cathedral have an air of class that sets [the campus] apart from all the other high schools. I was often caught by irate teachers staring dreamily out the windows during some of my more tiresome classes while admiring the fire and brilliance among the leaves at the heighth of fall. During winter I would watch the silent snow quickly falling to cover the brown earth as if it were shameful. In the spring as my freedom grew near I watched with great anticipation as the green buds appeared on the trees one by one.

The Cathedran, Unknown author

Cathedral is a "Life Preparatory School"

With ninety-seven percent of Cathedral High School's graduating seniors going on to college, Cathedral is a College Preparatory school. But it is also a life preparatory school.

"If all we did was prepare people for college, we wouldn't be doing our jobs," said Principal Fr. Patrick J. Kelly. He insists that the combination of Cathedral's curriculum and outstanding, involved faculty do more than just teach the mind: they prepare the person for life.

Providing a chance for success in college and life has not just been a recent goal at Cathedral. Cathedral's history points to the fact that it was a "College Preparatory" school even when there was no such term.

Nine of eleven members of the first graduating class in 1921 went on to college. Instead of college being the exception for a Cathedral student, it was and still is the norm. For seventy-five years it has been integral to the education that the majority of Cathedral graduates go on to college and have the necessary skills to succeed in life. Cathedral's tradition has been one of providing students with a strict and disciplined atmosphere. "The structure of this institution provides an atmosphere where the student has to be self-disciplined," Fr. Kelly said and that is why many parents choose Cathedral for their children's high school education.

"Former students return to Cathedral," Fr. Kelly said "to show the affection between students and faculty. We have so many kids come back and visit once they have graduated. I think that is a testament to our faculty. Often I hear them say, 'The faculty really cared about us.'"

Additionally, on a measured scale, Cathedral ranks well as a college prep school. "A great many of our students who do go on to college are able to test out of freshman English or math," Fr. Kelly said. "Sometimes a senior who may have been getting a "D" in Calculus here, is still prepared well enough to tutor students in college. It happens all the time."

Examples like that are not rare. Fr. Kelly likes to use another example to emphasize his point. "Often there are Cathedral students who have been given a chance because they received an academic scholarship or other financial aid. They went through the Cathedral system and now have plans for their lives and are living them very successfully. If Cathedral had not been here they would have been subject to the public school system and probably lost in the shuffle. I would like to think that we have given many kids a chance at success who otherwise might not have ever received that chance."

THE ALUMNI REACT

Loyal son of Cathedral Tom Keating, an *Indianapolis Star* columnist, began his April 30, 1976 column:

Cathedral Heritage Fades?

When it was announced last week that Cathedral High School was going to purchase Ladywood-St. Agnes School and open a coed facility at that location next fall, a great deal of comment was heard.

The parents of the girls at Ladywood expressed their displeasure in the newspapers and on radio and television, and Cathedral officials voiced their reasons for making the move.

But one group yet unheard from is that segment of the Cathedral alumni who feel excluded and ignored by the decision to close Cathedral and open another school with the same name at Ladywood.

Following is a letter to Cathedral board chairman Robert V. Welch from a young south side man named Mark Seal, who was graduated from Cathedral five years ago.

It pretty much sums up the feelings of a large number of Cathedral grads:

Dear Mr. Welch:

I am writing this letter to you in response to recent changes in the status of Cathedral High School regarding the purchases of Ladywood-St. Agnes and movement of Cathedral to that Northside location.

I must admit I am ignorant of the specific business details of the purchase, other than those which have been reported by The Indianapolis Star and News and also from discussions with friends of Cathedral.

It is not these details nor your personal involvement in the transaction which I wish to address, other than that you are in charge of the decision-making body from which these changes came forth.

I'm speaking from my heart in this letter because I truly love Cathedral, and I fear that I've lost something I sincerely put my heart into and which has given me so much in return.

The Cathedral from which I graduated only five short years ago was, I thought, one of the finest schools in the city. Certainly, her academic excellence and sports prowess added to the aura about Her.

But above these things in my mind was the unique attitude and spirit in which most of the students, faculty and staff conducted themselves each and every day. Going to school at Cathedral or working there was not a routine nor was it a task. I thought it to be an exciting experience.

The cornerstone of Cathedral's education was the excellent representation offered by all sides of the city and most economic statuses.

The gathering into one community of people with such diversified backgrounds was an education in itself. Each made a unique contribution to the school, each had his place in the community.

Now, this cornerstone is about to crumble.

Contrary to your remark in the newspaper concerning everything moving north, the other three sides of town still have some fine people and assets to offer Cathedral—enough that such a sweeping statement cannot be taken lightly.

Even if your seventy percent figure holds true concerning the retention of current students, is not close to one-third of a loss substantial?

The severe inconvenience in getting to 56th and Emerson for many students is sad indeed. But what seems sadder to me is the sterility of education which such a move carries with it. No longer will a variety of backgrounds and economic classes and, therefore, individuals, be educated at Cathedral.

No, the student at the new Cathedral, whether male or female will see only carbon copies of himself or herself as they look about at their classmates. This is most disastrous and most uncomforting to me.

The purpose of this letter has not been to scrutinize you personally, Mr. Welch. Rather, it has been to express my discontentment with the future of Cathedral in light of recent developments.

Perhaps some of these comments can be put to constructive ends. In any event, my prayers are with Cathedral, that Her spirit survives these devastating changes.

Sincerely, Mark Seal '71

Mark Seal, now Dr. Mark Seal, is a urologist and medical topics author living in Toledo, Ohio. He has updated his impressions:

I well remember the letter and the attention I received after it appeared in The Star. *Not all of it was good because there were those, including my boss at the time (an alumnus) who thought I was torpedoing Mr. Welch and a combined effort to save the school.*

I was persona non grata at the time, and it took years to resolve those feelings. My point was that the Cathedral I knew was a special place in which to grow.

In those days boys from my parish (St. Mark's) had provided three of the last four class valedictorians. Seven of the top ten students from my class were from Southside parishes. (I was not valedictorian, but our valedictorian, Jeff McKenna, was from St. Mark's. His brother Jim was valedictorian the year before.) Cathedral gave me the chance to receive the Notre Dame Club of Indianapolis scholarship, which led to my medical degree.

(Mark Seal was co-captain of the 1970 Irish football team, Coach McGinley's first.)

The old school, Brother James Sullivan.

Brother James Sullivan, Bob Welch and Pat Fisher before the transition.

Woodland paths, sturdy, serviceable school buildings with ample room and the charm of Ladywood and the Fletcher estate gone by marked the new school.

Three historic graduates of Cathedral: Stanley Boyle: recipient of the first Cathedral degree in 1921; Terry Woehler, last grad in the old building and Linda Baker, first grad on the new campus.

Graduation Day, Class of '72.

'72-'73 Regional Champs. On left, Asst. Coach Butch Branson; far right Coach Jean Ancelet.

Spirit!

1973 Irish, State Runner-up.

The Aquinian Chapter of the National Honor Society illustrated Cathedral's ever-growing emphasis on academics.

Greg Cox and his tuba in a time of outstanding musical achievement for the Irish.

The Brothers of Holy Cross, now in trim business suits, soon to part from the school they had carefully nurtured since 1918.

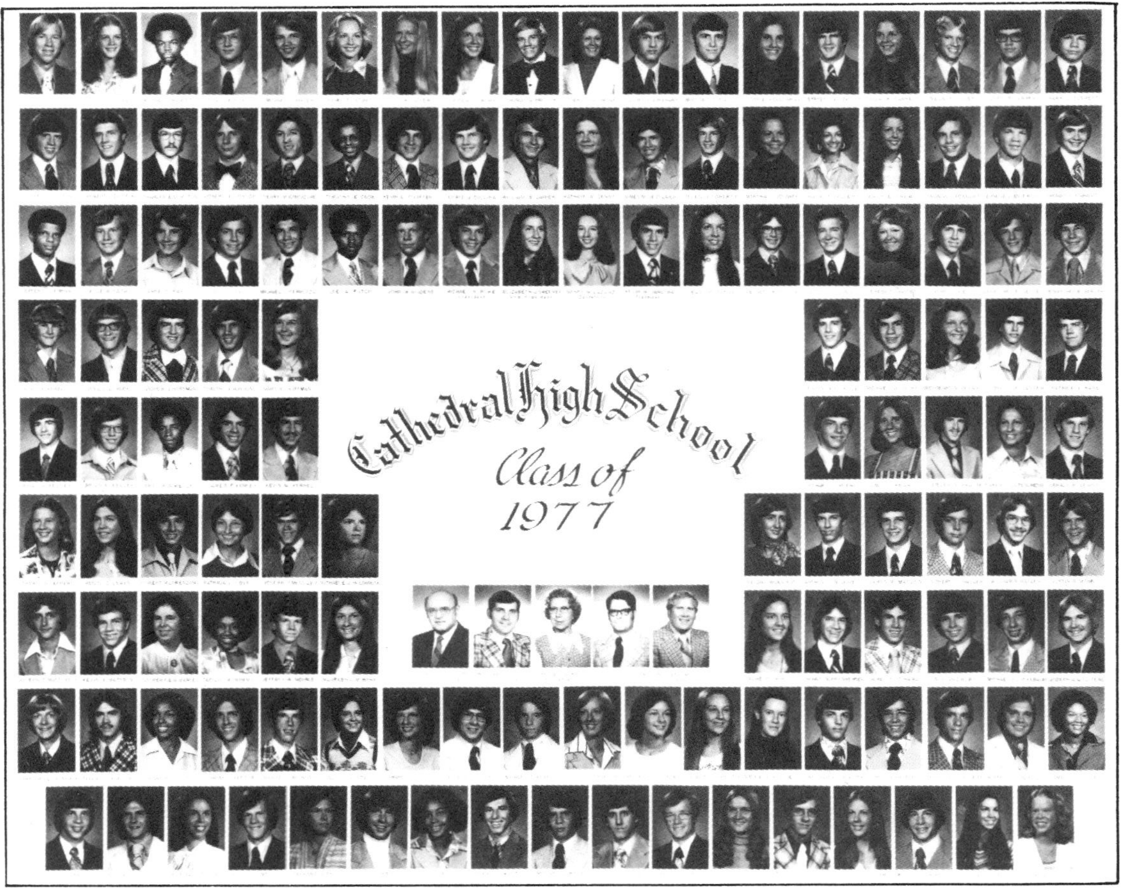
Cathedral High School
Class of
1977

General Joe Lutz

Dr. James Muller, International Physicians for the Prevention of Nuclear War

THE EIGHTIES

1979–1980

The Class of 1980 was the first class to come together as one group on the new campus, a class which started out together and had no personal recollections of old schools. What a difference a year made! The attitudes were decidedly more positive, with new developments happening in a climate of hope. Many people had a similar hope for the country and the world as they entered the eighties. The U.S. Hockey Team's defeat of the Russians to win the gold medal at the 1980 Winter Olympics seemed to give Americans some sense that the country was not falling apart after all. A similar attitude developed at Cathedral, as fear for Cathedral's future gave way to expectation and confidence in what was to come.

With Brother Pedro's retirement, Mike McGinley was appointed president of the school. By this time Mike had served in just about every capacity which the school had to offer—teacher, head football coach, principal, business manager, and now president. The 1979-80 school year is also remembered as the year in which Cathedral announced her first lay principal having no previous connection with Cathedral. Mr. Donald Stock led the school into the eighties.

Although the 1980s took Americans and the world forward towards new horizons, they also gave many mixed messages. There was hope, but terror still struck at the heart of people all over the world when they received news of the assassination of Archbishop Oscar Romero of El Salvador in March of 1980. In December of the same year three American nuns and a lay missionary would experience the same fate. Liberal and conservative Catholics began to debate the role of the church in Third World countries. The debate of "Liberation Theology" dominated Catholic news for most of the early eighties as death squads killed thousands of men, women and children, not only in El Salvador but throughout Central America.

In New York City, John Lennon was murdered in December of 1980. The deaths of Archbishop Romero, John Lennon and the American missionaries in 1980 set the tone for future world events. It was not until after their deaths that the attempted assassination of President Ronald Reagan took place in April of 1981, just three months into his administration.

One month later Pope John Paul II would have a similar experience. On the same day as the attempted assassination of President Reagan, Indiana University won another national championship under coach Bob Knight. Along with the game, the Academy Awards went on TV, as scheduled, the evening of the assassination attempt. Both events served as a comforting distraction for Americans who had watched the assassination attempt in slow motion over and over again throughout the day and evening news. Reagan's recovery seemed like something out of a John Wayne movie and served as a symbol of strength and hope. Pope John Paul II's recovery and his open forgiveness of his attempted assassin served as an example of faith and courage. It was a living demonstration of the Christian message.

In 1980 and 1981 Hollywood brought us two films which sadly and perhaps unknowingly pointed to the future of American society. *Kramer vs. Kramer* and *Ordinary People* were excellent examples of the dysfunctionality taking place in American families long before "dysfunction" became a household word.

Films like *E.T.* took us on a fantasy ride with the irony of people crying harder for a make-believe character than for the starving children in the world. There were scores of films dealing with the ever-controversial Vietnam War.

In 1982 recession hit America hard, and new words such as "bag ladies," "street people," and "food shelters" crept into our vocabularies. As the eighties unfolded, Nuclear freeze, *détente*, *perestroika* and "Star Wars" dominated international news.

The eighties also brought AIDS, STDs, more poverty and more world hunger. On the political front the United States refused to participate in the 1980 Olympics in the Soviet Union, and the Soviet Union returned the favor when they refused to participate in the 1984 Summer Olympics in the United States. The two superpowers were finding less common ground and "peaceful coexistence" appeared threatened.

One year following the 1984 Olympics, as has been said in an earlier chapter, Dr. James Muller of Harvard Medical School won the Nobel Peace Prize for his role in the International Physicians for Prevention of Nuclear War, which had evolved earlier in the eighties. Dr. Muller was the first American to speak freely on Soviet TV. In remembering his experience at Cathedral, Dr. Muller wrote, "The Christian values of hope and peace which were nurtured at Cathedral eventually led me to my work with Soviet physicians to found the International Physicians for Prevention of Nuclear War."

Dr. Muller actually visited Cathedral twice during the 1980s. His first visit had been to receive Cathedral's most coveted award, the Chartrand ring, named after Archbishop Chartrand, Cathedral's founder. At the time Dr. Muller received the award, Jack Baker, Frank McKinney, General Joe Lutz, Harry Binder, Bill Shover and Bob Welch were also honored, all in the same evening.

As has been said earlier in this book, the evening discussion between General Joe Lutz and Dr. Muller, reflecting divergent points of view, was a reflection of the diversity which existed and continues to exist at Cathedral High School. That kind of diversity can be heard any week in the classrooms or halls of Cathedral today.

The second time Dr. Muller came to Cathedral, he roamed the school cafeteria to talk with students during lunch about the threat of Nuclear war. Shortly afterwards, there was an all-school assembly featuring Dr. Muller, who left soon for Oslo, Norway to receive the Nobel prize. He enjoyed the school assembly, especially the pointed questions from the audience. At a later date he wrote, "I was thrilled to have the opportunity to speak at Cathedral High School and to note amongst the students the same spirit and intellectual curiosity which had characterized Cathedral in the past. The session in the Cathedral auditorium immediately prior to our trip to Oslo for the Nobel Prize was the most stimulating audience discussion that I encountered. I know Cathedral High School has an excellent past, and from what I can see, the excellence continues into the present." The Cathedral student body had sent Dr. Muller off to receive his prize with tremendous respect and great pride in being connected to the same high school that this world renowned worker for peace had attended.

Involvement seemed to mark the eighties. Cathedral students volunteered in many different ways in the decade of the eighties. The Christian Service program was set up with the Class of 1980 and has continued to this day. The program places senior students in various hospitals, nursing homes, educational centers and other places which can benefit from volunteers, with the students giving three to five hours a week at various jobs. In 1989 the Christian Service Program was recognized by the United Way as "Best Long-Term Volunteer Program" of its kind in the Indianapolis area. Students have given thousands of hours throughout the community through the Christian Service Program in the past fourteen years.

In many ways the program aided career searches for those students who wanted to know more about a particular field. Many students who served at Methodist, Riley and St. Vincent's hospitals have gone into one form of medicine or another. For other students it was a matter of commitment to the program and the community, even if they did not particularly like the volunteer assignment they received. Whether playing cards with senior citizens in a nursing home or entertaining terminally ill children, Cathedral students involved themselves in the community.

In addition, teacher Jo Cavanaugh generated new enthusiasm for the canned food drive, which brought thousands of cans and other food items to those in need at Thanksgiving. By the mid-eighties fifteen to twenty thousand cans (and boxes and other food items) were collected each year and given to such places as the Gleaners Food Bank, Holy Cross food pantry, and other food distribution charities. But that was not all. Simultaneously with the food drive, the Senior Class would start its drive to collect new and used toys for the Central State Hospital Teen Toy Shop.

Through bake sales and collections in the cafeteria, the Senior Class was able to take hundreds of dollars worth of toys to Central State Mental Hospital, so the patients would have something to send home to their loved ones at Christmas. Senior students went out to the hospital every Monday after Thanksgiving to help patients pick out gifts, wrap them and send them out in the mail. This program will finally come to an end next year, when Central State Hospital will close its doors under Governor Bayh's order.

There is even more. Three weeks before Christmas, every religion class adopted a family to help meet that family's needs for the holidays. These families were never in short supply, coming from various inner city parishes which knew of individual needs. These parishes had once sent large numbers of students to Cathedral High School, so it was fitting that Cathedral students do what they could to help. The families were always grateful and often brought to tears by the students' generosity.

There have been other student fund drives for the hungry, scholarships, and homeless shelters just to name a few charitable projects beyond those just mentioned. All came out of the eighties, with the exception of the canned food drive, which some say goes all the way back to the days of the Great Depression, when Cathedral students learned to share what little they had.

Being involved not only meant volunteering for charitable organizations and the like by a few people. On the contrary, being involved at Cathedral in the eighties meant belonging to anything and everything for many. Student government, sports, academic competition, after-school clubs, the school paper and yearbook, numerous retreat programs, spiritual direction, peer counseling, music, band and drama programs made it difficult for students not to find their niche. Someone once commented looking at the filled parking lot at 7:00 p.m. in the middle of the school week, "Our kids never seem to go home. How many other places do you think you could look out over the school parking lot with nothing special going on and see a parking lot practically full because most of their students are so involved?" That situation is what one could find at almost any time, and became even more true in the late eighties and early nineties.

Cathedral not only survived the seventies, but it also ended the decade on a significantly high note. In the fall of 1979 Chairman of the Board Robert V. Welch established the Cathedral Committee On Priorities—CCOP. This committee brought together Board members, teachers, administrators, parents, alumni, and community leaders to set in motion the school's list of priorities. From social service programs to athletic and academic programs, the committee worked well together to develop a plan for the future. All extracurricular programs were included, such as band, drama, debate and computer facilities. The committee was designed not only to dream a little, but also to look realistically at the future in order to give the school direction for the eighties.

The CCOP was developed by Bob Welch and chaired by Vice-Chairman of the Board, Rev. Clem Davis. Many excellent ideas and recommendations came out of the committee. Perhaps more importantly, the group helped to strengthen the Cathedral family by involving as many people as possible, demonstrating collegiality at its best.

The following year a ten million dollar campaign was kicked off by the Board. The drive was headed by American Fletcher National Bank president Harry Binder. Although the campaign did not fully realize its goals, the CCOP moved forward to implement many of the recommendations offered by the committee. Although some recommendations were put on the back burner, a great deal was accomplished in the early eighties. Sports facilities often remained last on the list of priorities in order to take care of more pressing issues such as providing faculty with competitive salaries while trying to keep tuition costs down, and making class sizes smaller. The gym, a real need and great desire of many, remained a dream for the time being. This was difficult for many who wanted the sports facilities updated immediately. However, the priority was to provide quality education, and the Board never lost sight of their mission to do just that.

The CCOP remained a focal point of reference for all future development for the late eighties and early nineties. Most programs and facilities were upgraded in the nineties— athletics, drama, arts, and computers. The gym still remains an unrealized dream, but it is on the horizon.

With the CCOP and the capital campaign underway, the '79-'80 school year moved forward. Two new coaches joined Cathedral that year, Bob Pychinka and Lance Rhodes. Rhodes went on to experience tremendous success as head wrestling coach, and he remains at Cathedral today. The '79-'80 school year also saw the return of Tom O'Brien as head basketball coach. Pychinka did not have the same kind of success and left Cathedral after two years as head coach. In O'Brien's first year back, his team went 9-14, but they were, after all, young. Only two years later he took his State-ranked team to the final four. He stayed until the '83-'84 school year, re-establishing pride and glory in the basketball program once again. There will be more on these coaches and their teams later.

The class of 1980 did not necessarily leave their mark on Cathedral through their athletic prowess, but through their attitudes and values. The football, basketball and baseball programs had mediocre seasons at best. However, the '79-'80 boys tennis team led by P.J. Kervan, Tom Jeffers, Eric Riegner, Pat Jeffers, Brian Thinnes, Scott Schaefer, and Eric Neal won the first city title since arriving at the new campus. They were 12-1.

Under Mary Clark, another new coach that year, the girls sports program showed the most promise of any team in '79-'80, as they won their first City title in volleyball, while posting a 24-3 record. Team captains Cindy Cassel and Jackie Glenn led their teams to many exciting victories. Post-season honors were earned by Felicia Broadus, named to the All-City Team. Honorable mention honors went to Cindy Cassell, Ann and Jackie Glenn, and Tere Alicea.

The boys cross country team also saw success; they were the first cross country team to advance to the regionals in twelve years. All-City and All-Sectional honors went to Dennis

McDowell. The team had a disappointing Regional, but neverthe-less had a very successful season.

It should be noted that although the football team had a disappointing year, as has been said, two senior players, Drew Ahlers and Tom Mackall did earn All-City honors.

The wrestling program, which was rebuilding under Rhodes, saw captain Jimmy McGinley win city and regional championships.

The '79-'80 school year saw Meredith Kemper appointed editor of *The Megaphone* and she brought creativity and social consciousness to *The Meg* once again.

The school was visited that year by a Cardinal from Uganda, a country which was seeing murder and torture of its people. The school plays in the '79-'80 school year were *The Gift of the Magi,* starring Kim Wurster and Jim Risch. Wurster would go on to become a professional actress. The plays *Dorian Gray* and *The Kentucky Marriage Proposal* starred David Scheidler. Scheidler has gone on to become a Holy Cross Catholic priest. Multi-talented Kevin Flynn and Lori Butler starred in *He and She.* Jude Kennedy and Kevin Flynn stole the show in the spring musi-cal, *South Pacific.* The show also starred Julie Ong, Casey Hayes and Dave Kasberg.

Perhaps the most significant development of the 1979-'80 school year was the establishment of the Senior Retreat Program by religion teacher, Jo Cavanaugh. Mrs. Cavanaugh and Principal Don Stock went with several senior students to be a part of Scecina's Christian Awakening Program. At that time Cathedral did not have a retreat program of any kind. The experience which Cavanaugh, Stock, and students John Christ, P.J. Kervan, Mary Madden, Jeff Suttner and Arnold Dumal experienced led to the development of Cathedral's Senior Retreat Program. It remains one of the most successful programs at Cathedral today.

The program is voluntary, involving approximately forty seniors per retreat. There were only a couple of retreats a year when it first started out. By the mid-eighties and especially in the nineties, there were usually three to four senior retreats per year, allowing virtually everyone to attend. The staff who make up the retreats is unique in itself: at least four teachers, and often more, attend the three all day and all night retreats. The setting, off-cam-pus, provides a real break for seniors in their last year of high school. According to retreat director Jo Cavanaugh, "the Senior Retreat Program is one of the finest things we do at Cathedral. It has changed many lives over the years." Concerning the retreat she said, "it is a great opportunity for seniors to get in touch with themselves and God and set priorities." It must be noted that families and friendships are often enhanced or renewed as the result of the Senior Retreat Program. Not everyone loved the retreat, but the vast majority who attended the retreat would claim it as a significant milepost in their lives.

CHS graduates who are in college return to work the Senior Retreats. If not for them, the retreat program could not be effective. The very fact that they return to work high school retreats while they are in college is testimony to the impact and importance of the program and their sense of being part of the "family."

Many CHS graduates have returned time and time again to work the retreat program, people like Rob Hoaglin '85, Matt Wire '86, Kevin Kervan '88, Brian Murphy '88, Molly Cain '89, Joe Behringer '91, Matt Larner '91, Carrie Caito '92, Jay Zmhral '92 and any of a number of the Scheidler clan, especially Maria '85, and Elsa '88.

A couple of footnotes must be added here about the Senior Retreat program. People from Scecina helped out on the first couple of senior retreats, especially a Scecina graduate named Bob Brown, and Fr. Ron Ashmore. Although not from Scecina, Rev. Jeff Godecker was also instrumental in the early retreats, so much so that he became very close to several Cathedral students and concelebrated the '81 Baccalaureate Mass. In 1992 he returned to say the Baccalaureate Mass in the absence of Archbishop Edward T. O'Meara, who had died earlier that year. Fr. Godecker has been a good friend to Cathedral. He currently serves as Director of Religious Education for the Indianapolis Archdiocese.

It must be noted that Archbishop O'Meara was not only very kind to Cathedral, he was very generous as well. He publicly and financially supported the school, giving at a very crucial time a significant contribution of fifty thousand dollars to CHS. During the Diamond Anniversary Campaign he made another contribution of an undisclosed amount. Archbishop O'Meara was a dear friend to Cathedral High School during his reign from 1980-1992.

The 1979–80 school year ended on a fresh note. Cathedral High School saw her first female valedictorian, Kathleen Morrison. Little did anyone know at the time that Kathleen was the beginning of a trend for the eighties. From 1980 to 1989 there were seven female valedictorians. The salutatorian in 1980 was also a female, Jennifer Swiergiel. There were seven female salutatorians in the eighties as well.

The Board of Trustees award in 1980 went to one of Cathedral's truly outstanding student leaders—Jeff Suttner. Suttner was instrumental as a student leader in the CCOP and was available to help out in all areas. As Student Council officers, Suttner, and John Christ, another outstanding student leader, led the entire student body into the decade of the eighties willingly and smoothly. They had the respect of their peers, and the faculty and administration alike. Physics and math teacher Paul Brown gave the Baccalaureate address to the class of 1980. His dry sense of humor and his entertaining and creative methods for teaching math and physics endeared him to the class.

The class had been led by class officers Mike Healy, Bobbie Smith, Meredith Kemper, and Katie Gallogly. Senior Joe Vande Bosche was a school leader without an official title, but one who was well known for gathering people together to accomplish a goal and to have a good time. An outstanding student, Joe led a group fondly referred to as "The Vigilantes." This spirited group included characters like Jim Ryan, Tom Mackall, Mike Healy, Mike Diehr, Perry Page, Kevin O'Donnell and the smilingest one of them all, John Lorenzano.

Lorenzano was killed in 1992 fighting a fire at the Indianapolis Athletic Club for the Indianapolis Fire Department. John Lorenzano, who also served as a drug and alcohol counselor for St. Francis Hospital, will remain one of Cathedral's true and genuine heroes, remembered always for his smile.

The class of 1980 set an example for all future classes of the eighties in more ways than one. Other classes emulated them and built on some of the traditions they had established. Above all else they were a kind group, with big hearts, and their traditions of spirit, hope, pride, and having a good time while learning, grew throughout the eighties and into the early nineties. They were trend-setters, living their lives with purpose and meaning. Whether they realized it or not at the time, they lived the Christian message and showed the community what a Cathedral High School student was all about.

1980-1981

When discussing characters and character no class stands out more than the Class of '81. They were a great group of people, unique in their thoughtfulness. Their retreats were a tremendous success, taking up in spirit and tradition where the Class of '80 left off. With people like Paul Radspinner leading the way, the Class of '81 led a spirited group called IRAC—Irish Rowdies At Cathedral. That group lasted until 1986, when some of the school spirit seemed to fade.

In other respects this class was much like the Class of '80. The football team had a another long season by posting a losing record of 3-7 during Bob Pychinka's last year as coach. No one was more disappointed with the record than tri-captains Bill Brady, Tom Page and Mike Richey. One of the few highlights was Randy Knox's receiving All-City honors. Brady went on to an excellent college career at Wabash and Page played his college ball at Earlham.

The boys tennis team also experienced a disappointing year, failing to win another City Team title, though Mike Farrell and Phil Yaggi did win the Doubles Championship.

The girls cross country team was coached by Kevin McDowell. This team, which had a 9-4 record, watched junior Susan Morrison advance to the State Finals as Mr. Kevin McDowell completed his last year coaching the Irish. He compiled a 44-7 record while at Cathedral.

The wrestling team improved dramatically in Coach Lance Rhodes' second season. They were 11-2-1, capturing a Sectional Championship for the first time since 1970. Football captain Bill Brady was also captain of the wrestling squad. John Maio and Eric Hofmeister won City titles, and John Maio, Mike McGinley, Roger Wood, and Tom Page all won Sectional titles. Andy Cope made it to the Semi-State and Eric Hofmeister advanced all the way to the State Finals.

The boys basketball team improved, but their record (14-10) did not show it. Actually, very few points separated them from having an outstanding season. The next year would be their year, with only one senior, Chris Burnett, graduating.

The girls basketball team had a dismal 7-11 season. Highlight performance in track in '81 went to junior Beth Happel, who was a State Finalist in the hurdles. Next year she went on to win it all to become a State champion. The boys track team had a tough schedule, but they still managed to break twelve varsity and freshmen records.

The girls tennis team also improved, but was still a year or two away from greatness. The baseball team and the golf team both posted winning seasons, though no records were broken and no championship won.

The sports story of the year at Cathedral involved a gymnastics team of three tiny sophomore girls named Beth Arbuckle, Karen Duffy, and Kelly Doyle. Although all three girls contributed to a fantastic season, this story is about Kelly Doyle, the last in a family of girls who had always been enthusiastically associated with Cathedral. Kelly Doyle's accomplishments were truly spectacular.

Although Kelly's sisters Rita, Jo Ellen, and Mary Ann all served as cheerleaders for Cathedral, Kelly was the only one who attended the school. Cathedral, of course, was not a co-ed school until 1976, shortly after the older girls had graduated from St. Agnes, (Rita and Jo Ellen) and Our Lady of Grace (Mary Ann). Besides being a gymnast, Kelly was also a cheerleader.

This incredibly talented athlete captured an unprecedented five Gymnastic Medals in the State Finals to earn the Overall State Championship title. Doyle, Arbuckle, and Duffy all earned college scholarships for their gymnastic abilities. More importantly, they are remembered for their love of life, kindness and consideration.

Kelly's sister, Rita Doyle O'Malia remembers making cheerleading quite well. She said, "My dad was so excited when I made cheerleading because that was the closest he would ever get to the Cathedral football team." Since there were six girls and no boys in the Doyle family, being a cheerleader for the Irish was the best Mr. Doyle could hope for.

During the 1980–81 school year Principal Don Stock came into his own. Students who took the time to know him liked him; he worked many retreats and attended almost every single sporting event and other extra-curricular activities.

Like other principals of Cathedral, Don had his own style. He would always start an assembly by trying to quiet the crowd before he made a few comments, raising his hands above his head and crisscrossing them by waving them back and forth, a signal for the kids to quiet down. It never worked. The kids all raised their hands above their heads, crisscrossed them, and waved back. This became a ritual before every assembly and one which Mr. Stock himself would laugh at on occasion.

Don Stock helped initiate many new programs while at Cathedral, including the famous Academic Olympics for eighth graders. Enrollment went up every year he was principal; he supported his teachers and parents seemed to trust him. He was a family man both to his immediate family and to the Cathedral family, trying to involve himself in as much as he could handle.

He left Cathedral in 1984 and was elected by the Senior Class that year to speak at their graduation, an honor which deeply pleased him. At last word Don Stock was Superintendent of Catholic Schools in Michigan.

One of the plays at Cathedral in '80-'81 was *Arsenic and Old Lace.* Another play, *Christmas Dream,* was directed by students Lori Butler and Jennifer Hamilton.

In the fall of 1980, Cathedral held her first Walk-a-Thon, and students raised thousands of dollars for their school. In January of '81 *The Megaphone,* under editor Mary Below, did something extraordinary. Junior staff members for *The Megaphone* went to Washington D.C. to cover the inauguration of Ronald Reagan. Juniors Mike Vore, Jon Schwantes, Jim Wilson, and Paul Georgescu all made the trip. They were in the Oval Office with Dan Rather, Andy Rooney and other famous personalities when President Reagan announced the release of the hostages from Iran. This was a unique story for a high school paper, especially *The Meg.* Schwantes went on to become the editor of *The Megaphone,* and, possibly influenced by his trip to Washington D.C., a political reporter for *The Indianapolis News.* He and another CHS graduate, Joe Fahey '71, cover the Indiana State House.

The school year came to an end with Baccalaureate and Graduation Ceremonies. It was the first time Baccalaureate Mass had been rained out, and it took place in the auditorium; senior religion teacher Jim Obergfell gave the Baccalaureate Address. Music was supplied by teachers Kevin McDowell and Paul Brown and senior students Lori Butler and Jude Kennedy. At honors night in '81 Bill Brady was awarded the Al Feeney Award. Student Council President Sue Matthews was honored with the Board of Trustees Award. Sue Matthews and Ellen White, President of the Senior Class, were two of the finest young women to ever grace Cathedral High School. "Responsible," "thoughtful" and "ethical" are words which describe them well. As a matter of fact, those words describe the class of '81 as well as any. Sue Matthews Harris returned to Cathedral in 1992 to address the National Honor Society. She is a nurse-counselor for hemophiliacs who have the HIV/AIDS virus. Ellen White Quigley is practicing law in Indianapolis.

A few stories related to the 1980–81 school year:

When John Hornak returned from his Senior Retreat, he told a story at the closing about his dad dropping him off to attend the retreat. "Go find yourself, John," his dad had said. John looked up to the audience at the retreat closing and to his dad and said, "Well Dad, I did." His story was both funny and meaningful, but to do it justice only John could tell it.

Another person who has returned to Cathedral to help out over the years has been Letitia Miele '81, news reporter for Channel 8, WISH-TV news. She has been a part of Cathedral's career day on several occasions, drawing some of the largest crowds of students.

The '81 prom was held at the Athletic Club; Doris Bagios was crowned the queen. Dean Burger and Elise Vander Bennette were co-valedictorians and multi-talented Jude Kennedy was salutatorian.

George and Louise Kovatch may have had the most profound impact on the class of '81. They team-taught biology and the class of '81 turned out more people in some field of medicine than perhaps any other class ever. Many students from this class who pursued those medical careers credit George and Louise Kovatch and chemistry teacher Glen Mauger for their interest and success in medicine.

George Kovatch, better known by some as Brother George, served many years at Cathedral, downtown and at the 56th Street Campus. He loved to challenge students, never hesitating to let them have it when they did something wrong. He was devoted to Cathedral and to her students. He and Louise left Cathedral in 1987, and there is simply no way one could give enough accounts of George's years to do him justice. Everyone has his or her own George Kovatch stories, which will be told for years to come. Memorable teacher and coach, George Kovatch was truly a unique and unforgettable personality, characteristic of that fine time in the school's history.

1981-1982

The 1981–82 school year saw "Iron Mike" McGinley enthusiastically welcomed back as head football coach for the Irish. Some say the title "Iron Mike" came along when he was still an assistant under Joe Dezelan. Mike McGinley had a way of getting the most out of his players. He did this through some grueling calisthenics, commonly referred to by one of his assistant coaches as "McGinley cals." Sprints, running in place, laps, falling down, getting up, more laps, more sprints, and on and on it went. According to long-time assistant coach Jim McLinn '70, this grueling program helped build mental toughness and gave Cathedral teams a psychological edge over other teams. Time after time McGinley produced teams which would destroy larger and more talented squads. When one looks back on Mike's career, it almost appears that he got maximum effort from the less gifted teams. The success of Mike's State Runner-up teams of '73 and '76 were largely due to the maximum effort put forth. And the '86 team which won the State Championship was also largely made up of people who simply gave everything they had to give. This is not to say that there was no talent on these teams, because there was; he simply knew how to maximize it.

The 1981–82 school year saw the smallest graduating class since Cathedral had moved to the new campus—119 students. Ironically, the next incoming freshmen class had over two hundred. The small senior class left a rich legacy, most notably that of the basketball team led by seniors Ken Barlow, Tim Hoffman, Jeff Ewing, Brad Montgomery, Tim Healy, Rob Taylor, and Chuck Knox. Underclassmen Scott Hicks, Shelton Smith, Carl Daniels, and Scott Fath played very significant parts also, as the basketball team went all the way to the State Finals.

It was one of the most exciting basketball seasons ever, not just for Cathedral but for the entire state of Indiana. There was incredible talent throughout the state, but especially in the Indianapolis area. One of the greatest basketball games in Indiana basketball history took place that season in the city tourney at Tech High School. Cathedral took on an outstanding Howe team with talented stars Lawrence Hayes, Marx Clark and Greg Cheatham. The standing-room-only crowd watched four overtimes slowly pass before the Irish came out on top. The Irish were without their big man Ken Barlow for all four overtimes; he had fouled out in the fourth quarter. Scott Hicks took over and sank two free throws with thirteen seconds to go to make the final score 71-70. It was Hoosier Hysteria at its best, and the crowd went crazy giving a standing ovation to each team between overtimes, particularly the last one. There was tremendous applause for both teams at the end of play for the talent, determination, and genuine good spirit shown throughout the game. Both teams were a class act.

Howe, Washington and Cathedral had all been ranked in the Top Ten of the state throughout the season, so the City Tournament was a prelude of what might happen in the State Tourney later on in March. Cathedral played Washington in the first round of the City Tourney, avenging one of their only two losses of the year. After beating Howe in the four-overtime, second game of the tourney, Cathedral took on Arlington for the championship game, which was an anticlimax after the earlier actions, with a score 62-49. Not to be outdone, Arlington came back at the end of the season to upset the Irish right before the State Tourney began.

The Irish team was nicknamed the "cardiac kids" by the media throughout the State Tourney because there were so many close games. Page upon page could be written about the '81-'82 basketball season, with a squad so outstanding that it merits its own book.

The Sectional matched up Cathedral and Arlington once again. This time the Irish came out on top but they did not look like the same team that won the City title. Winning the Sectional title at Hinkle Fieldhouse set the Cathedral team up for a rematch with the Howe Hornets in the Regional. After losing in the City Tournament to the Irish in four overtimes, the Hornets would be gunning for Cathedral, that was obvious. In the afternoon game the Irish looked strong again as they confidently came away with the victory. Later that evening Cathedral went against Washington for the third time. Washington had earlier won the first game; Cathedral had taken the second. Washington was led by stars John Sherman Williams and Darren Fitzgerald. Interestingly enough, Williams was a cousin to Cathedral's Scott Hicks, and the two cousins had a great respect for one another but they were competitors on the court. In another come-from-behind victory, Cathedral managed to win the Regional when Washington's Fitzgerald missed a long shot with three seconds to go: score 61-60.

Cathedral advanced to the Semi-State, where the team soundly defeated Connersville and Muncie Central. The Irish looked stronger than ever, and it appeared that no one would stop them for the State title; certainly the Cathedral team was the media pick to win it all at Market Square Arena in Indianapolis. The stage was set for the Irish to take on a talented Plymouth team, starring Scott Skiles.

The loyal Cathedral followers were so used to winning that it never occurred to them that their team might lose at this point of the season; after all, even when the Irish were behind in key games they always found a way to win.

There was a difference heading into the final four this time. The Irish were going into the game without their great defensive player, Tim Hoffman, who was out with mononucleosis. Hoffman, who had also missed the Semi-State games, was good on the boards and excellent from the foul line. He was always good for about ten points and a half-dozen rebounds per game, but he was most noted for his great defensive play.

Hoffman's own personal dream of playing in a State Championship game was shattered by his illness, and his team felt his absence. The Irish started off the Plymouth game looking timid, and as the game progressed, Cathedral consistently turned over the ball. In addition, the team only shot 36 percent from the foul line, when their normal percentage was 70 percent of their free throws. Cathedral was shocked in the afternoon game by losing 59-62 and the chance of becoming the first Catholic school to win a IHSAA State Basketball Championship.

Their fine effort, though, did not go unrecognized. Throughout the month of March the entire Indianapolis community supported the Irish. *The Indianapolis Star* and *The News* wrote numerous times about the character and the class Tom O'Brien's Irish team often displayed throughout the season. O'Brien and the team were especially cited for the way they handled the loss at Market Square Arena. When the Irish team came out of the showers to watch the second afternoon game they went straight to the Plymouth team, already sitting down, to congratulate them on their win. It was just another display of what a first class program Tom O'Brien had put together. He deserves great credit for the positive image the '81-'82 basketball team projected to the Indianapolis community, and beyond.

The accolades continued. Ken Barlow made First Team All-State and Scott Hicks made Second Team All-State. Barlow was named to the '82 Indiana All-Star Team. Hicks was an All-State selection again in '83 and he made the '83 Indiana All-Star Team. Both Barlow and Hicks played their college ball at Notre Dame.

There are several other noteworthy events concerning the '81-'82 basketball season which must be mentioned. There were more pep rallies than one could count during the entire basketball season, but never more than in the month of March, when they occurred every Friday and Monday. No one ever saw a Cathedral pep rally if they did not see Kevin Flynn and Ute Finch and company in action. They entertained the student body all year long, with Flynn playing a host of different characters such as the likes of Evangelist Ernest Anige.

The first pep rally going into the State tourney involved a special guest, Joe Montana, quarterback for the San Francisco Forty-Niners and MVP of the Super Bowl, which had taken place only a few weeks before his visit at Cathedral. The former Notre

Dame star enthusiastically wished the school and the team well as they headed into the tournament, even taking time to talk about his own high school days playing basketball. The kids went crazy, especially the girls. The entire school community appreciated Board Chairman Bob Welch's success in getting Montana to come to Cathedral.

Another pep rally during the month of March involved members of the CHS class of 1932. The group who visited the school for the pep rally included the legendary Charley Hill and John Ford, one of the great stars of the '32 basketball team. With a group of other 1932 classmates they reenacted a cheer made popular in their day. The men lined up facing the back side of the person before them, rotating their arms like the wheels of a locomotive slowly spelling out the word C-A-T-H-E-D-R-A-L, going faster and faster all the while spelling out C-A-T-H-E-D-R-A-L, until they could go no faster. The student body loved it and showed great respect for the graduates who were celebrating their fiftieth anniversary in 1982. Before the pep rally was over the students started chanting "Charley! Charley! Charley!" for Charley Hill, the leader of the pack of 1932.

The last pep rally brought many celebrities together for the send-off to the State Final Four. Archbishop O'Meara, Mayor William Hudnut, Chairman of the Board Bob Welch, and future Chairman of the Board Dan O'Malia were all there. Television cameras and newspaper reporters were everywhere. In addition, several representatives from McDonald's fast-food were also there to Honor Ken Barlow, who received McDonald's All-State Award.

There was an interesting twist to that pep rally. The microphones did not work, and for well over five minutes the Fighting Irish Band had to play the CHS fight song until an alternative system could be found. This was known to happen on many occasions at important functions during this period, often driving the people planning the events crazy. On one such occasion the microphones went out on wrestling coach Lance Rhodes, who, irritated by this continual problem, quickly announced to the crowd, "If it worked, it wouldn't be Cathedral."

During the basketball season of 1981–82 the media visited the school at least once a week or more, especially in the memorable month of March, and Indianapolis was well aware of Cathedral.

The success of the basketball season did not necessarily transfer to the success of other events at CHS that year. The junior-senior prom was an event that is not likely to be forgotten any more than the basketball team's going to the state finals. The special evening took place at the Columbia Club, but, dismayingly, the band failed to show up for the event. While one teacher headed home to get his stereo, a three-piece band finishing a wedding reception on the third floor agreed to come up to the top floor to play at the prom. It wasn't exactly what the class had planned, but they made the best of it. Sharon Hartman was crowned Prom Queen.

The school year came to a close with Glenn Mauger speaking at graduation ceremonies. He was chosen by the seniors to be their speaker in this first year that a faculty member spoke at graduation ceremonies instead of the Baccalaureate Mass. The Archbishop "switched places," speaking at Baccalaureate Mass under a new routine which has remained in place to the present. Beth Happel was the valedictorian and Lisa Aracher was salutatorian, while Kevin Flynn was awarded the Board of Trustees Award. No one has ever been more deserving of the award. Ken Barlow was awarded the Al Feeney (today the Joe Dezelan) Award for the most outstanding student athlete. If awards had been given at that time (as they are today) for both male and female, Beth Happel most certainly would have been the female recipient. Beth won the State Championship in hurdles and was a high school All-American who held the low hurdles state record for ten years, with a time of 13:95.

More noteworthy events of the 1981–82 school year:

The Mud volleyball tournament at Homecoming, which became a raucous disaster, involved almost the entire student body. Many teachers were also covered with mud from head to toe and the showers in the school building were completely clogged. It got to the point where no one was allowed back into the building. Parents arrived to pick up their sons and daughters and they were furious about how things got so out of hand, but no one was hurt, and by the time the entire mess was cleaned up everyone laughed at what a good time it had been.

Pretty Carrie Greene, who had been nagged all year about the way she styled her hair by her cheerleading coach Cathy George, was crowned Homecoming Queen.

Prosecutor Steven Goldsmith visited Cathedral to talk about drugs and alcohol.

Bob Considine started a column in *The Megaphone* called "Considine's Cuisine." The restaurant review has continued in *The Megaphone* to this day, under a number of different titles.

A Glimpse of the Eighties

Kevin Flynn, '82 reflecting back on his days at CHS, penned the following comments: The best example I can think of to describe what it was like to be at Cathedral during the 1981–82 season is the movie Hoosiers. *It is hard to share the experience of following your team on the road from game to game and cheering as loudly as possible until your voice was so hoarse that it couldn't be heard. That experience was true for football, basketball and even wrestling. Cathedral ruled the sports pages all week long, and its teams led the students on a roller coaster of emotions throughout each season.*

The students were the same as they had been for generations. They were proud to be "Irish," and they were leaders at school, in sports and in the community. Upper–classmen like Paul Radspinner, John Christ and Mary Ferruza (Rosanne Rossanna Danna) stirred up the fans and led the student body in spirit well ahead of our class. We followed in the same tradition. Underclassmen like Nora Welch, Matt Considine and others picked up the spirit where we left off. In fact, our class, and the classes ahead of us and behind us got together on many occasions on and off campus and became close friends. Much of this enthusiasm was from the student body's rallying together to support their Irish on the court or the field.

The teachers were a part of the student body, too. Doc Wellman, Jim Obergfell, "Ma" Beyer, Glen Mauger, Kevin McDowell and others had earned the respect of the students with their down-to-earth styles of teaching. They were our friends and they expected a lot from each of us. We had to be prepared for class or risk kneeling for the period in Glidden's AP English or looking dumb in front of Morgan's Calculus class.

Pasting up our senior yearbook allowed a few of us to reflect just before graduation on our four years. We laughed at our attempt to create the World's Largest Milk Shake for the Sophomore Homecoming Dance and joked about George Kovatch's "farm." We found fun pictures of the mud volleyball match, Ken Barlow cutting down the net at the City Finals, and assorted Homecoming Queens like Karen Flynn, Carrrie Green and Carla Courter. Dave Kasberg even managed to find a picture of me in a grass skirt and coconut bra on the set of South Pacific.

Every once in a while I pull out that 1982 Cathedran *and a rush of memories fills my head—the sounds of laughter and glimpses of heartbreaking times. It is hard to believe, but when I run into my classmates on the streets or at Mickey's these days, no one seems to have changed much since those early days in the 1980s.*

1982–1983

The school did not start off with any particular expectations except perhaps those put on the Senior Class by itself and teachers hoping for high achievement. The Senior Class, an incredibly bright class with a number of people scoring well over 1200-1300 on SAT tests, did not disappoint anyone. With the likes of Karen Hoffman, Mary Kay Steinmetz, Dan Nicholich, John Leo, Tony Zappia, Shari Kennedy, Terri Catterson, Joe Grabow, Jim Risch, Angie Price, Jenny O'Brien, Debbie Dreiband, Cathy Martin, Annie Christ, Roger Wood and David Scheidler leading the way, the class of '83 was serious about learning. Surely they were one of the most intelligent and hard-working classes of the Eighties. They were a creative bunch as well, and athletics were important.

In the fall of '82 the football team led by All-State player Vince Freeman, and supported by seniors big "Jimbo" Kane, John and Jeff Haigerty, Dennis O'Hara, Vince Rago, Andy Cope, J.T. Snyder, John Jeter, Jim Marchino, Steve Glogoza, John Greenwalt, Roger Wood, Mike Boyle, Grady McIntire, Tommy Smith, Dennis Kelly, and a great little kicker named Chris Dugan, won the last City title.

The City Championship was won by defeating Roncalli 7-6. Thanks to a great pass by Dennis O'Hara, and a tremendous fingertip catch by John Jeter in the end zone with only thirty-nine seconds left in the game, the Irish earned a great victory. Roncalli had one of the best defensive units in the state, led-by nose man Andy Mappes. The Roncalli team held the Irish to only twenty yards rushing. Conversely, Roncalli rushed for 215 yards, led by All-State back Kenny Gillum, who gained 213 of the yards on thirty-two carries. Still, Roncalli was unable to put the ball in the end zone and had to settle for two field goals. They tried a third field goal but it was blocked by junior Joe McGinley. O'Hara, known to come through in a clutch, made some big plays and passed for 125 yards and the winning touchdown to Jeter.

With the win over Roncalli, Cathedral ended the season 9-1. This was an outstanding feat in McGinley's second year back, considering the Irish started out the season a 34-0 loser to Hobart. The win over Roncalli earned the team a place in the Sectional opener with Northside rival, Chatard.

The Chatard game was brutal—three quarters went by without a score by either team, In the fourth quarter Cathedral had the ball on Chatard's twelve yard line and was close to scoring when they were slapped with back-to-back fifteen-yard penalties. The penalties took them completely out of scoring position even for a field goal.

Shortly after Cathedral had given up the ball to the Trojans, Chatard threw a pass for what would turn out to be the winning touchdown. The receiver for Chatard and the defender, Brian Elson for Cathedral, were both going for the ball, and it appeared that Elson was going to intercept it. Instead, he was knocked aside by the Chatard receiver, who caught the ball. His momentum carried him forward as he headed for the end zone all alone, scoring. Fr. Kelly and Joe Dezelan claim to this day that offensive interference should have been called on the Chatard player. No one took the loss harder than Brian Elson. He carried the weight of the world on his shoulders for days, because he felt responsible for the loss. No football player ever had more heart than Brian Elson. In recalling the incident for this book, Elson said, "not a week or two goes by that I don't think about the touchdown play for Chatard; it was probably the worst thing that ever happened to me in my life." Then he quickly added, "If that is the worst thing to ever happen to me then I guess I have had a pretty good life. People bring it up all the time," he said.

Brian loved the game of football and he went on to an outstanding career at Butler University, where, interestingly, he became teammates with some of his high school rivals from both Roncalli and Chatard. In his Butler days Brian Elson was part of two Heartland Conference titles, and a trip to the Division Two Playoffs.

There is one note concerning the Roncalli game that must be recalled. On one play in the game Roncalli fumbled on Cathedral's five-yard line. It was scooped up by 5´-9´´, 195-pound Vince Freeman, who finding himself unable to lateral, ran the ball faster than he had probably ever run in his life. Persisting, he scampered ninety yards and was finally tackled on Roncalli's five-yard line as the crowd roared and chuckled at the same time at the "Little Big Man's" courage. He was not about to give up his once-in-a-lifetime opportunity to run and possibly score a touchdown.

Due to a clipping penalty, the play was brought back to mid-field where Cathedral took over the ball. It was a happy moment of glory for Vince Freeman, one he will never forget. Vince Freeman was an All-State player who made the All-Star team. He went from Cathedral to Butler University, where he had a very successful career.

There was no officially declared City Champion from 1984-1991. In 1991 it was decided that a City Champion should once again be declared. The new winner is determined by how many city games are won and lost, a system which works to Cathedral's disadvantage, since the Irish play so many out-of-city teams. In 1991 the Irish football squad was runner-up in the State Tournament and in 1992 they won the State title. However, in neither year were they City champs because they did not play enough city teams.

Responding to excellent teachers like Nick Morgan, Judy Birge, Ruth Beyer, Judy Ney, Glen Mauger, Bob Glidden, and Melinda Luckey Bundy, the class of '83 took every challenge presented to them.

The class was led by a serious but carefree individual named John Matthews. With Kay Wiles, Bob Mooney and Nora Welch leading the way, too, they held many unofficial and impromptu class meetings at the Mooney Barn and anyplace else that struck them, including the pond by O'Malia's grocery.

When this group celebrated senior skip day they had almost one hundred percent attendance, and they all went to the same place on Geist Reservoir, even managing to make the radio shows in the afternoon to claim such a fantastic feat.

The '82-'83 basketball team was excellent, but not good enough to repeat a trip to the Final Four. Nevertheless, there were some great games. The Hall of Fame Classic at New Castle matched super stars Scott Hicks of Cathedral and Steve Alford of New Castle together in what turned out to be a genuine classic indeed. Alford scored thirty-five points for New Castle, and Hicks scored thirty-two for the Irish. Before six thousand screaming fans, Cathedral won the sixth Hall of Fame Classic 71-69.

A little over a month later the two teams met again. Alford had another outstanding game scoring thirty-seven points before a home crowd of nine thousand fans. Hicks, who was nursing a sore ankle, scored only seventeen points, but he hit the one that counted the most when he scored on an outside jumper with eight seconds to go to win the game 68-67 in overtime. New Castle hit 25-25 free throws that game and had only six turnovers, but the Irish prevailed to prove to themselves and everyone else that they were "for real."

Alford was chosen Mr. Basketball at the end of the season and went on to star for Indiana University. Hicks also made the Indiana All-Star team and later starred at Notre Dame. It had been another great basketball season for Cathedral and the state of Indiana. The Irish were eliminated in the sectional that year by Broad Ripple, ending all hopes of seeing yet another great game between New Castle and Cathedral in the tournament. More importantly, it ended all hopes of getting back to the Final Four once again to win that State Championship title. As great as the CHS basketball teams were in the eighties, they never did get back to the Final Four. As a matter of fact, they never got past the Regionals again. Nevertheless, they were great basketball teams to watch and infused a new and exciting spirit at Cathedral.

The boys tennis team won another City title and the girls cross country team, led by Mary Matthews, also celebrated a City Championship.

The wrestling team came in third in the state led by heavyweight Andy Cope, who ended the season as the State Heavyweight Champion. The third-ranked team left coach Rhodes with great hope for the future, since most of the team were underclassmen.

Ruth Beyer was elected by the Senior Class to speak at graduation ceremonies, and the class cheered her loudly and graciously after her talk.

Ruth "Ma" Beyer was loved by all of her students for her wit and intellectual charm, but perhaps what endeared her to her students most of all were her motherly instincts and her kind and gentle way of letting people know when they were out of order. Jimmy Cain '85 related a story which typifies Ruth's gentle nature. Jimmy would often try to get away with dress code violations, especially when he wanted to wear a new sweater. One day when he was wearing a new sweater, he came into class and everything was fine. As the class period went on, Mrs. Beyer was discussing Greek Mythology. Without any rising intonation in her voice, she paused for a moment, looked up over her reading classes hanging on the end of her nose and said, "Mr.Cain, I like your sweater. It is very becoming on you. By the way, you are out of dress code."

A former student of Ma Beyer's, John Christ '80 wrote of her, "I have an image of a lady who taught us a subject referred to as 'English' but which, as every high school student can tell you, encompassed everything from grammar and composition to literature and vocabulary. In the midst of this serious study, we would pause once in a while to talk about the best 'junk' books to read in the summer or to comment on the fall of the Nixon Administration and its relevance to Greek Tragedy or perhaps to make an extremely bad joke out of the word 'defeat'." Gentle were her ways but Ruth Beyer's lessons remained forever.

In the spring of '83 Beatriz Luengo, an exchange student from Spain, was crowned Prom Queen. Beatriz returned from Spain for her ten-year reunion over Labor Day Weekend, 1993.

One hundred and thirty eight seniors graduated in '83. *The Megaphone*, led by co-editors Ce Ce Mallet and Dan Williams, was dominated by stories about cheating, stealing, smoking, drugs, alcohol, apathy, senior privileges and "senioritis," a word invented to describe what happens to seniors in the second semester of their senior year.

There were many nicknames with this bunch which were heard on a daily basis, the most famous being Dennis "Crash" Kelly. Names like Plucker, Moondog, Shitzi, Hodgie, Wags, Bags and Rags resounded in the halls. Then there were monickers like Sharbear, Jimbo, Stymie, Slider, Hoffnut and L.D. And finally there was Nora "Flora" Welch and Amy "Blamey" Sneddon. Their affection for nicknames may be one reason why the class of '83 connected so well with Ruth "Ma" Beyer.

Karen Hoffman and Mary Kay Steinmetz were honored as valedictorian and salutatorian of their class, and the Board of Trustees award went to Karen Hoffman. The class of '83 were and are a close group although many miles separate them.

The spring musical in '83 was *Oliver*, an outstanding performance, which, interestingly enough, involved many of the junior and senior football players. Having some of the toughest guys in the school in the spring musical was unique in itself, and Kim Wurster gave a memorable performance as Oliver.

An excellent "Peanuts" comic-strip skit at Thanksgiving featured many members of the class playing Snoopy, Woodstock, and the other famous characters, including Matt Cohoat as Charlie Brown.

The final scene had all the people sitting at a long narrow table reminiscent of Leonardo da Vinci's "Last Supper" as everyone silently listened to Linus (David Scheidler) tell the student body about the meaning of Thanksgiving. The Thanksgiving assembly ended with Michelle Ross singing "America the Beautiful." It was an excellent display of the creativity, imagination, wit, charm, and confidence so characteristic of the entire class of '83.

A few related notes concerning the 1982–83 year must be mentioned. David Scheidler will be ordained a Holy Cross priest in April of 1994. He is the first CHS student in quite some time to become a priest.

The book *Crime and Punishment* was a favorite for most of the seniors as it was taught by great English teachers, Ruth Beyer and Bob Glidden.

Also in the spring of 1983 Rev. Patrick J. Kelly celebrated the twenty-fifth year of his ordination to the priesthood. There was an all-school celebration following an outdoor Mass. Since Fr. Kelly has a great love for classical music, the Junior Class gave him a new stereo to celebrate his anniversary. It remains in his first-floor sanctuary at this writing and can often be heard by those walking past.

1983–1984

The 1983–84 school year was marked by a much different cast of characters. Athletic prowess was evident in this diverse group, which included 15-20 percent non-Catholics and students from all over central Indiana, thus refuting the theory that Cathedral wasn't as diverse on the new campus as it used to be. The classes of the eighties and early nineties, with mixtures of male and female, Catholic and non-Catholic, black and white, were as diverse as any group of people that ever came through CHS in her entire history.

In the fall of 1983, the cross country team saw senior Matt Debono lead classmates A.J. Ratz, Mark Cline, Kieran Tansy and others to many victories. Debono, a bright young man and a great runner, made a trip all the way to the State Finals. When he graduated from Cathedral he attended Wabash with a very promising future. Matt Debono, however, was struck down by a disease called aplastic anemia in his freshmen year at Wabash and died a year and a half later in June of 1986. Friends like Mickey McDaniel were loyal to him to the end. This courageous and well remembered young man faced his death with complete knowledge and understanding of his disease, giving others great courage and a genuine feeling for the value of life.

Led by juniors Claudine Debono, Hilary Snyder and Susan Duffy and supported by freshmen Cindy Troy, Cathy Bradshaw, Elizabeth Crisp, Tina Welch and Julia Hill, the girls cross country team began a new era of success under coach Robin McCart.

While the cross country teams were encountering much new success, the boys tennis team went on to post yet another city title under senior players Kurt Riegner, Kerry Beidelman, and an outstanding junior player, Art Boyle. Two other juniors, Joe Broeker and Tim Coyne also made up the varsity squad, along with sophomores Tim McNulty and Barry Schneider.

The girls tennis success was largely built on the talents of Kathleen Boyle '84 and her sister Meg '86. The team posted their first City title since 1977, the first year CHS had a girls Team. Kathleen Boyle went all the way to the State Individual Final Four. The girls tennis program has gone on to unprecedented success since that year—eleven City titles, numerous other titles and a State Championship in 1986.

There were great expectations for the football team in the '83-'84 school year, expectations not fully realized. The optimism was in large part caused by the tremendous talent on the team, which was led by seniors Joe and Mike McGinley, Brian Elson, Dale Speckman, Clarence Todd, Reggie Jones, Ken Oskins, Jeff Day, John Marbaugh, Mickey McDaniel, Bill Nichols, Grant Drook, Rob Clevenger, great punter Bob Welch, and soccer star and football kicker Marc Behringer. The season opened with a heartbreaking loss to Lawrence North 7-6. CHS went on to post five straight convincing victories, including one over long-time rival Scecina, 28-7. This was the last time the two schools would meet on the football field. This brought an end to a great rivalry, a rivalry which saw friends go together to the Halloween-season games to sit on opposite sides and included co-social events and close friendships.

There are many children today whose fathers attended Cathedral and whose mothers attended Scecina. There are even more Cathedral and Scecina graduates, male and female, who have remained close friends since their high school days. It was a sad day which saw the end of the rivalry, one which had been good for both schools in general and for the Catholic community in particular.

After five straight victories, the Fighting Irish of 1983 went into the Chatard game with great optimism. It turned out to be a devastating evening, as Chatard went on to beat the Irish 26-0. This was the only team to shut out the Irish, who averaged almost twenty points a game. Toward the end of the season a trip to Lancaster, Ohio, also turned out in the negative. The season ended at 7-3, a respectable but disappointing season for such great talent and initial promise.

A young but successful volleyball team posted a 19-8 record led by only two seniors, Collette Cassell and Annette Kinn. Juniors Witney Shewman, Maura Mooney, Katie Blocher, Kris Kennelly, Theresa Haragan and Christy Torzewski helped make the difference, along with sophomore Anita Hodgson. On the horizon in J.V. that year were Cathy Guye, Trisha Mooney, Pattie McShane and Angie Rathz.

There were plenty of experienced players on the 1983-'84 boys basketball team to give hope for a great season, perhaps to even go places in the State Tournament again. Veteran players from the Final Four team of '82 included Shelton Smith, Carl Daniels, and Terry Buford. They were joined by Clarence Todd, Reggie Jones, Jeff Wuensch, Dan Voss, Kevin Long, Mike Rolles, Brian Lloyd and Frank Collins. The season ended with sixteen wins and six losses, including two losses (once in the Sectionals) to a tough Arlington team.

The girls basketball team posted a 12-8 season, and the boys young baseball team showed much growth despite their 13-16 record.

The girls softball team ended the season 12-16 for coach Russ Sarfaty.

The boys and girls track teams fared well, with outstanding performances by City champs Brian Lloyd (300 lows) and Steve Morrison (2400 meter). Sophomore Sectional champ Pete Bynm went all the way to the State Finals in the 110 highs. Annette Kinn was Sectional champ in the discus and shotput.

The golf teams, although young, did very well while being coached by Jim McLinn. The boys soccer team, led by All-American Marc "Sparky" Behringer, Pat Curran and Greg Archer wound up fourth in the State. Behringer went on to play for Indiana University and was co-captain of the 1989 National Championship team there.

Wrestling Coach Lance Rhodes continued to build a wrestling program that has remained unmatched in Indiana. His first State Champion was '83 graduate heavyweight Andy Cope. Perhaps the team which had the greatest chance for a State title, at least up to that point of Rhodes' career, was the '83-'84 team. With the likes of Joe and Mike McGinley, Tim Walsh, John Maio, Mark Clevenger, Gene Boyd, Brian Elson, Kevin Troy, Tim Peiffer, Steve Troy, Nick Rohrman, Chris Blume, and Gilbert Durham, the team seemed poised to win it all. It did not happen. Rhodes could not have been more disappointed.

There are many characteristics which could be attributed to coach Lance Rhodes, but what most marks him is his dedication and determination to win. He is intense beyond explanation and he instills the "killer instinct" it takes to win in an often brutal individual sport.

Although the State title still eludes him, and though his opponents sometimes vilify him, Rhodes' contribution to Cathedral's wrestling program will never be matched.

There are several noteworthy items concerning the 1983-84 school year which need to be mentioned, including the Peer Counseling Program which began under the leadership of Debbie Bhagwandin. This program matched senior students with freshmen students throughout the year to help the younger Cathe-dralite make the transition to high school.

Editors of *The Megaphone* were senior Jenny Hahn and junior Lisa Jochum. A fire in Loretto Hall unfortunately destroyed many of the old Cathedral football pictures.

Highlights of the year included Anna Lamberti placing first in the state piano competition for the second year in a row, Stacey Loner and Tony Ross starring in *Annie Get Your Gun,* and the big Homecoming Week toga extravaganza, when seniors, purposely late for first period, ran up the hill screaming, yelling, and wearing togas, much to the administration's consternation and to the delight of the student body.

The 1983–84 school year also saw the death of Michael Duffecy, who originated the Cathedral Fight Song in the 1920s, the Student Council active with co-presidents Mickey McDaniel and Greg Archer, and Kurt Riegner as valedictorian and A.J Ratz as salutatorian. The Board of Trustees Award went to Richard Bryant, who headed from Cathedral to the Naval Academy. Principal Don Stock announced he was leaving Cathedral, and it was at this graduation that he was honored as speaker.

Following Stock's retirement, Rev. Patrick J. Kelly was appointed Principal of Cathedral High School and remains in that position to the present day. Kelly has been involved with Cathedral from the early days when the Brothers of Holy Cross first decided to leave Cathedral in 1972. In his twenty-three years at Cathedral, perhaps Fr. Kelly's greatest enjoyment has come from serving as chaplain to the Fighting Irish football team. He has been a good friend to hundreds of students. Fr. Kelly wears many hats in his service to Cathedral and to the community, including being chaplain to the Indianapolis Colts.

1984–1985

The school year started off with a cloud hanging over the heads of the senior class. It wasn't until the end of the year that everyone would realize just how dark that cloud was. This particular school year was such an unusual one, tinged with highly personal tragedies, that it is forever recalled in those terms by people in attendance at that time, and it needs to be dealt with in detail.

The Class of '85 found out at the end of their junior year that classmate Ryan Updike had cancer; his leg would have to be amputated. The Junior Day of Recollection focused in large part on Ryan and fear for what was going to happen to him.

Ryan returned to school his senior year and most people seemed optimistic. School proceeded for the class in some respects as it had for other classes in the early eighties. The Class of '85 were bright, fun, serious, and creative. Looking back, though, it is quite easy to see that in some respects, fear ruled them. Some felt that that fear had lifelong consequences for them.

The unconscious fearful mental climate was, in the beginning, clearly related to the illness of their classmate Ryan. In the beginning of the fall semester of their senior year Ryan went to all his classes, although he tired easily. Often he sat with Fr. Kelly in his office, as the two became good friends; in fact, most of the Senior Class became regulars in that office and became close friends to their principal in this unique year for the school.

One senior who got to know Fr. Kelly well that year was Scott Altherr, a senior athlete and scholar and one of the captains of the football team. He was a class officer and a genuine leader to all. Scott wrote his college essay to Wabash College on Ryan Updike, emphasizing the courage Ryan displayed and what he was going through as the year progressed and Ryan's condition worsened.

Students eventually became aware that this loved classmate of theirs was going to die. His hope was to make it to graduation; it was, of course, everyone else's hope as well. Ryan's good friends Art Boyle, Jimmy Cain, Tommy Cline and others were as loyal to their friend as one might ever witness. But it was Scott Altherr who stopped to ask Fr. Kelly one day if he thought Ryan was scared of dying. Fr. Kelly's response was, "Sure, wouldn't you be?" Scott's response was, "Not if I was going with someone."

That conversation took place in late spring, just a month or so before graduation. A week or two later Scott Altherr took off school on a Friday afternoon to go pick up his sister Maureen, who was returning from IU for the summer. On his way there he was in an accident and was killed.

The news of Scott's death came at the end of the school day. The impact devastated the community, especially the Cathedral family. Several teachers commented that Scott had come by their rooms before he left for IU to say good-bye as if he were leaving for a long time. The student body arrived at school on Monday morning and there was almost complete silence throughout the day in the halls. Scott was buried on Tuesday morning.

Later that same evening Ryan Updike died from the cancer he had been battling for almost a full year. He did not make it to graduation. Along with Ryan's family, Fr. Kelly, Art Boyle, Tom Cline, and Jimmy Cain were with Ryan when he died. Acting on the advice of the people working at the hospice, Fr. Kelly told Ryan it was okay to let go and that Scott was there for him. Moments later a tear dropped down Ryan's cheek, and he died. His funeral was on Friday. Two times in the same week the Cathedral family was saddened beyond words. Fr. Kelly once again was called upon to perform the services. His homilies for both boys funerals were amazingly effective; there was not a dry eye at either event. It was, and is at times like these, that Father Kelly is most masterful.

The cortège at Scott Altherr's funeral came through the CHS parking lot to circle around before heading to the church. In an incredibly moving scene, the entire student body waited in complete silence surrounding the parking lot for over a half hour before the cortège arrived. Three days later they lined up again for Ryan Updike's cortège, which circled the school after his funeral. As the cortège stopped, a group of senior boys got out of their car to enter the school. They returned with one balloon for every senior student, each carrying the name of a classmate.

They released the balloons on a beautiful sunny day, and the entire student body watched with sadness and also with relief—that one of the most mournful weeks in CHS history was over.

It was not, of course, really over. All of this took place only two weeks before the prom and less than a month from graduation. The remaining days of school were difficult to say the least. The prom was held at the Atkinson Hotel downtown. The school was so stunned by the boys deaths that it was not really prepared to deal with the aftermath of both events. Perhaps for this reason the kids let loose at the prom. Sick and drunk students at the prom sincerely worried the manager, and he called Father Kelly the next day to inquire after them, concerned about the welfare of the students.

Fr. Kelly was so upset that he said there would be no more proms while he was principal. He had a change of heart the next school year, but the 1985 prom was the last open prom, when students could arrive and leave anytime they wanted. As of 1986 the prom was a closed affair. Students had to arrive for dinner and the dance with everyone else at the same time and no one was allowed to leave until it was over. The students did not like it, but at least they had a prom. The following year, 1987, the parents put together an after-prom, which meant that students and their dates arrived for the prom for dinner and dance and then headed for the Natatorium until 4:30 a.m. The overnighter ended with Mass; then the kids were free to go.

The success of this new program was largely due to the efforts of math teacher and Junior Class Moderator, Lisa Ford. Mrs. Ford brought parents together to become much more involved. For the most part the prom and after-prom has been a success.

Because of the boys' deaths and what happened at the '85 prom there was no senior skip day that year. Not wanting to experience any more tragedies, Fr. Kelly put his foot down and told the seniors if anyone took a skip day he or she would not be allowed to go through graduation ceremonies. Respecting Father Kelly, no one skipped. It was the only year in the eighties that there was not a senior skip day.

To paint the class of '85 as a bad group would not be fair at all. This was a very caring group who were sensitive to others, showing understanding and courage throughout the year. Besides their own personal battles which are typical of those common to seniors in high school, they seemed to take on the battles of the world as well.

The class of '85 were handsome, charming, fun and very intelligent but logical to a fault—they sometimes used logic to suppress emotions. They had plenty to be emotional about, so it is easy to understand why logic tried to rule. When logic did not rule, denial often surfaced. Experiencing joy and genuine sorrow and all the emotions in between, this class was a favorite of many teachers, perhaps because of all that the students had been through or perhaps because they showed all the elements of human behavior.

There are many other notable events which took place during the 1984-'85 school year which must be recognized.

In sports, the boys' tennis team brought home its fourth consecutive City title with players Tim Coyne, Joe Areddy, Mike Stegemeier, Art Boyle, and Kevin McGrath. They ended the season 9-6.

The girls cross country team had an excellent year, win-

ning their third City Championship and a Sectional championship. They were second in their Regionals and they placed ninth
in the State Finals. This team was led by seniors Claudine Debono
and Hilary Snyder and underclassmen, Sheila McDermott, Ann
Bradshaw, Cathy Bradshaw, Katie Turner, Julia Hill, and Cindy
Troy. They were coached by Robin McCart and Mike Armstrong.
Because they were so young and talented, and made up of very
bright students who knew when to be serious and when to have
fun, this team had a promising future.

The boys cross country team was led by senior captain
Steve Jamell, along with other senior runners Mark Cavanaugh
and Brad Apple. They posted a 6-2 record and a second place finish in the City Tourney. With only three seniors, this group was
also looking to the future.

The volleyball team, coached by Denise Farrell and led by
senior co-captains Whitney Shewman and Maura Mooney, had an
excellent season posting a 22-8 record. They had key losses to
Roncalli in the City Tourney and to Chatard in the Sectional, but
they had beaten Chatard earlier in the season. They also beat Fifth
Ranked Ben Davis that year, and they brought home the Lawrence
Central Tourney trophy—a long-awaited accomplishment.
Whitney Shewman went on to play volleyball at Notre Dame.

What was accomplished on the football field that year was
amazing to say the least; the team had an outstanding 9-1 season
with only eight seniors involved. Led by seniors Scott Altherr,
Gene Boyd, Scott Trieloff, Mike Dooley, Tom O'Hara, Matt Guye,
Robert Walsh and Avery Borders, the squad surprised everyone.
They beat Lawrence North for the first time in Cathedral history,
and they upset highly ranked Lafayette Jeff. Their only loss was to
archrival Chatard in a heartbreaker 28-21 victory. The Irish beat
up on Chatard all night long, but Chatard made the big plays,
earning a berth to the State Tournament and winning the State
title.

However, Cathedral held the Number One position in the
final State ranking. In the mid-eighties only a few teams were invited to a playoff berth, and Cathedral did not get a spot because
they had been beaten by Chatard. It wasn't until the next year that
all teams were allowed into a real playoff tournament. Like all the
other fall sports teams, the future football team looked very bright
because the teams were so young.

The fall of 1984 saw the first girls golf team formed. It finished a respectable season, considering it was going against very
established programs. The team was made up of juniors Kim

Skiles and Ann Hebenstreit, sophomore Chrissy Pauley, and freshmen Amy Skiles and Molly Williams.

The Irish wrestling program had another outstanding season, winning its fourth consecutive City title. They finished the season 16-0. The climax of the season saw the wrestling team defeat eventual State Champion Delta. The team won their fifth straight Sectional and their third straight Regional, followed by their first Semi-State Championship. Matt Moll, Sean McGinley, Gilbert Durham, Steve Troy, Scott Altherr and Gene Boyd all qualified for the State tourney, where CHS placed tenth. Gene Boyd was crowned Runner-up at 185 lbs.

The boys basketball team was up and down all season long. The young team, led by senior Terry Buford, beat some state ranked teams and lost to less talented ones. Posting a 12-11 record, the Irish managed to win the City Championship and made it to the Sectional finals.

The girls basketball team finished a 12-7 program, with Stephanie Webb as MVP. They made it to the final Sectional game, where they were defeated by Number One-ranked Warren Central 53-46. Other seniors on the team were Maura Mooney, Whitney Shewman, and Mary Ann "Boomer" Smith.

The Irish baseball team posted a winning record of 16-13 under new head coach Keith Perin. Although they did not win any titles, they did defeat State-ranked Roncalli twice and State-ranked Ritter once, also defeating a very strong Ben Davis team that year. The team included seniors Tim Coyne, Chris Cleveland, Bob Hodgson, Steve Jamell, Jeff Wuensch and Steve Lee. On the horizon, soon to become a star pitcher, was sophomore Brian Conway.

The girls tennis team was one year away from a dream season. Nevertheless, they won the City title once again and their Sectional as well. Meg Boyle, a junior, was named First Team All-State and Amy Boyle, a freshman, was named Second Team All-State. Lisa Jochum and Maureen Brady were the only seniors on the team, so there were great expectations for this bunch, which also included Ann and Cathy Bradshaw, Meg and Mandy Harvey, Michele Leighton, Nicole Karto, and Jennifer Areddy.

The boys track team was young and successful, breaking six new school records. Records were set by Pete Bynm, David Jones, David White, Brian Lloyd, Tony Harris, Herbert Gary, and Evan Gibbons.

The girls track team only posted a 4-3 record, but showed

great improvement for a young team.

The boys golf team won a City Championship and junior Mike Williams was Medalist. First Team All-City honors went to Mike Williams and Paul Hibbit. Steve McDaniel made Second Team All-City.

The team in the newly popular sport of soccer had another successful season finishing the year 9-2-1. They defeated state powerhouses Carmel and North Central. They were led by seniors Tim Archer, Steve McDaniel, Albert Moore, Kevin Finister, Steve Lee and David Marbaugh.

The girls softball team finished the season 13-8. The Mental Attitude award winners were Katy Blocher and Susan Duffy.

In spite of some events which went wrong during their senior year, there was recognition. The 1984-85 Sportsmanship of the Year Award was given to Cathedral High School by the referees' association.

Graduation at Cathedral

Graduation in 1985 was held downtown at the Circle Theater because the Cathedral church on North Meridian street was closed for extensive renovation. Graduation ceremonies have remained at the Circle Theater ever since. Heidi Weas was valedictorian and Stephanie Webb was salutatorian.

Cathedral graduation ceremonies have been described by most people who have attended as the very best in the city. With the Indianapolis Symphony Brass Quintet providing the music and the traditional bag pipe rendition of *Amazing Grace* and *Auld Lang Syne* by former teacher Larry Everhart, graduation ceremonies are particularly personal and meaningful. In addition, the speeches given by the valedictorians and salutatorians have always been memorable.

In more recent years a senior Student Council representative starts off the ceremony by leading the crowd in prayer and the singing of "America the Beautiful." The principal introduces the valedictorian and salutatorian. After their speeches, a Senior Class officer introduces the faculty graduation speaker. Closing remarks are made by the President of the School who welcomes each new graduating class as Cathedral alumni.

Diplomas are passed out by the principal, president and Chairman of the Board as each name is called out by the class moderator. Recitation of the Irish Blessing by the senior class moderator closes the ceremony. On a few occasions, special citations or honorary diplomas have been awarded to various individuals. Other schools would be hard pressed to match the pride, tradition, and overall feeling of a Cathedral graduation.

In 1985 a special citation was given to principal Rev. Patrick J. Kelly for all that he did to help the Senior Class through their very trying year. It was presented by Senior Class officer, Elizabeth Byers. Elizabeth also introduced faculty speaker Glenn Mauger, who was chosen once again to give the graduation address. He did a masterful job given the nature of what had transpired throughout the year. The parents of Scott Altherr and Ryan Updike received their sons' diplomas for them. It was an emotional ceremony.

Elizabeth Byers, who had won the spirit award her senior year at Cathedral went on to Purdue where she graduated Phi Beta Kappa as a math major. Elizabeth went back to school to become certified to teach and then returned to Cathedral where she currently teaches math. An outstanding high school and college student with an outgoing personality, Elizabeth Byers is the first female graduate to come back and teach at Cathedral full time. Having had wonderful math teachers like Nick Morgan and Lisa Ford, Elizabeth Byers knows what it takes to pass on great math skills to Cathedral students.

The following comments were written by Elizabeth Byers concerning the importance of having the excellent math teachers Cathedral provided:

When I was a sophomore in honors geometry, Nick Morgan had us write down what we wanted to be when we grew up. I remember having no idea. He told us that even if we changed our minds one hundred times between now and then it was important for us to have a long term goal in the back of our minds so that our days at school had a definite purpose. He was the first person to encourage me to become a teacher. I learned more about learning that year than any other year in high school. I learned about setting goals, and that it's okay to change your mind. One doesn't have to know all the answers as long as he or she is willing to figure the answers out.

Lisa Ford taught me about dedication. She demanded that we work up to her high standards. That gave me self-discipline and a sense of responsibility in my academic studies. On return visits to school after graduation, I got to see the "human" side of Lisa Ford, her concerns for her students and her love for teaching. I have used Lisa Ford as a direct model in my role as a teacher.

I try to keep my attitude as caring as Lisa's and Nick's and to make my students think about the other aspects of life that high school provides so that they learn about more

*than just "math"—that they learn to think, to reason, and to
set goals for themselves.*

Some other noteworthy events throughout the 1984–85
school year included a gift to the school from the Senior Class. The
class had a concrete platform poured for an outdoor altar behind
Loretto Hall where Baccalaureate Mass is held. A stone dedicating
the altar to Ryan Updike and Scott Altherr sits at the front of the
platform.

The drama department put on *Night Must Fall*, which
starred Karl Kenzler, Maria Scheidler, and Monica Hartman. Also
joining the cast were Edward Scheidler, Rob Hoaglin, Jane Fox,
Libby Christopherson, and Amy Osburn.

The spring musical was *Kismet*, starring Kevin Terry,
Monica Hartman, Karl Kenzler, and Michelle Bennett. Thyra
Metz, Natalie Hessong, and Kathleen Hannon were a few of the
dancers performing in the play.

The Megaphone editors were Mike Melliere and Lisa
Jochum. They made *The Megaphone* a weekly paper for the first
time.

The Shamrauction netted $242,000 and saw guests Arch-
bishop O'Meara, Prosecutor Steven Goldsmith, and Olympic
Champion Greg Louganis attend the successful evening.

Mrs. Gerry Kennedy once again came through with tremendous decorations as chairpersons Dan Hasbrook and Rita
O'Malia led the way in organizing the event.

Led by sophomore Tom Watson, the Model UN team of
'85 won great praise for their political wisdom and diplomatic
expertise. Two years later the Model UN Team, led once again by
Tom Watson, would win the equivalent of a State Championship
Title.

The debate team was led by sophomore Libby Christopherson, Anita Hodgson and Rosemary Buting, but only Hodgson
and two others, Sean Lemeiux and Tracy Doherty, would make it
to the State Finals.

Natalie Hessong was homecoming queen. Elizabeth Byers
was crowned Senior Prom Queen and Meg Boyle was honored as
the Junior Prom Queen.

Heidi Weas was the Board of Trustees Award winner and
Scott Altherr won the Joe Dezelan Award for the most outstanding student athlete. His parents received the award on his behalf.

One day in class, early in the year, senior Lori Nester
called her religion teacher by the name by which she had always
known him, Uncle Jim. For most of the year many senior students

also referred to him in the same manner. It was only one of the reasons he was so fond of the class of '85.

It rained the night before the Baccalaureate Mass. The next morning the weather looked ominous. However, Fr. Kelly decided to go ahead and try to have the Mass outdoors. As Fr. Kelly said early that morning, "I have faith that Ryan and Scott will make the sun come out so let's go ahead and set up for the Mass." It happened just like Fr. Kelly said it would. The clouds gave way to sunshine by the time the Mass started at mid-morning. When the sun came out it was as if the cloud which had hung over the heads of this class were finally lifted so they could let go and move on. The class of '85 left Cathedral with their heads held high acting out the theme of the banner which hung on the altar at the Baccalaureate Mass: "We came as many . . . We leave as One."

1985–1986

The 1985–86 school year started off on the wrong foot as far as the students were concerned. There was hope that the school year would go a little more smoothly than it did the year before. In some respects it did and in other areas it did not.

There were too many new rules and less and less freedom. As far as the students were concerned, the school was over-reacting to the turmoil of the year before them. Rules were tighter; there was no doubt about that. Early dismissal was abolished and everyone had to remain at school from first through seventh periods. An already strict dress code would be strictly enforced. Moreover, the prom was to be strictly regulated, as has been said. In the scale of life, these were small problems but to typical seniors in high school these problems were enough to create some negative feelings toward the school.

The positive spirit which emerged in the early eighties seemed to diminish significantly, and an attitude of "us versus them" began to develop. One teacher described the class of '86 as "rebels without a cause".

Still, there were many people in this class who were just as, or more, conscientious as any group who came before them. They were a charitable group who extended themselves when doing acts of service, collecting more money and toys for the Central State Hospital program than any class before them and any class since. They overwhelmed families at Christmas with gifts and food, and several volunteered over their Christmas break to help out at Holy Cross Catholic Church.

Whether because of many new restrictions or out of fear of what happened to the class before them many people in the class of '86 became uneasy, apathetic, or even angry. A negative feeling began to emerge within the student body as a whole. There had been rumors going around that Cathedral was hurting financially, and this added to the feelings which were developing.

Perhaps the school in 1986 represented society at large. In some respects people seemed more self-centered and in other respects more giving. That may seem to be a contradiction, but the statement fits the Cathedral class of '86 and the country as a whole.

Self doubt came into the picture as Americans watched the shuttle blow up in living color on TV. People seemed less trusting of one another as the "yuppies" emerged to take all that they could get with no regard for others. On the other hand we saw thousands of people volunteering their time to help those who were less fortunate.

The malaise in the country was felt at the personal level by students. They were receiving reports that the opportunities for them when they graduated from college would not offer the same advantages as for those who went before them. On a much smaller scale, the changes which were taking place at Cathedral were representative of what might become of their future: less freedom, limited choices, and no assurance that things were going to get better. Again fear, this time of a different kind than for the class before them, began to rule them. The reactions to this fear was unpredictable. Some would laugh at it, some were angry because of it, and others simply became apathetic to it. Still others embraced it and saw it as a challenge to combat.

Like the class of 1984, the class of '86 was loaded with athletic talent. The football team started off the season playing Cincinnati Moeller at the Hoosier Dome. Moeller was considered to be one of the top teams in the country—from the high school in Cincinnati where Notre Dame coach Gerry Faust had been head coach. An enthusiastic crowd watched as the Cathedral boys played well but lost the game 24-0. Cathedral played one of the toughest schedules in the state in the fall of 1985, also including 5-A State Champion Warren Central. The Warren game brought out a tremendous crowd for both schools. The Cathedral boys played their hearts out but lost to Warren on the last play of the game when the Warren quarterback, Jeff George, threw a desperation pass which was caught in the end zone for the winning touchdown.

One of the most significant plays of the game came when Cathedral's Pete Bynm ran for over twenty yards carrying two or three Warren players with him into the endzone for the leading score. The entire team headed for the endzone to pile on Pete and to congratulate him for what appeared to be the winning touchdown since time was running out. As a result of excessive celebrating in the endzone when Bynm scored, Cathedral was slapped with a fifteen yard penalty for delay of game. The team had to kick off from their own twenty-five yard line. That gave Warren Central great field position. George had been hit hard all night long by the Irish defense led by senior Moe Gardner and junior Derrick Brownlow, and company. Nevertheless, George led his team down to the one yard line and on the last play of the game, on fourth down, George completed a touchdown pass that ended Cathedral's dream of upsetting the Number One-ranked team in the 5-A division. It was truly an outstanding high school football game.

The season came to an end when the Irish were surprised by a stubborn Roncalli team in the Sectional final. Roncalli went on to win the 3-A State Championship.

More players, perhaps, from the '85 team went on to play college ball than from any other previous team. Gardner and Brownlow would end up at Illinois, become All-Americans and play professional football. John Lindgren, Tony Harris, Joe Pindell, Chris Peck, Tim Maschek, Blaine "Woody" Bishop, Bobby Brady, Billy Peebles, Jimmy Allen, Scott Evans, Pete Guye, and Nick Melloh, all went on to play college ball.

The Irish had beaten number three Bloomington South that year and a tough Ben Davis team, thus ending the season 7-3.

Other sports events at Cathedral in '85-'86 included the girls cross county Team's fourth City Championship and their second Sectional Championship title. Coached by Robin McCart and Mike Armstrong, they ended the season finishing ninth in the state, with runners Bridget Kelly, Katie Turner, Ann Bradshaw, Julia Hill, Cindy Troy, Mary Boyer, Cathy Bradshaw, and Sheila McDermott delivering strong performances.

The boys cross country team won the City title for the first time since 1962 and also the first time in nine years that someone other than Chatard had won the title. Chatard had a tremendous program in the eighties, but Cathedral was making headway. The

Irish were led by co-captains Matt Wire and Ron Nolton and sophomore Brian Cleverly. Also on the starting team were Jerry Harkness, Connor Welch, Bob Moriarity, and Shane Nolton.

The Irish soccer team ended the season 9-2-1 and gave great hope for the future.

The rebuilding volleyball team finished their season 23-14 and placed second in both the City tourney and the Sectional. The mental attitude award went to junior Trish Mooney and the most valuable player awards went to Patty McShane and Anita Hodgson. Coach Denise Farrell was optimistic about the future.

Girls golf finished 10-2, a credible performance for the first full year. The team included Ann Hebenstreit, Amy Skiles, Amy Fischer, Chrissy Pauley, Kim Skiles and Molly Williams.

The boys' tennis team once again won the City title, with outstanding senior leadership provided by Barry Schneider, Tim McNulty , and Evan Moss. Moss, Schneider and McNulty currently coach the boys tennis team at Cathedral.

It was a dismal year for the basketball team, which ended the season 11-10, truly a long season for Coach Steve Hodgson. The same held true for Coach Jim Williams and the girls basketball team, which ended the season with eight wins and ten losses.

The wrestling team was another story, posting a 20-0 dual meet record. The team claimed the fifth City title in six years and beat Delta for the second year in a row, also winning the Sectional, Regional, and Semi-State titles. The Irish wrestlers finished a remarkable but disappointing second in the State tourney. Freshman Lance Ellis won the state title at ninety-eight pounds. In his four years at Cathedral Ellis went 177-0 for the longest winning record in the state and won four State titles. Mark Clevenger also won a state title at 177 pounds. Bob Sweeny took fifth, Gilbert Durham captured fourth and Steve Troy was also a state finalist.

Not to be outdone by anyone, the girls tennis team was truly outstanding. The team, which had as much charm and grace as it did athletic talent, won the State Tennis Championship. Led by senior, Meg Boyle '86, and her sister, sophomore, Amy Boyle '88, no athletic group at Cathedral had ever displayed more class than the tennis team of 1986.

The team of seven also included sophomore Ann Bradshaw, '88 and her sister, junior Cathy Bradshaw, '87. Another sister act on the team were twins, Meg and Mandy Harvey '88. The other player on the starting team was Michele Leighton '88. Meg and Amy Boyle played number one and two singles, in that order. Ann Bradshaw was the number three singles.

Meg and Amy Boyle went on to play tennis at Miami University where their older sister Kathleen '84, had also participated. Ann Bradshaw continued her tennis at Notre Dame.

The 1985-86 school year included a "Brain Game" team which went all the way to the state finals by beating North Central—champions seven out of the last ten years. The Irish team lost in the final game to Perry Meridian. It was the second time Cathedral had advanced to the state finals since arriving on the new campus. The team included seniors Laura Polley, Scott Underwood, and Frank Baukert and junior Tom Watson. Senior A.C. Dumal was the alternate.

As spring rolled around, Carol Cleveland was crowned senior prom queen and Jenny Zeunik received the same honor for the juniors.

The spring musical was *Bye, Bye Birdie* staring Karl Kenzler. The senior class gave a thousand dollars that spring to have the altar from the old St. Lawrence Church moved to Cathedral and set up outdoors by Loretto Hall on the platform which the class before them had built. It remains still in the spot where every Baccalaureate Mass is held.

Graduation took place at the Circle Theater once again—seniors heard from salutatorian, Ann Hebenstreit and valedictorian, Kim Skiles. Monsignor James P. Galvin, a long time friend to Cathedral, received an Honorary diploma and was thrilled to be included in the class of 1986. The graduation address was given by senior religion teacher Jim Obergfell, who had been graciously introduced by Class President Anita Hodgson. The seniors recognized Ruth "Ma" Beyer who had celebrated her last year at Cathedral, retiring as head of the English Department. She passed that honor on to Jo Kissling who was new to Cathedral in 1985 but who remains Department Head at this writing.

Not only did Cathedral lose Ruth Beyer that year, but it also lost Bob Glidden and Judy Ney. All three teachers had taught for over twelve years at Cathedral. All three people, along with Melinda Luckey Bundy, were the core of the English Department from the mid seventies to 1986. It had been a tremendous department but only Melinda remained.

Most students who had these teachers would say they were among some of the very best teachers they ever had in high school or in college. Cathedral had always been known for its strong English Department; in earlier days some thought the school could never match the English Departments put together by the Brothers of Holy Cross. However, this group, Beyer,

Glidden, Ney, and Bundy were as good as any group to come before them. Bob Glidden brought with him some of the antics of the Brothers from the old school, such as making students kneel throughout an entire class for infractions.

Cathedral was fortunate to find teachers like Jo Kissling and Nancy Niblack Baxter to carry on the role of those people who were now gone. Another strong addition to the staff was John Hannon. Judy Ney returned one year later to teach part time, and Cathedral felt fortunate to get her back. Melinda Luckey Bundy never left, remaining into the nineties as witty and sharp as ever at her teaching job.

One other person who must be discussed when mentioning English achievement is Betsy Barnard.

Betsy came to Cathedral in 1980 to pioneer a highly successful program for college-bound students with learning disabilities. Betsy's Language Support program has been a model for other schools throughout the city and state, and even some surrounding states. Betsy has put Cathedral ahead in the race to educationally address learning disabilities. Her contribution to her students is even more clearly measured by the continuous success stories of so many of her former students in college and beyond.

The 1986 school year saw Latin being taught at CHS once again, when Sr. Mary Patrice came to Cathedral. A dedicated Sister of Charity, she no longer teaches but she still serves Cathedral working in the office in the early morning hours. Sr. Mary Patrice has been in education for over fifty years.

The school year also saw Jim McCoy pen a full page article featuring an interview with Dr. Jim Muller, the 1985 Nobel Peace Prize winner, for *The Megaphone* prior to his visit to the school.

Music education continued to evolve at Cathedral under Larry Everhart. Chris Hair came in first in the State Music Contest playing a tuba solo, and Joe Welch and Bernard Tord also received a first place award for their trumpet duet. Other significant band members who participated in 1985-'86 were Phil Caito, Mike Kennedy, Mark Hinkle and Frank Baukert.

The Megaphone staff, headed by Pam Povinelli and Marty Dezelan put in many long hard hours getting out a fine high school newspaper. They took their job seriously and could often be found at Cathedral well into the night piecing the paper together with faculty advisor Mike Armstrong.

1986–1987

Not only did the 1986–87 school year start off with many new people in the English Department, it also started off with a concerned faculty. A pay freeze, additional classes to teach, and more rumors of the school's financial troubles were unsettling. In addition, things appeared out of control when students arrived on the first day of school to find that schedules were not available for most of them. It was an ominous sign, but things got better and the year went on as usual.

In the summer prior to the 1986–87 school year, Cathedral High School went to a pre-paid tuition plan. This was designed to give some indication of just how many students would be attending Cathedral in the fall and to clear up any financial problems concerning tuition payments. The plan also provided much-needed working capital for school improvements. In the short run, this plan created some problems, but overall it was one of the best moves the school could have ever made. Other schools began to follow Cathedral's tuition plan.

Because of the many rumors concerning Cathedral's finances and the trouble with scheduling problems at the start of the school year, President Mike McGinley gave a "State of the School" report to dispel all rumors concerning both matters. It helped answer many of the questions people had and gave encouragement to students that Cathedral High School would be around for a long time to come.

Only a couple of months into the school year tragedy struck Cathedral once again. On October 27, 1986, junior Colleen Hafner, a varsity cheerleader, was killed in an automobile accident, only a year and a half after Scott Altherr and Ryan Updike had died. It was another difficult time for Cathedral but especially for Colleen's sister, Tanya, who was in her senior year when Colleen was killed. Students began to wonder when this sort of thing was going to stop. Colleen was described as a happy-go-lucky, fun-loving, kind-hearted person who enjoyed what she did, and who loved Cathedral High School.

The 1986–87 school year remained a difficult year for some faculty members who were disgruntled by the pay freeze and other concerns. Aside from these events, it was a great school year for most of the students. The Senior Class had much to do with keeping a positive attitude for the entire student body and the faculty. There was not a faculty member around who did not treasure this senior group of '87. With people like Cathy Bradshaw, Sue Choi, Matt Caito, Libby Christopherson, Elizabeth Crisp, Kerry Flaherty, and Tom Watson leading the way, the Senior Class made their mark during the 1986–87 school year. As was the case of the class of '83, those people academically in the middle might have found themselves at the top of almost any other class. The academic and intellectual power of this class was as impressive as that of any class in all the eighties. Leadership abounded in the class of '87 with people like Jerry Harkness, Tom Watson, Erin Healy, and Rowdy Taylor leading the student body and the Senior Class. There were many other leaders in clubs and organizations, students like Sandra Walton, Kerry Flaherty, Libby Christopherson, Cathy Guye, Derrick Brownlow, Cathy Bradshaw, Cindy Troy, Julia Hill, Matt Gardner, and Matt Caito, just to name a few who made a difference while at Cathedral.

The '86-'87 school year turned out to be exciting in more ways than one. The football team had a Cinderella season and won the 3-A State Championship. This team may have been short on talent compared to the '85 team but they had all the heart in the world needed to make them the champions they were to become. The team was led by a young man who breathed fire every time he stepped on a football field. He instilled a winning mentality in each one of his teammates—a fearless leader on the field no matter what team they played. Derrick Brownlow was respected by his teammates who knew quite well that they would not have been the team they were without him.

Brownlow loved his coach Mike McGinley and gave much credit to him for the team's success. Brownlow shed a few tears at the all-school assembly celebrating the Championship season when he thanked Mr. McGinley, and told him that he loved him. Brownlow went on to a spectacular college career at Illinois where he became an All-American. In 1992 Mike McGinley was voted into the Indiana Football Hall of Fame. At a celebration in his honor, many of Mike's former players returned to pay honor to the man. Brownlow, now a pro football player, once again told the audience how much he cared for McGinley and how important Mike had been in his life. Most of the '86 Championship team was in attendance for the now-retired coach's celebration.

Other members of the '86 championship team included a gutsy little quarterback named Pat Jansen. Other senior players besides Janssen and Brownlow included Sean Fahey, Kerry Altherr, Chris Clemons, Pete Guye, Scott Mencer, Jimmy Allen, and Leroy Spells. Juniors team members made up a significant number of players. People like Woody Bishop, Bobby Brady, Robert Beatty, Eric Guhl, Shawn Spellacy, Nick Melloh, Sean McGinley, Billy Peebles, Al Keogh, Scott Evans, Frank Moosbrugger, Brad Elson, Scott Richards, Paul Petigrew, and last but certainly not least, John Crisp.

Sophomores included Mike Alerding, Tony Slocum, Scott Bordenet, Tom Christian, Sam Schmutte, Eric Debrota, Mike McGinley, Scott Oskins, Chad Hohne, Tony Jordan, Mike Funk, Dave Elson, Hugh McGowan, Dan Spellacy, Kevin Newbold, Brian Collins, and Eric Altherr. An important person to this team was Marc Caito, the team's manager. The coaching staff behind Mr. McGinley included two men from McGinley's 1976 state runner-up team—Vince Lorenzano and Jimmy O'Hara. Both men would move on from Cathedral and became competitors in the years ahead. They both returned to speak at the dinner for Mike McGinley at his celebration into the Indiana Football Hall of Fame.

The girls cross country team placed sixth in the state at South Grove Golf Course. The team was led by seniors Cathy Bradshaw, Julia Hill, Cindy Troy, Diane Schmutte, and Mary Boyer. Juniors Sheila McDermott, Ann Bradshaw, Katie Turner, Bridget Kelly, Gina Jamell, Marni Creager, Lisa Mattasits, Mary Orth, Molly Michau, Elsa Scheidler, and Sharon Henn added a dimension of strength to the team. This particular group of girls brought humor and fun to each other and the team. If any group of people in a sport had fun it was this group. From summer camps and into the season, no group of people seemed to enjoy being together more than this one. Although their sense of humor was considered by some to be a little strange, they showed wonderful imagination and creativity in all the years they were together. They even went on to create a video reflecting on their cross country experiences.

The boys cross country team won their second city title in a row with help from newcomer Mike Mundy and seniors Connor Welch, Jerry Harkness, and Bob Moriarty. Outstanding juniors Tom Fisher, Doug Clarke, Brian Clevery, Rodger Ward, Mike Baukert and Pat Walsh added strength to the team and gave hope to the future for more titles. Mike Mundy went all the way to the state finals but had a disappointing finish.

The boys and girls cross country teams of the eighties shared a genuine camaraderie. They set a tone for future teams and left behind a rich legacy of fun, games, and unique traditions.

The boys tennis team went on to post their sixth city title in a row. The team was made up of players Slater Hogan, Chris

Gregson, Kevin McGath, Joe Areddy, John Bradshaw, Jason Murdoch, Pat Murphy, and Jon Gray.

The girls golf team completed their third season with only one loss while the young volleyball team finished 18-11. All state player Cathy Guye and other senior players Trisha Mooney and Angie Rathz went onto successful college careers. The boys soccer team led by seniors Cory Cline and Mike Cunningham posted a disappointing 5-8 season record. The girls basketball team had a good season but came up short of winning any titles. The boys basketball team led by co-captains Steve Nester and Pat Jansen posted a disappointing 10-10 season.

The wrestling team was up to its old tricks of winning. They posted a perfect season with twenty-one wins and no losses. Winning another city title, and every invitational they were invited to, the Irish team also won Sectional, Regional and Semi-State titles. The best chance Coach Lance ever had of winning a title was with this team. They sent seven people to the state finals. According to Rhodes, at the end of the first round on Friday night he was sure they had the tournament won. However, it was not to be. Saturday turned out to be a disappointing day. Only Lance Ellis would win a individual title and Matt Moll would come in third. The team once again came in third. If Lance Rhodes never experiences the kind of disappointment he felt after the state tournament in '87, it will be too soon.

The girls softball team did not win any major titles, but it was reported that they had a great deal of fun in the '87 season.

The Irish baseball team set a new school record, winning twenty seven victories against only five losses. The Irish lost the City title to Roncalli, a team they had beaten earlier in the year. They came through for coach Keith Perin in the Sectional beating North Central and Scecina for the title. They lost the Regional to a tough Beech Grove team. The team was led by junior pitcher Brian Conway, and seniors on the team included co-captains Pat Jansen and Kerry Altherr. Jansen was the star quarterback on the State Championship football team. Other seniors who played a significant role on the team were Steve Nester, and Bill Richards. Underclassmen were plentiful on this team and gave great hope for the future. Players like Rich Andriole, Brian Ross, Chris Koehler, Brian Collins, Jeff Duval, Chris Bell, Ara Manooshian, Kevin McGrath, Ted Taylor, Kyle Muehlbronner, Paul Pugh, Damon Keller, Brian Cleverly, and Andy Weas would join Brian Conway again in the '88 season.

Like the wrestling team, the girls tennis team found that winning was becoming a habit. The girls won yet another City and Sectional title but they were unable to repeat as State Champions. They were defeated in the Regionals by eventual State Champion North Central. The only person missing from the State Championship team of '86 was Meg Boyle; it proved to be a significant loss.

The boys golf team won nine matches with three losses. John Crisp was excellent, posting a thirty-three in the city tourney. Seniors Tim Delagrange, David Monsey, Wes Spewak, and Chris Gauss, and juniors Sean McGinley and Kevin McMullen completed the team.

The girls and boys track seasons were interesting as the girls were led by senior Cindy Troy. She won the city in the 3200 meter run. New school records were posted by Sheila McDermott, Roberta Price, and Cindy Troy throughout the season. The boys track team had some outstanding moments which took Tom Fisher all the way to the State Finals. This team also included a young man named Chris Huffins. Huffins would go on to become an All-American at the University of California, Berkley, and become one of the top contenders for the decathlon in the United States. Huffins' goal at the time of this writing is to make it to the Olympics in '96. Chris used to tell people all the time when he was in high school that one day he would participate in the Olympics. He was coached at CHS by Mark Worrell, himself a graduate of Cathedral in 1978.

With all of the success of the sports teams in '86-'87 it is hard to imagine there was time for anything else. The Drama Department put on several successful plays featuring many fine actresses and actors. In plays like *If a Man Answers* Libby Christopherson and Lara O'Dell were outstanding in their roles as mother and daughter. Chris Quigley, Craig Mulvaney, and Andy Wyand also had important roles, as did Sara Noll and Charlton Browning.

The play *The Dining Room* brought many new faces to the stage. People like Katie Coles, Hilary Strahl, Candy Howard, Mike McCarthy and Laney Phillips were among those getting experience. The spring musical also starred Katie Coles in a play called *Shadows From The Inside.* A host of other people were also included in this play about a young girl who is new to her school, struggling to be accepted.

If the year was marked by anything other than sports, plays and the like, it was the intellectual curiosity of those in the Senior Class. Enter The Foreign Relations Club, which was formed by Sr. Mary Ann Stewart to enhance skills for the Model UN program. Students would gather in Sister's room after school to discuss and debate the issues of their time. Led by Tom Watson, Matt Caito, Matt Gardner, Dylan McKenna, Libby Christopherson, Pat Murphy and others, this group fascinated many of their teachers. At times there were twenty to thirty people sitting in Sr. Mary Ann's room after school carrying on with each other about the world in which they lived. It was most impressive because there was no apathy in this group whatsoever. In many respects, people in this group challenged their classmates to want to know more about what was going on in the world. They were a powerful influence on their class and the student body as a whole.

Most of the people who participated in these discussion groups were involved in the Model UN program led by Sr. Mary Ann. The Model UN Team of '87, led mostly by seniors, went on to win the equivalent of the State Championship. This happened toward the end of the school year. Some of the people mentioned above made a significant contribution to that effort, especially Tom Watson. One of the greatest pep rallies ever held at CHS in the eighties was not for football, basketball, or even wrestling. Although Lance Rhodes was known for putting on some pretty good pep rallies for the wrestling teams, the best pep rally was for the Model UN Championship team. It was an outstanding affirmation of intellectual pursuits and an acknowledgment of something other than sports. The seniors in particular were strong in their support for those who returned from the Model United Nations with so many trophies.

As the school year progressed, another St. Patrick's Day came and went with Larry Everhart serving as band director for what would be his last time. Everhart had become an institution at Cathedral over the years, and he put together many first class bands. Perhaps more importantly, Larry taught hundreds of students, whether they were in the band or not, to truly understand and love all kinds of music through the freshman music appreciation class, which he had taught for many years. Larry also served as a symbol for the Fighting Irish when he played his bagpipes on graduation day and other such events. Although he no longer teaches at Cathedral, he still plays his bagpipes at every graduation ceremony, where his performance is one of the highlights of the occasion. Everhart returned to Cathedral to play his bagpipes on September 13th, 1993, to help the Senior Class and the entire student body celebrate Cathedral's 75th Anniversary.

The class of '87 should always be credited for having brought great spirit back to Cathedral after a rough year in '86.

Everyone was aware of it as the administration developed a new attitude of working with students. The adversarial relationship between the student body and administration seemed to completely disappear, except when dealing with the issue of prom and the fine arts. The person writing this account will never forget the class of '87 because they were kind, considerate, challenging, intellectually curious, and so much fun. They redefined school spirit and set the school on course for the late eighties and early nineties.

As spring rolled around another junior-senior prom was held. Senior class president Erin Healy was crowned Prom Queen and Tory Callaghan was crowned Junior Prom Queen. Baccalaureate Mass and graduation ceremonies went on as scheduled. Libby Christopherson penned the class poem on the back of the Baccalaureate Mass program. Valedictorian for the class of '87 was Cathy Bradshaw. Cathy was also the Board of Trustees Award winner for being an outstanding student leader and for her dedication to excellence in all that she did in her four years at Cathedral. Cathy also won the Joe Dezelan Award for being the most outstanding student athlete. This was the second time in two years both awards went to one person, both of whom were girls. The winner of both awards in '86 was Anita Hodgson. She was the first person honored with both awards.

Salutatorian for the class of '87 was Sue Choi. She brought many people to tears as she reflected on friendships and her four years at Cathedral. Assistant football coach and Business teacher Jim O'Hara gave the graduation speech to the class to close out the year.

There is one more interesting note to the 1986-87 school year. On the day in which National Honor Society members were inducted they heard a different kind of speaker. He was chosen by Mrs. Lisa Ford, head of the National Honor Society to address the student body and the adult audience. The strength and fitness coach from the Indianapolis Colts, Tom Zupancic, gave one of the most inspiring motivational talks ever witnessed at such an event. Zupancic graduated from Cathedral in 1973. He had not been a member of the National Honor Society when he was at CHS in the seventies, but he certainly was impressive in 1987.

Playing in the Big Events

Cathedral graduate athletes have participated in most major sports classics including the Super Bowl, National Basketball Association All-Star Game, World Series, the post-season bowl games including the Rose, Cotton, Fiesta, Sugar and Orange bowls. Graduates have also earned the Pulitzer Prize and Nobel Peace Prize.

The Big Event: Shamrauction

In 1978, Cathedral's single largest fundraising event for student scholarships was launched under the direction of then Development Director, John Short. Each year, co-chairs of this event provide the dedication and commitment, along with hundreds of volunteers, to ensure its success. This gala raises well over $200,000 annually through the support and generosity of the families and friends of Cathedral High School. There are many key people who have worked behind-the-scenes of the Shamrauction, but three individuals stand out: Gerry Kennedy, Rob Hoaglin, '85, and Jenny Matthews. Co-chairs have included:

1978 Harry Bindner, Mary Young	1986 Dan Quigley, Gretchen Cain
1979 Charles Stimming, Norma Winkler	1987 Larry Conrad, Mary Lou Conrad
1980 Mike Schaefer, Carolyn Welch	1988 Mark Stephens, Glendys Moosbrugger
1981 Chris Duffy, Mary Bindner	1989 John Short, Betsey Harvey
1982 Dan O'Malia, Eileen Christ	1990 Jim Alerding, Rosie Houk
1983 Gary Drook, Irene Welch	1991 Gary Zmrhal, Paula Lee
1984 Bill McGowan, Lou Ann Steinmetz	1992 Steve Schaefer, Marcia Bozic
1985 Dan Hasbrook, Rita O'Malia	1993 John Davis, Carol Boyle
	1994 Tom McNulty, Jo Ellen Dascoli

1987–1988

During the 1987–88 school year it was realized that the class of 1991 would be the smallest to enter Cathedral on the new campus and possibly one of the smallest since the 1940s. One hundred and twenty-six freshmen started off the 1987–88 school year, and only one hundred and fourteen would graduate.

There are several explanations for the small class size. One revolves around demographics—the low number of students in the grade schools in the mid-eighties, particularly parish schools in Indianapolis. Fewer than twenty students graduated from St. Matthews, a large feeder school for Cathedral, in 1987 when in the past the school was graduating well over forty eighth graders a year.

Another explanation may have been that Cathedral that year charged a fifty dollar, non-refundable fee to take the entrance exam. This was considered to be a huge mistake and the next year it was done away with. A more plausible explanation is that rumors were still circulating that Cathedral was in dire straits financially. In addition, the school lost more than a half a dozen popular and excellent teachers for one reason or another. A few other teachers had talked about leaving and that did not help.

Finally, open house in the fall semester of the '86-'87 school year was scheduled on a Sunday afternoon at the same time the Indianapolis Colts were playing a sold-out home game, resulting in a very poor turnout.

Whatever the explanation for the small freshman class, the 1987–88 school year began with a small group which would later be credited with taking a chance to come to Cathedral despite all the rumors and all that happened in the mid-eighties. Some people believe this group of stalwarts may have saved Cathedral High School from closing its doors.

To avoid another small freshmen class, Cathedral became assertive in her approach to getting eighth graders to take a look at the school, reinstating free entrance exams to entice students and parents to at least set foot in the school. A committee was also formed to plan an effective, well-timed and well-structured open house event, giving eighth graders and their families a good look at Cathedral's current students. The student body was given significant responsibility for selling Cathedral to prospective students.

A speech given by senior Sheila McDermott at the open house in the fall of 1987 had a tremendous impact, especially on a particular eighth grader from St. Pius named Katie Quinn. Katie, Class of 1992, went on to become president of her class both her junior and senior year and she never forgot Sheila's speech. Katie was given the honor of speaking to eighth graders at open house when she was a senior, and she recalled Sheila McDermott's speech four years earlier. Katie's speech had a similar impact on the class of 1996, one of the largest classes to enter Cathedral in her entire history. Two hundred and fifty-eight freshmen entered Cathedral in the fall of 1992.

One additional effort was made in the 1987-88 school year to help promote Cathedral to the community at large. A public relations campaign featuring Cathedral graduates writing letters of support for the school was developed and initiated by senior religion teacher Jim Obergfell. These letters, run in newspapers, were an unknown public relations quantity, so it was a risk for those people who first agreed to participate in the letter writing campaign. Only four people were featured in the first letter writing campaign: a young lawyer, Denise Clark '79; the 1985 Nobel Peace Prize winner, Dr. James Muller '61; a senior law student from IU, Eric Riegner '81; and a freshman at Notre Dame, Cathy Bradshaw '87. The effort has since snowballed, as over one hundred Cathedral graduates have participated in this tremendous program. The campaign had an impact on Cathedral in more ways than one. Incoming classes in the late eighties and early nineties began to swell and good feeling re-emerged in the community, thus enhancing the efforts of the development office and bringing many Cathedral graduates who had been disenchanted with the move to the 56th Street Campus, back into the fold. The letter writing campaign continues to this day.

In the midst of everything that was going on at Cathedral at the beginning of the 1987–88 school year, a significant change took place. After being Chairman of the Board for sixteen years, Robert V. Welch resigned as chairman. He remained on the board until his death in the fall of 1992. Bob Welch had been Cathedral's only Chairman of the Board from the time the Brothers of Holy Cross left Cathedral in 1972. Much has been written and said concerning Bob Welch's impact on Cathedral, which can never be overlooked. Although it has been said many times before, it has become much clearer to this writer through all the research for this book that if it had not been for Bob Welch, Cathedral would not be here today. Robert V. Welch did indeed save Cathedral

High School. It would be hard to accurately measure his love for the school, but suffice it to say that most of his adult life was genuinely devoted to Cathedral.

With Mr. Welch's retirement, the Board of Directors appointed a new Chairman of the Board. Enter Daniel J. O'Malia, president of O'Malia Food Markets, a 1965 graduate of Cathedral and a Xavier University graduate. Dan had taught English at Cathedral in the mid-seventies as he finished his Masters Degree at Butler University. After leaving Cathedral, he went to work in his father's grocery business. When Mr. O'Malia took over as Chairman of the Board in the fall of 1988, all was not well, but when he resigned as chairman five years later, Cathedral appeared stronger than ever. He remains on the board and is still active in all that goes on at the school.

When Dan retired as Chairman of the Board in the fall of 1992, Michael G. Schaefer became the third Chairman of the Board at Cathedral. A 1943 graduate and an original board member from 1972, Michael G. Schaefer had been a good friend of Mr. Welch and CHS for many decades.

The 1987–88 school year brought much success athletically. The girls cross country team won another city title and a second place finish in the regional. It was the last year for top runners Ann Bradshaw, Katie Turner, Jane Nohl, Sheila McDermott and Bridget Kelly.

The boys cross country team, led by Tom Fisher, Doug Clarke, and Brian Cleverly, came in second in the city.

The soccer team was disappointed, losing in the first round of the State Tournament to Warren Central; but they did enjoy a significant win over Park Tudor in regular season play.

The volleyball team had only three seniors: Tory Callaghan, Eileen Caito, and Michelle Dinn; the players coming along behind them would dominate area volleyball in years to come. Amy Greer, Suzay Smith, Stephanie Keefe, Amy Van Winkle, Leah Lentz, and Mindy McGinn were outstanding players, most of them going on to play college volleyball.

The girls golf team finished their season 9-3 led by seniors Molly Williams, Michelle Leighton, Amy Skiles and Amy Fischer.

Another remarkable season was in store for the boys tennis team, which posted an 18-2 record. Led by Slater Hogan, John Bradshaw, Joe Areddy, Eric O'Bryan, Jason Murdock, Kevin McGrath, Kevin McMullen, Matt King, Ara Manooshian, Tony

Murdock, and William Brandt, the team won another City title under coaches Jim Williams and Paul Farrell.

The football team was looking to repeat as State Champions in the fall of 1987, but what began as a very good start in that direction did not end with the Championship. In the first game of the season, the Fighting Irish defeated Ben Davis, the eventual 5-A State Championship team by a score of 7-6. Overall, the Irish ended the season 8-4. They lost a heartbreaker 28-29 to New Palestine in the final game of the Sectional on a missed extra point which would have tied the game and sent it into overtime.

Senior Nick Melloh was All-City, All-Metro, and All-State. Bobby Brady was All-City, as was Woody Bishop. Brad Elson was also All-Metro. Melloh went on to play college ball at Butler, while Brady had a fine college career at Wabash. Woody Bishop was an All American at Ball State and is currently playing professional ball for the Houston Oilers. Kicker Damon Keller had a fine career at Ball State, while Billy Peebles captained his team at Evansville and Scott Evans played at St. Joe's. Underclassmen on this team who would later go on to play college ball included Chad Hohne and Bill Wheeler at Evansville and Jon Hill and Eugene Murray at Butler.

Under new coach Howard Renner, the talented boys basketball team showed a marked improvement over the previous season. Outstanding seniors like Sean Woods, Noble Duke, Monty Dupree, and Tom Kane were supported by great shooters juniors, Kevin Newbold and Brian Poytner and sophomores Ryan Greenwood and Steve Lee. A great win over Lawrence North saw five-foot ten-inch Noble Duke run circles around six-foot eleven-inch Eric Montross, and Coach Jack Kiefer of Lawrence North gave a tremendous tribute to Duke and the entire Cathedral squad for the emotion and effort the fighting Irish put forth throughout the game.

In the second game of the Sectional, Cathedral defeated North Central and seemed certain to go on to claim the Butler Sectional title. The final Sectional game brought Cathedral and Chatard together for a rematch. The Irish had beaten the Trojans earlier in the season by ten points. The heavily favored Irish were defeated in the final game by Chatard by a resounding 71-55 score. It was quite an upset considering Cathedral had been playing so well, and no one seemed to take the loss harder than Noble Duke. He gave his heart and soul to every game he played for Cathedral. Sean Woods was selected as an Indiana All-Star and went on the to the University of Kentucky, where he was a star guard for the Wildcats.

Under new coach Linda Allen, the girls basketball team started off the season with a bang by defeating long time rival Chatard. However, it was not necessarily an indication of things to come. The girls basketball team finished the season 8-13, losing a heartbreaker 50-53 to Arlington in the final game of the Sectional.

The wrestling team once again came in second in the state, finishing the season 19-1. Junior Lance Ellis captured his third State Championship, remaining undefeated three years in a row. Cathedral was down in the final round of the State Finals by one-and-a-half points with Ellis and Sean McGinley left to wrestle. Ellis won his match, but McGinley lost his bout in the final seconds as the Fighting Irish came in second once again. This may have been coach Rhodes' last chance to win it all—the team was laden with seniors. All but two members of the team graduated at the end of the year, with only Ellis and Chris Caito returning.

The boys track team, led by Doug Clarke, Brian Murphy, Chris Huffins, and Tom Fisher, extended themselves to record performances. Chris Huffins set the school record for the long jump with a jump of 23 feet and 6.5 inches and broke the old record which was held by Mark Clayton '79. As was mentioned earlier, Huffins is currently one of the top contenders in the USA decathlon competition. Tom Fisher broke the nine-year-old record in the 1600 meters with a time of 4:27.02.

The girls track team, coached by Robin McCart and Jim Nohl, did not experience as much success as they had found the previous year. The seniors on the team said good-bye to Mr. McCart, a person for whom they had developed a great deal of respect.

The baseball team captured a City Championship on a grand slam homerun by junior Eric Altherr, winning the game against Ritter by a score of 12-11. The team was led by outstanding pitcher Brian Conway, considered to be one of the best in the state. Seniors Chris Koehler and Paul Pugh were also considered to be some of the most outstanding players in the state. Pugh hit over .500 his senior year. Conway's pitching career earned him a four-year scholarship to Notre Dame, where he had one good season as a freshman before a career-ending injury in his sophomore year. Other seniors on the CHS team in 1988 included Andy Weas, Chris Bell and Kevin McGrath. Juniors Brandy Hampton and Tim Lyons, along with Altherr, were considered to be impact players for the Irish.

The girls softball team was exciting but young. They won no titles. Gina Jamell, Katie Turner, and Eileen Caito were the only seniors on the team.

The girls tennis team won the City and Sectional titles once again, but they were defeated in the Regional by North Central. This was the end of the road for the remaining members of the 1986 championship team. Amy Boyle, Ann Bradshaw, Meg and Mandy Harvey, and Michele Leighton graduated at the end of the year.

The boys golf team did well but no championships were won.

The 1987–88 school year saw a group of charitable students take on a number of projects for the less privileged. Spirit ran high in the highly competitive senior class, with students constantly challenging one another in this class, especially academically.

Interest in the Model UN program and debate continued to grow in the '87-'88 school year. Debate coach Mrs. Judy Ney took her students to area schools to give examples of debate. On one such occasion at a local Catholic grade school, Sheila McDermott and Debbie Booker thought they would display what one should not do in a debate. Sheila, with a charm which only people who knew Sheila would understand, asked a very impertinent question of Debbie. "Debbie," she said, "are you wearing any underwear today?" Sheila knew exactly what she was doing: she immediately captured her audience and they paid attention to the entire debate. Mrs. Ney admits to being embarrassed and caught off guard, but she had great faith in Sheila and what she was doing. Sheila McDermott, who won the Board of Trustees Award in 1988, was one of a kind, and Cathedral has not seen the likes of her since. There was not a teacher in the building who did not love Sheila McDermott, except perhaps Mr. Rhodes. She had challenged his view of women and his overall conservative dog-eat-dog doctrine. Actually, there was no genuine dislike between them.

Principal Fr. Kelly remembered Sheila's creative spirit when he reflected on one day during spirit week of her senior year. Fr. Kelly said, "I'll never forget her roller skating through the halls while wearing that football helmet." Mrs. Nancy Baxter remembers her clearing the AP English room of all furniture and bringing in a huge parachute on which all students had to sit and hold the edges. She was illustrating the need to "hold to each other" in a book she was reporting on. It was one of the most creative reports that was given in that teacher's five years. That was Sheila McDermott; creative, imaginative, fun, exciting, silly, serious, and sensitive.

Sheila McDermott returned to Cathedral to deliver the main speech at the induction ceremonies for the 1993 National Honor Society. Once again, Sheila captured the attention of her audience by her off-beat, but meaningful speech, vintage Sheila McDermott.

A new roof had to be put on the school during the 1987–88 school year at a cost of $75,000. It could not have come at a more inopportune time. There was a heavy storm one night before the roof was finished and it leaked so much that school had to be canceled. The roofers had clogged the drain spouts causing ceiling tiles to collapse throughout the building. The next day all was well and dry. In February of the same year, the student body sat in a pitch black school building for over two hours as the electricity was knocked out by a severe storm. All forms of communication were out. After students were escorted by flashlight to eat lunch in the cafeteria, school was dismissed to resume the next day.

Ann Bradshaw, valedictorian of her class, was named one of the top forty students in the state of Indiana. Her sister Cathy had earned the same award the year before.

Also in the spring of 1988, Anna Marie Fish won the prestigious Prelude Award for her ballet performance of "Carmen." The class of 1988 was a very talented group, as pointed out so well by salutatorian Joe Areddy. It was believed by many that it would be a long time before Cathedral would see another class like the class of 1988 again. That did not end up being the case as we will see later. In many respects, the class of 1988 exemplified all the characteristics for membership into the National Honor Society: Service, Leadership, Character, and Scholarship.

Two outstanding publications in the 1987–88 school year were *The Megaphone,* which was edited by Angela Moorman, and *The Cathedran,* which was guided by English teacher Mrs. Nancy Baxter, with the help of Michelle Kempf as the editor, and with tremendous help from seniors Debbie Booker, Joan Wagner, Katie Turner, Mike Crowley, Sean Harmon, and juniors Katie Spahn and Katie Lockman.

In the spring of '88, Vice Principal Sr. Thomas More, initiated a process for an evaluation of the school by the federal government. School President Mike McGinley and Principal Rev. Patrick Kelly overwhelmingly endorsed the effort. In February of 1989 the U.S. Department of Education sent a team of evaluators to Cathedral, and they appeared to be very impressed. The school was notified in the spring of 1989 that it had been selected as a "School of Excellence" as recognized by the U.S. Department of Education. The lengthy but rewarding process put a feather in the "habit" of Sr. Thomas More and Cathedral High School. The award brought tremendous prestige to Cathedral and is also seen as another significant reason enrollment continued to increase in the late 80s and early 90s. Fr. Kelly and Sr. Thomas More went to Washington D.C. in the fall of '89 , to meet with President George Bush, and to receive the award from the Secretary of Health, Education and Welfare at a ceremony in the White House Rose Garden. With this award Cathedral was sitting on a solid foundation as it headed into the nineties.

Other significant events during the 1987-88 school year included Senior Retreats, considered by this class to be a great success which brought them closer together.

English teacher Nancy Baxter started a tradition of having her students over to her house for dinner, with everyone portraying different characters they were studying in AP class. Her students loved it and popped up all over the Northside seeking directions to her home, dressed as Christopher Columbus, Pope Leo X, Rasputin or other such characters.

Over two hundred thousand dollars was raised at Shamrauction. The spring musical was *Sagebrush Sal*, starring Candace Howard. The play involved a great deal of audience participation.

The Prom Queen for the seniors was Tory Callaghan and for the juniors, Molly Cain. Doug Clarke won the Joe Dezelan Award. Lance Rhodes may not have won the state wrestling championship in '88 but he was selected by the Senior Class to be their speaker at graduation ceremonies. Class president Vickie Schneider, who had worked for Mr. Rhodes as a valkyrie for the wrestling team, had the honor of introducing him to her classmates.

The Mothers Club, as usual did an outstanding job hosting at the Baccalaureate and graduation receptions. Though often an unrecognized group, the Mothers Club is an integral part of the Cathedral experience. Besides taking full responsibility for receptions following Baccalaureate and graduation ceremonies, they also host Honors Night, Parent-Teacher night, and the National Honor Society Induction receptions. In addition, they do various fundraisers, gather materials for the craft booth at Shamrauction, provide the faculty with a beautiful Christmas luncheon, and help man the bookstore among many other activities. In recent years, they paid for the restoration of the cafeteria, supplied different items on the school's wish list, and helped to pay for students to go on senior retreat if they could not afford it.

One significant contribution they made was a beautiful spirit stick with a glass enclosed plaque showing which classes have won the award for each year. The spirit stick is dedicated to the four CHS students who died in the mid-eighties: Matt Debono '84, Scott Altherr and Ryan Updike '85 and Colleen Hafner '88. All four students had displayed tremendous spirit during their years at Cathedral.

All mothers serving Cathedral, both on old and new campuses, deserve heartfelt gratitude. Historically, when one group of dedicated mothers leave when their sons and daughters graduate from Cathedral, another excellent group always seems to take their place. The very special Mothers Club of today clearly points out why "She Is Still Dear Old Cathedral."

1988–1989

A time of beginnings and endings may be an appropriate way to describe the 1988-89 school year. When the U.S. presidential election came to an end, so did the negative campaigning which only helped divide the country. The election marked the beginning of a new U.S. Administration for the first time since the 1980–81 school year when Ronald Reagan was elected and took office.

Some of the highlights of the 1988–89 school year at Cathedral included the new Spiritual Direction Program initiated by Religion Department head Sara Koehler. The objective of the program was for students to have a chance to meet with a teacher on a regular basis to discuss their faith and other concerns. Participation in the program the first year was small for both teachers and students, but it was considered a great success in terms of quality. The next year more people became involved, and each year thereafter it has continued to grow.

In the beginning of the fall of 1993 the Spiritual Direction Program became so popular it was a mixed blessing for director Mrs. Koehler. This all-volunteer program has even developed to such an extent that graduates of Cathedral, community leaders, and parents are participating as companions to students.

One of the most significant highlights at the beginning of

the 1988–89 school year revolved around some of the best news that Cathedral had received in years. On September 15, 1988, Lilly Endowment awarded a five hundred thousand dollar matching grant to Cathedral, a dream come true for the school which had struggled financially in the mid eighties. This was the first sign that the school might possibly get itself out of debt since moving to the new campus. It was definitely seen as the beginning of a new era at Cathedral, one which was not plagued by financial crisis, a golden opportunity. If the school was ever going to get on its feet financially this was it. In the next year the Lilly matching grant became the Diamond Anniversary Campaign in which the school raised over 3.3 million dollars in a three year period. This campaign was headed by a very determined man from the Class of 1945: Jack Baker. He assured the success of the campaign by putting up his own money to hire a consulting firm to steer the way. If he was going to be in charge, he was not going to oversee another campaign which did not come to fruition. Jack Baker's impact on the success of the campaign deserves tremendous acknowledgment.

Throughout the 1988 fall semester there were rumors that Mike McGinley would leave Cathedral at the end of the school year. As it turned out it was indeed the end of Mr. McGinley's career at Cathedral High School. He retired at the end of the year after twenty-five years of serving in just about every capacity one could imagine.

Not only was it Mike's last year as President of Cathedral, it was also his last year doing what he loved, coaching football. Many of Mr. McGinley's accomplishments over a twenty-five year period have been recorded throughout this book: Mike McGinley saw Cathedral through some of her most difficult times as he made great personal sacrifices to ensure Cathedral's well being. Mike McGinley lived and breathed Cathedral all the years in which he was involved, especially Cathedral football. Cathedral said good-bye to Mr. McGinley at the end of the school year at a special assembly where he was honored by students, former football players, and coaches. A representative from the Mayor's office declared it Michael D. McGinley Day in Indianapolis and the Governor sent a representative to award Mike with the Sagamore of the Wabash, one of the most prestigious awards given to a citizen in the State of Indiana. The faculty held a special dinner party in the cafeteria for Mike and his family that same evening.

The wrestling team marked the end of another era. No, Lance Rhodes did not leave Cathedral. Lance Ellis did. Ellis, after four years under coach Rhodes ended his career at Cathedral in 1989 with the winningest record of all time in the state of Indiana. Lance Ellis posted 177 wins against 0 losses, and was, according to coach Rhodes, "simply the greatest high school wrestler ever." The media followed Ellis' pursuits with great enthusiasm throughout the entire tournament of his senior year. It will be a long time, if ever, before anyone surpasses Lance Ellis' record.

Two deaths saddened the Cathedral community during the 1988–89 school year. Melvin Brown '91, died in the summer between his freshman and sophomore year in a water accident in Kentucky. He was never forgotten—valedictorian Andy McGuire '91 remembered his classmate at graduation ceremonies three years later.

Several months later, teacher, counselor, computer expert Rev. Frederick Schmitt died in Germany over Christmas break. A large group of senior boys were shocked by Fr. Schmitt's death in his hotel only two days after the travel group had left the United States. He taught the boys to be independent and responsible for themselves—something they found useful in Germany when they lost their mentor. Nevertheless, many of the boys'parents wanted them home, so they returned as soon as possible. Fr. Schmitt's wit and intellectual curiosity made him a jack-of-all-trades. He knew the law as well as he knew good food, and he knew history, theology and computers and . . . as well as he knew his best friends. The boys at Cathedral were his best friends, nurtured and taught well by the man in the small office next to Father Kelly's. Fr. Schmitt encouraged the boys to develop a Spirit Club made up entirely of boys which helped the school in many ways when spirit seemed to be weak. The club was exclusive, and therefore controversial. Not all the boys felt welcome, not to mention the girls who were completely turned off by the whole idea. Nevertheless, Rev. Frederick Schmitt was a wonderful man who enjoyed his life as a priest and who had made a significant impact on three decades of young people, especially the boys at Cathedral High School in the late 1980s. He was ordained in 1959 and he died December 30, 1989.

The project of the IRISH sign which sits on the hill at the entrance of the school was originally built by the Spirit Club. The original sign, primitive but effective and made of concrete, fell prey to the elements year after year and was constantly in need of repair. At the time of their graduation, the Class of 1993 donated a more permanent sign which enhanced the IRISH spirit originated by Rev. Fredrick Schmitt and the Spirit Club of 1988–89.

The world of sports at CHS in the 1988–89 school year was a mixed bag. The boys cross country team, led by Brian Flaherty, Frank Otte, John Schuler, Roger Ward, and Matt Lamberti, captured another City title.

After losing many excellent runners due to graduation, the girls cross country team surprised everyone and also captured the City title. The traditions of the girls team were maintained and enhanced by Judy Clarke, Ginger Mobley, Maria Wodraska, Chris Weaver, Katie Lockman, Lisa Schmitz, Amy Cook, Patricia Smith, Alecia Scheidler, Kathy Baukert, and Shannon Poskon.

The boys tennis season closed with a record of 15-4 and ranked twelfth in the state. They captured their eighth City title. The team was led by John Bradshaw, Eric O'Bryan, Mike Dodson, William Brandt, Matt King, Rich Wurster, and Pat Gray.

The girls golf team won no titles, but it was recorded that they had a great deal of fun. The boys' soccer team ended with a record of 10-4-3 as they reached the "sweet sixteen" of the State Tournament. North Central ended Cathedral's season. Outstanding players on the team included Marvin Fundenburger, Colin Kress, Rich Moynahan, Greg Miller, Bill Leppert, and Garrett Hall.

The football team, with co-captains Chad Hohne and David Elson, had a disappointing season, finishing with seven wins and four losses. All-City players included Eric Altherr, David Elson, and Kevin Newbold, who also claimed All-State honors. One of the most exciting games of the season will remain in CHS folklore as a classic come-from-behind win against Hammond. The Irish team scored twenty-three points in the fourth quarter for a 26-24 victory, and Chad Hohne may have had the game of his high school career. Three of the teams losses that year were to 5-A teams: Warren Central, Terre Haute South, and Ben Davis—the eventual 5-A State Championship team. The other loss was to 3-A State Champion Roncalli.

The freshman team in the fall of 1988 went undefeated and unscored upon, amassing 162 points, while their opponents scored none. When this group became seniors in the fall of 1991, they were the Runner-up State Champions.

The 1988 volleyball team, the "CHS EXPRESS" as they were referred to, had an outstanding season and finished with a record of 29-4. They were led by seniors Suzay Smith, Carrie Hannigan, Andi VanWinkle, Lisa Zouvelos, and Mindy McGinn, and supported by an outstanding junior, Amy Greer. Other excellent players on the team included Stephanie Keefe, Leah Lentz, Mollie Peebles, Cathy Lekens, and Cindy Stuart. Suzay Smith was named First Team All-City, First Team All-Metro, and First Team All-State. Andi VanWinkle, Mindy Maginn, and Amy Greer were also named First Team All-City.

The "Coach of the Year" named by *The Indianapolis Star* was Denise Farrell. Mrs. Farrell would coach volleyball one more year before hanging up her whistle. Denise Farrell has served Cathedral as a coach, teacher, freshmen counselor, scheduling and computer expert, and super Irish fan. She is a true professional with whom students and parents alike feel comfortable, as they deal with problems which occur throughout freshmen year. In addition to her other assignments, Mrs. Farrell is also the director of the Peer Counseling Program, wearing many hats in the tradition of Cathedral teachers from the 1920s on to this day.

The boys basketball team made it to the final games for the City and Sectional titles, ending the season 19-9. Mark Poytner, Jimmy Saddler, Adam Holton, and Jon Hill were leaders of the team. Paul Lee and Ryan Greenwood would be leaders in 1990.

As mentioned before, Lance Ellis ended his career at Cathedral after the 1988–89 season; during his last year the wrestling team as a whole was not up to its usual ways of winning everything. Nevertheless, the young team which was led by Ellis and supported by Brian Funk, Jason Terry, Kevin Rider, Brett Croswell, Jim Dammon, and Roy Williams posted a team record of 12-6. Besides Ellis' tremendous accomplishments, Brian Funk finished sixth in the state and Jason Terry fifth.

The girls basketball team won no titles. Later in the spring, the softball team had a winning season.

A very young baseball team had only six seniors, including Brian "Chico" Collins, Danny Spellacy, Tom Christian, Eric Altherr, Brandy Hampton, and Tim Lyons. Underclassmen who made a significant impact included Scott Taylor, Matt Abriani, Brandy Hampton, Mike DeSanto, Corey Pasley, Tim Lyons, Mike Harmon, Danny Lyons, Mark Engel, Gene Murray, Danny Weas, Brian Stratman, Mark Kinn, and Darrell Osbourne. Although they did not win any titles, it was considered a successful season by first year coaches Ken Kaufman and his son Chris. They remain as the baseball coaches to the time of this writing.

The girls tennis team finished their season ranked sixth in the state. They won their seventh consecutive City title. The team included Judy Clarke, Karlanna Manders, Maureen Boyle, Katie Spahn, Susie Arnold, and Carrie Hannigan.

The boys golf team had an outstanding young golfer named Sean Rowen who was only a freshman with this group.

The girls track team got off to a slow start and that slow start had a significant impact on their not-too-outstanding season. There were individual accomplishments from Cathy Lekens, Ginger Mobley, Deborah Callaghan, and Tenise Gurnell.

The boys track team led by Jon Hill, Jeff Wheeler, and Roger Ward posted a 7-3 record.

One individual from the class of '89 who warrants special recognition for her grace, beauty, and gentle nature, is the talented Julie Harkness. At this writing, Julie is traveling with a national theatrical company.

Once again the Senior Retreats played a significant role in bringing the class closer together, especially the boys on the soccer and football teams, who had experienced a sense of dividedness up to the time of the retreat.

School plays included *Spoon River*, which starred Marcy Walsh, Marci Underwood, Lara O'Dell, Tracy Gauss, John Fischer and Derek Hobart. *Hello Dolly* was the spring musical, and it starred Allison Hugel as Dolly. The large cast also included John Fisher, Annie Doherty, and Derek Hobart.

The 1988–89 school year also saw another new band director. Randy Weaver did a nice job putting the band back together, but he left at the end of the school year. Matt Murdock came on the scene to take charge of the band in the 1989–90 school year, and he stayed for three years doing an excellent job of bringing stability back to the program, leaving after the 1993 school year.

A significant award was given to the Christian Service Program by the United Way for the best long-term Volunteer Program in the area. Senior religion teacher Jim Obergfell developed the program in 1980, a year after it was suggested by principal Brother Pedro Hearing shortly before he left in 1979. The students who were in the program at the time it won the award included Dianne Buck, Lauren Buckner, Marcy Walsh, Elizabeth Hahn, Karen Buzzelli, Katie McAllister, Allison Hughel, Autumn Marker, Marybeth Sampson, Lisa Paugh, Heather Martin, Candace Howard, Yvette Covington, Katie McGlinchey, Charles White, Don Hawk, and Brendan Moriarty.

The National Honor Society induction saw *The Indianapolis News* reporter Jon Schwantes '82 give an off-beat speech, *à la* Kevin McDowell, his former journalism teacher at Cathedral. Students loved it.

The Model UN Team was moving right along, as CHS brought home more trophies, including one for the best four-member delegation. This group representing Chile included Andy

McGuire, John Bradshaw, Scott Taylor, and Pat Beidelman. Barbara Goeben was presented with the Parliamentarian Award in 1989.

The Debate team in 1988–89 may always be seen by Mrs. Judy Ney as one of her most controversial, yet one of her best. With people like Hugh McGowan and Brian Flaherty leading the way they often put on a clinic for others to emulate.

A significant debate occurred in the auditorium between two teams of CHS students before an all-school assembly. Subject: the 1988 presidential election. The debate included a spirited exchange between Adam Holton and Hugh McGowan about tactics and partisanship being displayed during the debate. Although Hugh McGowan was justifiably reprimanded by Adam Holton for getting away from the original format set up for this particular debate, Hugh excited the crowd with his strong arguments. He was a master debater, one of the best to ever come through Cathedral High School.

The Megaphone staff, headed by editor Lara O'Dell, turned out an excellent paper. The staff included Katie Leo, Katie McAllister, Dianna Bennington, Toby Mattson, Candace Howard, John Fischer, Matt King, Chris Dahling, Allison Hughel, Steve Tanaka, Amy Moss, and Paul Cauchi. The paper's faculty advisor was English teacher John Hannon. Mr. Hannon first took over the newspaper in the fall 1986 and has provided *The Megaphone* with his leadership ever since, resulting in a superb high school newspaper year after year.

Student Council had been a significant factor all year long. With Hugh McGowan and Brian Flaherty leading the way, along with Candace Howard, Brendan Moriarity, Danny Spellacy, and Jenny Wurster, they set the tone for leadership throughout the entire student body. The underclassmen loved their leadership and antics throughout the entire year.

A very successful international dinner was held at Cathedral in the 1988–89 school year, and it set the tone for the future, as the foreign language clubs developed International Awareness Week at school. The prom came and went as Kim Van Noy was crowned Queen for the seniors and Jenny Wurster was crowned Queen for the juniors.

Practically speaking, the 1988–89 school year ended at graduation ceremonies. Michael McGinley was recognized once again before leaving Cathedral. Molly Cain, representing the senior class, gave Mike a watch, and in his final act as President of Cathedral Mr. McGinley had the honor of handing his first-born,

Michael, his diploma. Moreover, Mr. McGinley handed out three honorary diplomas to three of his dear friends, Rev. Patrick J. Kelly, Dr. Tom Brady, and Joe Mattingly. Each man had been a vital part of Mike's coaching years at Cathedral, thus, the honorary degrees.

Mr. Lance Rhodes, again the choice of the seniors class, delivered the Commencement address. John Fischer was salutatorian. Valedictorian Brian Flaherty, in classic Brian Flaherty style, gave a great speech comparing life at Cathedral to that of an ordinary sandwich. His sandwich represented the faculty and administration, his classmates and peers, and all that he had learned in four years at Cathedral High School.

1989–1990

The 1989–90 school year started off with great optimism for the decade of the nineties. An exchange student named Paola Fernandez from the Dominican Republic visited the school for the entire year. She was a talkative, hopeful and wise person, and she was as kind as she was beautiful. Returning to the Caribbean at the end of the school year after having made a major impact in the time she was at Cathedral, Paola has often reported back to her American teachers and friends that she learned a great deal from her life experiences while at Cathedral High School. Very few people, freshmen through seniors, will ever forget Paola Fernandez, who brought a fresh perspective and tremendous empathy for the people in her region of the world.

For much of Central America the 1980s ended as they began. In December of 1989 six Jesuit priests were brutally murdered in El Salvador, nine years after Archbishop Romero and four American missionaries had experienced the same fate.

The 1989–90 school year also saw significant changes at Cathedral. Little did anyone realize at the time that CHS was entering what some would eventually call the second "Golden Era" in the school's history. There have been so many positive changes and accomplishments in the nineties that it will be difficult to record them all, especially without the perspective that time provides. Nevertheless, it is important to recall as much as possible because this has indeed become a great period in Cathedral High School's history.

A new president for Cathedral came on the scene in the spring of 1989 and officially took over in the summer before the school year started. Julian T. Peebles, of course, was no stranger to Cathedral. He grew up in Cathedral parish downtown and was graduated from Cathedral High School in 1964. An All-City football player for one of Joe Dezelan's most powerful and winningest teams, he was also president of the Student Council and was the recipient of the Fr. Higgins Award, one of the highest awards given to a senior before graduation. As has been shown earlier, after four years at Butler, Julian returned to his high school alma mater to teach and help Joe Dezelan coach football. He left Cathedral in 1971 to pursue another career, but his heart was always with CHS. When Mike McGinley retired at Cathedral, the door was open for Julian Peebles to return to the place he never wanted to leave, doing what he had always wanted to do, help lead Cathedral High School.

Upon his arrival, Julian immediately took charge. Although there seemed to be some faculty apprehension about the arrival of a new head, to everyone's surprise the transition between Mr. Peebles and the faculty could not have been smoother. Insecurity turned into good will and the 1989-'90 school year got off to a great start.

The 1990s began to see the results of the Lilly matching grant and the Diamond Anniversary campaign. With Jack Baker at the helm, and with the assistance of Development Director Dave Allen and staff, the Diamond Anniversary Campaign would become one of the most successful fund-raising campaigns in the entire school's history.

With the success of the campaign Mr. Peebles endorsed and enhanced many of the programs and ideas which had been initiated over the years to encourage eighth graders to come to Cathedral. The results increased enrollment by significant proportions. From the fall of 1987 to the fall of 1993 Cathedral High School saw enrollment grow by almost three hundred students, a fifty percent increase.

In the fall of 1989 Mr. Peebles sent Sr. Thomas More and Rev. Patrick J. Kelly to Washington D.C. to receive the "School of Excellence" Award which had been announced in the spring of '89.

With the success of the Diamond Anniversary Campaign, the "School of Excellence" Award, and increased enrollment, Cathedral was in good shape heading into the nineties. However, Mr. Peebles did not rest on these laurels. He aggressively pursued the ISACS (Independent Schools Association of the Central States) accreditation initiated by Mike McGinley in the fall of 1986. With

Fr. Kelly, Sr. Thomas More, and the entire faculty and staff, Mr. Peebles helped bring recognition of the educationally significant ISACS to fruition in his first year at Cathedral.

Throughout the school year Mr. Peebles set new goals for Cathedral and charted her on a course for the nineties. In an interview in the fall of his first year *The Indianapolis News* called him "An Evangelist for Cathedral High School." It was clear Mr. Peebles was in love with his new job, and this, of course, gave a good feeling to just about everyone who came in contact with him. As the nineties unfolded, Mr. Peebles has overseen many significant changes for Cathedral, including exciting changes to the physical make-up of the campus, an expanded parking lot, a refurbished cafeteria and auditorium, five tennis courts, a softball diamond, a practice field for the soccer team, a better practice field for the football team, an enhanced fine arts program, and an updated computer lab.

Everyone seemed thrilled with many of the new changes, but the one group which seemed most happy were those people who had been screaming for years about the lack of attention given to the fine arts program. Excellent theater productions and visual arts programs have been produced in the nineties as a result of a new commitment to the fine arts program primarily initiated and supported by Julian Peebles.

Mr. Peebles also pursued many new benefits for the school's faculty, presenting to the Board of Directors a retirement program and a much enhanced health care plan, which were adopted. For the first time in Cathedral's history staff benefits and salaries were increased equal to, and in some cases exceeding public school increases. While the gap between public school salaries and Cathedral staff salaries remains, real progress was begun in this critical area. Julian Peebles seems committed to the faculty and he never misses an opportunity to credit them for the ultimate success of the school.

No one would have guessed how well Cathedral would do in sports in the 1990s—a story so impressive it will be difficult to record within the scope of this book. With championship after championship occurring throughout the early nineties, only the highlights of each year can be mentioned. Suffice it to say, the early nineties were indeed golden, financially, academically, and athletically. Which was the first "golden era" at Cathedral? It depends on whom one talks with from the various decades; still, by anyone's standards, the early nineties rank at the top of achievement periods for the school.

The world of sports at CHS in the 1989-90 school year saw the boys cross country team advance from the Sectional to the Regionals, although the titles still eluded the team.

The girls cross country team came in sixth place in the Sectional but did not advance to the Regionals. Individually, Chris Weaver did advance, finishing thirty-fifth in the Regionals.

The boys tennis team ranked thirteenth in the state and captured their ninth City title in a row, ending their season 16-4. Seniors John Bradshaw, Andy Matthews, Brad Smith, William Brandt, and Mike Dodson led the way. They were supported by underclassmen Tom Bradshaw, Brian Arnold, J.B. Boyd, Ryan Hasbrook, Dameon Bennette and Alex Cagann.

After Mr. McGinley's, and Mr. Vince Lorenzano's departures, new coach Rick Streif had his hands full with a football team which was having a difficult time adjusting. They started the season with a victory over Chatard but ended the season with a disappointing 5-4 record. After a great win over Warren Central, the squad lost the first Sectional game on a slushy field at Roncalli. The Irish played a great game, but a few critical penalties made the difference. One penalty involved a personal foul call which gave Roncalli the opportunity to score when they would have had to turn the ball over; the other saw a Cathedral touchdown run nullified by a controversial block below the waist.

Jon Hill was named first team All-State and All-Metro. He went on to a fine career at Butler. Toby Whitehead and Scott Paris also made First Team All-State and All-Metro. Gene Murray, Kevin Rider, and Mark Engel also had outstanding seasons. If the measure of a man is displayed by his character, then Mark Engel showed the entire community what it means to be a man. Mark Engel worked as hard as anyone in CHS history to be the very best he could be in everything in which he was involved, academically, athletically, spiritually, and emotionally. A silent leader of real magnitude, he handled loss and the lack of recognition with more maturity than most grown men. Living his life according to his values and principles, Mark Engel exemplified the ideal Cathedral man, and the quality of the man earned him the Joe Dezelan Award at the end of the school year.

The volleyball team achieved tremendous success in Denise Farrell's last year as coach. Although the team lost the City title to Roncalli, they turned around and beat them for the Regional Championship. They lost the Semi-State to eventual State Runner-up Champion McCutcheon in a heartbreaker 2-1.

Considered to be one of the top volleyball players in Indiana, Amy Greer was All-City, All-Metro, and All-State. All-City honors also went to Leah Lentz, Stephanie Keefe, and Kellyn Feeney. Other seniors on the team included Cindy Stuart, Kim Roberts, and Mollie Peebles.

Amy Greer also had a successful basketball and softball season and was declared Indianapolis' top female athlete of the year in 1990. There have been some excellent female athletes at Cathedral through the years, but the records of none compare to the overall accomplishments of Amy Greer. She was an All-City softball player in '88, '89 and '90. Moreover, in 1990 she made the Indiana All-Star softball team. She was first team All-City in volleyball in 1988, and 1989. In addition, she made the All-State volleyball team, 1989–90, plus the Central Indiana All-Metro volleyball team 1989–90. She was the CHS outstanding female athlete in 1990. She was the 1990 outstanding female athlete in Marion County and the ultimate honor came in the same spring of 1990 when Amy Greer was selected the top female athlete of the year for the entire state of Indiana by *USA TODAY.*

Amy Greer was a person who gave all she had to give to be successful in everything in which she was involved. Character, persistence, and a tremendous work ethic were her trademarks, thus, Amy Greer was also declared a winner of the Joe Dezelan Award. This marked the first time in which the Joe Dezelan Award was given to a male and female and the custom has continued ever since.

The girls golf team won the City Championship and made it out of Sectionals to advance to the Regionals. The team included Ann Marie Fischer, Patty Gable, Suzanne Delembo, Sarah Pavelko, Carrie Caito, Erin O'Brien, Beth Beiriger, Kathleen Gill and Jenny Schaefer.

The boys soccer team advanced to the Sweet Sixteen for the second year in a row. All-State honors went to Kevin Pugh, and Honorable Mention went to Matt Cheek, Garrett Hall, and Nick Shank.

The boys basketball team played some of the best teams the state of Indiana had to offer, but the team still posted a 12-10 record. Paul Lee received All-City and All-Sectional honors. Ryan Greenwood was All-City, Indiana Top Forty and Eastern Indiana All-Star.

The girls basketball team ended their season 8-11, and they claimed no titles.

The wrestling team went 12-3 and won the City and Sectional titles once again. Three Eastside boys advanced to the State Finals. Jason Terry finished his season 39-0 for a State Championship, Kevin Rider finished 33-3, and Brian Funk finished 33-7.

The boys baseball team co-captained by Mark Engel and Gene Murray won no titles, losing a heartbreaker to Chatard in the Sectional 6-7.

The girls softball team won its first Sectional ever and finished second in the city in a banner year for the Irish with many records being broken. The team had been led by seniors Amy Greer, Cathy McCarthy, Mollie Peebles, and Stephanie Keefe. Greer, Peebles, and Feeney made All-City.

The boys golf team won the City Championship on the efforts of sophomore Sean Rowen and Andy Matthews, Jason White, and Bobby Delagrange. Rowen was medalist in almost every match in which he participated.

The girls tennis team won another City and another Sectional title. The very young team was led by Karlanna Manders, Megan Caton, Maureen Boyle, Linda O'Bryan, Catherine Brandt, Debbie Dinn, and Chrissy Newcomb. They finished the season ranked Seventh in the state.

Current events in the 1989–90 school year included the historic collapse of the Berlin Wall, and the pro-democracy rallies in China which were destroyed in Tienemen Square by a ruthless military. As many as 3,600 student leaders and intellectuals were killed and as many as 60,000 injured. Hundreds were arrested. Also, the Supreme Court limited the power of states to outlaw desecration or destruction of the American flag. On the sports front Pete Rose was suspended for life from baseball for gambling. Tragically, Ryan White died of AIDS.

The Megaphone celebrated its seventieth anniversary with Jenny Wurster as the editor. The Model UN team continued to grow and won the most awards since the triumphant showing in 1987. Oustanding performances were put on by Jeff Zeunik, Julia Velonis, John Bradshaw, Andy McGuire, Ginger Mobley, and Brad Smith. Other oustanding performances included Eric Howard, Matt Holton, Brian Fischer, and Steve Pfanstiel.

The 1989–90 school year saw some interesting plays on the CHS stage, beginning with a student production of *Dracula*. It showed promise but seemed to disappoint the students participating in it. Pat Bieldelman was excellent as The Count. John Schlagenhauf was also good as the insane Reinfield. Shani Wyant was Lucy, and Joe Schmidt was Professor Van Halsing. The student director was Kristina Miller, as dedicated to Cathedral theater as any student ever.

Two great productions came to the CHS stage in the second semester. Thornton Wilder's *Our Town* found multi-talented Joe Schmidt playing the narrator and the soda jerk, Najla Munshower as Emily Webb and Christian Hobart as George Gibbs. Tim Fish, Alicia Scheidler, Bethany Bauer, Jessica Courter, and Mike Gill also starred, and the play was entirely student-directed by Kristina Miller and Pat Beidelman.

As good as *Our Town* was, the best was yet to come in this year of fine drama. Early in spring the *Wizard Of Oz* was put on stage by some of the best talent ever seen on a Cathedral stage including Pat Beidelman as the Scarecrow, Joe Schmidt as the Lion, Christian Hobart as the Tin Man, and Alicia Scheidler as Dorothy. They were all superb but one of the most believable characters was excellently performed by Sarah Otte, playing the wicked witch. She was as close to the character in the movie as anyone and was assisted by outstanding fellow witches Jessica Courter and Andrea Pfanstiel.

Miller, Beidelman, Schmidt, Scheidler, Hobart, Wyant, Courter, and many of the others who played different roles in the plays in the 1989–90 school year set a trend for the caliber of plays at CHS for years to come. In particular, Joe Schmidt and Pat Beidelman (who went on to drama success at Wabash College) showed as much confidence as any two people to ever appear on stage or behind the scenes.

And "behind the scenes" did become very popular in the 1989–90 school year, with technical crews performing their crucial work with a high degree of ability. Kristina Miller, Dan Tabling and Adam Miller also established the trend that all areas of theater work can be challenging and fun. Beth Welch, Jodi Dezelan, Paola Fernandez, Trey Thorne, Anthony Lillig, Justin Miller, Chris Caito, Jenny Balhon, Mike Thibault, Jeff Bray, Sarah Otte, John Pehler, Kathy McCarthy, Matt Lamberti, John Bradshaw, Jason Durkott, Brad Smith, John Schlagenhauf, Linda O'Brien, Christian Hobart, and of course unofficially, Pat Beidelman and Joe Schmidt worked "tech" with confidence and skill.

Other events which took place in the 1989–90 school year included Homecoming, with Rene Wyatt crowned Queen and Gene Murray honored as King. As spring rolled around the Student Council, headed by Mrs. Jo Cavanaugh, held the First Annual IRISH 500, which was incorporated with field day and talent show. It has become a very successful event over the past few years. Earth Day was celebrated in recognition of the first Earth Day in 1970. The prom came and went and saw Mollie Peebles crowned Queen and Jon Hill King.

Mark Engel, Matt Lamberti, and John Bradshaw were National Merit Scholars; all three headed for Notre Dame the following year along with Jason Konesco who received a four-year scholarship to play hockey.

The Board of Trustees Award in 1990 went to one of the most vocal and confident leaders the school has ever seen. With people like Amy Greer, Mark Engel, and some others, this award was a difficult choice to make. A young man of tremendous character and talent, Patrick Beidelman showed wisdom beyond his age to lead the entire student body through efforts involving the Student Council. A man of great faith, he also had charisma, strength, and courage, thus earning the ultimate Cathedral award.

Secretary and receptionist Mrs. Sharon Nester left Cathedral over halfway through the school year. The mother of three children who had been at Cathedral in the eighties, Mrs. Nester had been at her key desk post for over seven years. A few years after her last son graduated in 1987, she wanted to move on. She had been a mother, counselor, nurses aid, and Number One fan to students while she was employed at Cathedral. Mrs. Rosie Houk replaced her. Rosie graduated from St. Agnes Academy and was a cheerleader for the Fighting Irish in the early sixties. She had just finished serving as Shamrauction Chairman along with Jim Alerding, a Cathedral graduate in 1963 and fellow cheerleader. Mrs. Houk is known for always greeting people in a friendly manner no matter what is going on at the front desks. She serves in many capacities at Cathedral besides secretary and receptionist, and Cathedral is fortunate to have had both Mrs. Nester and Mrs. Houk serve faculty, students and parents so capably in the key position Marie Ferris originally held in the 1940s, 50s, and 60s.

As graduation drew near, the multi-talented class of 1990 picked a multi-talented individual to be their speaker. Mrs. Lisa Ford was best known at Cathedral for her tremendous math teaching skill and at winning almost every contest in which she entered her students. However, she did much more, and the class of 1990 recognized that more than anyone. Known to be difficult and challenging in the classroom, Mrs. Ford's expectations of her students were always very high. As a result, her students often found out that they could accomplish far more than they ever realized they could. Most of her students were unable to appreciate her until they were off to college and flying through math classes with relative ease. However, the class of 1990 saw Mrs. Ford's qualities long before they were off to college.

Lisa Ford came to Cathedral in the fall of 1981 and left the school at the end of the 1992 school year. Her departure was considered to be a tremendous loss to the school, not only because of her teaching, but because she was so involved in many other special events throughout the years, from prom to Shamrauction. Students who were taught by Mrs. Ford in the eighties and nineties are never likely to forget her.

The valedictorian for the class of 1990 was Mark Engel. John Bradshaw, brother to Cathy '87 and Ann '88, both valedictorians of their classes, was the co-salutatorian with Patty Gable. Londe Dezelan, Joe's wife, received an Honorary Diploma.

Other significant events during the 1989–90 school year included a speaker from the University of Loyola, Chicago. Frank Bucaro shared his wit and wisdom with the students. He challenged their thinking, insisting that values are caught not taught, and that we are all examples to one another.

Dick Nuttall came to Cathedral after retiring from IPS where he had been employed for thirty-five years. He has taught Freshmen English ever since his arrival, but he has done much more. He immediately involved himself in the lives of his students and remains one of the most influential people in their lives at CHS. Mr. Nuttall genuinely appreciates Cathedral and has helped others realize just what a jewel she is.

In February of 1990, Cathedral celebrated Black History Month and Shamrauction. Both were successful. In late spring Mrs. Ford's math team placed more students in the Marion County Math Contest than any other school for the seventh year in a row.

Also, in the 1989–90 school year, Joe Griffin, a retired policeman who had not attended CHS, died. In his will he left $153,776 to Cathedral High School. Joe's younger brother did attend CHS in the forties, but when Joe was in high school his family could not afford the school's tuition. Joe was the sole survivor of his family who had immigrated to the United States from Ireland, and he left his money to Cathedral and St. Meinrad Seminary.

With the early success of the Diamond Anniversary Campaign, Cathedral had a major celebration at the all-school class reunion in August of 1990. With Bob Welch '45, Jack Baker '45, Dan O'Malia '65, Julian Peebles '64, and '32 graduate Charley Hill at the front of one of the largest all-school reunions ever, they burned the school's mortgage. This signaled the turning point in Cathedral's overall financial picture, since the mortgage had been hanging around the neck of Cathedral High School like an albatross and kept her from realizing some of her dreams in the late seventies and all of the eighties. The mortgage burning ceremony will remain a genuine marker in Cathedral history because from that point on the school has been on the move to update itself in all areas.

The Sportsmanship award is held by Father Patrick Kelly, Cathedral's principal, and Athletic Director Jean Ancelet.

Baccalaureate, '87.

Kelly Doyle, Cathedral's first gymnastics champion.

Claudine and Matt Debono.

Cathedral Merit Scholarship Semi-Finalists Terry Black, Heidi Weas, Stephanie Webb, Scott Lively and Matt Guye.

City cross-country champs in 1982 (standing) Mitzi Lyons, Mary Renee Dandridge, Michelle Dougherty and Susan Duffy. (seated) Shawn Priller, Claudine Debono, Mary Matthews and Susan Boyer.

Cathedral High School 1982 basketball team, which went to the State Finals.

The 1985 prom with Natalie Hessong, David Marbaugh, Mr. Obergfell, Chris Blume and Prom Queen Elizabeth Byers.

1986 State tennis team.

Ryan Updike

Scott Altherr

1986 wrestling team with (left) Asst. Coach Bill Pruitt and (far right) Lance Rhodes. The Valkyries are at the feet of the team.

1986 Champs—AAA State Champions.

One of Mike McGinley's greatest moments—hiked high above the heads of John Crisp and Scott Mencer.

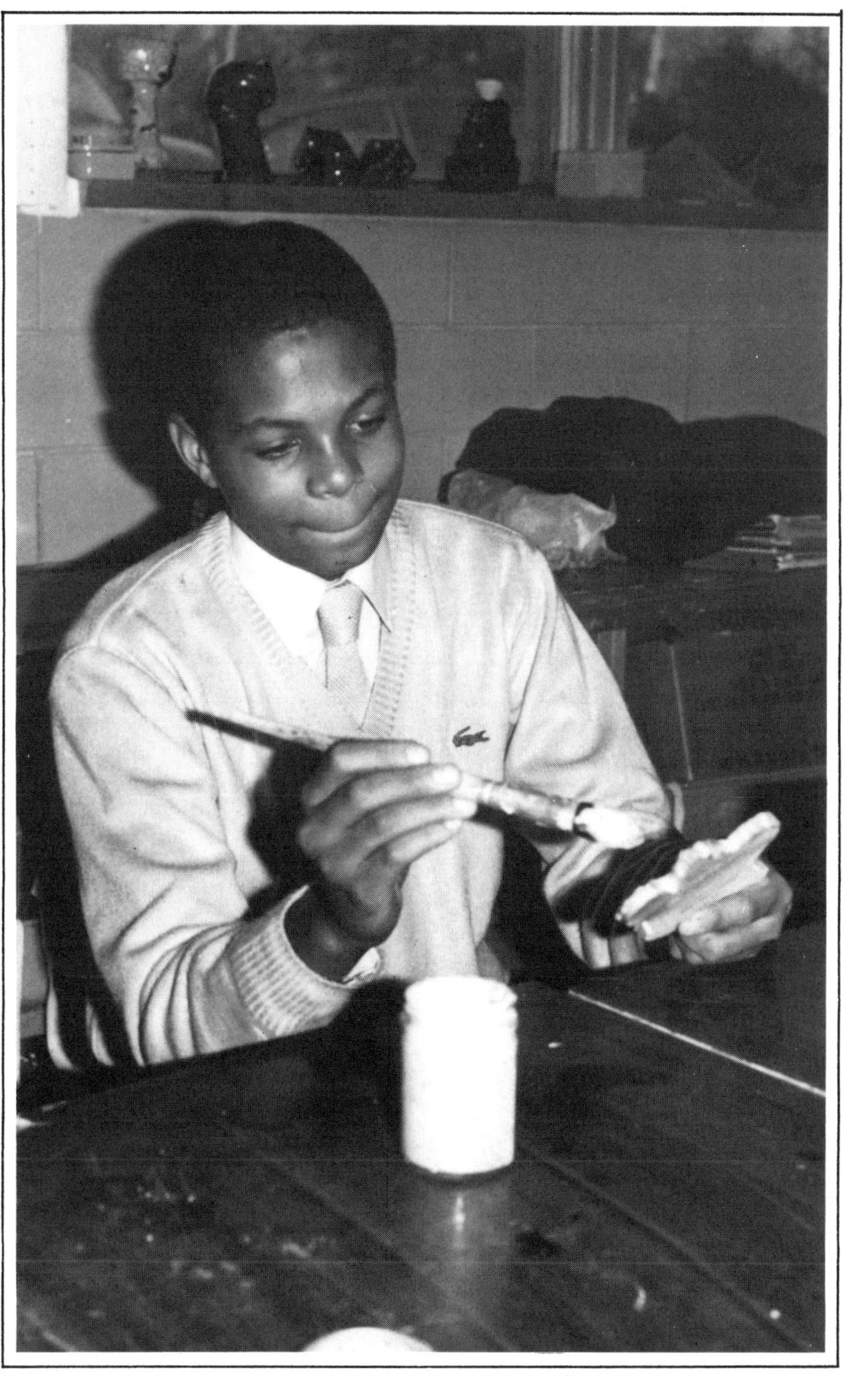

Michael Green '87 paints his creation in the expanded art program.

Father Kelly and Sister Thomas More hold the banner which symbolizes a height of national recognition in the late eighties.

Mike McGinley with his sons Sean and Patrick and daughter Moira at an appreciation dinner.

Triumphant, jubilant girls volleyball team in 1989. Denise Farrell (r, back) was coach.

(above) Junior Day or Recollection is a spiritual experience and a celebration of positive Christian values.

Active altruism: Vikki Schneider, Tory Callaghan and Karen Jung.

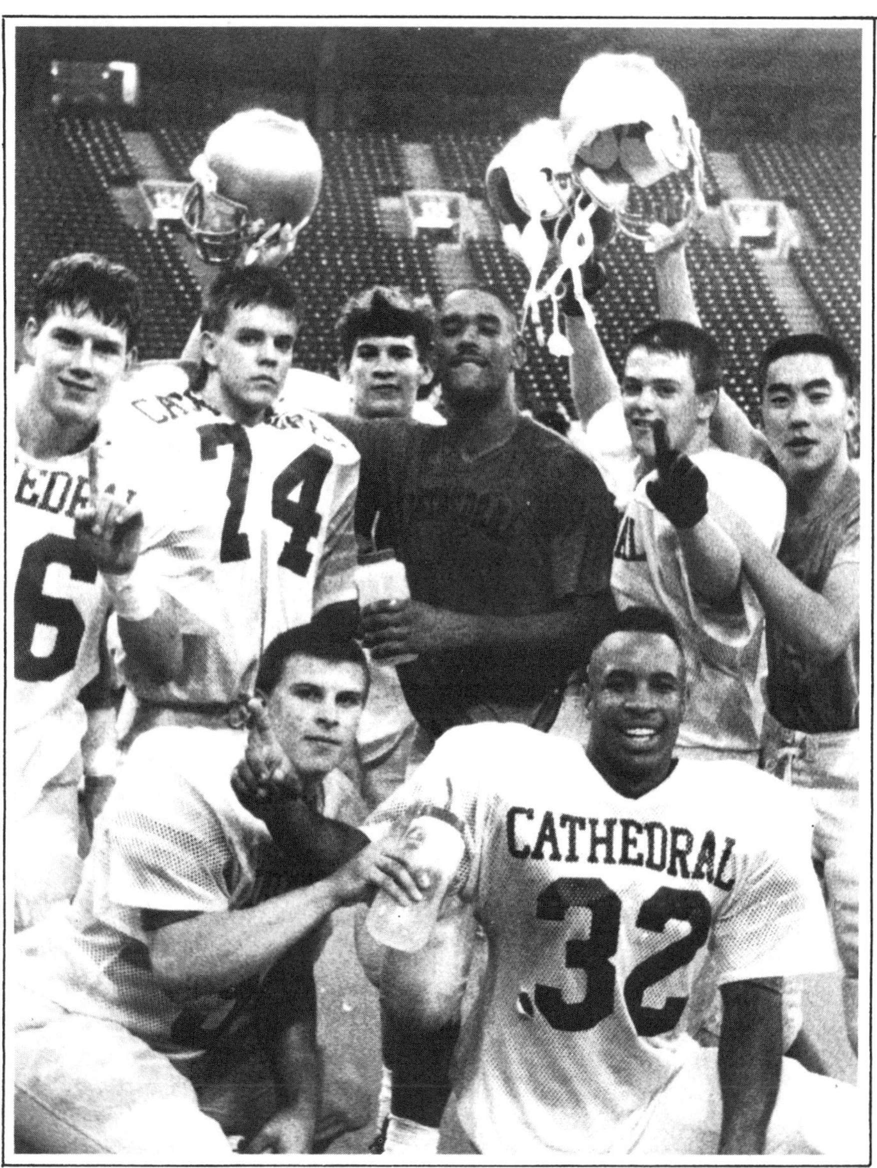

Time: Fall, 1989. Place: The Dome. Cathedral vs. Warren Central (l to r) front row: Kevin Rider, Jeff Coleman, (back row) Michael Hannigan, Ryan Williams, Jason Emmons, Desmond White, Scott Taylor Chris Wuensch.

Lance Ellis has been called the greatest high school wrestler in Indiana history.

THE NINETIES

1990–1991

When the students returned to CHS in the fall of 1990, they saw a newly landscaped entrance into the school. In addition, they saw a cafeteria and gym which were freshly painted and clean. Other significant changes would begin to happen by the end of the year, including the upgrading of the sports facilities and parking lot mentioned earlier.

In the fall of 1991, the Cincinnati Reds won the World Series. By the time spring rolled around the United States was in and out of a war with Iraq.

The 1990–91 school year was a smooth one, relatively speaking. Spirit was high and the small senior class along with the senior-led Student Council did an excellent job of leading the entire student body. The Class of 1991 was an enigma. Even though it was the smallest class in recent history, it was made up of a good many strong and unique personalities, so strong that one would be hard pressed to give a general definition of this group. Although they were unified in expression of spirit for the school, they were not as unified as a class. Nevertheless, in this unique group there were many wonderful individual personalities. Gentle, kind, bold, boisterous, candid, angry, fragile, and strong are just a few words to describe some of the many personalities which existed among them. Despite the diverse personalities, respect for one another began to emerge as the year developed.

Athletics brought the school close together during the 1990–91 school year as it always seems to do, and the Senior Class was often responsible for the spirit which ignited the school. This particular class won the spirit stick all but one year they were at CHS. To a large extent Andy McGuire was responsible for this spirit along with classmates Joe Herron, Chris Wuensch, Laurie Alerding, Matt and Jenny Larner, Tim Fish, Matt Davis, Alicia Scheidler, Najla Munshower, Kenny Roseman, Chris Burke, Lisa Bookwalter, James Conlu, Lisa Dahling, Matt Hahn, Nikki Henson, Christy Matthews, Kerry McAllister, Sasha Rogers, Carrie Wright, Laurie Williams, Jenny Weed, Melanie Richardson, Matt Davis, Ginger Mobley, Jenny Schnieders, Christy Matthews, Brett Croswell, Alyssa Hunt, and Maryanne Wisler, just to name a few.

The football team in the fall of 1990 had a disappointing season of 5-4, beginning with a major defeat by Chatard 33-13. The season ended in the Sectionals, again with a loss to Chatard, but this time it was a heartbreaking score of 6-7. Seniors on the team who shared their disappointment included Mike Hannigan, Ryan Williams, Mike Uber, Dan Weas, Kraig Maxey, Brett Croswell, Chris Nancrede, Clay Sheets, Tony White, Ken Roseman, Chris Bryne, Chris Wuench, Jose Evans, and finally, Jim Koers, a senior with real individual courage, who exemplified the ideal Cathedral athlete.

Despite a disappointing football season, spirit was still strong for other sports. The girls cross country team won their second City title in a row. Seniors on the team included Cathy Baukert and Ginger Mobley. Other stars included juniors Chris Weaver, Maria Wodraska, Claire Otte, and Lisa Schmitz. The boys cross country team claimed no titles, but seniors Sean Donnley and Steve Pfanstiel put forth fine efforts.

The girls on the volleyball team enjoyed their season, winning the City Championship, Sectional Championship, and Regional Championship. First year coach Jean Kesterson won the "Coach of the Year" award given by *The Indianapolis Star*. Seniors on the team included Cathy Lekens, Kellyn Feeney, Amy Moss, Leah Lentz, and Kelly Kennedy. Outstanding underclassmen included Sheri Osterhaus, Molly Davis, Jill Dascoli, Monica Borgo, Jackie Schaefer, all juniors. Sophomore standout Jody Dascoli and Freshman Molly Murray were also important to the team's efforts. Fan support had been tremendous all season long.

The boys tennis team won yet another city title, the tenth in a row. Led by junior co-captains Tom Bradshaw and J.B. Boyd, who were supported by Dameon Bennette, Brian Arnold, Ryan Hasbrook, Greg McDaniels, David Bradshaw, Jeff Hague, and Jason Kendrick, they had no problems repeating as City Champions.

The soccer team included a pretty junior girl, Sarah Ritter, four senior boys, Kevin Pugh, Nick Shank, Chris Burke, and Matt Davis, with the rest underclassmen. The Irish team finished second in their division behind Carmel, the eventual State Runner-up Champions.

The boys basketball team were runners-up in the City and the Sectional once again but the highlight of the season was beating Anderson High School in the Wig-Wam. Seniors on the team were Kenny Roseman and Matt Holton. The girls basketball team had only one senior on it, Debbie Dinn. Freshman LaKiesha

Brown was named All-City. Junior Jackie Schaefer was named honorable mention all-city, as was sophomore Jody Dascoli. With these two, the future looked promising

The wrestling team posted a 17-3 season record and won their eleventh City title in twelve years, also capturing another Sectional title. They came in second in the Regional and the Semi-State. State finalists included Brian Funk, Jason Terry, and Ryan Hasbrook.

The girls softball team, coached by Linda Allen and Mike Feeney, captured their second Sectional title in a row with only two seniors on the team, Kellyn Feeney and Christy Matthews. Up-and-coming players to look forward to included Carrie Caito, Jackie Schaefer, Shannon O'Malia, Amy Engel, Chrissy Collins, Kara Lathrop, Carolyn Rhodes, Kerri Freije, Becky Steiner, Ellen Murphy, Tracy Matthews, Molly Murray, and Katie Peebles.

The baseball team won a Sectional championship, led by Mike Harmon, Matt Larner, Brian Stratman, Dan Weas, and Juan Lopez. These boys, along with Tim Egan, Chance Hair, Eric Froehlke, Terry Peebles, Bob Hill, Bryan Keefe, Ryan Rizzo, Jon Holloway, Johnny Adams, Mike Luedeman, Darren Keller, J.B. Boyd, and Eric Gurnell had a genuine love for the game of baseball.

The girls tennis team won again the City and Sectional title. Composed of only three seniors, Debbie Dinn, Kerry McAllister, and Molly Farrell, they were boosted by other members of the team including Kindy Smith, Jenny Balhon, Catherine Brandt, Sarah Hanke, Molly Davis, Megan O'Bryan, Tracy Dinn, Jenny Leighton, Maureen Boyle, Linda O'Bryan, and Meghan Caton.

The boys track team posted their best record since 1988. They were led by seniors Tim Fish, Sean Donnelly, and Steve Pfanstiel.

Strong individual performances were posted in girls track by sophomore Moira McGinley and junior Maria Wodraska. Senior Deborah Callaghan was the City Champion in the high jump as well as a qualifier for the Regionals. Other seniors on the team included Ginger Mobley, Kathy Baukert, and Christina Hegyi.

The 1990– 91 school year featured the school's first career day in well over a decade. Mr. Tom Greer, assistant vice-principal, organized the event which included many CHS graduates representing over thirty different possible career choices. People representing various careers included Judge Jerry Zore '59, *The Indianapolis Star* columnist Dan Carpenter '65, and WISH-TV reporter Letitia Miele '81.

Dean of Students Tom Greer, assistant principal, counselor, computer and scheduling expert, and general overall trouble-shooter came to Cathedral in 1988. He appears just about everywhere. Some students have actually claimed that there must be two or three of him, because no matter where they go he is there. Dedicated, loyal, and completely committed to the well being of the students and the school, Tom Greer has made Cathedral High School a better place because he is there. With his endless responsibilities, he is a permanent and not always fully recognized fixture at Cathedral.

The 1990–91 school year also saw the fourth band director in four years since Larry Everhart left. Matt Murdock arrived on the scene in the summer of 1990 and helped bring stability back to the band program once again. He stayed until the end of 1993. In his first year he took his small band to the Veterans Day and St. Patrick's Day parades, also developing a jazz band for the first time in years.

Speech and debate teams were oustanding in the 1990-'91 school year with award winning underclassmen like Maureen Kaiser, Brian Potts, Claudia Choi, Michelle Evans, and Bridget McClelland leading the way. Seniors Clay Sheets and Matt Davis also gave fine performances.

Flowers for Algernon and *Up the Down Staircase* were well attended plays which starred Matt Hahn, Jeff Barnosky, James Brightman, Sarah Neal, and Andrea Pfanstiel in *Flowers* and Alicia Scheidler and Jacob Prell in *Staircase*.

The Model UN team celebrated its tenth year at CHS by putting together a large number of delegates in the IUPUI contest. Cathedral delegates were invariably good and competitive, even with each other; thus they sometimes canceled each other out. Their great performances and strong preparation didn't win awards but added to the school's luster.

In the spring, Frank McKinney '57, Chairman of Bank One and Olympic Gold Medal Winner, gave a speech at the National Honor Society Induction in which he challenged all the students to have a dream and a goal. "Do not intend to live by accident," he said, "intend to live with a purpose." His son, Bob, a member of the junior class, and the entire audience listened to him attentively.

The Megaphone put out another fine paper with Deborah Callaghan as the editor. The yearbook was organized by Andrea Pfanstiel, Krista Kuhns, and Matt Hahn. After sophomore David Mazelin died, a poem expressing many of the feelings shared by his classmates was penned by his friend Matt Kissling for the yearbook. David's presence remains strong in the memories of the class of 1993, of which he too was a member.

Spring also rang in another prom, where Sasha Rogers was crowned Queen and Clay Sheets was crowned King. For the juniors, the same honors went to Kathleen Gill and Todd Greenwood.

Mrs. Jo Cavanaugh was in full swing with her group called ACTS. She led volunteer students to perform all kinds of community service projects from working in food kitchens, to involvement with Holy Family Shelter, Gleaners Food Bank, nursing homes, and other charitable sites. The individuals involved with her during the 1990-91 school year included Bob McKinney, Sarah Hack, Lacey Fages, Kindy Smith, Megan Hofheinz, Emily Austin, Kristen McMullen, Jay Zmrhal, Chance Hair, Bob Bergin, Ann Margaret McAninch, Karlanna Manders, Tracy Roberts, Darrell Bains, and Alisa Clinard.

Four members of the chess team qualified for the state finals: Steve Pfanstiel, Christian Hobart, Paul Goyette, and Chris Gill.

Former band director Brother Eugene Weisenbach died having taught at CHS in the fifties, sixties, and early seventies. He was primarily responsible for the many excellent bands which came out of those eras, serving as a legacy for all future bands to come.

In late May of 1991, Archbishop Edward T. O'Meara said his last Baccalaureate Mass at Cathedral. He had been a part of that service for ten years. Archbishop O'Meara died later that fall.

Graduation ceremonies were beautiful once again. Steve Pfanstiel was salutatorian and Andy McGuire was honored as the valedictorian. Andy spoke of his class accomplishing the tasks "of becoming what a Cathedral graduating class should be." Lance Rhodes was selected to address the students for the third time in four years and encouraged them to look for the heroes in their lives. President of the Senior Class and former wrestler under Mr. Rhodes, Joe Herron, introduced Mr. Rhodes to his classmates. The Board of Trustees Award went to Andy McGuire, a young man who exemplified the ideal Cathedral student all four years of his high school career as academic all-star and leader. He was voted as one of the top forty students in the state of Indiana by *The India-*

napolis Star. The Joe Dezelan Awards went to Jim Koers and Kellyn Feeney and the Athlete of the Year awards went to Kellyn Feeney and Kenny Roseman.

The year ended on a high note, as the smallest graduating classes in decades moved on to some of the nation's best colleges and universities and opened the doors at Cathedral to one of the largest enrollments in over twenty-five years.

1991–1992

As the world continued to change in the Soviet Union and elsewhere, so did Cathedral High School. The football field, although still rough, was complete. The soccer field and tennis courts were near completion, and by the end of the year even the softball diamond would be dedicated and ready to use. New sports teams came to Cathedral in the 1991–'92 school year—the Irish developed new winning traditions in swimming, hockey, and rugby. Continued interest in Cathedral made her "The Choice of the '90s" as declared by Mr. Peebles.

The Senior Class did not realize when they arrived at school in the fall either the success the year would bring, or how different they would be spiritually, emotionally, and intellectually at the end of that year. Their hearts touched one another as they also grew closer together as a class. With people like Monica Borgo and Tom Bradshaw, this class also knew how to have fun.

If the athletic teams during the 1991–'92 school year should be labeled by any single name they should be called "champions"! Championships of significant proportions were earned during the school year; the football team won Sectional, Regional, and Semi-State titles and were the runner-up State Champions in the 3-A division. The volleyball team took City, Sectional, and Regional titles, while the boys soccer team won third in the state losing to eventual State Champion Carmel 0-1. The girls golf team also won a City Championship, and the boys tennis team brought back to the school their eleventh consecutive City Championship and Sectional and Regional championships. The boys and girls cross country teams both won City titles, and the girls first-ever swimming team also took the City title. The boys and girls basketball teams finished their seasons with City titles and Sectional titles as well, and the wrestling team won another city trophy, their eleventh in twelve years. The first-ever rugby team came in third in the state, and the girls tennis team took another City title. The gifted senior class provided most of the talent on these teams, but underclassmen were also significant contributors.

In football the team was led by seniors Terry Peebles, Bob McKinney, Chuck McCarthy, Lamarco Pate, Brian Hofmeister, Chris Abriani, Jeremy Gardner, Terry Ford, Craig Hauser, Ryan Hasbrook, Matt Logue, Damon Smith, Matt Cain, Marcus Thorne, Jeff Coleman, and Alvin Middlebrooks. Underclassman on this team who made a significant contribution included Will Dinwiddie, John Adams, John Clamme, Darren Keller, Jamil Stafford, David Ray, Rik Hagarty, Jon Holloway, Mike Luedeman, Brian Ford, Ryan Kinn, Bryan Keefe, Jim Hannigan, Darren Gerlach, Aaron Logue, Damon Hope, Derek Spriggs, Alex Scheidler, Mark Hurley, Jeff Risser, Chris Strykowski, Brenden Fitzgerald, and Jeremy May. All-State honors went to Bob McKinney, Brian Ford, and Marcus Thorne. All-City honors also went to Thorne, McKinney, Ford, and Jeff Coleman, Chris Abriani, Chuck McCarthy, Terry Peebles, Ryan Hasbrook, and Jon Holloway

The turning point of the season came against 5-A Warren Central, as the Irish beat the Warriors in the Hoosier Dome 31-7. The Hamilton Southeastern game was too close for comfort, but the Irish won on a bitter cold night 3-0. On another bitter cold evening Cathedral beat Evansville Memorial 13-12. In a hard fought battle the team was not so lucky against Fort Wayne Dwenger in a heartbreaking loss for the State Championship 27-35. The runner-up Irish team had every reason to be proud of their accomplishments. Though he did not not know it at the time, Coach Rick Streiff would return to the Hoosier Dome one year later in another State Final game.

From the '91 team, seniors Peebles, McKinney, McCarthy, Huaser, Thorne, Coleman, and juniors Dinwiddie, Adams, Clamme, Holloway and Brian Ford, all went on to play college ball.

The championship volleyball team was led by five seniors: Monica Borgo, Jackie Schaefer, Sheri Osterhaus, Amy Moss, and Jill Dascoli. They were aided by underclassmen Molly Murray, Molly McCarthy, Caryn Jones, Jody Dascoli, Lisa Borgo, Kellie Greer, and Moira McGinley. This was coach Jean Kesterson's second Regional Championship team at Cathedral, in the year in which she celebrated her one hundredth victory. Named First Team All-City were seniors Monica Borgo and Jackie Schaefer, along with junior Jody Dascoli, and sophomore Molly Murray. Schaefer was also selected to the First Team All-Metro, and Honorable Mention All-State. Lisa Borgo was selected as an Academic All-State player.

The girls swimming team, winning a city championship in its maiden year, was made up entirely of underclassmen. Freshman Katie Hasbrook was the overwhelming star of the team, which also included juniors Marget Arthur, Maggie Linville, and Kelly Arbuckle.

Seven seniors made up the Third-in-the-state soccer team. They included Garrett Hall, Jay Zmrhal, Jon Stites, Matt Cheek, Jamie Richter, and Matt Petrili. Important underclassmen included Chris Iams, Ryan Smith, Scott Zmrhal, Matt Lockman, Ross Bobenmoyer, Justin Miller, and Birt Hampton. Coach Paul Schroeder was named "All-Metro Coach of the year." Cheek, Hall, and Smith were named to the All-Metro team. The soccer team played a superb game, losing to Carmel on the same bitter cold night that the Irish football team defeated Hamilton Southeastern 3-0. The Irish fans were heavily represented at the old CYO field for the soccer game, with numb feet and hands then they quickly headed for the Hamilton Southeastern football field for the second half of that game.

The boys championship tennis team was led by an exchange student from Germany named Tim Mussenberg, with co captains, J.B. Boyd and Tom Bradshaw. Other significant members of the team included Dameon Bennette, Brian Arnold, Greg McDaniel, and David Bradshaw.

Coached by Joe Molony and Steve Jamell, the championship cross country teams were led by seniors Chris Weaver and Maria Wodraska. Other significant runners included Linda Petigrew, Nicole Nolton, Katy Hair, Deirdre Brill, and Gina Schuler, for the girls. The boys team included Tim Merchant, Sean Rowen, Paul Long, Peter Sakon, Joe Dascoli, Mike Solomon, Chad Mobley, and Arin Neuks.

Coach Howard Renner's championship boys basketball team was led by Todd Greenwood, Steve Bryant, Steve Reed, Derek Miller, RaasSahn Milton, Brian Ford, Chris Peoples, Jermaine Ball, Geoff Faerber, Artie Taylor, and Keesh Brewer. They were presented with the championship trophy by Mayor Stephen Goldsmith. Jermaine Ball would go on to Evansville to play college basketball. Coach Linda Allen's girls championship team was led by Jackie Schaefer, Moria McGinley, Molly Murray, LaKeisha Brown, Jody Dascoli, Lynn Radzilowski, Monica Borgo,

Caryn Jones, Kissy Dawson, and inspirational team leader Amy Engel. Brown, Schaefer, and Dascoli all made All-City.

"Coach of the Year" Lance Rhodes' wrestling championship team included State Finalist seniors Jason Terry and Ryan Hasbrook, and freshman Dan Pleak. Other significant members of the team included Ryan Smith, Tony Alerding, Trent Gill, Aaron Cook, Chris Funk, Joe Dascoli, Scott Dillinger, John Arbuckle, Will Dinwiddie, Adam Walsh, James Kaufman, Marcus Thorne, and Terry Peebles.

The girls City Championship golf team included Academic All-State player Erin O'Brien, along with Carrie Caito, Sarah Pavelko, Laura Caito, Kathleen Gill, Tina Watson, Beth Beiringer, Katie Peebles, Nicole Meisburger, Meghan Spellacy, and Tisa Meyers, for the girls. For the championship boys Matt Hughes, Andy Van Noy, Sean Rowen, Bobby Delagrange, Mike Wolf, Matt Jaimet and Tim Merchant made up the excellent team. Sean Rowen took his third City title, and he placed eighth in the state competition. The girls team was coached by Greg Bamrick and the boys team by Bill Mattingly.

Although the track teams won no titles, Moira McGinley and Maria Wodraska set new school records, with Moira placing first in the City in the 3200 meters. Chris Weaver placed second in the 800 meters.

The girls championship tennis team was led by Maureen Boyle and Meghan Caton, Linda O'Brien, Molly Davis, Sarah Hanke, Kindy Smith, Catherine Brandt, Jenny Leighton, and Tracy Dinn. They were coached by Dr. Pat Bradshaw and Paul Farrell on the new tennis courts. It ought also to be said that if it had not been for the efforts of Paul Farrell, the tennis courts at Cathedral might never had become a reality. Maureen Boyle and Meghan Caton went on to capture the State Championship Doubles title. Maureen was the last member of one of the most influential tennis families ever to attend Cathedral.

On May 28, 1992, the softball diamond was dedicated with a first pitch thrown by sports enthusiast and Chairman of the Board, Dan O'Malia. The girls had a good season, but no titles were won. Carrie Caito made All-State and was selected as an Indiana All-Star. All-City honors went to Carolyn Rhodes, Carrie Caito, and Kara Lathrop. The boys baseball season did not turn out as all had hoped, but seniors Terry Ford, Terry Peebles, and Eric Froehlke all hit over .400 for the season. Terry Ford and Eric Froehlke made All-City, and Bobby Hill was selected as an Academic All-State player.

The athletically talented Senior Class was equally charming, witty, intelligent, and handsome. With six National Merit Scholars and ten commended scholars, the class of 1992 was a gifted and challenging group. National Merit Scholars, the most the school produced in any single year in over fifteen years, included Tom Boyce, J. B. Boyd, Tony Ragucci, Heidi Hughes, Tom Bradshaw, and Erin O'Brien. There was also a larger-than-normal group of National Commended Scholars which included Jennifer Balhon, Chuck McCarthy, Megan O'Bryan, Andrea Pfanstiel, Kelly Scanlon, Mike Tabor, Marcus Thorne, Sean Terry, and Robbie Johnson.

With Katie Quinn, Chuck McCarthy, Sheri Osterhaus, Jamie Coles, Jay Zmrhal, Tim Egan, Damone Johnson, Maria Wodraska and J. B. Boyd leading the way, this class carried enthusiastic school spirit to a higher dimension. There were so many types of leaders in this class without official titles, people like Molly Davis, Ellen Murphy, Megan O'Bryan, James Brightman, David Weilhammer, Bob McKinney, Tony Ragucci, Bob Hill, Amy Engel, Tom Boyce, Kathleen Gill, Kristen Kennedy, Chris Branson, Kelly Scanlon, Caleb Clarke, Kathryn Landis, Aaron Cook, Michelle Evans, Matt Cain, Jeff Bray, Rob Adams, Leslie House, Andrew Hasbrook, Claire Otte, Tracy Roberts, Michael Browning, Krista Kuhns, Shannon McNulty, Marcus Thorne, and Chris Bittinger to name a few.

The Senior Retreat added to the process of growth which this class eagerly welcomed. This class of '92 was humorous, serious, determined, spiritual, sensitive, thoughtful, and candid. One of the senior religion teachers was in awe of them, admiring them all tremendously. He could not wait to get to school on a daily basis because he looked forward to what was going to transpire each new day. He pushed them and they pushed him back, and for that he loved them.

Due to the very successful retreats, strong personal relationship were developed between most members of this class. Teachers like Jo Cavanaugh, Sarah Koehler, Dick Nuttall, and Gary Spurgin, better known as the "God Squad," mentored the seniors on every Senior Retreat. Whether it was with *The Megaphone*, yearbook, tutoring, drama, speech, debate, sports etc., this class was as involved as any class to ever come along; some of them could be found at school well past 6:00 p.m. on any given evening, sometimes just sitting around together with peers and faculty members having conversations about important issues, and sometimes talking about nothing in particular.

Tragedy and significant losses for almost a year started in the fall of 1991 when Nicole Armstrong, who had just graduated in May of the the same year, was killed in an auto accident. Unfortunately, that was only a small example of events to come. On Thanksgiving eve, long-time English teacher at CHS, Mrs. Melinda Bundy lost her husband after a long battle with cancer. On Christmas Eve, 1987 graduate Amy Kervan, was also killed in an auto accident. In February firefighter, John Lorenzano '80 was killed fighting a fire at the Indianapolis Athletic Club. Early that summer Jesse Hair, assistant baseball coach, and father to Chance Hair '94 was also killed in an auto accident. In mid-summer, former business manager at CHS, Bill Welch died. Later that summer Matt Cheek's father was killed in an auto accident. Matt graduated in '92 and his mother, Donna, taught at Cathedral for two years.

That was not all. On the day when most people from the class of '92 were getting ready to leave for college, classmate Bob Hill was killed in an auto accident. He ranked fourth in his class and was heading to what surely was high academic achievement at Hanover. Still more tragedy lurked ahead only a few weeks into the 1992–93 school year. In September, 1992, less than one year from the date when Nicki Armstrong was killed, Bob Welch '45 and Frank McKinney '57 were killed in a plane crash. The significance of these two men to Cathedral has been told many times.

Other significant events involve taking a look at the lighter but also meaningful side of the 1991–92 school year. Mrs. Ney took Megan O'Bryan, Katie Quinn, Tim Egan, and J. B Boyd to put on fine debate clinics for grade school students around the city. Mrs. Koehler developed a group called "Races Working Together" to promote racial harmony. One of the results was celebrating Black History Month in February. A wonderful trip to Central State Hospital was made with about twenty seniors who had collected and purchased toys for patients at the hospital so they would have something to send home to their loved ones. Chris Branson, Kelly Scanlon, Heather McDonald, Ellen Murphy, Molly Davis, Megan O'Bryan, and Jamie Coles were just a few of those who participated in this activity.

It was an important year for the cheerleaders at Cathedral High School. Often neglected and unappreciated, the girls on the cheerleading squads have the longest season in all of high school sports, and it is a demanding sport. From early fall to late spring their season is exhausting. Any teacher sticking around school late into the evening could often find cheerleaders like Chrissy Collins and Shannon O'Malia lying in the hallways doing homework, sleeping, eating fast food and junk food, while waiting to practice late into the evening. The 1991–92 squad, coached by Lisa Walters, earned one of six "Excellence Awards" at a summer camp at Ball State. Later they went on to capture the National Cheerleading Association Regionals. Shortly after Christmas they headed for Dallas, Texas to compete in the Nationals, where they placed thirty-fourth out of 109 teams. Besides seniors Chrissy Collins and Shannon O'Malia, the team included seniors Delisa Brown, and captain Amy Walsh. Other very significant members to the team included underclassmen Molly Bozic, Julis Albers, Christy Phillips, and Krista Delgallo.

According to cheerleading captain Amy Walsh, the team realized the responsibility of setting the pace for school spirit. The girls set the goal at the beginning of the year to have cheerleading respected the same as any other sport. Amy Walsh said, "We earned that respect and brought prestige to the program. Getting to the Nationals was something we all wanted. We worked hard to reach our goal and we achieved it. I am very proud to have been a Cathedral cheerleader. I hope we have set a standard for all future cheerleaders that they be respected for their hard work, dedication and discipline, just like all other athletes."

In early fall, Shakespeare's *Romeo and Juliet* played to packed houses in the CHS auditorium. It was considered by some of Cathedral's harshest critics to be excellent. Senior Christian Hobart and sophomore Casey Senden played the two leading characters and Ann Margaret McAninch was Juliet's nurse. Other starring roles were played by seniors James Brightman, Kenny Becker, Ryan Feeney, Sean Terry, Andrea Pfanstiel, and Adam Williams, with important roles played by juniors Claudia Choi, Craig Stoughton, and Jacob Prell.

In mid winter there were three student-directed one act plays, *The Lottery, Baker's Dozen,* and *An Occurrence at Owl Creek Bridge.* These plays gave many students who had no previous experience a chance to try drama. The Senior Class grabbed at the opportunity to participate in these plays. Senior participation exemplified one more time just how involved they were at Cathedral. Senior directors Andrea Pfanstiel, Jeff Bray, and James Brightman did a great job putting these productions together.

The Spring Musical, *Joseph and the Amazing Technicolor Dreamcoat* was called the "greatest musical triumph of Cathedral High School to date" by long time drama student James Brightman. It starred Megan Hofheinz and Casey Senden, Jacob Prell and a huge supporting cast, including Matt Cain playing the king *à la* Elvis Presley. James Brightman also excelled.

The Megaphone put out a fine paper with Jennifer Balhon as editor and with wonderful socially relevant articles by Michelle Evans.

As spring rolled around another successful prom came and went as seniors Maria Wodraska was crowned Queen and Chris Branson King. For the juniors the honors went to Marget Arthur and Willie Gholston. At the Irish 500-talent show-field day, seniors watched with sheer delight as Matt Cain, James Brightman, Rob Adams, and Tom Bradshaw's band had colorful make-up on their faces and played "It's The End Of The World As We Know It." The best part of the talent show came when seniors did a skit imitating teachers. Chris Branson played Judy Birge and the seniors went wild. One could not tell the difference between Branson and Birge as illustrated by the picture they had taken standing next to one another. The senior class loved Judy Birge, and so has almost every class she has ever taught in her long-time association with Cathedral.

Judy started teaching at the school when it was still Ladywood back in 1972—so she has been in the building longer than anyone associated with the school. Judy has several trade-marks. Bandanas, Diet Pepsi, tennis and golf stories, love for politics and talk of who's who, clear enunciation of the word *bourgeoisie*, sun dresses and sun glasses on top of her head, earth shoes, knee-high hosiery, love for East Coast schools, and one of the most original Government programs in the state, have made her an institution at Cathedral High School. Most students report that political science classes in college are a breeze because of Judy Birge's teaching.

Besides Judy Birge, there are five teachers who deserve recognition for their continued dedication to Cathedral. Glen Mauger, Melinda Luckey Bundy, Dan "Doc" Wellman, Judy Ney, and Jim McLinn all came to the 56th Street campus from the old school downtown. They remain significant in helping Cathedral maintain her heritage. Mauger celebrated twenty years at CHS last year, Wellman and Bundy celebrate twenty years this year, Jim McLinn and Judy Ney are in their nineteenth year.

McLinn, Ney, and Bundy have been mentioned frequently in this book. Jim McLinn's humor and love for stories, and Judy Ney's highly principled life and love in watching her students grow, and Melinda Bundy's charm, quick wit, and love for her extended family at Cathedral High School, have had tremendous impact over the years. Mr. Mauger and Doc Wellman are both legends in their own time. Doc Wellman's love for history, especially the Civil War, has been contagious; hundreds of students have absorbed the fascinating details and importance of history. His loyal attendance as scorekeeper for the boys basketball team has provided him with something he loves doing outside the classroom. What he is best know for however, is his genuine love for IU sports, and in particular, IU Basketball. In the winter of '93 Doc Wellman received an IU flag signed and presented to him at Cathedral High School by his hero Bobby Knight. "Doc" guarded that flag the rest of the evening.

No teacher earns the respect of his or her students like the man who is often covered with chalk dust at the end of each day, Glenn Mauger. His serious, yet humorous methods of teaching chemistry have endeared him to hundreds of Cathedral graduates who were constantly challenged by his teaching. Whether celebrating "mole day" or finding nicknames for each of his students, Mr. Mauger has consistently found a way to teach his students chemistry so they can understand it, relating his subject to their lives. Molly Davis, a 1992 graduate who attends Notre Dame said, "His class was the only science class I ever liked because he made it interesting and fun, but very demanding. Mr. Mauger was a great teacher."Moreover, Glenn Mauger has taken a personal interest in all his students, especially when they needed extra help. He is one of the first teachers to arrive in the morning and one of the last to leave, and he has been doing that for over twenty years now.

In May of 1992 Cathedral said goodbye to a great class. Baccalaureate Mass was rained out, so services had to be held in the auditorium. Fr. Jeff Godecker said the mass and gave a beautiful homily. Honors night recognized J. B. Boyd with the Board of Trustees Award, and the Joe Dezelan Awards went to Maria Wodraska and Marcus Thorne. The Athlete of the Year awards went to Terry Peebles and Jackie Schaefer.

A beautiful, sunny day ushered in Commencement. Ceremonies took place at the Circle Theatre once again. Tom Boyce, voted one of the top forty students in the state of Indiana and selected as an Indiana Academic All-Star, was valedictorian of his class. He spoke about the new beginnings he and his classmates were about to undertake outside the walls of Cathedral High School and read his own poem about change. Salutatorian Erin

O'Brien gave a wonderful speech urging everyone to learn to accept challenges. The faculty speaker Jim Obergfell was very graciously introduced by class president Katie Quinn. Before introducing him, much to her credit, Katie kindly paid tribute to the entire Cathedral faculty. Mr. Obergfell echoed the students' speeches in encouraging the class to have courage to deal with all of the challenges and changes which would forever exist in their lives.

Dan O'Malia, who retired as Board Chairman shortly after the 1992 graduation, presented his daughter Shannon with her diploma, and President Julian Peebles did the same to his son Terry. After all the diplomas were handed out, President Julian Peebles and Chairman of the Board Dan O'Malia caught Jim Obergfell completely off guard and presented him with an Honorary diploma from Cathedral High School for his service to the school. Overwhelmed and grateful, Obergfell was thrilled to have received the honor and to have had the opportunity to share it with the class of 1992, genuinely one of his favorites.

1992–1993

With the incredibly successful year of 1991–92 gone by it was hard to imagine that the 1992–93 school year could get any better, but it did. No, the school did not experience as many championships, but the ones she won were "oh so sweet." The senior class had no National Merit Scholars but some of the most determined and hard working people the school has ever seen. Desire, dreams, diligence, heart and soul define many of the people in the class of 1993. As in all other years, the Senior Class set the tone for the entire school: positive and full of accomplishment. Of course, it wasn't all positive with some of the group being typically rebellious, but they did a masterful job in setting a good example for all those who where to follow in their footsteps.

At Homecoming the seniors put on a pep rally which would equal any of the best from the past. With their rendition of "We are the Seniors" to the music of "We are the World," the senior class showed themselves united in their support for their teams and each other. With Sean Fisher as Bob Dylan, Claudia Choi as Tina Turner, Nicole Nolton as Cindy Lauper, Greg McDaniel as Michael Jackson, Scott Fels as Huey Lewis, Jon Holloway as Willie Nelson, Willie Gholston as Stevie Wonder, Scott

Kraege as Bruce Springteen, and Taryn Walker as Diana Ross, spirit shook the auditorium and amazed the rest of the student body. It was only a small example of the closeness this group would eventually experience throughout the year. In large part the Senior Retreats reinforced the closeness felt at the year's beginning.

The football team had a single-minded goal: to get back to the Hoosier Dome to settle some unfinished business from the year before. No one gave them a prayer at the beginning of the season—they had lost so many talented seniors from the year before.

Pejoratively speaking, it looked like it was going to be a long season; the squad looked terrible in their first game of the season and were blown away by archrival Chatard 0-31. As it turned out, it was indeed a long season. But it was a glorious one, as it developed into a classic case of watching the Irish spirit carry a determined team to reach their goal. "Carpe Diem" was their motto, and they did indeed "Seize the Day" as they won the crowned jewel which they had barely been denied the year before, the 3A State Football Championship.

After the awful Chatard defeat, the team won the next two games and then they lost to 5-A powerhouse Ben Davis. That was it. The team went undefeated the rest of the season, including avenging the loss to Chatard in the Sectionals 17-5. The Irish squad had improved immeasurably in a short period of time. The loss to Ben Davis was the game which made the difference, for it was there that the Irish gained the confidence of realizing that they were a very good team. Although the score was 27-10 in favor of Ben Davis, that score does not tell the story. A few bad calls by referees against the Irish may have made the difference in the game. Still the team learned something about themselves that night and they never looked back, learning from their loss, and growing.

Outstanding senior leadership by John Clamme, Brian Ford, Mike Luedeman, Johnny Adams, Jon Holloway, Bryan Keefe, Will Dinwiddie, Darren Keller, Jamil Stafford, Dave Ray, Rik Hagarty, Ryan Kinn, and excellent managers Matt Weber and Cliff Cavorsi created an atmosphere of excellence.

Underclassman, many of whom were impact players, included juniors Brandon Reardon, Jimmy Hannigan, Darren Gerlach, Aaron Logue, Chris Dobrota, Jeff Risser, Hannibal Wright, Derek Spriggs, Chris Kaufman, Jason Pugh, Matt Mescall, sophomores Dan Pleak, Tony Alerding, Scott Dillinger, Chris

McGee, Jeff Banks, Mike Seall, Antoine Butler, Steven Adams, Franco Ditillo, Ray Lee, Vince Druding, Bob Koers, Micah Davis, Mike O'Bryan, and Tom Riley.

Various All-State honors went to Brian Ford, Jimmy Hannigan, John Clamme, Ryan Kinn, and Jon Holloway. All-City honors went to all the people mentioned above and Darren Keller. Brian Ford was named the Defensive Player of the Year by *The Indianapolis News;* he was also selected for the All-Star Team.

The football team, as it has done so often throughout the school's history, set the tone for the spirit, involvement and over-all good feelings which were generated at Cathedral in the 1992-93 school year. This marked the second year in a row in which the student body had the experience of supporting their team all the way to the State Finals, only this time they came out on top; what a wonderful experience it was.

Coaches Rick Streiff, Doug Armstrong, Chris Kaufman, Mark Deal, Scott Symmonds and Ken Kaufman did an extraordinary job of getting the boys to seize the day! In five years at Cathedral High School, head coach Rick Streiff has had some difficult seasons, but in that same short period of time he took two teams to the State Finals and ended with a State Championship.

Perhaps because of football, retreats, or something else entirely, the boys in the Senior Class were as close to one another as brothers. One teacher commented that he had never seen such a close knit group of boys in all his years at Cathedral, yet there had been many close-knit groups in his time.

Football was not the only event going on at Cathedral in the 1992-93 school year. In the fall semester the drama department put on a fine production of *The Lion, The Witch, and The Wardrobe* which involved over fifty people in the play. Later, drama teacher Terry Fox put on *Scapino*, which also involved well over fifty people. In the spring semester Fox's production of *Once Upon A Mattress* was highly impressive. The color and pageantry were fun to watch, as was the huge cast. Great performances were put on by the whole cast, but the starring roles by freshman Lauren Cregor, and upperclassmen Precious Gholston, Chris Gill, and Megan Hofheinz were outstanding.

One of the best aspects of Fox's productions is that they have involved so many people on a regular basis, and the creativity, imagination, and talent which have been displayed by his students have been commented upon by the audiences.

The 1992-93 school year saw language clubs continue to grow under the leadership of longtime and dedicated teachers like Lucia Fedor and Gary Spurgin culminating each year in their highly acclaimed International Week and Dinner. The Marching Band also saw an increase in numbers, as did the choir. Speech and debate teams were excellent—Precious Gholston went to the State Finals and Claudia Choi went to the Nationals in Florida. *The Megaphone,* under editor Arin Nueks asked many hard questions and brought a variety of social and school issues to the forefront to be discussed and debated. A few seniors were not satisfied with what they considered to be "fluff" journalism so they started an underground newspaper. It drew mixed reactions.

As mentioned before, some sports teams did not experience the marked success as the year before them, but other sports programs did well. Although the girls cross country team did not win a title, Deirdre Brill won the Individual City Championship. The girls swim team captured their second City Championship in a row, once again starring Katie Hasbrook, Marget Arthur, Kelly Arbuckle and Maggie Linville and freshman—Katie Johnson. The soccer team was stopped by North Central in the Sectionals. Matt Lockman and Ryan Smith were both named All-State players. The volleyball team won a City and Sectional title but they were not able to repeat as Regional Champions. Molly McCarthy, Molly Murray, Jody Dascoli, and Caryn Jones were selected as All-City players. All-State honors went to Jody Dascoli and All-Metro honors went to McCarthy, Murray, Dascoli and Jones.

The boys basketball team went 4-15 and looked to brighter days in the future. The girls basketball team posted a 14-8 record and earned a Sectional Championship. All-City honors went to Keisha Brown, Jody Dascoli, Lynn Radzilowski, and Kissy Dawson.

The Cathedral-Chatard Blues hockey team ended third in their division. In the two-year-old program the hockey team has produced three Indiana All-Star players—Christian Browning, Marc Konesco, and Mark McAllister, all from the class of 1993. Senior Will Dinwiddie was named an All-State player for the Rugby team. The softball team lost to Roncalli twice in the season, once in the City tournament. They also lost to Lawrence North in the Sectional. They ended the season 14-3.

The baseball team won the 1993 City Championship and Coaches Ken and Chris Kaufman saw three of the team members selected as academic All-State players—Mike Luedeman, Ryan Rizzo, and Darren Keller. All-City honors went to Bryan Keefe, Darren Keller, and Jeremy May.

The wrestling team won another City Championship, and the Sectional and Regional titles. They were second in the Semi-State and placed fifth in the State Tournament. State finalist included seniors Ryan Smith and Joe Dascoli and sophomore Dan Pleak.

The boys golf team won the City title under the leadership of captain Bob Delagrange.

The boys and girls tennis teams won City titles, but both teams were stopped by North Central in the Sectionals. The boys City Championship team included David Bradshaw, Greg McDaniel, Ben Garten, Tim Trevathan, Pete Madden, Andrew Autojay, Mark Gisler, and Bill Spalding. Girls Championship team included Meghan Caton, Kindy Smith, Jenny Leighton, Johanna Newcomb, Sarah Hanke, Tracy Dinn, and Catherine Brandt.

Other individuals who merit recognition for their accomplishments during the 1992-93 school year include junior Ryan Vertner, winner of McDonald's "Black History Makers of Tomorrow Award." Ryan was one of ten people selected nationwide for character, scholarship, and community service.

Brandie Metz was crowned queen of the Miss Indianapolis Teen Scholarship Pageant. She won the Senior Achievement Award and the Top Talent Award as well. She was also a finalist in the Indiana Young Woman of the Year Award. Her sister, Thyra Metz '87, had won the award when she was a senior at Cathedral.

English Teacher Nancy Baxter finished her fourth book in the *Heartland Chronicles* series and travelled to Pittsburgh when her book *The Movers* was chosen a Waldenbook Preferred Reader selection there.

The spring ritual of prom came on a beautiful evening. Sara Hack and John Clamme were crowned prom Queen and King for the seniors. For the juniors Sarah Weber and Tim Merchant received the same honors.

Honors night at Cathedral saw a variety of people take significant awards. Athletes of the year awards went to two great ones in Jody Dascoli and Ryan Smith. The Joe Dezelan Awards deservingly went to Jody Dascoli and her twin brother Joe Dascoli, both representing the ideal student athlete at CHS.

The Board of Trustees Award went to Molly Bozic. Having been president of her class for three of the four years she was at Cathedral and vice-president the other year, Molly Bozic exemplified the ideal Cathedral student through her character, work ethic and spirit, and through her service and dedication. She was indeed one-of-a-kind.

As the year came to an end, the Senior Class shone once again, only this time it was at the Irish 500-Talent Show-Field Day. The highlight of the talent show featured Lisa Borgo, Eileen Kiefer, Bridget McClelland, Bridget Mooney and Moira McGinley imitating the rock group Guns'n Roses. One had to be there to honestly appreciate this performance. Freshman Shannon King and junior Allison Hampton were also good.

Toward the end of the year senior class officers Molly Bozic, Brandie Metz, Willie Gholston and Tom Grossman decided on a gift to the school from their class. They purchased a new IRISH sign for the front of the school and spent many hours cleaning up the hill and re-painting the gold lettering on the stone sign on 56th street. In addition, they had the cross on top of the school gold leafed—symbolically, and permanently leaving a positive mark on Cathedral High School from the class of 1993.

Whether helping to plan the Baccalaureate Mass or cleaning up the surrounding grounds where it was held, no one worked harder than Senior Class President Molly Bozic. Idealistic and high achieving, she worked diligently to realize her dream: going to Notre Dame.

The altar was set and Archbishop Daniel Beuchlein came to celebrate the Mass. His homily touched many of the seniors. Laura Shanabruch said she felt as if the Archbishop was "talking right to her," and most everyone in the congregation felt the same way. The overwhelming response from people at the Mass was that the Archbishop spoke to them, and not at them. This was clearly appreciated by the students as they listened attentively to everything he had to say. With senior participation, the mass was beautiful.

Before the Archbishop gave his final blessing President Julian Peebles stepped to the podium to officially welcome the archbishop to Cathedral High School and to thank him for coming. Mr. Peebles also took the opportunity to thank the Senior Class for their gifts to the school and to tell them that their legacy to Cathedral High School would always be recognized through their symbolic offerings.

Senior class Vice President Willie Gholston took to the podium next and presented a number of gifts from the class of 1993 to the archbishop as a sign of their appreciation for celebrating their special mass. One of the gifts was a Cathedral baseball cap. The Archbishop took off his miter and as he put on the baseball cap everyone laughed and applauded. After mass the archbishop stood by to greet many of the graduates and their families. In a little over one hour Archbishop Daniel Beuchlein endeared himself to the Cathedral family. It was a beautiful day for the Irish.

Once again graduation ceremonies took place at the Circle Theatre. Alex Scheidler led the audience in prayer before everyone joined in to sing "America the Beautiful." Salutatorian, Molly Bozic gave a speech emphasizing that genuine leadership can only come about through one's own example. She was followed by Valedictorian Brandi Metz who spoke about finding the jewel within oneself by living consciously. Mr. Peebles recognized their exceptional speeches toward the end of the ceremony as two of the best he had ever heard. French teacher Gary Spurgin was chosen by the Senior Class to be the Commencement speaker. He had been involved with this particular class for several years in a variety of different ways. In his speech, he described the Senior Class as a book by highlighting them in different chapters. Upon leaving the Circle Theatre, students and their families stood around in the beautiful summer weather taking pictures. It was another special day for the Cathedral family.

1993–1994

With the successful classes of '90, '91, '92, and '93 and the promise already displayed early in this current year by the class of '94, it is easy to understand why the 1990s have been called the second "Golden Era."

From the beginning of the year, the Senior Class was ready to disprove the negative image they developed in their first three years. Perhaps, like younger siblings in a family, they were just waiting for the very successful classes of '91, '92, and '93 to leave so they could show everyone who they were and what they wanted to become.

As this book went to press, the Senior Class has taken charge of the school, as is the tradition of every senior class. They have already displayed leadership, courage and growth, taking on challenges and setting a positive tone, with of course, some normal rebellious exceptions that only prove this is still Dear Old Cathedral.

On September 13, 1993, Cathedral celebrated her Seventy-fifth Anniversary. It was seventy-five years to the day since the school opened her doors. With help and guidance from Assistant Principal Tom Greer, the Senior Class put on a tremendous all-school assembly outdoors to celebrate the Diamond Anniversary.

With representatives of each decade in attendance, including Robert Worth from the first graduating class of 1921, the assembly watched and listend to speeches, presentations, Irish dancing, and music, to celebrate the birthday. Cathedral High School Day was declared in the City of Indianapolis by Steven Goldsmith and in the State of Indiana by Governor Evan Bayh. Proclamations were presented to the school by representatives of each man's office, Mrs. Caress Garten, mother of Ben '93 and Matt '96 for the mayor, and Tom Jeffers '80 for the governor. Following the assembly there was a cookout almost entirely prepared and served by the Senior Class.

Class President Rob Heisserer was greatly assisted by the other class officers, Michelle Rollins, Kevin Gill, and Tracy Matthews. Kerri Freije, David McGinley, Krista Delgallo, Laura Caito, John Alvarado, and several others helped to make it another proud day for the Irish—a day Joseph "Joe Bish" Chartrand, the founder, would have loved.

For the Homecoming pep rally, seniors made up their own lyrics to a song from the play *Grease*. Girls dressed in poodle skirts and the boys slicked back their hair and rolled up their shirt sleeves. Performances by Kathleen Fischer, Steve Weilhammer, Casey Senden, and many others, showed creativity, imagination, and talent in the tradition of Cathedral pep rallies. Jessica Greathouse was crowned Homecoming Queen and Mike Soloman, King.

The first of the Senior Retreats took place shortly after homecoming. The retreat was extraordinary as one person described it. Another student simply said, "I needed something like that so badly." then she added, "it felt so good." Like other years, the first Senior Retreat often sets the tone for the rest of the school year. If that is the case with this class then it will indeed be an exceptional year.

The world of athletics at Cathedral in the fall of 1993 has started where many of the great teams of the early nineties left off.

The boys tennis team won another City Championship, the team's fourteenth in a row. The team was led by David Bradshaw—the last of the Bradshaw family, one of the most successful and influential families academically and athletically in the 1980s and 1990s at CHS. The championship team also included players Bryon Gill, Pete Madden, Andrew Autojay, David Hanke, Bill Bissmeyer, and David Miller.

On October 5, 1993, the girls and boys cross country teams both won the City Championships. Coaches Steve Jamell and Mark Worrell were elated, celebrating well into the evening. Deirdre Brill was the Individual City Champion for the second year in a row. She was aided by the efforts of Jessica Greathouse, Katy Hair, Kathryn Hammel, Molly Maguire, Mary McNeely, and Gina Schuler to secure the City title. The boys Championship team included Chad Mobley, Craig Moore, Tom Miller, Steve Kempf, Chris Kiefer, Kevin Kubacki, and Mike McKenna.

Another State Championship for the football team seemed almost too much to ask for, especially since Cathedral was bumped up to the 4-A division because of the school's increased enrollment. Nevertheless, Cathedral folklore is filled with stories where "never say never" has been proof positive that anything is possible for the Fighting Irish of Cathedral High School.

With other promising opportunities in sports, and talk of *Grease* being the spring musical and the full array of extra-curricular activities underway, the school's usual wide range of achievements seemed assured.

Whether championships and awards are won or not, it is the life-building experiences that count; the Cathedral family has certainly learned that lesson well over the past few years. If Cathedral students are able to pull off some of those storybook victories and success stories as the year emerges, no one will be surprised, and everyone will join in the celebrations. If games and events are lost, everyone will be there to support one another. That is what makes the Cathedral family unique.

There should be no attempt to forecast the history of Cathedral High School because the future will create its own untold stories and records. Through faith, families, friends, and faculty we hope Cathedral will continue to serve future generations in both the Catholic community and the City of Indianapolis, as it has since 1918. The excellence, traditions, pride and spirit, the service, the dedication, the honor in attending and being a part of the school, and the commitment to the community will endure.

One only needs to listen to Cathedral graduates to realize that these qualities are the hallmarks of a Cathedral High School education. Staying loyal to her original mission, the school has guided three generations incredibly well over the years. Through wars, depressions, recessions, chaos, uncertainty, fear, broken families, a devalued society, heartbreak and jubilation, Cathedral has been there. As long as Cathedral High School stays true to her mission and is guided by true and just principles, she will not only continue to be here in the future, but also will thrive and remain one of the premier high schools in the city of Indianapolis, the state of Indiana, and the United States of America.

IPSA DUCE NON FATIGARIS

"UNDER HER LEADERSHIP WE SHALL NOT TIRE"

There are many staff members who have been with Cathedral for a number of years who have not been mentioned in this book and must be recognized, people like Darlene Conway, Mary Croswell, Susan Lord, Jean Boyce, Belinda Speck, Jenny Matthews, Sr Francis Borgia, Mary Jane Janssen, Judy Rail and Sr. Marie Benson. These devoted people have always been there when they are needed. And four individuals who work so hard to keep Cathedral beautiful and funtioning include Larry "was up" Ison, Don Christian, Charlie Newport, and Fr. Jack Okon.

Teachers serving the school today, like those in the distinguished past, have significant impact on the school and her students and should be recognized. These people include Ed Lyle, Peter Berg, Doris Cantrell, Kathy Bethuram, Shirley Stockdale, Mary Bruinsma, Jan Duggan, and Cyndi Dietz. And Bonny Hannigan, Oather Daniels, and Barbara Fitzgerald. Tee Fonseca, Sr. Sue Freiberger, Nancy Hartman, Karen Hebert, Sr. Jenny Howard, Sr. Lynn Matteson, Sandi Sheetz, Carla Leppert, Becky Meyer, Vicki Perry, Tom Peterka, and Cynthia Reid. Marcia Reynolds, Sharon Sipe, Kathy Thomas and Barbara Velonis add their own unique talents.

Like the Brothers of Holy Cross, whose legacy is always with us, these teachers have succeeded in making a significant difference for young people. Many Cathedral teachers, however, unlike the Brothers of the Holy Cross, have families of their own; yet they have not wavered in their commitment to their students. Today's teachers have to find a balance between the needs of their own families and their Cathedral family. They have done this masterfully and they have often incorporated the two into one, thus enriching the larger Cathedral family.

One only needs to listen to the testimonials given by Cathedral graduates to realize the importance of a strong faculty. Whether they were taught by Brothers of Holy Cross, other religious, or a lay faculty, students remember teachers as the heart of the school experience. The following comments by Cathedral graduates illustrate this point so well.

> *Probably the greatest attribute of Cathedral is her faculty. The teachers have a genuine concern for their students. They helped me to realize my potential and instilled in me the self-confidence I need to achieve my goal.*
> —Molly Cain '89

> *I learned not only lessons, but discipline; along with math and English, I was taught moral values and a sense of purpose. I became aware of the community around me and realized a responsibility to get involved in that community.*
> —Judge Charles A. Wiles '52

> *It was through the encouragement and prodding of a fantastic teacher that I learned not only about trapezoids and parabolas but, more importantly, I learned a very valuable lesson in life—to believe in myself and my own God-given abilities.*
> —Mary Below '82

> *The teachers at Cathedral are of the highest quality. However, their most important characteristic is that they care. They care not only about the quality of education their students receive, but the quality of life their students have.*
> —Mike Bigelow '85

I remember a faculty that was supportive of the student body and that challenged them to be active and not passive participants in the world, especially when dealing with questions of social justice.

—Joe Vande Bosche '80

What lingers in each of us is a sense of values—lifelong lessons of faith, hope and charity—of wanting to make each of our families, our neighbors, churches, and workplace a little better.

The board, administration, faculty, and parents work hard to teach more than books, consequently challenging her students to live their lives with a spirit of generosity, and pride. Cathedral graduates owe a tremendous debt of thanks to our parents, teachers, and classmates who continue to challenge us decades after we graduate.

—John D. Short '70

The open diaolgue between students and teachers on issues of social justice, economic justice, and world relations encourages students to recognize that an understanding of these issues is as important as mastering the concepts and theories of their chosen profession.

—Denise Clark '79

The involved and dedicated faculty was also part of our family which makes me look back on Cathedral with fondness. Open and thought-provoking discussions, empathetic talks, and personal attention were the norm. I know that my high school years at Cathedral were indeed rich because of the education that touched not only my intellect but my heart.

—Sue J. Choi '87

I best remember the teachers at Cathedral. They seemed to care about me as a person and not just a number in their grade books. They were always willing to take extra time during or after class to explain questions or problems I had or just to talk about life in general.

—Megan M. Alerding '86

*The faculty at Cathedral helped prepare me for the impor-
tant things in life—social integration, a sound education, a sense of
human kindness, a sense of value for myself and others.*
—Michael L. Harrison '64

*There are many reasons for Cathedral's success in educa-
tion. One of the most important is the faculty. The faculty members care and have a sincere concern for each individual student's
success .*
—Carl E. Daniels '84

*When asked what Cathedral means to me, I think of the
faculty because they gave me their caring and dedication, their experience, and their values. Once I had left the school, I found that
they were not just my ex-teachers, they were my friends as well. I
look back and find that I learned so much in my four years at Cathedral. The most important things, however, weren't found in the
books; these things came from the people I met along the way.*
—John M. Christ '80

*The devoted, high-caliber faculty of Cathedral guided us
through, just as the present faculty is doing for Cathedral students
today. The result, a good education and a sound development in
moral and ethical values, which stand the test of time so well.*
—H. Jack Baker '45

*In my daily contacts or discussions with one Brother or
another, I became impressed with the hard fact that it is not expected of each student that he aim to be a genius by the time of
graduation; to the contrary, it is ideally hoped that each student
reach or attain his or her potential—the academic, personal, and
moral level—bearing in mind that each student's potential differs.*

*To meet, or satisfy one's potential, I learned at Cathedral
High School that three principles be pursued:*

*1) In your every day life, whether it is work, study, or con-
tacts with your fellow man, use common sense.*

*2) Whatever the task with which you are encountered give
it your all—work hard—a maximum effort always.*

3) Zealously guard and protect your moral person. Avoid any conduct which might question your integrity.

Cathedral High School is totally responsible for my grasp of these principles, from which I greatly benefited, and for which I have been extremely grateful to this day.
—John C. O'Connor '34

The Cathedral faculty was among the finest in the country. Not only did they make learning exciting, but they were always accessible, helpful and friendly.
—Judge John F. Hanley '73

Dedicated teachers, a supportive administration, lots of encouragement from our parents, and help from each other when we needed it most—these were the hallmarks of our Cathedral experience.

I am sure each one of us was affected in some way or another by a special teacher, coach, or staff member who went that extra mile, gave that extra effort, or showed that extra concern. Their example taught us to show the same support and encouragement to each other.

Those who shaped our Cathedral years gave us more than facts and figures. They gave us the most important, intangible lessons of caring, love, and Christian values.
—Cathy Bradshaw '87

I do not think one can imagine the strength, wisdom, and concern the faculty of Cathedral exhibits to her students. The faculty is approachable, supportive, and giving of their free time. The teachers get to know their students on a personal and academic level.

My time at Cathedral was not just a four year academic education. Cathedral is a life long experience. Her values, traditions, spirit, and pride will always live on in my memories, my friends, and in me.
—Stephannie M. Keefe '90

My teachers and my peers taught me lessons about living and learning, loving and growing. The spirit and the pride, the tradition and the values are what make Cathedral so much more than just a place to receive an education. It is more than just a building with desks and classrooms. Cathedral High School is a family of administrators, coaches, teachers, and students who share a genuine concern for one another.
—Katie M. Quinn '92

With these comments let this book come to an end. Let us leave the challenge of perpetuating the legacy of her mission and philosophy to Board members, administrators, teachers, students, alumni, parents and friends of Cathedral so that twenty–five, fifty, or even another seventy-five years from now, the torch will have been passed to a new generation, and she will still be

"Dear Old Cathedral!"

A NOTE FROM JIM OBERGFELL . . .

There are so many people I would like to thank, but I would especially like to express my gratitude to the following:

—To Bill Shover, whom I am proud to call my friend, for inviting me to co-author this book with him, and for graciously allowing me to share his dream to permanently record a history of Cathedral High School.

—To Julian Peebles, Fr. Patrick Kelly, and Sr. Thomas More for encouraging and supporting me in my efforts, and for granting me this unique opportunity. Along with them, I would also like to thank Jim McLinn for serving as a sounding board throughout this project.

—To all my former students whose impact on me has touched my heart and soul, and has left an indelible mark in my mind. Your were the best teachers I ever had.

—To my 1993-94 senior religion classes for their understanding and patience during the 1st quarter of this school year. I could not have finished the book without their support.

—To Molly Bozic, '93, Jay Zmrhal, '92, and Deborah Callaghan, '91, for their research, kindness and advice.

—To Nancy Baxter who challenged me, who treated me with respect, and who was always open and honest with me. A true professional, she was kind as she was genuine. It was a sincere pleasure to work with her.

—To the many faculty members who supported, challenged, encouraged, and listened to me throughout this whole project.

—Most importantly, to my daughter Anna, CHS class of 2002, and my wife Nancy, who made many sacrifices over the past six months to give me time to finish the book. Without their challenges, patience, understanding, and genuine love and concern, my part in this project would not have been possible. Sweet dreams!

Thank you.
Jim Obergfell

In the nineties the Cathedral High band stepped out just as spiffily as it had in the twenties.

Father Patrick Kelly. Singular devotion, growing out of a long religious tradition.

Christopher Columbus, Mary, Queen of Scots, Pope Leo X and friends at an AP English Renaissance dinner. The humanities are alive and well.

Former Fire Prevention Chief Charley Hill,'32, Chairman Dan O'Malia, '65, Former Chairman Bob Welch, '45, Diamond Anniversary Chairman Jack Baker, '45, and President Julian Peebles preside at the historic burning of the Cathedral mortgage.

Images of the nineties: (clockwise) Micah Shrewsberry, Franco Dattilo, Bryan Keefe and Steve Adams lead the baseball squad around the field. Cathedral honored Board Chairman Danny O'Malia at a farewell dinner (here he cuts the cake the daughter Colleen.) Carolyn Rhodes swats one at a softball match; Paola Fernandez was a contributive exchange student in the nineties.
(many nineties photos courtesy of Chris Kaufman.)

The brain team crushed Brebeuf in the early nineties.

One of Cathedral's finest groups: the '93 Championship cheerleaders. (back) Christy Phillips, DeLisa Brown, Chrissy Collins, (middle) Shannon O'Malia, Julie Albers, Molly Bozic, Amy Walsh. (front) Krista DelGallo.

Paula Glover '93 on her way to Indiana State College and a promising career in teaching.

Boys and girls together now, Andrew Hasbrook and Katie Quinn.

The cast of "Once Upon a Mattress" was not a cast of thousands; it only looked that way in 1993.

The Cathedral faculty and staff, Christmas '91.

Moira McGinley and opponent take the hurdles with gusto.

The one and only Larry Everhart.

Board Chairman Mike Schaefer (left) with Valedictorian, Class of '93 Brandie Metz and Salutatorian Molly Bozic, President Julian Peebles and Principal Patrick Kelly.

Jerry Cranney, Effie Quinn, Ray Schworr, Notre Dame Coach John MacLeod, and John O'Conner at a Dezelan luncheon.

Champion athlete Amy Greer '90.

Cathedral's famed history teacher and visitor of dead Presidents' graves, Doc Wellman, receives a tribute from an admiring friend.

Maria Wodraska shown at a track meet, wonders where the ecstacy is after so much sporting agony. The hand on her shoulder is that of her supportive father.

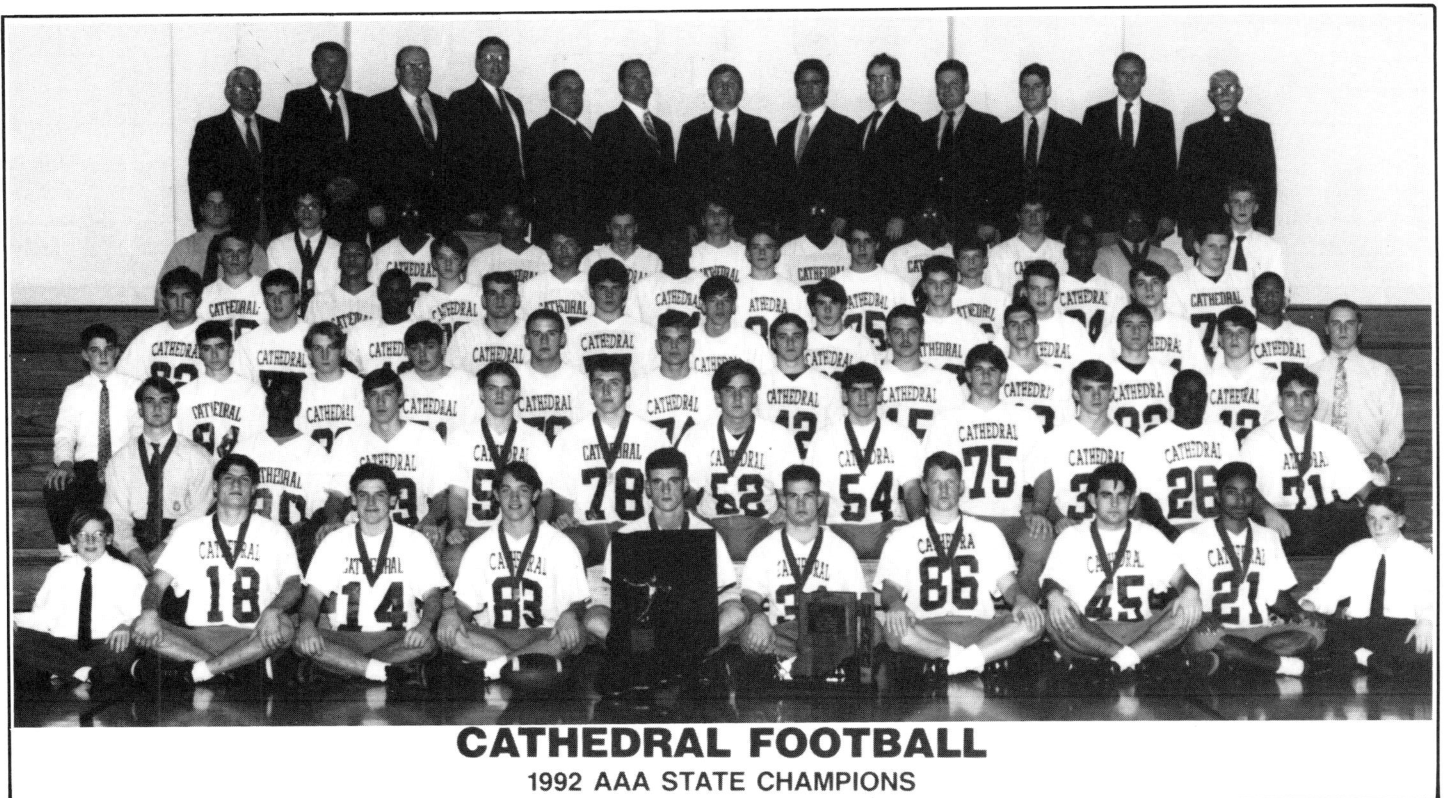

From "The Insects" to the Dome: 1992 State Champs.

Parochial Power Tradition Continues
as Three Catholic High School Teams in Finals

Collectively, they represent just five percent of the 312 IHSAA-member schools that play football. But what a punch the 16 Catholic schools pack.

For the 10th straight year, the parochial schools will be represented at this weekend's celebration of the best of Indiana high school football. Cathedral, Ritter and Fort Wayne Luers—all state runners-up in 1991—will play for state titles again Friday at the Hoosier Dome.

Ritter is a surprise returnee in Class A; Luers in 2A and Cathedral in 3A are not. And it will be no surprise if at least one of the three captures the title that eluded them a year ago.

Since 1983, at least one state title each year has gone to a Catholic school. Since the post-season party began in 1973, the Catholic schools have been represented at the finals in total of 18 championships.

The numbers are noteworthy, especially since most of the Catholic schools are lumped into classes 2A and 3A, including Cathedral, Chatard and Roncalli in the same 3A sectional. There are none in 5A and only one in 4A.

(Cathedral was elevated to 4A competition in 1993.)

What also won't be a surprise this weekend will be the grumbling that usually accompanies the continued football success enjoyed by the small but proficient minority. It was particularly noticeable last year when five Catholic schools reached the finals and two repeated as state champions.

More a near-constant murmur rather than a thunderous roar of discontent by fans, coaches and administrators from public schools, it nonetheless is nettlesome to the Catholic schools. Understandably so, they believe their players and coaches deserve praise for their accomplishments rather than criticism.

"The kids hear that stuff, but we try to keep it as a non-factor," said Coach Andy Johns of Fort Wayne Dwenger's three-time state champs. "I think there's more talk in Indianapolis than anywhere else."

Call it envy, call it distrust, but the whispers of illegal recruiting are always audible. Some may be founded, but Cathedral coach Rick Strieff made an interesting point this week.

If the Catholic schools are illegally recruiting and taking all the good players from the public schools why are none of the 18 Mr. Football semi-finalists from a Catholic school?"

The "are they or aren't they" argument could last for days with no winner. Suffice to say that penalties by the IHSAA have been few despite all the finger pointing.

As it stands, call it an uneasy co-existence 50 years after Catholic schools were admitted to IHSAA membership. And as much as the public schools may grumble and IHSAA officials may express concern about keeping a level field of play, there is an appreciation for what the Catholic schools provide to the state football tournament—money.

From the sectional level to the dome, the fan support is significant. Everybody benefits. Perhaps that's why a move to force the Catholic schools to play one class above their enrollment figures in the state tournament appears to have lost momentum for now.

"It generated a lot of discussion in our district but over-whelmingly, people were opposed to it." said Steve Riordan, principal of Lawrenceburg and an IHSAA executive committee member.

The reasoning behind the proposal was that some public schools in the middle classes and most of the Catholic schools play a steady diet of larger opponents during the regular season. Then they feast on schools of similar size in the tournament.

Cathedral, for instance, played five 5A opponents during the regular season including perennial power Ben Davis. Ritter played four 5A opponents, none from Class A.

In the Illinois state tournament, Catholic schools play one class above their actual enrollment. But unlike Indiana, not every school in Illinois qualifies for the state tournament.

One reason for establishing an all-comers state tournament in Indiana in 1985 was to allow schools to build their regular season schedules based on conference affiliation, geographical situation and level of competitiveness. Unlike previous formats, the specter of the post-season is not an overriding consideration when building a regular season schedule under this format.

To change it, whether it be for Catholic schools or all schools, would be a mistake. The present system is fair. Moreover, it rewards the schools who strive to excel. Isn't that what the extracurricular aspect of education is supposed to be about?

(Reprinted with permission from *The Indianapolis News*, November 25, 1992 by Jim Russell)

Religion is the Heart and Soul of Cathedral Life

In an interview Mark Mooney '22, long detached from his Indianapolis upbringing and friends at Cathedral, asked: "Is Cathedral still a Catholic school?"

In the Webster definition and in daily life Cathedral remains, as it has for seventy-five years, a family of students, teachers, and administrators who practice the Catholic life.

The roots of Cathedral were nurtured by the Congregation of Holy Cross who, beginning in 1842, had evangelized northern Indiana and established a number of churches.

The invitation from Fr. Chartrand in 1917 to the Congregation of Brothers of the Holy Cross at Notre Dame, Indiana was with the full understanding that Cathedral High School's mission was to educate and nurture religious beliefs.

And while its student body, in increasing numbers, attracts students of other religious denominations and some without theological enrichment, the school, for three-fourths of a century, has served as a mission for the teachings of Christ.

Though religion is not, in the words of Hammerstein "drummed into their dear little heads," the example of religious belief has caused many students to invite God into their lives through the ministry of the Roman Catholic Church.

One of the revered ministers of the Church through his service at Cathedral was the late Rev. Frederick A. Schmitt.

Fr. Schmitt first taught at Cathedral in 1986 and extended his lessons by taking students on tours of Europe. He said: "At Cathedral there is a relational interplay of the faculty and students through their community service which is an extension of God's love."

Fr. Schmitt once said, "Cathedral must resist mediocrity. Its excellence is needed most in carrying out Christ's work." In Cologne, on December 30, 1989, Father Schmitt suffered a fatal heart attack while accompanying students on a holiday tour.

His service to Catholic education at Terre Haute Schulte, Roncalli and Scecina Memorial high schools is testimony and recalls the service of the Holy Cross Brothers of 1842 who reached out, inspired and enlarged the communities of Catholic life.

That spirit remains at Cathedral as it has since 1918. Christ is a constant companion of the Cathedral student. From its rewritten mission in 1972 when Cathedral continued without its beloved Brothers of Holy Cross, Cathedral remains a Catholic school as it was when Mark Mooney entered in 1918.

Graduates who became priests:

John Basso '30
Edward Bauer '32
Paschal Boland, O.S.B. '38
Richard Brune '51-'52
Fenten Cantwell '50
Thomas Carey '34
Chris Cheesborough,
Thomas Clarke '34
Anthony Conway '39
Patrick Evard '50
Ronald Ferguson '51
James Hannigan '44
Carl Herald '35
James Hickey '31
James Hill '42
Harry Hoover '39
Herman Lutz '50
John Lynch '37
Robert Minton '38
John McQuiston, S.J. '32
Herman Mootz '34
James Moriarty '40
William Munshower, '50
Thomas Murphy '50
Ralph Pfau '29
John Quinn '44
Francis Reeves '29
Timothy Sexton, O.S.B. '34
John Shaughnessy '32
Bernardine Shine, OSB. '34
Walter Sullivan, O.S.B. '33
Donald Walpole, O.S.B. '43
Marand Widolff '34
Carl Wiberding '33

Graduates who became Brothers of Holy Cross:

Brother Majella Hegarty
Brother Cyril Ward
Brother Columba Curran
Brother Francis of Assisi Davis
Brother Thaddeus Gottenmoller
Brother Quentin Hegarty
Brother Eric Landers
Brother Camillus Kirsch
Brother Edwin Mattingly
Brother Leonard Leary
Brother Timothy Hickey
Brother Fernand Hickey
Brother Keric Cain
Brother Valens Chrisman
Brother Alberto Neff
Brother Thomas Corcoran
Brother Roy Smith
Brother Joseph LeBon
Brother Arthur LeBon
Brother Keric Dever
Brother Joseph Cain
Brother Walter Davenport
Brother Edward Boyle
Brother Edward Daily
Brother Michael Becker
Brother William Wickham
Brother John Lang

(Other priests and brothers are not verifiable at the time of publication.)

***"Greater Love than this no man hath,
that a man lay down his life for his friends."***

Cathedral Dead in World War II

Raymond Becker, ex. '33
Herman Billerman, ex. '36
Jerome V. Blackwell, '43
Philip J. Carmody, '43
Michael J. Casserly, ex.
Louis Cesnik, '37
Julian J. Commons, '40
Paul J. Commons, '39
Thomas J. Connor, '39
Robert L. Corum, '41
Michael Dean, '38
Francis English, '33
Thomas Fish, '39
Paul J. Foltz, ex. '38
Leonard R. Fort, '27
Thomas A. Gedig, ex. '33
Alfred Greig, '39
Frank J. Hearne, '41
George J. Hoffman, Jr., '32
Thomas W. Holmes, ex. '39
John F. Hyland, '39
William J. Keeney, ex '37
Paul Kestler, '32
James P. Kiernan, '36

Henry Langsenkamp, Jr., '25
John R. Lents, ex. '41
Edward Linne, ex. '26
Edward J. Long, '40
Edmund McAtee, ex. '34
Erwin McGinnis, ex. '37
Charles McGuire, '30
Raymond J. McManus, Jr., '39
Furl C. McMillen, '41
John R. Mansfield, ex. '34
Frank A. Metzger, ex. '40
George M. Murphy, '29
John F. Payleitner, '41
James L. Pritchard, '43
Hubert Pryor, '36
Quentin L Quinn, ex. '37
Bernard J. Reilly, ex. '35
Edward L. Roney, '43
Thomas F. Ruckelshaus, '23
Philip A. Scott, '43
Frederick Strack, ex. '33
Joseph E. Taylor, ex. 41
Bernard J. Tuohy, ex. '41
William Turner, ex. '39

HEADS OF CATHEDRAL HIGH SCHOOL

From the founding in 1918, until 1964, Cathedral High School was operated by the Diocese/Archdiocese of Indianapolis. The school has been privileged to have these great educators and religious leaders as superintendents and principals:

SUPERINTENDENTS:
1924-39 Rt. Reverend Peter Killian
1939-45 Reverend Thomas J. Finneran
1945-51 Rt. Reverend Richard Kavanagh
1951-55 Rt. Reverend James P. Galvin
1955-56 Reverend Bernard W. Gerdon
1956-64 Reverend James P. Higgins

PRINCIPALS
1918-22 Brother Bernard Gervais, CSC
1922-25 Brother Austin Carroll, CSC
1925-28 Brother Ephrem O'Dwyer, CSC
1928-34 Brother William Mang, CSC
1935-37 Brother Richard Grejczyk, CSC
1937-39 Brother Agatho Heiser, CSC
1939-42 Brother Marcian Karsky, CSC
1942-47 Brother Benedict Gervais, CSC
1947-53 Brother Regis Regensburger, CSC
1953-59 Brother Pedro Haering, CSC
1959-62 Brother Giles Martin CSC
1962-66 Brother James Sullivan, CSC
1966-73 Brother Douglas Roach, CSC
1973   Bernard Melevage
1973-75 Michael D. McGinley '60
1975-79 Brother Pedro Haering, CSC
1979-83 Donald M. Stock
1984-   Father Patrick Kelly

BOARD CHAIRMEN:
1973-87 Robert V. Welch '45
1987-92 Daniel J. O'Malia '65
1992-   Michael G. Schaefer '43

PRESIDENTS:
1973-77 Robert V. Welch '45
1977-79 Brother Pedro Haering, CSC
1979-89 Michael D. McGinley '60
1989-   Julian T. Peebles '64

Cathedral Football: Indiana's Most Successful Program

Brother Gregory blew the first whistle as a Cathedral football coach. Since that November 2 afternoon in 1919 when a group of Cathedral underclassmen took to the field at Northwestern Park, Cathedral teams through 1992, have played 699 varsity games. They have won 483 games, lost 197 and tied 19 for an overall winning 71 percent.

Motley-clad in uniforms and floppy headgear that would invite litigation with today's standards of safety, the yet-unnamed team lined up against players, mostly from Shortridge High School. The opponent was "the heavy" (as *The Megaphone* reported) Northwestern Athletic Club. They, equally ill-attired and equipped, bowed, 12-0. A second game, a grudge contest, was played on Thanksgiving Day and Cathedral won again, 12-6.

The record showed that Mark Mooney scored the first touchdown; that big Tom Ruckelshaus and captain George Sadlier "were outstanding in their play."

Mooney, interviewed for this book, went on to Notre Dame after graduating in 1922, Cathedral's second class. He lived away from Indianapolis after his college days and now resides in Tampa, Fla.

From Mooney's historic touchdown to the 1992 State Championship, Irish football teams have won more varsity football games than any other high school in the state of Indiana.

The football record of the old Elkhart High School was discontinued after it was split into Central and Memorial high schools in 1972. Elkhart had amassed an impressive record, but with the division of the school, the Blue Blazers' records ended.

Second to Cathedral's victory total is old foe Evansville Reitz with a dozen fewer victories than the Irish.

In the Indianapolis area respected rival George Washington High School has earned 369 victories, with only three varsity coaches, Henry Bogue, Joe Tofil and Bob Springer. The Continentals played football first in 1927, eight fewer seasons than Cathedral. In competition against each other since 1928, Cathedral leads in victories 28-15 with three ties.

These two schools of football tradition has contributed a son to coach the other school to success. Joe Dezelan, a 1933 graduate of Washington, won 182 games for Cathedral.

Washington's Coach Bob Springer—like Dezelan a member of the Indiana High school Football Hall of Fame—has won

242 games for the Continentals and Sacred Heart Central. Springer, a member of Cathedral's 1952 graduating class, was an All-State end and was a standout at Purdue. Cathedral's winning percentage of 71 percent also is the highest among long-time football-playing schools. Cathedral's winning percentage is even more impressive as the school had not had a "home" field except for 1949-1976 when Cathedral played at the CYO Field on West 16th Street.

Cathedral Football
"Through the Years"

Year	W	L	T	Coach	CHS	OPP
1919	3	0	0	Brother Gregory	26	6
1920	5	0	0	Al Feeney, George Sadlier	179	8
1921	5	1	0	Al Feeney, Mark Mooney	241	13
1922	7	0	0	Al Feeney, John Trenck	152	0
1923	4	3	0	Brother Vincent, Earl Whiteman	116	69
1924	6	0	1	Brother Vincent, Joe McCarthy	184	26
1925	3	4	0	Brother Vincent, Dave Harmon	78	64
1926	5	2	0	Joe Sexton, "Bo" Egan	73	34
1927	7	1	0	Joe Sexton, Emmet Miller	132	26
1928	4	4	2	Joe Sexton, Emmet Amsden	87	76
1929	2	5	0	Joe Dienhart, George Pfeiffer	45	88
1930	8	0	1	Joe Dienhart, John McCreary	160	23
1931	9	0	0	Joe Dienhart, Johnny Ford	247	18
1932	3	6	0	Joe Dienhart, Bernie Breen	51	109
1933	4	6	0	Joe Dienhart, Bill Daugherty	100	105
1934	7	1	1	Joe Dienhart, John McMahon	210	50
1935	6	1	1	Joe Dienhart, Jim McNamara	121	68
1936	3	4	2	Joe Dienhart, Bob Fitzgerald	111	92
1937	2	5	1	Joe Dienhart, Sal Iozzo	60	55
1938	7	2	0	Joe Harmon, Joe Fitzgerald	127	38
1939	6	4	0	Joe Harmon, Jim Fitzgerald	81	51
1940	5	4	1	Joe Harmon, Ott Hurrle	103	110
1941	2	7	0	Joe Harmon, Dilger and Sage	68	197
1942	3	6	0	Milt Peipul, Bob Kasper	97	158
1943	4	4	1	John Janzaruk, John Grande	78	94
1944	7	2	0	Joe Dezelan, Phil O'Connor	142	54
1945	8	1	0	Joe Dezelan, Mike Carr	214	76
1946	8	1	0	Joe Dezelan, Joe Zore	196	34
1947	4	5	0	Joe Dezelan, Bill Holmes	95	90
1948	6	3	0	Joe Dezelan, Mason and Schmutte	165	177
1949	3	5	1	Joe Dezelan, Accomando and Mussio	74	80
1950	8	1	0	Joe Dezelan, Gene Mangin	194	21
1951	9	1	0	Joe Dezelan, Springer and White	210	67
1952	9	0	0	Joe Dezelan, Stroud and Battreall	205	58
1953	6	3	0	Joe Dezelan, David Latz and David Maley	166	98
1954	7	2	0	Joe Dezelan, Farrell and McGinley	143	82
1955	5	5	0	Joe Dezelan, Wade and Schoening	127	141
1956	7	3	0	Joe Dezelan, Long and Gallagher	142	122
1957	5	4	1	Joe Dezelan, Grimm and Braun	119	112
1958	6	4	0	Joe Dezelan, Galbreath and DeCroes	170	106
1959	10	0	0	Joe Dezelan, Brezette and Richart	255	52
1960	8	1	1	Joe Dezelan, McGinty and Smith	210	86
1961	9	0	1	Joe Dezelan, Tofil, Dezelan and Steinmetz	226	43
1962	8	1	1	Joe Dezelan, Schmutte and Rosner	184	61
1963	9	0	1	Joe Dezelan, Harrison and Peebles	244	18
1964	9	1	0	Joe Dezelan, Ross and Wishmire	186	105
1965	5	4	1	Joe Dezelan, McCullough Caskey and Carson	125	115
1966	5	5	0	Joe Dezelan, White and Kern	183	124
1967	4	6	0	Joe Dezelan, Swartz, Siler and Hewitt	138	178
1968	9	0	1	Joe Dezelan, Weimer and Casey	226	58
1969	8	2	0	Joe Dezelan, Schaefer and Weber	210	114
1970	7	3	0	Mike McGinley, Seal and Ericksen	168	84
1971	6	4	0	Mike McGinley, Weinmann and Wise	157	124
1972	8	2	0	Mike McGinley, Svarczkopf, Robisch and Weber	193	101
1973	11	1	0	Mike McGinley, Zapp and Kelley	275	113
1974	6	4	0	Mike McGinley, Bob Willis	119	133
1975	8	2	0	Mike McGinley, Terry Woehler	200	138
1976	12	1	0	Mike McGinley, Mattson and Stirling	352	138
1977	8	2	0	Mike McGinley, Bowling and Fillenwarth	256	126
1978	8	2	0	Mike McGinley, Cassell and Washington	198	126
1979	5	5	0	Bob Pychinka, Mackall and Glogoza	140	107
1980	6	4	0	Bob Pychinka, Page and Brady	163	107
1981	6	4	0	Mike McGinley, Knox and Dreiband	290	158
1982	9	2	0	Mike McGinley, O'Hara Hargerty and Freeman	216	130
1983	7	3	0	Mike McGinley, Todd and Troy	197	118
1984	9	1	0	Mike McGinley, Boyd and Altherr	221	115
1985	6	3	0	Mike McGinley, Gardner and Lindgren	175	104
1986*	12	2	0	Mike McGinley, Brownlow and Guye	315	114
1987	8	4	0	Mike McGinley, Melloh, Guhl and Brady	251	140
1988	7	4	0	Mike McGinley, Elson and Hohne	229	141
1989	5	4	0	Rick Streiff, Clemons and Rider	162	120
1990	5	4	0	Rick Streiff, Hannigan and Koers	163	180
1991	11	3	0	Rick Streiff, McKinney, Coleman and Hauser	299	186
1992*	12	2	0	Rick Streiff, Ford, Keller, and Luedeman	337	182
1993	8	4	0	Rick Streiff, Hannigan, Pugh, Reardon, and Risser	291	171

* - IHSAA STATE CHAMPIONS (3A)   **TL: 492 200 19**   **12,843 6,824**

The Football Opponents

In football, Cathedral has competed against two amateur teams (1919), Dayton University preps (1920 and 1925) and 85 high school opponents. Cathedral teams have defeated seven high school teams from Ohio, Illinois and Kentucky.

Of Cathedral's 78 Hoosier high school opponents only four have a winning advantage in a series of more than eight games. They are: Chatard (7-10), Evansville Reitz (3-6),Lafayette Jefferson (6-7) and Warren Central (3-5).

In the 699 games played, Cathedral teams have scored 12,402 points as opposed to the 6,636 points of their opponents: a 17.7 to 9.5 per game scoring average.

The single-game scoring record is held by Mark Mooney '22. In 1920, during the fifth game played by the Irish, Mooney scored five touchdowns and 14 points-after–touchdown against Boys Prep School, now Park Tudor School. The 44 points scored may be a single-game record for an Indiana high school player.

Tony Hinkle and the Cathedral Men

Other than Cathedral team coaches, no one coached and inspired more Cathedral graduate athletes than the legendary Paul Daniel (Tony) Hinkle of Butler University.

During his years at Butler—from Irvington to Fairview—"Hink" coached more than 200 former Cathedral athletes in football, basketball and baseball.

Hinkle's teams won 1,046 varsity games—a pinnacle that no other National Collegiate Athletic Association coach has ever achieved. His Cathedral athletes captained 16 Bulldog teams. Coach Hinkle was the only coach ever to coach national championship teams in two sports—Butler basketball in 1928, and the Great Lakes Naval Training Station football team during World War II. Fran Royse, a star of the undefeated 1922 Irish team, was first to play for him in 1924. As Hinkle's first letterman from Cathedral, Royse was considered one of the finest Bulldog halfbacks ever, at Irwin Field on Butler's old Irvington campus.

"Coach Hinkle had a pipeline that seemed connected to Cathedral," Bill Sylvester '46 quipped. In 1946, the Butler football team boasted thirteen Irish athletes, six of them starters.

Sylvester played football at Butler, succeeded Hinkle as head football coach and became the school's director of athletics three years after Tony's retirement.

"Sub" as Bill was known during his football and varsity basketball-playing days at Cathedral, caught the winning touchdown pass with twelve seconds to play against Tech in 1945.

"Hinkle always liked Cathedral guys because of their combative spirit," Sylvester recalled. When Cathedral had no place to practice in the late 1920s and early thirties, Hinkle arranged for Irish teams to practice at Butler at no cost. That relationship was suspended as a possible infraction by then North Central Association, the accrediting body that monitored college athletics prior to the formation of National Collegiate Athletic Association.

Perhaps part of Hinkle's respect for Cathedral athletics was the influence of another Cathedral graduate, Jim Morris '31, long-time Butler athletic trainer and Hinkle confidant.

Morris went on to become trainer at Butler University in 1938 after graduation. Jim was more than just a physical therapist to athletes (he also was a "patsy" for high school athletes who needed his advice as well as therapeutic skills).

In 1969 he was named to the Helms Hall Athletic Trainers Hall of Fame. He ministered to athletes for more than fifty years. Long-time friend and veteran Bulldog Coach Tony Hinkle called Morris "one of the most highly-respected men in his profession in the United States." In 1988, more than 100 Cathedral athletes who played for Coach Hinkle honored him at a luncheon and awarded their mentor an honorary block "C" for years of association. A plaque, signed by Hinkle's Cathedral players, is on display in the Fieldhouse that bears his name.

At a memorial service held on the basketball floor in the Hinkle fieldhouse his many successful teams shared how "Tony" had insired them. Jim Doyle '46 served as a pallbearer. Doyle led the Bulldog basketball (1947-50) teams to winning seasons and, like Sylvester, kept a life-long relationship with his coach.

"Tony Hinkle coached Cathedral coaches including Joe Dezelan, Cleon Reynolds, Mike McGinley, Tom O'Brien, Julian Peebles and so many of the school's athletes we felt he was one of us," Doyle said.

Coach Hinkle shepherded his players and always arranged transportation for them to go to Mass while on the road. Doyle recalled: "Several years ago Coach Hinkle called me and reported that, for the first time, a Butler player, a Catholic, didn't attend Mass. Hinkle was stunned. "But," he quickly added, "the kid didn't go to Cathedral, Jimmy.'"

*Cathedral grads from the mid '40s who played for Butler's Tony Hinkle.
(bottom) Joe Qualters, Bill Kuntz, unknown;   (seated) Bill Sylvester, Dave Kenny, Jeke McHugh, Jim McLinn;
(standing) unknown, Bob McAllister, Jack Elder, Jim Kavanaugh*

Jim McLinn, . . . Jr.

September 27, 1958, a five-year-old first grader from Our Lady of Lourdes grade school stands at the fence at the CYO stadium, enjoying popcorn with his grandpa. Hearing a thunderous roar behind him, he turns to see the commotion. Forty-some warriors dressed in gold pants with blue jerseys, putting on yellow leather helmets, pass by him through the gate and onto the playing field. "Who are they, Grandpa?" he asks. "That, my boy, is THE Cathedral Fighting Irish, the best high school football team you'll ever see." It was at that point that the love affair began with this thing they call Cathedral.

Of course, since birth I had heard stories of my dad, Jeke McHugh, Bill Sylvester, Bill Kuntz and the other "legends" of the '45-'46 athletic heritage. I was, even then, caught up in the mystique. "I'll play for the Fighting Irish someday," I reported to Grandpa. "You better," was his simple reply. As I write this thirty-five years later, with the last twenty spent as teacher, coach and counselor at Cathedral, I feel fortunate that my dreams as a young boy have come true beyond what I could have imagined. By the way, Cathedral won that night by a score of 21 to 13. Thanks, Grandpa.

As I look back at my personal involvement with Cathedral, memories that flow back are always connected with one person who made the experience unique. I remember running in the hall on 14th street with Bill Hurrle after we had finished our "entrance exam." In my four years as a student, besides my friends, the Brothers of Holy Cross and the coaching staff (Joe Dezelan, Mike McGinley, Tom O'Brien, and Garry Donna) were the most influential people. Brother Raymond steered me toward a college major in English and Coach Dezelan told me as a senior to come back to Cathedral to teach and coach. When Coach Dezelan gave you an order, you blindly followed without question.

I owe my return to Cathedral as a teacher to Michael D. McGinley. As a senior at Butler University, I received a call from him one day to come in and talk about a position teaching English, Speech, Health and Physical education. It was a done deal; Papa Joe's orders would come true and I could not have been happier. I remember my first class as "the teacher." As the bell rang, there in front of me sat twenty all-male freshmen (we were still on 14th street) waiting for me to fill their heads with grammar. "What in the hell am I doing here? What did Coach Dezelan get me into?" I thought. Somehow I survived, because Cathedral taught me how to face adversity and overcome it.

And so, "Dear Old Cathedral, here's to you . . ." Congratulations on seventy-five glorious years of service. I want to thank you for being my life for the last thirty-five years. I can only hope to be around to help celebrate your Golden Anniversary. If not, grandpa and I will be there at the football games.

About the Authors . . .

Bill Shover is a graduate of Cathedral High School (1946) and Butler University (1952) and an army veteran (1946-1948.) After serving as Assistant Public Relations Director for *The Indianapolis Star,* and *The Indianapolis News* he came to the *Arizona Republic/ The Phoenix Gazette* in 1963 and is the Director of Public Affairs for the papers.

Shover, along with Glenn Hawkins and the late Jack Stewart, helped to found the Fiesta Bowl in 1968 and Bill was its president 1978-79. Among his many honors, including an Honorary Doctorate in Public Service from Grand Canyon College (1982), he values awards given for active service to youth: the Good Scout Award of the Theodore Roosevelt Council of the BSA and the Big Brother of the Year recognition given by Valley Big Brothers.

While in Indianapolis, Shover was a founding member of the "500" Festival and director of the Indiana-Kentucky All-Star Basketball Game from 1953-1962. He is married to the former Mary Jane "Murny" Kunde and is the father of sons Kevin and T.A. and daughters Sandra (Mrs. John Moses) and Lisa. He has six grandchildren.

James Obergfell is a native of Indianapolis, growing up in St. Philip Neri and Holy Spirit parishes on the east side of town. He is a graduate of Indiana University, where he has also done graduate work. For the past fifteen years he has taught religion to seniors at Cathedral High School, where he also became an honorary graduate of the Class of 1992.

During his tenure he has initiated and directed the much honored Service Program and Cathedral's public relations campaigns. He is the senior class sponsor and is in charge of all Baccalaureate and Graduation ceremonies, Cathedral Archives and pictorial history. Jim Obergfell has been chosen three times by his students to give the graduation address. No one has known Cathedral students better or is more uniquely qualified to tell their stories. Jim is married to the former Nancy Lorenzano and has one daughter named Anna.